</ G0 AMW.075

OXFORD MEDIEVAL TEXTS

General Editors

J. W. BINNS   W. J. BLAIR
D. D'AVRAY   M. LAPIDGE

VITA EDWARDI SECVNDI

THE LIFE OF EDWARD THE SECOND

VITA EDWARDI SECVNDI
THE LIFE OF
EDWARD THE SECOND

RE-EDITED TEXT
WITH NEW INTRODUCTION, NEW HISTORICAL NOTES,
AND REVISED TRANSLATION BASED ON
THAT OF N. DENHOLM-YOUNG
BY

WENDY R. CHILDS

CLARENDON PRESS · OXFORD

OXFORD

UNIVERSITY PRESS

Great Clarendon Street, Oxford OX2 6DP

Oxford University Press is a department of the University of Oxford.
It furthers the University's objective of excellence in research, scholarship,
and education by publishing worldwide in

Oxford New York

Auckland Bangkok Buenos Aires Cape Town Chennai
Dar es Salaam Delhi Hong Kong Istanbul Karachi Kolkata
Kuala Lumpur Madrid Melbourne Mexico City Mumbai Nairobi
São Paulo Shanghai Singapore Taipei Tokyo Toronto

Oxford is a registered trade mark of Oxford University Press
in the UK and in certain other countries

Published in the United States
by Oxford University Press Inc., New York

© Wendy Childs 2005

The moral rights of the author have been asserted
Database right Oxford University Press (maker)

First published 2005

All rights reserved. No part of this publication may be reproduced,
stored in a retrieval system, or transmitted, in any form or by any means,
without the prior permission in writing of Oxford University Press,
or as expressly permitted by law, or under terms agreed with the appropriate
reprographics rights organization. Enquiries concerning reproduction
outside the scope of the above should be sent to the Rights Department,
Oxford University Press, at the address above

You must not circulate this book in any other binding or cover
and you must impose this same condition on any acquirer

British Library Cataloguing in Publication Data
Data available

Library of Congress Cataloging in Publication Data
Data available

ISBN 0-19-927594-7

1 3 5 7 9 10 8 6 4 2

Typeset by Anne Joshua, Oxford
Printed in Great Britain
on acid-free paper by
Biddles Ltd, King's Lynn, Norfolk

DA
230
.V58
2005

PREFACE

There have been three previous editions of the *Vita Edwardi Secundi*, in 1730, 1883, and 1957. The last, by N. Denholm-Young for Nelson's Medieval Texts, also included a translation and is still, justly, widely used, although out of print. My first task, therefore, is to record what changes have been made in this new edition. First, the Latin text, classicized by previous editors, has now been wholly revised from Hearne's eighteenth-century transcript, and returned as far as possible to fourteenth-century orthography. The text has also been provided with a full *apparatus criticus*. The introduction is entirely new, and takes account of the many works on the reign since 1957; I have also provided new and more extensive historical notes, an index of quotations and allusions, a concordance with previous editions, and a new general index. The translation has been fully checked and a number of changes have been made for accuracy and style, but this is the part which bears the strongest links with N. Denholm-Young's edition of 1957. In numerous passages his choice of words was difficult to improve.

My many obligations to other scholars, past and present, will be apparent throughout the introduction and the historical notes, and I am grateful to them all. Here, however, I would like particularly to thank the staff of the Bodleian Library, Oxford, who willingly made Hearne's transcription in MS Rawlinson B. 180 available to me, and also provided a photocopy, which made the work of checking the text so much easier. I would also like to thank all friends and colleagues who have answered questions, large and small, and those who have unconsciously helped by prompting my thoughts and further questions in general discussions. Among my colleagues at Leeds, I would particularly like to thank Dr Catherine Batt, Dr W. Flynn, Mr Ian Moxon, Professor Ian Wood, and Dr A. D. Wright. Among those outside Leeds, my thanks are due to Dr Paul Brand, Professor Chris Given-Wilson, Dr J. R. Maddicott, Professor Seymour Phillips, and Professor Michael Prestwich, some for responses to direct questions, some for comments on conference papers as long ago as 1995. Particular thanks must, of course, go to the General Editors of Oxford Medieval Texts. My debt here is great and twofold. One is to the present editors, who have made excellent suggestions for improvement in the later stages of the work, and have seen the edition to the press. The second is to those who were editors when I began, Dr Diana Greenway, Miss Barbara Harvey, and Professor Michael Lapidge. Their encouragement, advice, and criticism in the early stages were invaluable. My debt to Miss Harvey is particularly great, not only for her encouragement to undertake the edition, but also for her continued interest and comments which have saved me from error and led to great improvement. I would also like to take this opportunity to thank Mrs Ann Dale and Mrs Margaret Walkington, who helped with early typing of the text, and to thank Dr Bonnie Blackburn for making further valuable suggestions as she copy-edited the text.

When I started the new edition a decade ago, I certainly did not expect it to take so long. Unfortunately, it was overtaken by other demands, but perhaps the delays have made it a better volume, as I have had greater opportunities to seek advice. Any errors which remain will show where I failed to take it.

W.R.C.

July 2003

CONTENTS

ABBREVIATIONS

Ann. Lond.	*Annales Londonienses*, in Stubbs, *Chronicles*, i
Ann. Paul.	*Annales Paulini*, in Stubbs, *Chronicles*, i
Anon.	*The Anonimalle Chronicle 1307–1334, from Broth-erton Collection MS 29*, ed. Wendy R. Childs and John Taylor, Yorkshire Archaeological Society Record Series, cxlvii for 1987 (1991)
Aylmer and Cant, *York Minster*	G. E. Aylmer and R. Cant (eds.), *A History of York Minster* (Oxford, 1977)
Barrow, *Bruce*	G. W. S. Barrow, *Robert Bruce and the Community of the Realm of Scotland*, 3rd edn. (Edinburgh, 1988)
BIHR	*Bulletin of the Institute of Historical Research*
BL	British Library
Bracton, *De Legibus*	*Henrici de Bracton de Legibus et Consuetudinibus Angliae*, trans. S. E. Thorne from the edition of G. E. Woodbine, 4 vols. (Cambridge, Mass., 1968–77)
Brid.	*Gesta Edwardi de Carnarvan, auctore canonico Brid-lingtoniensi*, in Stubbs, *Chronicles*, ii
The Bruce	John Barbour, *The Bruce*, ed. and trans. A. A. M. Duncan (Edinburgh, 1997; repr. with corrections, 1999)
BRUO	A. B. Emden, *A Biographical Register of the University of Oxford to AD 1500*, 3 vols. (Oxford, 1957–9)
Brut	*The Brut*, ed. F. W. Brie, EETS, original ser., cxxxi (London, 1906)
Cary, *Medieval Alexander*	G. Cary, *The Medieval Alexander* (Cambridge, 1956)
CChR	*Calendar of Charter Rolls*
CChW	*Calendar of Chancery Warrants*
CCR	*Calendar of Close Rolls*

CDS	*Calendar of Documents relating to Scotland*, ed. J. Bain, iii (Edinburgh, 1887)
CFR	*Calendar of Fine Rolls*
Chaplais, 'Duché-Pairie'	P. Chaplais, 'Le Duché-Pairie de Guyenne: l'hommage et les services féodaux de 1303 à 1337', in his *Essays in Medieval Diplomacy and Administration* (London, 1981), ch. 4
Chaplais, *Gaveston*	P. Chaplais, *Piers Gaveston: Edward's Adoptive Brother* (Oxford, 1994)
Chaplais, *Saint-Sardos*	P. Chaplais (ed.), *The War of Saint-Sardos (1323–1325): Gascon Correspondence and Diplomatic Documents*, Camden Society 3rd ser., lxxxvii (London, 1954)
Childs, 'Resistance and treason'	W. R. Childs, 'Resistance and treason in the *Vita Edwardi Secundi*', in M. Prestwich, R. H. Britnell, and R. Frame (eds.), *Thirteenth-Century England VI* (Woodbridge, 1997), pp. 177–91
Childs, '"Welcome"'	W. R. Childs, '"Welcome, my brother": Edward II, John of Powderham, and the chronicles, 1318', in I. N. Wood and G. A. Loud (eds.), *Church and Chronicle: Essays Presented to John Taylor* (London, 1991), pp. 149–63
CIPM	*Calendar of Inquisitions Post Mortem*
CMI	*Calendar of Miscellaneous Inquisitions*
Cod.	*Codex Iustinianus*, see *Corpus Iuris Civilis*
Cole, *Docs. Illus.*	H. Cole (ed.), *Documents Illustrative of English History in the Thirteenth and Fourteenth Centuries* (London, 1844)
Cont. Trivet	*Nicolai Triveti Annalium Continuatio; ut et Adami Murimuthensis Chronicon, cum ejusdem continuatione: quibus accedunt Joannis Bostoni Speculum Coenobitarum et Edmundi Boltoni Hypercritica*, ed. A. Hall (Oxford, 1722)
Corpus Iuris Canonici	*Corpus Iuris Canonici*, ed. A. Friedberg (Leipzig, 1881)
Corpus Iuris Civilis	*Corpus Iuris Civilis*, ed. P. Krueger, T. Mommsen, and R. Schoell, 3 vols. (Berlin, 1900–4)
CP	G. E. Cockayne, *The Complete Peerage*, revised V. Gibbs *et al.* (London, 1910–59)

CPL	*Calendar of Papal Registers, Papal Letters*
CPR	*Calendar of Patent Rolls*
Davies, *Opposition*	J. Conway Davies, *The Baronial Opposition to Edward II: Its Character and Policy. A Study in Administrative History* (Cambridge, 1918)
Decretal. Gregorii IX	*Decretalium Gregorii IX*, see *Corpus Iuris Canonici*
Decretum	Gratian, *Decretum*, see *Corpus Iuris Canonici*
Denholm-Young, 'Authorship'	N. Denholm-Young, 'The authorship of the *Vita Edwardi Secundi*', *EHR*, lxxi (1956), repr. in his *Collected Papers* (Cardiff, 1969), pp. 267–89
Denton, *Winchelsey*	J. H. Denton, *Robert Winchelsey and the Crown 1294–1313: A Study in the Defence of Ecclesiastical Liberty* (Cambridge, 1980)
Dig.	*Digesta Iustiniani*, see *Corpus Iuris Civilis*
DNB	*Dictionary of National Biography*
Doherty, *Isabella*	P. Doherty, *Isabella and the Strange Death of Edward II* (London, 2003)
EcHR	*Economic History Review*
EETS	Early English Text Society
EHD	*English Historical Documents*, iii: *1189–1327*, ed. H. Rothwell (London, 1975)
EHR	*English Historical Review*
Eubel, *Hier. Cath.*	C. Eubel, *Hierarchia Catholica*, i: *1198–1431* (Regensburg, 1913)
Fleta	*Fleta*, ed. H. G. Richardson and G. O. Sayles, 3 vols., Selden Society, lxxii, lxxxix, xcix (London, 1953, 1972, 1984)
Flores	*Flores Historiarum*, ed. H. R. Luard, 3 vols. (RS, London, 1890)
Foed.	*Foedera, Conventiones, Litterae et Cuiuscunque Acta Publica*, ed. T. Rymer, ii (RC, London, 1816–69)
Fryde, *Tyranny*	N. Fryde, *The Tyranny and Fall of Edward II 1321–1326* (Cambridge, 1979)
Gransden, *Historical Writing*	A. Gransden, *Historical Writing in England*, i: *c.550–c.1307* (London, 1974); ii: *c.1307 to the Early Sixteenth Century* (London, 1982)
Green, *Alexander*	P. Green, *Alexander of Macedon, 356–323 B.C.: A*

	Historical Biography (Berkeley and Los Angeles, 1991)
Haines, *Orleton*	R. H. Haines, *The Church and Politics in Four-teenth-Century England: The Career of Adam Orle-ton c.1275–1345* (Cambridge, 1978)
Hamilton, *Gaveston*	J. S. Hamilton, *Piers Gaveston, Earl of Cornwall 1307–1312: Politics and Patronage in the Reign of Edward II* (Detroit, 1988)
Hamilton, *Plutarch: Alexander*	J. A. Hamilton, *Plutarch: Alexander. A Commentary* (Oxford, 1968)
HBC	*Handbook of British Chronology*, 3rd edn., ed. E. B. Fryde, D. E. Greenway, S. Porter, and I. Roy (RHS, London, 1986)
Hearne, *Trokelowe*	T. Hearne, *Johannis de Trokelowe annales Eduardi II. Henrici de Blaneforde chronica et Eduardi II vita a monacho quodam Malmesburiensi fuse enarrata* (Oxford, 1729)
Hist. Roff.	*Historia Roffensis*, text and trans. for 1321 in N. Pronay and J. Taylor, *Parliamentary Texts of the Middle Ages* (Oxford, 1980), pp. 161–3, 166–7
HMC	Historical Manuscripts Commission
Inst.	*Institutiones Iustiniani*, see *Corpus Iuris Civilis*
Itin.	*The Itinerary of Edward II*, ed. E. Hallam, List and Index Society, ccxi (London, 1984)
Keen, *Laws of War*	M. Keen, *The Laws of War in the Late Middle Ages* (London, 1965)
Kingsford, *Song of Lewes*	C. L. Kingsford (ed.), *The Song of Lewes* (Oxford, 1890)
Lanercost	*Chronicon de Lanercost*, ed. J. Stevenson, Banna-tyne Club, lxv (Edinburgh, 1839)
Lay Taxes	M. Jurkowski, C. L. Smith, and D. Crook, *Lay Taxes in England and Wales 1188–1688*, PRO Handbook, xxxi (London, 1998)
Le Baker	*Chronicon Galfridi Le Baker de Swynbroke*, ed. E. M. Thompson (Oxford, 1889)
Legg, *Sarum Missal*	J. Wickham Legg, *The Sarum Missal. Edited from Three Early Manuscripts* (Oxford, 1916; repr. 1969)
Let. Bk. E	*Calendar of Letter-Books Preserved among the*

	Archives of the Corporation of the City of London: Letter Book E, ed. R. R. Sharpe (London, 1903)
Lib. Cust.	*Munimenta Gildhallae Londoniensis; Liber Custumarum*, ed. H. T. Riley (RS, London, 1860)
List of Sheriffs	*List of Sheriffs for England and Wales from the Earliest Times to A.D. 1831*, PRO List and Indexes, ix (London, 1898)
Lunt, *Financial Relations*	W. E. Lunt, *Financial Relations of the Papacy with England to 1327* (Cambridge, Mass., 1939)
Lydon, 'Impact'	J. Lydon, 'The impact of the Bruce invasion', in A. Cosgrove (ed.), *A New History of Ireland*, ii: *Medieval Ireland 1169–1534* (Oxford, 1987), pp. 275–302
McNamee, *Wars*	C. McNamee, *The Wars of the Bruces: Scotland, England and Ireland, 1306–1328* (East Linton, 1997)
Maddicott, *Lancaster*	J. R. Maddicott, *Thomas of Lancaster 1307–1322: A Study in the Reign of Edward II* (Oxford, 1970)
Murimuth	*Adae Murimuth Continuatio Chronicarum*, ed. E. Maunde Thompson (RS, London, 1889)
OMT	Oxford Medieval Texts
Parliamentary Texts	*Parliamentary Texts of the Later Middle Ages*, ed. N. Pronay and J. Taylor (Oxford, 1980)
Patterson, *Chaucer*	L. Patterson, *Chaucer and the Subject of History* (London, 1991)
Phillips, *Pembroke*	J. R. S. Phillips, *Aymer de Valence, Earl of Pembroke 1307–1324: Baronial Politics in the Reign of Edward II* (Oxford, 1972)
PL	*Patrologiae Cursus Completus. Patres . . . Ecclesiae Latinae*, ed. J. P. Migne, 221 vols. (Paris, 1844–64)
Plac. Abb.	*Abbreviatio Placitorum*, ed. G. Rose and W. Illingworth (RC, London, 1811)
Prestwich, *Ed. I*	M. Prestwich, *Edward I* (London, 1988)
PRO	Public Record Office, London, *see* TNA
PW	*Parliamentary Writs and Writs of Military Summons*, ed. Sir F. Palgrave, ii (RC, London, 1827–34)
RC	Record Commission
RHS	Royal Historical Society

RP	*Rotuli Parliamentorum*
RS	Rolls Series
Sext.	*Sexti Decretalium*, see *Corpus Iuris Canonici*
SHR	*Scottish Historical Review*
Smith, *Appointments*	W. E. L. Smith, *Episcopal Appointments and Patronage in the Reign of Edward II* (Chicago, 1938)
SR	*Statutes of the Realm*, ed. A. Luders *et al.*, i (RC, London, 1810)
Stones, *Anglo-Scottish Relations*	E. L. G. Stones (ed.), *Anglo-Scottish Relations 1174–1328: Some Selected Documents*, OMT (1970)
Stubbs, *Chronicles*	*Chronicles of the Reigns of Edward I and Edward II*, ed. W. Stubbs, 2 vols. (RS, London, 1882–3)
TBGAS	*Transactions of the Bristol and Gloucestershire Archaeological Society*
TNA	The National Archives, London (formerly Public Record Office)
Tout, *Chapters*	T. F. Tout, *Chapters in Medieval Administrative History*, 6 vols. (Manchester, 1923–35)
Tout, *Ed. II*	T. F. Tout, *The Place of the Reign of Edward II in English History*, 2nd edn. (Manchester, 1936)
TRHS	*Transactions of the Royal Historical Society*
Vita, 1st edn.	*Vita Edwardi Secundi*, ed. N. Denholm-Young (London, 1957)
Walther, *Carminum*	H. Walther, *Initia Carminum ac Versuum Medii Aevi Posterioris Latinorum* (Göttingen, 1959)
Walther, *Proverbia*	H. Walther, *Proverbia Sententiaeque Latinitatis Medii Aevi*, 5 vols. (Göttingen, 1963–9)
Willard, *Parliamentary Taxes*	J. F. Willard, *Parliamentary Taxes on Personal Property, 1290–1334* (Cambridge, Mass., 1934)
Wright, *Reynolds*	J. R. Wright, *The Church and the English Crown 1305–1334: A Study Based on the Register of Archbishop Walter Reynolds* (Toronto, 1980)

INTRODUCTION

THE MANUSCRIPT

i. Hearne's transcript

THE chronicle known as the *Vita Edwardi Secundi* (a title given to the work by its first editor, Thomas Hearne) is now known to us only through Hearne's transcript made in 1729. The discovery, editing, and loss of the manuscript were fully described from Hearne's own letters and papers by its second editor, Bishop Stubbs, and only a résumé is necessary here.[1] Mr James West of the Inner Temple acquired the manuscript among others which had once belonged to Gervase Holles, a life-long collector of manuscripts who died in 1674. When and where Holles had acquired it, and precisely how it came to West, are now unknown. The manuscript contained a number of chronicles and chronicle extracts and some miscellaneous writings. In October 1728 West lent it to Thomas Hearne for a pronouncement on its age and authorship. In January 1729 Hearne described it to West as being composed of two distinct parts, probably originally separate and possibly first bound together by Gervase Holles in the seventeenth century. The first part was largely made up of a chronicle which ran from 1066 to 1347 and was essentially a compilation of known chronicles, but the second part contained an independent 'large and full' chronicle of the reign of Edward II, which Hearne decided to transcribe for publication. By July 1729 he had finished his transcription and by January 1730 it had been printed.[2] Already nine leaves were missing from this second part: two for the year 1316, six which covered 1322 from the execution of Lancaster in March to the rebellion and arrest of Robert Ewer at the end of the year, and one for 1324 between the attempted escape of Maurice Berkeley from Wallingford castle and Robert Bruce's request for a full treaty. Hearne kept the manuscript a little longer as he found the first part, although mainly a compilation, more interesting than he had at first thought and decided to transcribe that too. (Stubbs identified the sources of this part as mainly the Premonstratensian Barlings chronicle to 1282,

---

[1] Stubbs, *Chronicles*, ii, pp. xxxi–xliii.   [2] Hearne, *Trokelowe*, pp. 95–250.

Geoffrey le Baker to 1336, and the *Eulogium Historiarum* down to 1347.)

Hearne returned the manuscript safely to West in June 1730, but in January 1737 a fire in the Temple burned several chambers, including West's, together with many of his books and manuscripts to the total value of £1,800. The Temple fire was described as a 'public loss', just as the fire at the Cotton Library had been. West's losses presumably included this manuscript, which has not been seen since. Thus the manuscript, containing one of the most interesting and important accounts of the reign of Edward II, is now preserved for us only in Thomas Hearne's transcript of 1729 and publication of 1730.

Hearne's transcript of the section now known as the *Vita Edwardi Secundi* is to be found in the Bodleian Library, Rawlinson MS B. 180. This transcript and Hearne's marginal notes are faithfully reflected in the publication of 1730 and it is clear that Rawlinson B. 180 served as the printer's copy. Hearne's paragraph marks, commas, and brackets are all clearly later additions superimposed on his original transcript, which was written as one continuous piece with only full stops and question marks as punctuation.[3] On his transcript Hearne also marked up the folio numbers, the line endings, and the original paragraph marks of the fourteenth-century manuscript. These marks are all still visible in Rawlinson B. 180 but were not transferred to the printed version. From them it is possible to reconstruct the line lengths and lines per folio of West's manuscript. Rawlinson B. 180 has itself lost a leaf since 1730, and for the final passages on the queen's refusal to return to England we are now dependent on Hearne's printed copy alone.

Hearne's transcript of the first part of West's manuscript is also in the Bodleian Library, as Rawlinson MS B. 414. From a study of these transcripts together with Hearne's letters and notes, Stubbs described the original manuscript borrowed from West as of 165 written leaves (making no allowance for the losses Hearne noted). Fos. 1–62 contained the consecutive derivative chronicle from 1066 to 1347; fos. 63–84 contained a long extract from William of Guisborough (called Hemingburgh by Hearne); fos. 85–91 contained scraps from William of Newburgh (which Hearne did not transcribe) and a list of the abbots of Malmesbury, written in a 'modern hand', according to

---

[3] Apart from the inset of the verses, the only exceptions to the writing as a continuous piece without paragraphs come with new paragraphs at the beginning of 1316 (this is also the change to fo. 126 of the original manuscript), and at the beginning of 1320.

Hearne. Finally fos. 92–165 contained what we now know as the *Vita Edwardi Secundi*, which Hearne described as beginning with a large illuminated letter E. There is a minor problem with this folio numbering, but the shape of the manuscript is clear.[4] Hearne also recorded that at the end of the *Vita* there was a deed relating to Malmesbury Abbey, which he copied, and that on the *recto* of the last leaf appeared

$$\left. \begin{array}{l} \text{G. Holles} \\ \text{meis, mihi} \end{array} \right\} \; 1648.^{5}$$

Hearne and Stubbs both expressed regret at the loss of the leaves, and we can only echo them. The loss of the long passage for 1322 is particularly unfortunate; we are left with only the beginning of the author's lament for Lancaster in 1322, and we lose entirely any comments on the further executions, the parliament at York, and the Scottish expedition. The loss of the passage for 1323 deprives us of Harclay's execution, and possible further comments from the author on acceptable resistance and treason.

ii. The date of West's manuscript

Hearne described the whole manuscript as being written in a four-teenth-century hand or hands, and his experience and general accuracy as an editor have led subsequent scholars to accept his view. However, West's manuscript itself was certainly not written early in the fourteenth century nor by the original author of the *Vita*. In his manuscript the section on Edward II was followed without any break by a short continuation down to 1348, which was drawn mainly from Higden's *Polychronicon*. Since Hearne made no comment on a change of hand for that continuation, it is likely that one hand wrote the whole section 1307–48. If so, the text of the *Vita* which comes down to us must be the work of a scribe writing sometime after 1348.[6] It is nonetheless just possible that the two parts of this text were

---

[4] On Rawlinson B. 180 Hearne wrote 'fo. 92' twice at the beginning of his transcript (on fo. 162 top left margin, fo. 162ᵛ mid-right margin at line 13). There is sufficient text between them to make clear that he is not referring to material on the same folio. Subsequent folio numbers follow consecutively and at regular intervals from the second mention of fo. 92, but are crossed through to fo. 123 inclusive as if for correction. The *Vita* must therefore have been contained either on fos. 91–165 or 92–166 of the original manuscript.

[5] Stubbs, *Chronicles*, ii, pp. xxxviii–xxxix.

[6] Ibid., p. xlv.

written by different scribes, as there appears to be a different usage of paragraph marks in each: Hearne regularly marked paragraph marks in his transcript of the text for 1307–26, but recorded none in the continuation to 1348. However, even if the two sections had been in different hands, it is still clear that the text for 1307 to 1326 cannot be the author's original text. A number of the simple errors which Hearne found in the manuscript indicate slips which are likely from a copyist but unlikely to have been written by the author; and the few places where words in the text are so garbled as to make no sense are extremely unlikely to have been written by the original author, even in an unrevised text.

Hearne was a careful transcriber. As well as marking folio numbers, line endings, and paragraph marks, he made about 500 marginal notes on the wording of the manuscript which indicate that he had looked particularly closely at the text. His notes fall into four main categories. First, a word or words in the margin followed by *MS* indicate the original manuscript spelling where Hearne had incorporated a correction directly into the text as he made the transcription (*c*.320 instances). Secondly, a simple *sic* in the margin records where he thought something in the manuscript was odd but did not change it (*c*.39 instances). Thirdly, *F.* (*faueo*) or *malim* with an alternative shows that he favoured another reading but had made no change in the text (*c*.90 instances). Finally, a variety of comments (*malit nonnemo* . . ., *malint forsitan alii* . . ., *potest etiam* . . . *legi, siue* . . ., *uel* . . ., *nescio an* . . ., *conieceram* . . ., and *adieci* . . ., *addidi* . . .) indicate other possible alternative readings and some additions of words to make sense (*c*.78 instances). There remain a few mistakes noted by later editors which were not commented on by Hearne. It is now impossible to be sure in these cases whether Hearne accurately transcribed a faulty text without making a note or whether he himself made some of these errors, as for instance where a letter is misread, as in the desires of the rich being as *pernis* (thighbones) rather than the more likely *pennis* (feathers).

Most errors are easily explicable copying mistakes, where, for instance, *ut* may be a misreading of the abbreviation for *uel*, or a *titulus* (and therefore an abbreviated *m* or *n*) is missed. With minimal adjustment the text makes sense, but there are a few instances where the errors are less easily explicable and where the manuscript does not make sense. It is easy for copying errors to creep in at any time, but if, as is almost certain, the text was copied as a whole after 1348, the date of the copy possibly compounds the problem. A major shift in script was taking place in the mid-fourteenth century and a young copyist, particularly if he copied fast or lazily, might have increasing difficulties in reading a manuscript written decades before, possibly by someone trained in the 1270s and 1280s.

iii. The date of composition of the Vita

There has naturally been much more debate about the more interesting question of the date and method of composition of the original text than there has been about the date of the manuscript copy. Since the author himself tells us nothing about this, everything has to be drawn from internal evidence. It has been generally accepted that the author finally stopped writing sometime between December 1325, when the narrative of the chronicle ends, and late September 1326, when Isabella invaded, an event about which the author appears to know nothing. This completion date was accepted with only minor reservations by Stubbs, Denholm-Young, and Gransden, and there is no reason to dispute it.[7] Stubbs (although reserving the possibility of a later date) noted that the text indicated no knowledge of the final disasters of the reign and the accession of Edward III, although the author used the literary convention of forward comment.[8] Denholm-Young further elaborated the arguments for completion by 1326, pointing out that it was unnecessary to associate the passage against purveyance *sub anno* 1316 with the *Speculum Regis*, written (as it was then believed) between 1330 and 1333; that the text was without doubt written before 1334, when the next Gascon pope was elected, before 1329, when Robert Bruce died victorious, before 1327, when Edward III became king, and before October 1326, when Walter Stapledon was murdered; otherwise the author's forward comments concerning those figures and his use of *rex senior* for Edward I make no sense at all.[9]

However, it has also often been accepted in the past that the

---

[7] Ibid., pp. xliv, xlv; *Vita*, 1st edn., pp. xvii–xviii; Gransden, *Historical Writing*, ii. 31. Professor Given-Wilson, the most recent writer on the dating of the *Vita*, accepts this as the *terminus ante quem* while arguing convincingly for contemporaneous composition: see C. Given-Wilson, '*Vita Edwardi Secundi*: Memoir or journal?', in *Thirteenth Century England*, vi, ed. M. Prestwich, R. H. Britnell, and R. Frame (Woodbridge, Suffolk, 1997), pp. 165–76, at 165–72.

[8] He also remarked that the content became fuller as it approached 1325, as it often does as a writer nears his own time, but this is not in fact marked in this chronicle after 1322.

[9] *Vita*, 1st edn., pp. xvi–xviii.

chronicle was probably written as one piece in the months immediately before it finally breaks off. It has been seen as a memoir of a man in retirement in 1325–6, suddenly cut short, possibly by his death, with passages left unexpanded and unrevised. Several passages end in the word 'etcetera', which might suggest that the author intended to go back to write more.[10] Lack of revision is suggested by the story of Gaveston, which contains a number of repetitious passages; and the most obvious unrevised passage is on the death of the earl of Gloucester at Bannockburn. It is also true that the work has several characteristics of a literary memoir in its conscious writing for posterity, in its tendency to follow a narrative through as far as possible, and in its extended commentary and recapitulation. Yet certain discontinuities, a lack of information about future events, some detailed paraphrases of debates, occasional verbatim passages, apparent changes of opinion, and the tenses used indicate a greater immediacy in the writing. Both Stubbs and Denholm-Young acknowledged this and accepted the possibility that the author had kept notes on which he based his final text. However, in the end both editors emphasized their view that the author was writing at the end of a career, from an accurate and well-stocked memory as much as from notes, and perhaps with access to a library for some of his verbatim material.

There is, however, good reason to challenge this view. If the author's occasional summing-up is (as Denholm-Young says) careful not to go beyond the point in his narrative, why can we not take that at its face value and accept that he is summing up exactly to the end of his knowledge so far, rather than using an unnecessarily artificial literary device? Moreover, just as his comment on England possibly never having again a Gascon pope makes nonsense if it was written after 1334, so his warning to Despenser under 1313 to beware of Lancaster and leave England to escape makes nonsense if he already knew of Lancaster's death in 1322. There are other suggestions that the author lacked information at the time when he was writing. With his tendency to run a story through if he could, it is odd that he should record Gaveston's execution and the Dominican retrieval of his body in 1312, without noting his subsequent burial in 1314 if he had known that. Other retrospective annalists noted *sub anno* 1312

---

[10] See below, pp. 122–3, 166–7, 174–5, 212–13. These might, however, equally indicate that the author was drawing on newsletters or alluding to biblical or other well-known sources, which he did not intend to repeat.

both Gaveston's execution and his burial two years later.[11] His writing of summer 1313 also provides an untidy record of the Canterbury election in two sections. He clearly stopped writing when the king and queen were still abroad, after 23 May and before 16 July, and his first note of Winchelsey's death on 11 May certainly shows no knowledge of Reynolds's provision on 1 October. His later bitter tirade about this makes it extremely unlikely that he would not have expanded on Reynolds's appointment, if he had known of it when he first mentioned Winchelsey's death. His narrative of Edward Bruce in Ireland is chronologically accurate but is similarly spread over two years with other material interspersed between the events.

If we allow greater weight to the notion of notes or a journal and are prepared to see compilation and composition as continuing throughout the years of the reign, why not take one step further and accept the *Vita* as a fully contemporary chronicle, written up bit by bit as time passed? This solves the problems, raised by previous editors, of the historic present and of forward comments which do not go beyond the year they refer to. It solves the problems of repetition and lack of revision. It also explains the slight, but perceptible, changes of attitude to individuals as time passes. It is unlikely that an author looking back over a decade and a half could chart these nuances so carefully, especially if his recollection was coloured by the outcome of the events of 1321–2. The appearance of a 'memoir' comes from the fact that the author was not merely a 'jotter' but a man with an analytical tendency, a literary mind, and an interest in the value of history. He wrote, as he tells us, with a view to explaining to posterity why things happened the way they did. He thus takes time every so often to sum up Edward's achievements and to comment extensively on the developments of his reign so far. Professor Given-Wilson has recently provided an extremely convincing argument for the *Vita* as a 'journal' of a man who wrote up his thoughts regularly through the reign, and provides many more instances to uphold the case.[12] Even if some readers still prefer to argue for a final composition in 1325–6, it seems clear that the author must have been using contemporary notes to such an extent that the work closely reflects his attitudes as events took place rather than simply

[11] See for instance *Brid.*, p. 44.
[12] Given-Wilson, '*Vita Edwardi Secundi*: Memoir or journal?', pp. 165–76.

in retirement. Once its immediacy is recognized the *Vita* becomes even more valuable to historians, in charting very precisely one informed observer's reactions over two decades to the changing political scene. It reveals his times of hope and despair, his changes of attitude to individuals or groups in response to particular circumstances, his growing disillusion with Lancaster, and both his tolerance and exasperation with the king.

We might then legitimately ask whether it is possible to see exactly when he wrote each passage. When did he first begin, and how did he continue? Did he write regularly or at erratic intervals? This is not easy to work out. The closer the examination the more the discontinuities appear. The initial decision to write probably came around 1310–11, although possibly as late as 1312–13, and was no doubt prompted by the drama of the exile or the murder of Gaveston. Certainly the events of the first three or four years seem telescoped in time and are written with almost exclusive attention on Gaveston. It would not be difficult to postulate a man who watched the growing trouble with Gaveston and who, either when it erupted in 1310 with demands for general reform, or when it culminated in the Ordinances (or even possibly when events had moved further to Gaveston's death) decided that these were unusual times and worth recording for posterity. Exactly where the first break in writing comes is nonetheless difficult to assess. For instance, it would be possible to read the first section to 1311 as a backward look prompted by the need to explain the appointment of the Ordainers and the king's current campaign in Scotland. The following reflection on Gaveston's unpopularity, which repeats some of the earlier remarks about his Gascon origin, the earldom of Cornwall, and his arrogance, strongly suggests discontinuity, and that this is a new passage written some time after the previous one; this would explain the repetitions. However, it might also be possible to argue for the passage as a final reflection summing up the situation in late 1311 in which repetitions were acceptable. Either would be possible. Professor Given-Wilson has made a further suggestion, that the passage 'so that the condemnation of one may may instruct others, and the downfall of the one condemned become a lesson to others' may indicate that this section was written as late as 1313, after Gaveston's death. Yet, shortly afterwards, the author writes as if Piers is still alive: 'I fear that his pride will bring about his ruin.' The condemnation in this passage may therefore be the exile in

November 1311 rather than the death in June 1312.[13] The *Vita* abounds in such problems, and its internal dating may take some time to work out in detail. Professor Given-Wilson has made a very plausible possible division into eight sections written up in general every two or three years, but has warned that these sections may themselves have depended on notes made more frequently. It may prove impossible to work out the precise dating more closely than this, but the importance of this view of the *Vita* is immense. It means that we can use the *Vita* more subtly, to monitor constantly changing attitudes to central politics and personalities.

iv. Contemporary historical sources of the Vita

The text appears to be unique and totally independent as a chronicle. The author did not plunder any of the chronicles known to modern scholars; nor was his work quoted by other writers of the Middle Ages or beyond. As N. Denholm-Young said, 'he reveals no sources and leaves few traces'.[14] His lack of dependence on other chronicle sources is not surprising if he was writing contemporaneously up to 1326, since most known major fourteenth-century accounts of Edward's reign were written after 1327. Those composed before 1325 include the *Annales Londonienses*, the early sections of the *Annales Paulini,* and possibly the continuation of the *Flores Histor-iarum* by Robert of Reading (although Dr Gransden has argued for this as a retrospective chronicle written at the behest of Isabella and Mortimer). None of these has verbal similarities with the *Vita*, although inevitably they cover some of the same events.

The author does reveal clear traces of documentary sources. He quoted five verbatim, three of which can be traced and are clearly quoted accurately. Only the clause in the Ordinances which exiled Gaveston was from a mainstream political document; the other four were ecclesiastical in origin: the letter of 'a certain regular of admitted authority' against the king's oppressions, the decretal of Boniface VIII 'Concerning Penalties' cited after the seizure of the cardinals by Gilbert Middleton, a letter of support from Henry of Lancaster to the bishop of Hereford, and the letter from the bishops asking Isabella to come home in 1325.[15] The balance of these documents suggests that

---

[13] Ibid., pp. 175–6; and see below, pp. 26–7, 28–9.
[14] Denholm-Young, 'Authorship', p. 267. See also *BRUO*, iii. 2224–5.
[15] See below, pp. 34–7, 129–31, 142–5, 232–3, 244–7.

he may have had access to an ecclesiastical library rather than to an aristocratic muniment chest, but he also paraphrased Lancaster's letter of excuse in 1317 and the accusations against the Despensers in 1321.[16] In both he isolated the issues neatly and accurately, which suggests that he also had access to these documents and time to peruse them. Other documents, perhaps newsletters, are suggested by the unrevised passage on Gloucester's death at Bannockburn which indicates two attempts to adapt another source, and by the use of *etcetera* after details of the battles of Myton-upon-Swale and Boroughbridge.[17] Otherwise he seems to write from his own experience and from information given by associates close to events, as he occasionally suggests with phrases such as 'I heard' rather than the more general *ut dicitur*.[18] The accuracy of his chronology and his understanding of the often intricate issues he describes confirm that he was on the spot, or had excellent informants, especially for the middle years of the reign.

v. The authorship of the Vita, *and its literary sources*

Hearne associated the *Vita* with Malmesbury Abbey because a list of abbots of Malmesbury ('in a modern hand') and a copy of a charter of an abbot of Malmesbury were written on the blank sheets at both ends of the text in West's manuscript. This proves only, of course, that West's manuscript probably belonged to the Abbey at some time. How the text of the *Vita* got there is quite unknown. It is always possible that the original author or a later owner of the text or the owner of the copy of the text was a corrodian, or a visitor, or a benefactor of the abbey. The *Vita* itself was certainly not composed by a monk. The author had not the slightest interest in monastic life. Stubbs suggested a university teacher or a retired civilian.[19] Denholm-Young suggested a secular clerk and nothing is more likely. Someone so well informed could well be one of the fairly small group of educated professional clerks working in royal, baronial, or ecclesiastical circles, and if so he is likely to be someone whose name has come down to us in one context or another. After an ingenious piece of detective work, Denholm-Young suggested John Walwayn, DCL, canon of Hereford and of St Paul's, agent of the earl of Hereford, royal clerk from 1314, and briefly treasurer in 1318, who

---

[16] See below, pp. 136–9, 192–5.
[17] See below, pp. 90–3, 166–7, 212–13.
[18] See below, pp. 18–19.
[19] Stubbs, *Chronicles*, ii, pp. xliii, xlvi–xlvii.

THE MANUSCRIPT XXV

had retired and died by 1326.[20] In the absence of any evidence apart from that in the text itself, it was probably too audacious to name a name, and there are some problems in accepting Walwayn as the author. One might expect someone present at the parliament of 1316 to have written more positively about it. One might expect someone given to inveighing against the corruption of the papacy in providing unsuitable bishops and who was apparently disappointed in his hope of the bishopric of Durham (if Graystanes is correct in suggesting that Hereford put him forward in 1317), at least to have noted the appointment of Beaumont to that see. One might not expect someone who had lost his recently gained job during the purge of officials in autumn 1318 to have responded to that purge with quite such enthusiastic and vehement denunciation of government corruption. Yet Walwayn fits a substantial number of the criteria in training, west country connections, and career. If it is not he, then someone with a career very like his is needed to fit the bill.

From the text itself emerges a picture of an Englishman whose strictures on modern youth in 1315 suggest, if not old age, at least a certain maturity: a man at least in his forties and probably in his fifties. His strong criticism of corruption and simony in the Church, given vent when he recorded the appointments of Reynolds to Canterbury and Burghersh to Lincoln, have suggested a man frustrated in his career; but as this was a period when the debate over the wealth and poverty of the Church was vigorously aired he may simply be genuinely incensed at financial corruption in the Church. Elsewhere he certainly showed that he did not like to see Church wealth sucked into royal taxation. He admired Winchelsey's stand against Edward I, and he was critical of the clerical tenth granted to Edward II in 1316, writing that 'the goods of the church are the goods of the poor', and again that 'the wealth of the church . . . should be for the poor'.[21] This sounds less like the view of a man aiming at a bishopric than one strongly sympathetic to the views of the friars (although the two need not be mutually exclusive). However, he lamented corruption among the laity as much as among the clergy, and wrote throughout with a strong moralistic tone, especially castigating the sins of pride and avarice. The career of Gaveston allowed him free rein on the first and the career of the Despensers on the second. But he also referred generally to the

---

[20] Denholm-Young, 'Authorship', passim; Vita, 1st edn., pp. xix–xxviii.
[21] See below, pp. 132–3, 134–5; see also Gransden, Historical Writing, ii. 32.

aristocracy's greedy expansion of patrimony; to the corruption of
courtiers and of those who held the king's assizes; to Lancaster's
reputation destroyed by his allegedly taking a Scottish bribe of
£40,000; and to the greed of Stapledon when treasurer.

As all commentators on the *Vita* have remarked, the writer was
conventionally well educated. He used clear, uncluttered Latin, but
the whole text indicates a conscious intention to write literary history,
a commentary on the history of his times. As history was part of
classical rhetoric, this invited the medieval writer to use a number of
literary devices and ornamentations. Not only did the author of the
Vita make occasional use of the historic present (as at the battle of
Bannockburn), but he made more frequent use of direct speech
between characters to enhance the drama of events. He sometimes
used direct speech to a character in his narrative, as when he warned
Gaveston to beware of Lancaster in 1309, and more frequently to his
audience, whether to explain the hatred of Gaveston in 1312, or to
suggest that Stapledon would do well not to return to France in 1325.
His most ornate devices were reserved for his longer digressions,
which provided explanations of motives, laments, and homilies on
sin. There he used parallel constructions to produce both rhythms
and rhymes. Denholm-Young remarked that the author's use of
rhymed prose jarred on modern ears, but 'rhythmic cadence and
rhymed endings' were particularly suited to tirades.[22] Rhymed
couplets can also be found scattered elsewhere than in tirades,
often providing moralistic closures of episodes, as for example the
comments on the Welsh propensity for rebellion in 1316, and the
mistakes of the Bristollians, also in 1316.[23]

His phrasing, whether consciously or unconsciously, often echoed
biblical and liturgical vocabulary (*in conspectu . . .*; *manus . . . erat cum
illis*), and with many quotations and allusions. For his many biblical
allusions, the author drew most heavily on the Old Testament. He
cited almost all books except the later prophets, but used particularly
frequently the Books of Kings and the Psalms. His relatively few
references to the New Testament were mainly to Matthew and Luke,

[22] *Vita*, 1st edn., pp. xix, 99 n.
[23] Hearne and Stubbs drew attention to four of the earlier couplets by printing them as
verses, a practice which Denholm-Young continued (*Vita*, 1st edn., pp. 13, 23, 28, 29). As
not all examples of rhymes were so printed, and as to print them all would certainly 'jar the
modern ear', three of these four early examples have been returned to continuous prose in
this edition. Denholm-Young's rhyming translations are retained where appropriate.

with a scattering of examples drawn from the epistles. The author also had a highly developed legal sense. His familiarity with civil law is shown through a dozen references and clear allusions, and also through his use of civilian vocabulary such as *concussio, patrocinium, pedaneus iudex,* and *mala mansio*.[24] This is hardly surprising if Walwayn, DCL, were the author. Even if he were not, English common law treatises of this period such as Bracton's *De Legibus et Consuetudinibus Angliae,* copied and circulated after 1268, and the *Fleta* (*c.*1290) show Roman law to be well known to English lawyers, and several of the Roman law tags used by the author also appear in Bracton and *Fleta*.[25] His references to natural law also come ultimately from Roman law, possibly mediated through canon law. He made four specific references to canon law, and referred to Marcher law and the laws of war.[26] Throughout he was keen to discuss legality. His descriptions of the arguments of the barons and of the king frequently explain their legal points, and he seems to have a strong interest in the precise definitions of treason.[27] Beyond theology and law, he knew something of astrology, recording the explanations for the rains of 1316 given by those 'wise in astrology'.[28] He knew and quoted some of the contemporary moralistic Latin verses of his day,[29] and, not surprisingly, he was familiar with moralistic sermons against the vices. His denunciations of vices and his laments on people and events reflect strongly the sermon style of the time. His digression on avarice in particular seems to be closely modelled on sermons, even to the use of the exemplum of a 'good man', and elsewhere his use of *figura* in relation to material drawn from the Old Testament complies with the precise usage of the word advocated by a contemporary sermon theorist such as Robert of Basevorn.[30]

[24] See below, pp. 20–1, 156–7, 194–5, 242–3; these were pointed out by Denholm-Young, *Vita*, 1st edn., notes to pp. 10, 91, 114, 142.

[25] See e.g. below, Text, nn. 250, 336, 469.

[26] For further comment on his legal interest, see below, pp. lii–lv, and index of quotations.

[27] For further discussion of his views on treason, see below, pp. lii–lvii.

[28] See below, p. 122–3.   [29] See below, pp. 110–11.

[30] See below, pp. 132–3, 170–3. For the use of *figura* in sermons see Robert de Basevorn, *Forma Praedicandi,* cap. xlix, in T. M. Charland, *Artes Praedicandi: Contribution à l'histoire de la rhétorique au moyen âge,* Publications de l'Institut d'études médiévales d'Ottawa, vii (Paris, 1936), pp. 231–323. An English translation is available by L. Krul, 'Robert of Basevorn, *The Form of Preaching* (1322 A. D.)', in *Three Medieval Rhetorical Arts,* ed. J. J. Murphy (Berkeley and London, 1971), pp. 109–215, at pp. 205–7. I am indebted to Yuichi Akae for this reference to Basevorn.

The author was also familiar with classical Latin authors and Greek history. He quoted from Claudian, Horace, Juvenal, Lucan, and Palladius, and referred frequently to the Trojan War and the reign of Alexander the Great for comparisons. This again is not surprising. Forerunners of the 'classicising friars', such as John of Wales and Nicholas Trevet, were beginning to intensify interest in classical learning in England during his lifetime,[31] but the interest in classical material was far from new. It had been strong since the mid-twelfth century, and was shown not only in the direct study of classical texts, but also in new universal histories such as the mid-thirteenth-century *Speculum historiale* of Vincent of Beauvais, and in the retelling of classical stories in legendary histories, epics, and romances.[32] The range of classical literature and historical information available to English authors and their interest in it can be seen, for example, in John of Salisbury's *Policraticus* from the twelfth century, in the Franciscan John of Wales's *Breviloquium* on the virtues of ancient princes and philosophers and *Compendiloquium* of the lives of illustrious philosophers from the mid-thirteenth century, and in Ranulf Higden's *Polychronicon*, which was being written in Chester at about the same time that our author was completing his work.[33] These works themselves became, in their turn, sources of information on antiquity: John of Wales drew on John of Salisbury, and Higden drew on both. All were widely read and so helped to spread knowledge yet further. Preachers, who also used classical exempla, spread basic information about classical figures and history even beyond the literate classes.[34] By the reign of Edward II, through these various means, classical stories and allusions were pervasive and commonplace in the cultural baggage of literate society, and familiar in outline to many beyond it.

The Trojan War and the reign of Alexander the Great were

---

[31] B. Smalley, *English Friars and Antiquity* (Oxford, 1960), ch. 3.

[32] Ibid., pp. 15–26, 41–65.

[33] See John of Salisbury, *Policraticus*, ed. and trans. C. J. Nederman (Cambridge, 1990), pp. xix–xxi, and the prologue to Book I, pp. 3–8; J. Swanson, *John of Wales: A Study of the Works and Ideas of a Thirteenth-Century Friar* (Cambridge, 1989), pp. 101–6, 123, 164–6, 189, 196–200; J. Taylor, *The Universal Chronicle of Ranulf Higden* (Oxford, 1966), pp. 39–44, 72–81. For John of Wales's role as a forerunner of the English 'classicising friars' see Smalley, *English Friars*, pp. 51–5.

[34] This is visible, for example, in the Franciscan preaching handbook *Fasciculus Morum: A Fourteenth-Century Preacher's Handbook*, ed. and trans. S. Wenzel (University Park, Pa., 1989). For Alexander the Great there, see pp. 94–7, 98–101; for the Trojan war, see pp. 264–5.

particularly popular episodes from Greek history, accessible not only through Latin writers such as Virgil, Quintus Curtius, or Orosius and, more recently, Vincent of Beauvais, but through increasing numbers of romances. The drama of the fall of Troy encouraged one of the earliest vernacular romances, the *Roman d'Eneas*, a retelling of Virgil's *Aeneid* in Anglo-French for the court of Henry II.[35] Troy also provided the basis for Geoffrey of Monmouth's legendary *Historia Regum Britanniae* (*c*.1136), which traced the foundation of Britain to Brutus, descendant of Aeneas.[36] The reign of Alexander similarly passed from Latin histories into vernacular romances,[37] and by the 1330s romances of both Troy and of Alexander were to become available not only in French but also in English.[38] Aspects of classical history were thus familiar to both the author and many in his potential audience.

Our author drew on the Trojan war for the example of Achilles, who quarrelled with his fellow Greeks and failed to bring them help in their need (a parallel used for Lancaster's failure at Berwick); Achilles also had in Patroclus a close friend whose death he avenged (a parallel used for Edward's friendship with Gaveston). The fall of Troy offered parallels for the betrayal of the king and of a city (Berwick). The history of Alexander the Great provided two more parallels for treason, with Philotas's failure to tell Alexander of a plot, and Alexander's death by poison at the hands of traitors. Interpretations of these classical stories in the Christian world could be complex, and elements of this complexity are visible in the *Vita*. Aeneas, especially for the writers of foundation legends, was 'noble

---

[35] The literature on the story of Troy in the Middle Ages is substantial. Excellent brief introductions may be found in Lee Patterson, 'Virgil and the historical consciousness of the twelfth century: The *Roman d'Eneas* and *Erec et Enide*', in *Negotiating the Past: The Historical Understanding of Medieval Literature* (Madison, 1987), pp. 157–95, at 157–83; Lee Patterson, *Chaucer and the Subject of History* (London, 1991), pp. 86–99; F. Ingledew, 'The Book of Troy and the genealogical construction of history: The case of Geoffrey of Monmouth's *Historia regum Britanniae*', *Speculum*, lxix (1994), 665–704.

[36] The Trojan exiles appeared in the legendary histories of several northern peoples, linking them with antiquity and legitimizing their rulers; see Gransden, *Historical Writing*, i. 204 and note; Patterson, *Chaucer*, pp. 90–3. For the use of the *Aeneid* by Norman writers see Ingledew, 'The Book of Troy and the genealogical construction of history', pp. 677 and n., 682–5. For the development of Scotland's foundation legend in this period see below, pp. 224–5.

[37] Cary, *Medieval Alexander*, pp. 16–77. One of the best known 12th-c. retellings was the Latin *Alexandreis* by Walter de Châtillon, which our author may have known (see below, Text, nn. 72, 287, 336).

[38] Smalley, *English Friars*, pp. 21–6.

Aeneas', a prince who fought as long as possible against overwhelming odds, but for others, including in this period Trevet and Higden,
Aeneas was the cowardly betrayer of his city through his flight.[39] Our
author uses both 'noble Aeneas' and 'Aeneas the traitor' according to
need.[40] His references to Alexander were more one-dimensional: he
took the view that Alexander was simply the greatest conqueror the
world had ever seen, who was nevertheless betrayed by his followers,
but another view among moralists and theologians was that Alexander's overweening ambition and other vices brought his early death
as just punishment.[41]

   History was constantly in the author's mind. Apart from his
references to Greek history, he mentioned the conquests of England
by Julius Caesar, the Saxons, and the Normans, seeing all as the
outcome of internal discord. He cited British history through
Geoffrey of Monmouth and he alluded twice to the prophecies of
Merlin.[42] He referred to the characteristics of English kings back to
Henry II, and mentioned histories in Latin and French of Richard I at
Acre.[43] But, like any educated administrator or politician, he was
particularly sensitive to the political events of recent decades, and he
drew most parallels with events in the reigns of Henry III and
Edward I.[44] His information on Edward I's later reign would certainly
be first-hand and he might even be old enough to have childhood
memories of the aftermath of Henry III's civil war. In any case his
knowledge of that would undoubtedly feel immediate through
parental experiences, just as aspects of the war of 1939–45 still
seemed familiar to some in the 1990s. His world of allusion, however,
was largely sober and rational. Unlike a number of chroniclers he paid

---

[39] Ingledew, 'The Book of Troy and the genealogical construction of history', pp. 677
and n., 682–5; Patterson, 'Virgil and the historical consciousness of the twelfth century',
pp. 176–7.
   [40] See below, pp. 24–5, 168–9.
   [41] For the varying interpretations of Alexander's life, see Cary, *Medieval Alexander*,
pp. 83–105, 118–25, 173–81.
   [42] Geoffrey of Monmouth wrote his history *c.*1136. Tracing British origins to Brutus,
descendant of Aeneas of Troy, he provided the British with a direct link to the world of
antiquity; he then worked through legendary and historical British kings to the death of
Cadwallader in the 7th c. He inserted a section on Merlin's prophecies at book vii. 1–4 (*The
Historia Regum Britanniae of Geoffrey of Monmouth*, ed. A. Griscom (London and New
York, 1929), pp. 383–97). His work became very popular, and was incorporated in the early
sections of the popular Brut chronicle of England. For references to Merlin in the *Vita*, see
below, pp. 110–11, 118–21.
   [43] See below, pp. 62–3, 68–9.
   [44] See below, pp. 32–3, 76–7, 128–9, 158–9, 168–9.

no attention to portents and prophecies, and was scathing about the Welsh belief in Merlin.

The author's geographical point of interest is certainly the west country, but the exact focus is less clear, as Denholm-Young demonstrated. Some of the interest in the Marches after 1320 may be explained simply as that of the informed political observer, aware of the area's importance; similarly the large number of references to the earls of Gloucester, Hereford, and Warwick, to Amory, Audley, the younger Despenser, and the Mortimers may reflect their national role as much as their local one. However, the long narrative of the Bristol rebellion and of Llywelyn Bren's rising, the several references to Maurice Berkeley, the picking out of Giffard and Willington among those captured at Bannockburn suggest a stronger local interest. The Marcher passages are also well informed, as are the passages on Bristol and Bren. The author knew precisely why the Marchers hated Despenser, he discussed the details of Marcher law, and provided names of Marcher castles. His comments on the wild and rebellious Welsh also smack of local prejudice.[45] There are fairly long digressions into rebellions by Banaster (Lancashire), and Ewer (Hampshire and the south), but in these the author displays little specific geographical knowledge compared with his work on the west country. Within the west country, Denholm-Young argued strongly for the writer's interest in the earl of Hereford rather than the earl of Gloucester, although some of his points seem a little forced. The use, for instance, of 'bishop of that place' immediately after a reference to the city of Hereford seems quite acceptable as literary style, while if the author worked for Hereford, it seems discreet to the point of absurdity to make no personal comment on the earl, when he praises both Gloucester and Warwick.

The author's career had certainly placed him in political circles. He was too politically aware and politically informed, especially for the middle years, to be far from the centre. His paraphrases show that he has had access to important political documents. His information on each parliament is accurate; his appreciation of the points in the debates was sharp. He was indeed someone 'in the know'. He made the point that, although the magnates' debate was not made public in 1310, 'he heard' the outcome,[46] a more positive statement than the usual impersonal, 'as it is said'. Experience is suggested by his

[45] See below, pp. 56–7, 118–21.   [46] See below, pp. 18–19.

comment that mediators exaggerated the danger of civil war in 1312, and that mediators often twist the messages they bear.[47] Experience at the centre clearly left him critical of court corruption, and with admiration for Archbishop Melton, who maintained his integrity at court.[48] He maintained a relatively tolerant and balanced view of most political individuals, being able to rehearse the arguments both in favour and against the positions of Gaveston, the king, Lancaster, and the rebel barons. His position comes through clearly as that of someone highly critical of the court, and sympathetic to the baronage, but not sympathetic to baronial lawlessness and rebellion, and certainly not to Lancaster's flirtation with the Scots.[49]

THE REIGN OF EDWARD II AND THE VALUE OF THE *VITA*

i. The reign of Edward II

The reign of Edward II is one of the most dramatic in the Middle Ages. In his twenty-year reign Edward faced defeat in the Scottish war, failure in France, and utter disaster at home: repeated threats and open violence against his favourites, a revolutionary reform programme, civil war, and finally deposition. Part of Edward I's legacy (unfinished war with Scotland, a £200,000 debt, recent resistance from 1297 onwards) meant that his successor might expect a rough ride at first, but there was no inevitability that the reign should end in deposition. Financial and political developments under Edward I offered the potential for solving the problems he left. Ultimately Edward II brought about his own downfall. The reign exemplifies comprehensive breakdown in the relationship between king and barons. It is precisely here that the *Vita* is so valuable, since the author's predominant interest was in secular politics at the highest level.

ii. Recent historiography

Since the last edition of the *Vita Edwardi Secundi* in 1957, there has been no change in the position of the text itself as a major literary source for the reign. No new accounts or chronicles have been found, although a full text of the short continuation of the French prose Brut

---

[47] See below, pp. 54–5, 138–9. [48] See below, pp. 236–7.
[49] See below, pp. 168–75.

has been published for the first time.[50] However, a surge in the publication of monographs in the last three decades has led to changes in interpretations of the reign.

For a generation before 1957, when N. Denholm-Young wrote his introduction to the *Vita*, the works of J. Conway Davies and T. F. Tout held general sway. Both had emphasized constitutional and administrative developments, and in Tout's case his interest in administrative developments led to an interpretation which emphasized principled baronial opposition to what was termed 'household government'. Not all agreed. B. Wilkinson's work continued to emphasize the importance of broader constitutional ideas and Denholm-Young's short but forceful introduction to the *Vita* criticized the 'household theory' and did much to put personal politics at the centre once more. Denholm-Young took, perhaps, too extreme a swing when he denied the reformers any moral purpose and took so narrow a definition of 'constitutional' that he denied that the author of the *Vita* had any constitutional interest at all. However, his views marked a distinct move away from the constitutional emphasis of the previous generation of historians.[51] The surge of interest in the reign from 1970 brought excellent new studies, which have reassessed baronial motivations, Edward's inheritance, and his character, as well as the precise significance of many of the events. The interest in personalities is shown by the number of biographies, which have proved a useful approach to the politics of the reign. The best of them are wide surveys of the political world, providing a full context for the actions of their subject. J. R. Maddicott, J. R. S. Phillips, J. S. Hamilton, and P. Chaplais have looked at Lancaster, Pembroke, and Gaveston; R. Haines, J. Denton, J. Wright, and M. Buck turned to the bishops of the period. N. Fryde looked more broadly at the last years of the reign, drawing on work in the financial area. M. Prestwich's work has transformed views of Edward II's inheritance. More recently C. Valente has reassessed the documents of the deposition, P. Doherty has reassessed the role of Queen Isabella, P. R. Dryburgh has written on Roger Mortimer of Wigmore, and R. M. Haines has published a new study of the reign.[52] Works on

---

[50] *The Anonimalle Chronicle 1307–1334, from Brotherton Collection MS 29*, ed. W. R. Childs and J. Taylor, Yorkshire Archaeological Society Record Series, cxlvii (1991).

[51] *Vita*, 1st edn., pp. xi–xii.

[52] J. R. Maddicott, *Thomas of Lancaster 1307–1322* (Oxford, 1970); J. R. S. Phillips, *Aymer de Valence, Earl of Pembroke, 1307–1324* (Oxford, 1972); J. S. Hamilton, *Piers Gaveston, Earl of Cornwall 1307–1312: Politics and Patronage in the Reign of Edward II*

demography, economic history, numismatics, Scottish history, legal developments, parliament, and county communities have also steadily enhanced our understanding of the circumstances in which the political figures took their decisions. The importance of many of these works will be apparent in the notes to the text.

The biographical approach inevitably puts personal ambitions and antagonisms at the centre of discussions of baronial motivations. The rejection of an ideological attack on a 'system' of household government has been confirmed, but most modern authors stop short of claiming that the barons were uninfluenced by constitutional and political ideas. None returns unreservedly to Stubbs's view of the reign as an 'exceedingly dreary' one, in which there was 'a miserable level of political selfishness which marks without exception every public man', and 'an absence of sincere feeling except in the shape of hatred and revenge'.[53] The result is a much more balanced and believable view of complex political motivations. Personal hostilities between Gaveston and most of the other major barons, between Lancaster and Pembroke after 1312, between Lancaster and Warenne, and between Lancaster and Badlesmere had deep significance for the peace of the realm, but strong personal emotions did not mean that the great political figures ignored the ideas clearly visible in the treatises, documents, and actions of the period. They believed in good counsel, consultation, consent, justice, due legal process, the value of traditional offices such as constable or steward, the regular calling of parliament, and the regular changing of officials. The Ordinances encapsulated many of these beliefs and were important to others

(London, 1988); P. Chaplais, *Piers Gaveston: Edward II's Adoptive Brother* (Oxford, 1994); R. M. Haines, *The Church and Politics in Fourteenth-Century England: The Career of Adam Orleton c. 1275–1345* (Cambridge, 1978); J. H. Denton, *Robert Winchelsey and the Crown 1294–1313: A Study in the Defence of Ecclesiastical Liberty* (Cambridge, 1980); J. R. Wright, *The Church and the English Crown 1305–1334: A Study based on the Register of Archbishop Walter Reynolds* (Toronto, 1980); M. Buck, *Politics, Finance and the Church in the Reign of Edward II: Walter Stapeldon, Treasurer of England* (Cambridge, 1983); N. Fryde, *The Tyranny and Fall of Edward II, 1321–1326* (Cambridge, 1979); M. Prestwich, *Edward I* (London, 1988); id., 'The Ordinances of 1311 and the politics of the early fourteenth century', in *Politics and Crisis in the Fourteenth Century*, ed. J. Taylor and W. R. Childs (Gloucester, 1990), pp. 1–18; C. Valente, 'The deposition and abdication of Edward II', *EHR*, cxiii (1998), 879–881; P. Doherty, *Isabella and the Strange Death of Edward II* (London, 2003); P. R. Dryburgh, 'The career of Roger Mortimer, 1st earl of March (c. 1287–1330)', Ph.D. thesis (Bristol, 2002); R. M. Haines, *King Edward II: His Life, his Reign, and its Aftermath, 1284–1330* (Montreal and London, 2003). Unfortunately the last appeared too late to be fully absorbed into this volume.

[53] Stubbs, *Chronicles*, ii, p. lxxv.

besides Lancaster. Of course, the interpretation and strength of these ideas varied from individual to individual, and changed over the decades in response to events, but such variation does not necessarily mean that beliefs were not sincerely held. Practical politics is always a matter of compromise, and in the political world of the fourteenth century, as Maddicott remarked, few could afford to emulate Lancaster (immensely rich, holder of five earldoms, and a royal cousin) and stand for long against the king, losing all chance of patronage.[54] Indeed, Lancaster is a good example of the contradictions in a complex personality. His personal feuds and probable collusion with the Scots were combined with public piety and staunch adherence to the Ordinances, at least until 1318. Pembroke's career similarly illustrates the complexities of motivation and action: a staunch Ordainer and Gaveston's captor in 1312, he returned firmly to the king's side after Gaveston's capture and murder, which he saw as a stain on his personal honour. Despite his quarrel with Lancaster over the seizure of Gaveston and over land at Thorpe Waterville, he nonetheless worked to produce reconciliation between Lancaster and the king. His apparent vacillations could be the struggles of a man of principle looking for the best way to support his anointed king and the peace of the realm.[55] Of all the great figures the most radical reassessment has been in the position of Gaveston. His competence as a soldier and success as lieutenant in Ireland are now clear, and increasingly historians have questioned the significance, and even the existence, of a homosexual relationship between him and Edward.[56] P. Chaplais has argued cogently that the strongest bond between them was a sworn brotherhood, and this relationship alone would have been sufficient to raise Gaveston above all other men except Edward's blood brothers. But all authors still agree that the extremely favourable patronage granted to Gaveston, for whatever reason, was the prime cause of Edward's early troubles.

Just as views on baronial motives have become more complex, so have views on the difficulties inherited by Edward II. To many historians in the nineteenth century Edward I was the epitome of a successful king and Edward II's main problem would have been to live up to his father's reputation. J. Conway Davies drew attention to

---

[54] Maddicott, *Lancaster*, p. 326.   [55] Phillips, *Pembroke*, pp. 141–3.
[56] Hamilton fully accepts the homosexual relationship but argues that it was not of fundamental importance in the dislike of Gaveston (*Gaveston*, pp. 15–17, 109–12); Chaplais is more sceptical of the relationship (*Gaveston*, pp. 109–14).

more practical and interlocking problems of war and finance, but suggested that the main problem was baronial reaction against the strong prerogative rule of Edward I, which then centred upon who should control the administration. Thereafter others, including N. Denholm-Young in 1957, paid attention to the practical problems left by Edward I, but it has been left to M. Prestwich's work to reveal the full extent of these: a vast debt (now known to have been in the region of £200,000), an overstretched Exchequer organization, an unresolved Scottish war and anger at the prise, purveyance, and loans which financed it, an unresolved Gascon problem, and a baronage whose criticism of a demanding ruler over the last decade had met with some success. But alongside the deeper appreciation of the problems left by Edward I remains an awareness that Edward II also had the means to overcome at least some of them with the new taxation systems and the booming economy. While debate may continue over the exact scale of Edward II's inherited problems, it is not immediately clear that Edward II started at a substantially greater disadvantage than did his grandfather, his father, or his son. M. Prestwich's recent study of Edward I concluded that Edward remained a 'formidable king' and his reign 'a great one'.[57] Edward II's inheritance was more difficult than once thought, but by no means unmanageable.

Views have changed less on Edward's own shortcomings as king. We may feel justified in modifying the first part of Denholm-Young's judgement that 'Edward II sat down to the game of kingship with a remarkably poor hand' by pointing to the underlying strength of the English monarchy, but it is difficult to deny that 'he played it very badly'.[58] Ultimately it was not the burden of debt or the Scottish and French wars which destroyed him, but his own domestic political decisions, especially his reliance on favourites. Even his financial success brought criticism when it seemed to be for the benefit of his favourites. However, while interpretations of his kingship remain much the same, interpretations of his personal character have seen some change. This is particularly notable in the recent scepticism about his possible homosexual relationship with Gaveston.[59] It is also visible in comparisons of the depositions of Edward II and Richard II. These have sometimes implied that, while Richard's sins were those

[57] Prestwich, *Ed. I*, p. 567.
[58] *Vita*, 1st edn., p. ix.
[59] See above, n. 56.

of commission, Edward's were of omission, in that he simply left government to others. Stubbs drew from his sources the impression of a man with 'skilful hand rather than . . . thoughtful head', with 'a love of pomp' but 'no taste for discipline', a 'fine, tall, handsome man' with 'little self-restraint'.[60] H. Johnstone wrote on his love of 'rustic pursuits'.[61] Denholm-Young noted him as aimless, lazy, incapable, and out of sympathy with his subjects.[62] More recent views make Edward less negative, perhaps more complex, although no more successful. J. R. Maddicott discerned a man sometimes shrewd in political tactics, sometimes energetic in action, but with no vision or political judgement, little interest in the 'business of ruling', and lacking military ability;[63] and N. Fryde found evidence of sharp interest in the business of governing when it came to raising money.[64] Certainly, Edward's actions in defence of his prerogative, his military action and vengeance in 1321–2, and his success in obtaining money do not show a weak king in the conventional sense. Rather they show a man who had a clear idea of the power of kingship and a strong desire to exercise it, but unfortunately for him and the country, no clear idea of how to do this in the circumstances of the early fourteenth century, given his own love for his favourites and the uncompromising opposition of his cousin, Lancaster.

iii. The value of the Vita

The value of the *Vita* is clearly evident in the wide use that historians have made of it. As Denholm-Young wrote in 1957, particularly of the section on the middle years, 'there is hardly a sentence that has not been cited by modern historians'. T. F. Tout saw it as the strongest of the group of chronicles for Edward's reign, for its humanity, colour, and sympathetic critical comment, and A. Gransden has remarked that research since Tout's time has confirmed the author's 'wise judgments and factual accuracy'.[65] In all the recent works mentioned above, the *Vita* has continued to hold a prime position. Its value lies in its contemporary dating (which was not always evident to earlier writers), in the closeness of the author

---

[60] Stubbs, *Chronicles*, ii, p. xlix.
[61] H. Johnstone, 'The eccentricities of Edward II', *EHR*, xlviii (1933), 264–7; see also Childs, ' "Welcome" ', pp. 160–1.
[62] *Vita*, 1st edn., p. ix.   [63] Maddicott, *Lancaster*, pp. 89–90, 186, 253.
[64] Fryde, *Tyranny*, ch. 7.
[65] *Vita*, 1st edn., p. xi; Tout, *Ed. II*, p. 5; Gransden, *Historical Writing*, ii. 3.

to central politics, in the literary form chosen by the author, and in the demonstrable accuracy of his work. The first two aspects have been fully discussed above, but the latter two also deserve brief comment.

The author has chosen to inform his reader and posterity (both of which he mentions) by writing history rather than a simple annal. The work is a sophisticated, reflective commentary, looking for causation and motivation. Given its probable dating and the author's overwhelming interest in central politics, it thus becomes even more valuable. Alongside its well-informed narrative, it provides a running commentary of high quality on the great political figures, their shifting alliances, and their motives. The author devotes nearly half his narrative to the relationships of the king and his greater barons. He expands on the content of debates and arguments put forward at meetings between king and barons, and offers criticism and homilies on the vices of the period. Such a wealth of commentary provides not only insight into the concerns of the great, but also gives us one of our clearest insights into the reactions of those around them. The responses by this individual may well be representative of a larger group among his milieu: familiar with government, aware of personal and moral failings, sympathetic to the king's opponents, but also aware of the fragility of peace, terrified of civil war, and totally opposed to resistance which might slide into treason. The author also spends about one-fifth of his narrative on Scottish affairs. He has interesting comment on economic problems and information on the regional affairs of the west country. He offers some colourful comment on episcopal appointments and church corruption, but, unlike almost all other chroniclers of the time, he makes no comment on such *causes célèbres* as the dissolution of the Templars or the Franciscan heresies. The value of the text lies overwhelmingly in its commentary on central politics.

The author's chronology is almost entirely accurate. Although he offers few exact dates and is often allusive to meetings, a close parallel reading of record sources shows that his account of people present and matters discussed at meetings is almost always right. Such combined use of record and chronicle is essential for a full appreciation of the *Vita*, or indeed any chronicle. Writing generally, but no doubt with the *Vita* in mind, Tout wrote that 'on re-reading even the best known chronicles in the light of the study of records, many passages that hitherto had suggested very little become full of meaning'.[66] Because the author is accurate where we can check his information, we can reasonably accept information which cannot be checked, as in the unique record of Edward's second attempt to induce the pope to annul the Ordinances in 1317. The author is not, however, without faults. Some are trivial, as when he suggests that the clause concerning Gaveston was number 10 or thereabouts, when in the final contemporary version it comes at 20. The inaccurate transmission of numbers in medieval texts, however, is not infrequent and these mistakes could be the fault of a copyist, miscopying .x. for .xx. There are other mistakes, however, some of which seem a little odd if he was as close to central affairs as we think. He was wrong in his statements that one of Edward's motives for going to Scotland in 1310 was to avoid a French demand for homage and that it was the earl of Gloucester who was left as keeper of the realm in 1313.[67] Further, in 1318 the parliamentary summons came after rather than before the Leicester meeting (but otherwise the author's account of the abortive parliaments that year is vastly superior to any other chronicler's), and the judgement against Despenser was an award rather than the statute (but here the author is correctly reflecting earlier wording, since the Despensers' opponents initially asked for a statute but had to be content with an award when the king proved unwilling to accept a statute).[68] However, amongst the wealth of accurate information offered such mistakes are few and do nothing to undermine the chronicle's value.

iv. Chronological content

The reign may be usefully broken into three periods, 1307–11, 1311–22, and 1322–7. In the first period domestic politics were dominated by Gaveston, in the second by Lancaster and the Ordinances, in the third by the Despensers. The detail of the *Vita* is best for the middle period, but in all three the author has things of significance and importance to say.

The early section of the text from 1307 to 1311 centres almost completely on Gaveston. The author probably began to write about

---

[66] Tout, *Ed. II*, p. 4.
[67] Gloucester, however, was one of those appointed to open parliament when the king was late returning from France.
[68] The commons nonetheless called the award a statute in 1327. See Maddicott, *Lancaster*, pp. 284–5; M. Prestwich, 'The charges against the Despensers, 1321', *BIHR*, lviii (1985), 95–100, at 95, 97.

1310 or 1311, or possibly even as late as 1312, prompted by the crisis over Gaveston. This would explain the extended descriptions of why Gaveston was disliked, and it would also explain the sparseness of details on the first exile and return. Otherwise, if the author were writing throughout 1308–9, it is surprising, given his interest in constitutional matters, that he omitted all reference to the declaration on homage presented in 1308 and ignored the parliaments at Westminster and Stamford in 1309. Nonetheless, the text is valuable for this early period because, unusually, the author shows in greater detail than any other chroniclers how uncertain the barons were at this time and how their allegiances changed. In 1308 he records Lincoln's swing from support of Piers to opposition, Despenser senior's swing to the king, and Gloucester's inhibition at pressing for his brother-in-law's exile. After the first exile he records how Edward enticed many back to his side, including Lincoln and Warenne, but not Warwick, and he records Lancaster's first swing into opposition in 1309.

The concentration on Gaveston is broken after the appointment of the Ordainers in 1310 by the king's campaign against Scotland. The Scottish war is the author's second main interest, taking nearly a quarter of his narrative. This first passage on Scottish affairs is itself a microcosm of his historical and analytical method. He includes a brief but clear analysis of why England was at war with Scotland, comments on the difficulty for the English of Scottish terrain and tactics, shows some regard for Bruce as a tactician, and explains how Edward's action against Scotland was weakened by the domestic squabble over Gaveston. This brings him neatly back to a further discussion of the problem of Gaveston, and to a long description of the negotiations over the presentation and final acceptance of the Ordinances in 1311. His comment here on the relationship of Gaveston and the king is particularly interesting. He strongly castigates the king for immoderate love of Gaveston, but his emphasis makes clear that he saw its impropriety as lying in its diversion of patronage and favour from the king's normal advisers, not in any sexual relationship.

The narrative then moves smoothly into the second period of Edward's reign, dominated by the Ordinances, Lancaster, and the Scottish war. The author emphasizes that it was concern with the enforcement of the Ordinances that prompted Gaveston's capture, and describes in detail the turmoil which his murder provoked.

Uniquely he records Pembroke's personal crisis when Gaveston was taken from his custody, and his appeal to the earl of Gloucester and the University of Oxford over the stain on his honour. At this stage the author's analytical bent surfaces again as he explains why action against Gaveston had to be by Lancaster, whose wealth and blood made him the only earl powerful enough to stand against the king. The narrative then moves steadily through the rest of 1312 and into the beginning of 1313, charting important details of the subsequent negotiations between king and barons. This theme is unbroken except for the record of the birth of the future Edward III in November. The author closes this passage in spring 1313: the king's departure for France is followed by a dispiriting summary of his reign so far, a long obituary for Archbishop Winchelsey, who died in May 1313, and a sharp comment on the uselessness of the king's delay in reaching settlement with his opponents.

The writer seems to start again in the autumn of 1313 when the narrative of the reconciliation of the king and Lancaster is completed. Important comment includes an early statement on the elder Despenser's unpopularity because of his unjust actions as a royal official, and interesting speculation on how far the opposing barons might have gone if Edward had not compromised. At this stage the author was looking back to the clash between Henry III and Montfort to show how dangerous even justifiable resistance to the king could be. His final comment that the war subsidy of 1313 was granted to the king by the magnates illustrates his perception of parliament as an entirely aristocratic occasion. The rest of the year 1313 is filled with a very long tirade against papal corruption on the appointment of the unworthy Reynolds instead of the worthy Cobham to Canterbury.

In 1314 the narrative is almost entirely devoted to Scotland, a major concern in this middle period, and one in which the author was strongly interested. He records the loss of Edinburgh and Roxburgh, the Scots' attempt to retake Berwick, and the siege of Stirling Castle, which resulted in the battle of Bannockburn. His interest in domestic politics is still strong, however, and, unlike any other chronicler, he records in some detail the dispute over whether the king should go to Scotland without the backing of the barons in parliament, as required by the Ordinances. He describes the journey north, the battle, and the rout in detail, and finishes with a lament, which ends in his blaming the modern-day pride and envy of the English. The narrative makes clear how the loss gravely weakened the king, and describes his confirmation of the Ordinances, and the exchange of captives for the earl of Hereford. The year concludes with the final burial of Gaveston at King's Langley (another indication of 'journal' rather than 'memoir').

In 1315 the author's interest is still centred largely on Scottish affairs. He first describes further reforms with the purge of the court and price-fixing measures, but then returns to Scottish affairs with detailed reports of Maurice Berkeley's appointment as keeper of Berwick, John Botetourt's to the sea squadron to stop supplies reaching Scotland, and Pembroke's and Badlesmere's appointments to patrol the border. He records Bruce's siege of Carlisle and, in more detail, Edward Bruce's invasion of Ireland. (At this stage there was clearly no knowledge of Edward Bruce's subsequent failure.) The author then asks what prompted the Scots' attack on England, and sees it as God's judgement on the pride and deceit of the English. He particularly denounces the pride of young men, English deceit in not repaying debts, and the corruption of justice. He also makes his first reference to the great famine of the middle years, and sees this too as God's punishment. In the autumn of 1315 his interest changed to rebellions: those of Adam Banaster against Lancaster and of Llywelyn Bren against Payn Turberville in Gloucester's Welsh lands. He provides an extended discussion of Bren's rebellion and his motives, which forms one of the passages which points strongly to the author's west country origin.

Under 1316 the author remarks that the January parliament at Lincoln did little because of Bren's rebellion. This is a corrective to the modern historian's tendency to emphasize the importance of this parliament. However, despite his dismissive beginning, the author goes on to mention three important measures: the perambulation of the forest, the appointment of Lancaster as the king's chief counsellor, and the abolition of the price-fixing ordinance. His comment on the last shows clear appreciation of the relationship of supply and demand. It is followed by a more extended comment on the continuing dearth of corn, which had led to famine on a scale not seen, he says, for a hundred years. His discontinuity of comment on the scarcity of corn in 1315 and in 1316 (like the discontinuity on Gaveston's burial, Bruce in Ireland, and the Canterbury election) again suggests contemporary writing rather than hindsight. By far the greatest amount of space in the year is then devoted to the troubles at Bristol. As with his first comment on Scotland in 1310, the writer looks back to earlier years to explain the beginning of the outbreak and the situation by 1316. Bristol's final surrender is the opportunity for another homily on the uselessness of rebellion; the author believes that firm government would have solved the problem, but bribes and corruption delayed justice. From this he moves to a letter sent to the king's confessor about the hardship of prise, which is prefaced by a summary of the ideas on good kingship and tyranny. At this point two leaves were missing from West's manuscript, so we lose a passage which might have included an extended piece on the expectations of good kingship.[69]

When the text starts again the year is still 1316 and the author is in the middle of a discussion of the continuing dispute between Lancaster and the king, in which the households of each exacerbate rather than ameliorate the situation. This passage is extremely important as it records one of the earliest rumours of Lancaster's links with the Scots. It is followed by an unusually detailed account of the arguments in the Canterbury provincial convocation in October at which the bishops finally agreed on a grant for the king. This account shows a clear understanding of the modification of the papal bull *clericis laicos* and reveals the author's own views: he disapproves strongly of the use of church wealth by the lay power, since 'the goods of the church are the goods of the poor' and 'the wealth of the church . . . should be for the poor'.[70]

The year 1317 starts with an account of the embassy to Avignon to seek papal condemnation of Scotland. The author here offers a unique record, which may well be accurate, of the king's second attempt to persuade the pope to annul the Ordinances. It was unsuccessful because, as he records, the pope observed that the Ordinances had been made by trustworthy people and were unlikely to be detrimental to the kingdom or the Church. The second major topic this year is the worsening dispute between Lancaster and the king. The author reports Lancaster's failure to come to a parliament (probably the council of April 1317), the increasing distrust on both sides, Lancaster's hampering of supplies sent to the king at York, the king's rage at Pontefract, and the decision, brokered by Pembroke and the cardinals, to hold a parliament in January 1318 to sort things out. Here the author seems to be the only chronicler to note Lancaster's

---

[69] The two leaves seem to be the equivalent of about four pages of text in both Stubbs's and Denholm-Young's editions.

[70] See below, pp. 132–3, 134–5.

attempt to use his role as steward to military and administrative effect. The third major topic is the attack by Gilbert Middleton on the cardinals. The events are dealt with very briefly, but are followed by an extensive extract from the decretal 'on penalties', prompted by the awfulness of sacrilegious attacks on the clergy. Given the suggestion that Walwayn was the author and that he might have been an unsuccessful candidate for the see of Durham, it is interesting that he mentions only the cardinals' mission to Scotland, and not at all that they were travelling with Louis Beaumont, bishop-elect of Durham.

For 1318 his main interest lies in the king's reconciliation with Lancaster, which culminated in the treaty of Leake (1 Aug.). The author discusses the negotiations in considerable detail, and unlike any other chronicler shows his intimate knowledge of central politics by noting all the abortive parliaments of the year. The incident of the impostor is covered and the rise to prominence of new advisers recorded. As well as the Despensers, Amory, Audley, and Montague are named; this group of three is also specifically mentioned by the continuator of the *Flores*, who thought them worse than Gaveston.[71] The author also records one of the earliest instances of the queen acting as mediator this year. Domestic politics quite overshadows the loss of Berwick, which here was no more than one factor in a long list of those persuading the king to agree to a reconciliation he clearly hated. The reconciliation, however, brought a great deal of hope to the author and he counts the blessings now manifest in England: Robert Bruce has been excommunicated, Edward Bruce has been defeated in Ireland, the famine has ended, and the king has been reconciled with his barons. The entry for the year finishes with an approving account of the purge of officials in the autumn of 1318, and a tirade against the greed and corruption of officials—perhaps odd if the author was Walwayn, who lost his own job at this time.

Interest in 1319 lies again almost entirely with Scotland. A reasonably detailed account of the preparations for the siege of Berwick is followed by a long account of the Scottish raid south and the disastrous battle of Myton-on-Swale. With great lamentations and another tirade, against the greed and deceit of rich men, the author reports in considerable detail the accusation of Lancaster's collusion with the Scots: that he had been paid £40,000 to hamper the siege and to let the Scottish raiding forces go freely through his lines back to

[71] *Flores*, p. 178.

Scotland. Although the earl purged himself with an oath, it is quite clear from the intensity and length of the lament (taking up at least half the entry for the year) and from his bitter comment on the thorn turning into a lily and rust into iron that the author believed the rumours. The entry for the year ends with the two-year truce made with the Scots for the protection of Northumberland and to allow the king to go France to pay homage for Gascony.

In 1320 the entry begins with a comment on continued hostility between Lancaster and the court, a reference to the king's crossing to France, and a very long tirade against the appointment of the canonically underage Burghersh to the see of Lincoln. The rest of the year and the whole of 1321 are then taken up entirely with a long and detailed account of the next major domestic crisis—the Despenser war. Like a good historian (as with the Scottish war and the Bristol rebellion) the author recapitulates its origins in the marriage to Gloucester's sister, which had given the younger Hugh Despenser aspirations in the Marches. He explains the problem of the opposing claims in Gower, and includes a succinct but excellent summary of the individual reasons for the Marchers' hatred of the Despensers. It is notable that his narrative concentrates wholly on the Marchers. Although he mentions their sworn conspiracy with Lancaster (which must refer to the meeting at Sherburn) he gives no detail whatsoever on northern events; for that we must rely on the Bridlington chronicle. Particularly valuable are the detailed descriptions of the barons' threats to renounce homage and set up a *rector* instead of the king, and the warning, voiced by Pembroke in the August parliament, that the king should not break his coronation oath. The opposition to the Despensers was not, however, as solid as that against Gaveston, and the king's reaction was far more violent than in 1311. The author describes the king's counter-attack in some detail, sweeping with his narrative straight into 1322. He points to the lack of coordination between the Marchers and Lancaster, and to the melting away of rebel support, including the capitulation of the Mortimers and Berkeleys. At this point he offers a unique passage on the king's rejection of Harclay's plea for action against Scotland, saying that he would not move against the enemy abroad until he had conquered the enemy at home. A simple narrative covers the return of the Despensers, the clashes at Burton and Tutbury, the rebels' flight to the north (which he accepts as being to Scotland), the final battle at Boroughbridge and the subsequent execution of Lancaster at Pontefract. This is followed by the beginning of a lament for Lancaster. Clearly the author has little sympathy for him now, but the six leaves missing from the manuscript at this point mean that we lose all further comment on this.[72] This gap is the most unfortunate of all, because it covers the period of the further executions, the parliament of York, the annulment of the Ordinances, and the elevation to an earldom of the elder Hugh Despenser. The author's comments on these would have been well worth having.

The narrative begins again, still in 1322, with Robert Ewer's attack on Despenser senior's lands, and his arrest and death in prison. This is the beginning of the third main period of the reign, when Edward was back in the political saddle and the Despensers were dominant; it is interesting therefore that the author does not appear to show his usual animosity to the elder Despenser at this point. Perhaps relief at the end of civil war overwhelmed his earlier dislike of Despenser. However, although there was no serious political dissent left in England, violence continued, as is shown by Ewer's attack, and the attempt to release Berkeley from Wallingford castle, which took place about February 1323. There is then the loss of one more leaf, which would have covered the period of Harclay's treason.

When the narrative begins again it has reached 1324, probably late autumn, since the French truce made by the earl of Kent in September 1324 has already taken place. The author's concerns are Scotland and Gascony. He describes in detail the unsuccessful Scottish demands for a permanent peace treaty and the return of the stone of Scone, and the king's angry rejection of them. At this point he shows knowledge of recent Scottish propaganda in which Scota, the legendary ancestor of the Irish, was appropriated to provide Scotland with antique origins to match the legend of Brutus in England.[73] The narrative for the winter of 1324–5 is then taken up with unsuccessful negotiations with France.

In 1325 the narrator deals almost entirely with Anglo-French negotiations and the domestic problems which flowed from them. He is particularly interesting in his comments on the king's increasing harshness and cruelty, on the powerlessness of parliaments and other meetings (*parliamenta, tractatus et consilia*), and on the king's great wealth.[74] The king's wealth was remarked by several chroniclers at

[72] The six leaves seem to be the equivalent of about twelve pages of text in both Stubbs's and Denholm-Young's editions.
[73] See below, pp. 224–5.   [74] See below, pp. 230–1.

this time, and was the result of administrative and financial reforms encouraged under the Ordinances, but effected more stringently by the Despenser regime. The narrative for 1325 is quite full, and the author includes comment on such problems as who should be left in charge if the king were to go to France, whether Henry of Lancaster should be charged with treason, the wrangle between York and Canterbury over precedence when York was appointed treasurer, and the appointment of Ayrmin rather than Baldock to the see of Norwich. He records the arrangements for the king's son, the future Edward III, to do homage for the Gascon lands. The tone of his report of the queen's refusal to return and his short comment on the unpopularity of Stapledon, Baldock, and the two Despensers in France all indicate lack of knowledge of developments in the autumn of 1326. The chronicle finishes abruptly with a verbatim quotation of the letter from the bishops to the queen in December 1325, asking her to return to England.

v. Themes

There is much to explore in the chronological narrative, but two themes also stand out, the author's ready willingness to comment on the personalities involved in politics and his consistent comment on the validity and problems in resisting the king. These two themes will be explored further here.

a. Personalities

The personalities of high politics not only take up much space in his narrative, but the author was also clearly familiar with these figures. Although we do not know precisely what opportunities he had for his observations, the content of the narrative speaks for itself, and no one who studies the *Vita* doubts its value. Denholm-Young's comment that it is 'the best, and often unique, source for the character and doings of the protagonists' is a fair one.[75]

The author views the great political figures with both admiration and criticism. On the one hand he sees the barons as the king's chief support, without whom the king could do nothing of importance; vilification of them was tantamount to treason against the king; courtiers should beware of despising them because this was tanta-mount to despising the king; the drop in the number of earls from

[75] *Vita*, 1st edn., p. x.

fifteen to five or six had left the people leaderless.[76] On the other hand, he also notes the fickleness and susceptibility to flattery of soldiers, magnates, and the rich, and is critical of the lengths to which the rebellious barons went in 1321.[77] His barons are aware of and comfortable with political and legal issues and the concept of the good of the country, as his report of their arguments shows. Yet their actions were also guided by strong personal hatreds and feuds over property.

The author writes at greatest length on the favourites and on Lancaster, as might be expected, but he has clear opinions on others too. His views are a mixture of approval, disapproval, understanding, and even compassion. He particularly admires the earl of Warwick, who refused the blandishments of the king in 1308, and he comments at Warwick's death that there was no one like him for wisdom and good advice.[78] His comments on Gloucester, aged just 16 at Edward's accession and aged only 23 at his death, indicate understanding of the pressures individuals experienced. He reports Gloucester as unwilling to move against Gaveston, his brother-in-law, in 1308, yet one of the Ordainers in 1311; as providing Gaveston with a letter of commendation when he was exiled, but immediately regretting it and blaming this lapse on his youth and inexperience; as supporting the earls' first actions against Gaveston and giving Pembroke a tart reply when Gaveston was snatched from his protection, yet acting as mediator thereafter.[79] He was less engaged by the earl of Pembroke. Although he frequently mentions Pembroke's mediation and notes that he defended Lancaster's integrity despite their feud over Thorpe Waterville, he shows little sympathy for the way the earl was caught out in 1312, and suggests deceit in his mediation in 1321.[80] Among the others, he finds Amory ungrateful to the king, and Henry of Lancaster kind to those in trouble.[81]

Gaveston is viewed with unusual compassion, especially in the report of Piers's repentance before his death.[82] Reasons for his unpopularity are rehearsed. Although he was only a Gascon squire, he was given the earldom of Cornwall, a royal cousin as wife, acted as regent, and was made lieutenant in Ireland. He was extravagant, rude, and arrogant. His pride would have been unbearable even in a king's

[76] See below, pp. 48–9, 108–9.
[77] See below, pp. 16–17, 54–5, 196–7.
[78] See below, pp. 14–15, 108–9.
[79] See below, pp. 10–11, 36–9, 40–1, 44–7, 58–61.
[80] See below, pp. 44–7, 192–3.
[81] See below, pp. 208–9, 232–3.
[82] See below, pp. 48–9.

son. Nonetheless, the author, in one of his best known asides, states that he strongly believes that Piers might still have been safe if only he had been careful in his attitude towards the earls. Moreover, it was not just Piers's attitude that was the trouble, but that of the king himself. It was commonplace for great men to have close friends, which normally caused no trouble, but Edward went too far and ignored everyone else if Piers was in his presence. When Edward did make an effort to spread favour more evenly, it worked, as in 1308 when the king persuaded the earls to have Piers back by shrewd political tactics. But Edward did not continue that policy; he 'loved immoderately', and was rumoured to be willing to treat with France and even Scotland for Piers's safety, putting Piers's interests before the Crown's interests.[83] He focused on Piers to the detriment of any other policy; whether present or absent Piers upset the king's concentration on running the country. Gaveston's long shadow is apparent through to 1322. His strength is compared with Lancaster's in 1313; his reburial is recorded in 1314; his death is seen as a possible justification for Lancaster's links with the Scots in 1316; the king was reported as speaking of avenging him at Berwick in 1319; and he is seen as the ultimate cause of Lancaster's execution in 1322.[84]

The writer shows no such compassion for the Despensers.[85] Father and son are treated more clearly as two individuals than in many chronicles, but both are strongly criticized. For the author, the debate is less about any redeeming qualities they might have, and more about which of the two was worse.[86] The chronicle is interesting for identifying the elder Despenser's role in central politics early in the reign. References to him start under 1308, when he is described as hateful to the other barons for his desertion of their cause against Gaveston. In 1312 he is described as perhaps even less deserving than Gaveston, his injustices as a forester are criticized in 1313, and expanded on in 1321. Moves to oust him from court are recorded in 1314 and 1315, and the impossibility of reconciling him with Lancaster in 1318, 1319, and 1320.[87] The son is first mentioned under 1318 and from then frequent references underline his iniquities in the Marches, his greed, and his arrogance; he is also widely blamed for

---

[83] See below, pp. 28–9, 38–41, 42–3.   [84] See below, pp. 72–3, 101–3, 130–1, 214–15.
[85] When he was writing they were, of course, at first rising then at the peak of their power, with no turn of the wheel of fortune to prompt sympathy.
[86] See below, pp. 194–5.   [87] See below, pp. 52–3, 74–7, 100–1, 102–3, 194–5.

the king's meanness and for pressure against the queen.[88] It is
possible that the author had even more to say about their wickedness,
since some of the missing leaves covered crucial passages about the
events after Boroughbridge and the parliament at York, which would
give further stimuli to a discussion of the Despensers' role. Yet
compared with his unalleviated hostility in the earlier years, the
author seems to offer a more neutral tone at times in the 1320s. There
is even a favourable comment on the elder Despenser in 1325 when
he is described as shrewder and more experienced than other
magnates and therefore the most suitable man to leave in charge
when the king goes to France, although the author goes on to explain
that this was impossible because Despenser was so hated.[89]

The writer's attitude to Lancaster is also ambivalent and changes
within the chronicle. Lancaster was great, rich, but flawed. The
lament at Lancaster's death seems deeply felt, but rather because
great potential had been wasted, than from personal sympathy. The
author explains how Lancaster's five earldoms made him the obvious
leader in the execution of Gaveston; he describes him as a necessary
friend for the king in 1313; he records Pembroke's willingness to
defend Lancaster's integrity in 1317 despite their earlier estrange-
ment; and Lancaster's staunch stand on the Ordinances provokes
comparison with Simon de Montfort.[90] Yet there is little praise for
Lancaster. The author picks up on his possible collusion with the
Scots very early; it was excused in 1316 if Lancaster needed to save
his life, but in 1319 it is made a vehicle for a tirade against the avarice
of the rich.[91] There was no excuse for outright rebellion against the
anointed king, and in his final lament the author points to Lancaster's
faithlessness as the occasion of his fall.[92] His description of Lancaster's involvement in the rebellion of 1321–2 is oblique but interesting.
On the one hand, it confirms the view that Lancaster's stand was
riddled with personal emotions: the earl only agreed to work with the
rebels against the Despensers in 1321 provided they moved against
the father, his old enemy, as well as against the son; and he refused to
help at Leeds castle because of his dislike of Badlesmere. On the other
hand, it also shows that, for all his hostility to the king's court,

---

[88] See below, pp. 228–9, 230–1.
[89] See below, pp. 238–9. The Bridlington chronicler is more compassionate to the elder
Despenser, seeing him as a great man who acted foolishly in the end (*Brid.*, p. 87).
[90] See below, pp. 50–1, 72–3, 142–3, 168–9.
[91] See below, pp. 130–1, 138–9, 166–75, 210–11.   [92] See below, pp. 214–15.

Lancaster was reluctant to take up arms: he gave no practical help to the rebels in Wales in the summer of 1321, and he was so slow in showing support in the Marches after the fall of Leeds castle that the Mortimers and others gave up the struggle.[93] When his forces turned up at Burton-on-Trent it was too late. The pressures on Lancaster in 1321–2 were no doubt intolerable, but in allowing himself to be pushed into open rebellion for a cause already lost, his political ineptitude seems to have equalled the king's.

The author's views on Edward are for the most part moderate, although he disapproves of his actions. He remarks at one point that Edward had all the gifts necessary for a good king: he appears to think that Edward's legacy from his father was sound;[94] moreover, he was linked with French and Spanish royal houses, physically strong, tall, handsome. If only he had spent as much time on arms as on rustic pursuits and had not taken bad advice, he could have been successful. He sees Edward's shrewd use of promises and patronage in 1308–9 as politically skilful. He is less approving of Edward's delaying tactics in 1310–11 and 1313 because, although they might wear down opposition, they brought mistrust; he specifically mentions Edward's excuses as frivolous, and his illness as feigned. He seems to accept as reasonable Edward's determination to maintain his prerogative and his anger at being treated as if an idiot who needed his household appointed for him, but he also sees Edward's plan to send Gaveston to Scotland as stupid (*inane*), and his tactics before and at Bannockburn as poor. The author is critical of the relationship with Gaveston, not because it took place (he accepted that great men had close confidants), but because Edward's affection was extreme. A particularly interesting point is his remark that when Gaveston came back from exile in 1309 the king and Gaveston delighted in daily conversation. Since Higden mentions Edward as ready in speech, and Le Baker mentions Gaveston as sharp-witted, we might see the *Vita* as confirming the picture of two young men of similar quick-witted fast speech, delighting in each other's company, perhaps laughing at the duller wits around them and both indulging in the nicknames attributed to Gaveston. Nothing could be more calculated to offend than a king removed from his baronage in such a way.

---

[93] See below, pp. 190–1, 198–9.
[94] This is at odds with the findings of modern historians.

b. Kingship, resistance, and treason

One great value of the chronicle lies in the record of the arguments and threats used by each side in the various crises. This is especially apparent in the negotiations of 1310–11, 1312–13, 1317–18, and 1321.[95] These theoretical arguments may have been cloaking or justifying personal motives or they may have been sincere, but, whichever they were, the magnates' use of them shows what views were current, and that the barons were articulate and sophisticated in politics. In showing the strength of the arguments on each side, and in emphasizing the length of the debates and the delays, the author has immense value for us, as he underlines the complexities and difficulties in the political scene when a king and his leading subjects cannot cooperate. He understood that the divisions were far from simple on either a personal or a theoretical level, and he also noted both the need for mediation and the unfortunate fact that mediators were not always impartial.

Some of the author's most interesting comments on political ideas are voiced through the arguments of the king's opponents and advisers, but his own comments and allusions also illustrate the conscious political ideas of the early fourteenth century. Again, since we do not know exactly who he was nor for whom he wrote, it is not easy to assess how typical his views were; but as his career must have been somewhere near the political centre, his views may well reflect the general attitudes of others in and around government and aristocratic circles. He saw no need to spell out details of his assumptions, but relied on allusions, which suggests the currency of these ideas in the milieu in which he worked. Indeed, few of the ideas were new. By the early fourteenth century there was a considerable body of writing on political thought. Many of the author's words reflect ideas which can be found in writings, for instance, from John of Salisbury's extensive discussions in his *Policraticus*, through the political poem *The Song of Lewes*, to legal treatises such as Bracton's *De Legibus* (after 1268),

---

[95] See below, pp. 18–21, 32–3, 56–65, 136–43, 145–53, 190–5.

[96] John of Salisbury, *Policraticus*, ed. C. C. J. Webb (Oxford, 1909); see selections ed. and trans. by C. J. Nederman, in John of Salisbury, *Policraticus* (Cambridge, 1990); Kingsford, *Song of Lewes* (also trans. in *EHD*, iii. 899–912); *Henrici de Bracton de Legibus et Consuetudinibus Angliae*, trans. S. E. Thorne from the edition of G. E. Woodbine, 4 vols. (Cambridge, Mass., 1968–77); *Fleta*, ed. H. G. Richardson and G. O. Sayles, 3 vols., Selden Society, lxxii, lxxxix, xcix (1955, 1972, 1984).

and *Fleta* (after 1290).[96] Indeed the author's view that a king's duty is to rule well under the law and with consultation is very close to Bracton's legal view of kingship.[97] The significance of the ideas in the *Vita* lies less in their content than in the regularity and insistence with which the author comes back to them. They are of burning concern to him.

Ideas on kingship permeate the whole work. The king is recorded as articulating forcefully his views on prerogative,[98] and the author accepts that rebellion, civil war, and wrongly holding the king's castles against him are all morally wrong as well as likely to be unproductive.[99] On the other hand he is no upholder of absolute regal rights, and defends the king's opponents, although not in their most extreme actions. The view of kingship as a contractual office with responsibilities as well as rights is strong, both in the arguments put into the mouths of the barons and in the author's own comments. He thinks it worth recording the admonition on good kingship and tyranny in the complaint against prise in 1316. He clearly dislikes the extent to which the king's will had the force of law by 1325.[100] He notes the baronial argument that the king had not kept his coronation oath in 1310 and 1321,[101] that the king could not of his own will revoke what he and his barons had agreed together,[102] that the barons were working for the common good of the realm.[103] He does not even seem to disapprove of Lancaster's use of the powers of the steward against the king.[104]

Throughout the work the author lays much emphasis on the rule of law, acknowledging the complexity of this by referring variously to English practices, Roman law, laws of treason, natural law, the law of the Marches, and the laws of war. Lawful action and loyalty were the supreme virtues in his view: opposition was acceptable provided it was lawful, but it must not become treason. However, there was only a hairline division between lawful and unlawful action, and men might also feel conflicting loyalties—should they be loyal to the Crown or the king, to the king or their lord? At which point did an action stop being legitimate resistance and pass to breach of fealty,

---

[97] Bracton, *De Legibus*, ii. 19, 33, 304–6. For other aspects of Roman law also in Bracton, see above, p. xxvii, and below, Text, nn. 250, 336, 469.

[98] See below, pp. 38–9, 58–9, 64–5.   [99] See below, pp. 10–11, 32–3, 198–9.
[100] See below, pp. 230–1.   [101] See below, pp. 20–1, 192–3.
[102] See below, pp. 60–1.   [103] See below, pp. 62–3.
[104] See below, pp. 140–1.

and from there to outright treason?[105] Throughout the chronicle the
author shows himself to be intensely aware of the problem of treason.
Discussions of legitimate resistance, which were fairly commonplace
in canon and civil law, were familiar to him, and he struggles in his
judgements to make the difficult (perhaps impossible) distinction
between a legitimate breach of fealty and full-blown treason against
king and state.[106] Interest in these fine distinctions had undoubtedly
been stimulated by the ferocious punishment faced by some of
Edward I's recent opponents. After a long period in which resistance
to the king brought exile or fines, a horrendous death had emerged as
the penalty. Whether because of an increasing engagement with
Roman law ideas on the state and treason, or because political changes
within England led kings to feel more secure in crushing opposition,
resistance was becoming more dangerous. It therefore became more
important to define and defend the reasons for it.[107] The frequent
opposition in Edward II's reign and Edward's savage response in 1322
intensified the problem, and it is not surprising that in 1352 a
determined effort was made to define treason by statute.

The crises of 1310–11, 1312–13, 1321 and Lancaster's actions in
1317–22 provoked the author's fullest comments on resistance.
Justification for resistance included action for the common good, in
self-defence, and in response to the king's own breach of good
lordship (explicitly to his breach of his coronation oath).[108] Acceptable

[105] For comment on the author's legal interests, see above, p. xxvii. For a discussion of
lesa maiestas, *proditio*, and breach of faith in this text, see Childs, 'Resistance and treason',
pp. 180–9.
[106] The Roman concept of the impersonal 'state' is known and discussed in the 13th c.,
and Roman vocabulary is widely used to describe aspects of medieval government, but the
older ideas and vocabulary of fealty to the lord remain strong. For many, such as our author,
the boundaries between the two concepts are blurred. For further discussion of these
aspects, see Childs, 'Resistance and treason', pp. 177–91.
[107] For definitions of treason and a discussion of Roman law ideas see J. G. Bellamy, *The
Law of Treason in the Later Middle Ages* (Cambridge, 1970), pp. 1–58, and J. Dunbabin,
'Government', in *The Cambridge History of Medieval Political Thought c. 350–c. 1450*, ed. J.
H. Burns (Cambridge, 1988), p. 492. For the changing political circumstances in 13th-c.
England see D. A. Carpenter, 'From King John to the first English duke: 1215–1337', in
The House of Lords: A Thousand Years of British Tradition (London, 1994), pp. 28–43, at
pp. 29–35. For a discussion of the trend towards less harsh penalties in the 12th c., see J. A.
Green, *The Aristocracy of Norman England* (Cambridge, 1997), pp. 257–64.
[108] Self-defence, relations between lords and vassals, and action for the common good
were widely discussed by canon lawyers and theologians in the context of the causes of just
war. The ideas would therefore have been very familiar to the author and his circle. See F.
H. Russell, *The Just War in the Middle Ages* (Cambridge, 1975), pp. 44–7, 95–100, 131–8,
259–62. For the author's allusions to self-defence based on Roman law, see below, pp. 18–
19, 52–3, 58–9, 178–9.

resistance seems to be generally passive and refusal to do what the king wished. Positive action was more difficult to justify, but here too the author tries to categorize offences. On four occasions he uses the term *lesa maiestas*, which suggests he was thinking in Roman law terms, and each time the offence seems to be against the office and powers of the king. Although the author nowhere mentions the separation of office and person explicitly made by the magnates in their declaration in 1308, he is clearly aware of the distinction. More often he uses the term *proditio*, and this covered offences against the person of the king, his armies, his castles, or giving aid to his foreign enemies. This distinction, however, was not simple or complete. He records how the opponents of Gaveston insisted on his actions being treason (*proditio*) but since his actions did not displease the king, his treason must necessarily be against the crown. The author also struggled to come to grips with whether Lancaster's actions were best described as *proditio* or breach of faith. To the last he was reluctant to call Lancaster *proditor*.

The author's references to the Ordinances and parliament, two elements which gave the magnates the means by which to limit royal actions, are revealing. He clearly approved the making of the Ordinances and is the chronicler who mentions them most frequently. The making of the Ordinances in 1310–11 and their validity in the crisis of 1312–13 naturally take up much space, but there is much more. He also records the invocation of the Ordinances in relation to war in 1314 and 1317. Clauses in them are echoed, as when Lancaster objected to parliaments held in secret places in 1320. Warwick, as well as Lancaster, is praised for his support of them. The king's dislike of them is made clear, and the author offers the unique and probably correct record of Pope John XXII's refusal to annul them in 1317.[109]

The author's attitude to parliament is generally approving, and he clearly considered it an essential part of government through which consent could be expressed, but his parliament, as N. Denholm-Young pointed out, was a wholly aristocratic body. Despite references to actions in parliament being for the good of the realm and the people, the author makes no reference whatsoever to the commons in parliament, and even refers to the parliamentary subsidies of 1313 and 1319 as being granted by the earls and barons.[110] There is no reflection here of the assertion in the *Modus Tenendi Parliamentum*

[109] See below, pp. 134–7.   [110] *Vita*, 1st edn., p. x; see below, pp. 76–7, 160–1.

that the commons' voice was greater than that of the magnates.[111] Although he shows no interest in the parliaments of 1308–9, he mentions specifically at least two-thirds of parliaments which took place in the period covered by his surviving narrative, and he alone of all chroniclers records the abortive postponed parliaments of 1318. Frequently he notes the pressure on the king to settle important matters in parliament (often calling this the sounder advice), to call parliament before a war, or to make sure that all important men, including Lancaster, were present. He specifically notes the agreement in 1318 that the king would do nothing without assent in common parliament, and he clearly regrets that parliaments and colloquies were impotent in 1325.[112] Parliament provided a legitimate means of showing resistance to royal actions.

A further important element in the work is the frequency with which the author returns to the idea that the king might be restrained and even possibly removed, although he makes no mention of the declaration of 1308. His views on restraint are all the more interesting in a chronicle written before the deposition, as they show some of the stages by which the unthinkable became thinkable.[113] As early as 1310, during the struggle to exile Gaveston and obtain the Ordinances, the author voices the threats of the barons that they would not have Edward II as king. Similar threats were made again in 1321 over the exile of Despenser. The right of resistance and the belief that tyrants lost their legitimate right to authority and would therefore lose their kingdoms were often enough discussed by writers on political theories. They were also reflected in warnings given in the developing genre of mirrors for princes, and Rehoboam provided a useful example, much quoted by moralists, of a king who acted unjustly, ignored good advice, and lost most of his kingdom. These ideas would be commonplace to fourteenth-century political figures, but normally they remained somewhat conventional theoretical threats and, despite the threats by opposition barons to withdraw fealty and not have Edward as king in 1310, 1312–13, and 1321, it is not clear that they had any intention of replacing Edward with another king. The simple withdrawal of fealty by a large enough group of politically important figures might in itself make government impossible and bring the king

---

[111] *Modus*, cap. 23, in *Parliamentary Texts*, pp. 77, 89–90.

[112] See below, pp. 152–3, 230–1.

[113] See below, pp. 18–21, 32–3, 60–3, 192–3; see also Childs, 'Resistance and treason', pp. 184–5.

to the negotiating table. In this it was similar to the intention of
excommunication—to make government difficult in practice. Con-
straint by threats, by forced compacts like the Ordinances, through
parliaments, and by occasional shows of force was probably what the
king's opponents envisaged. Yet rumour may have exaggerated
intentions, and in 1312 Lancaster and his supporters felt obliged to
deny that they had ever contemplated replacing the king. The author's
own view at this time was that they contemplated not replacement, but
restraint as had been exercised against Henry III. It is possible that
some form of tutelage was discussed in 1321, when opponents
threatened to choose another for their *rector* to provide justice, but
there is still no record that anyone suggested choosing a new king.
Indeed, there would have been no obvious alternative to Edward II.
To 1312, his heir was his eldest half-brother, Thomas of Brotherton,
who was still a child. From 1312 he had direct heirs, but any
substitution would have meant a long minority. The possibility of
replacement became stronger as Edward's sons grew older, but,
nonetheless, our author never contemplates this possibility. Nor
does he ever call the king a tyrant, although his comments in 1325
that the king's will seemed unbridled and that the king was using his
will as law against reason, suggest that Edward was clearly seen to be
in danger of turning from *rex* to *tyrannus*. In charting how the political
community had debated ways of constraining a king for years before
1327, the author provides historians with illuminating background to
the final deposition. This is particularly important since the argument
that the author did not live to see the deposition seems unassailable;
his narrative of these arguments and threats therefore reveals contemporary opinion untainted by hindsight.

The *Vita Edwardi Secundi* is one of the most readable accounts of
Edward's reign, and one of the most valuable. It is not without its
faults, but the strengths far outweigh the problems. Compared with
other chronicles of the reign, the author's clearly informed narrative,
attempts to analyse motives, and extensive (and sometimes forceful)
comments offer an unusual combination, and one which has proved
attractive to historians. As N. Denholm-Young said, there are few
lines of the *Vita* which have not been quoted over the years, and it is
clear that its sharp and judicious perceptions have strongly coloured
the views of modern historians. Despite its long use, the text is far
from exhausted, and continues to offer new insights to the reign if we
ask it new questions.

Acknowledgement of the interest and importance of this text is shown by its three previous editions in 1730, 1883, 1957, one in each century. All are still serviceable. Thomas Hearne, who can be credited with the discovery of the text in that he recognized its interest, first published it as *Monachi cujusdam Malmesburiensis, Vita Edwardi Secundi, e codice MS. penes Jacobum Westum, armigerum*, in *Johannis de Trokelowe annales Eduardi II. Henrici de Blaneforde chronica et Eduardi II vita a monacho quodam Malmesburiensi fuse enarrata*, ed. T. Hearne (Oxford, 1729/30). The text was re-edited with some classicizing by Bishop Stubbs as *Monachi cujusdam Malmesberiensis, Vita Edwardi Secundi*, ed. W. Stubbs in *Chronicles of the Reigns of Edward I and Edward II*, Rolls Series, lxxvi, vol. ii (London, 1883). He kept Hearne's title, but established that the text was very unlikely to have been written by a monk. The third edition, with a parallel translation, for Nelson's Medieval Texts, the predecessor of Oxford Medieval Texts, was *Vita Edwardi Secundi, Monachi cuiusdam Malmesberiensis*, ed. N. Denholm-Young, Nelson's Medieval Texts (London, 1957). The subtitle was translated as 'by the so-called monk of Malmesbury', and Denholm-Young argued strongly for authorship by John Walwayn DCL.

i. Text

The orthography of the text presents problems since it is filtered to us through an eighteenth-century transcript. I have attempted to get as close as possible to the fourteenth-century manuscript by stripping away obvious classical spellings introduced by Hearne and by the later editors to return to known medieval conventions (thus *coepit* and *conquaestum* return to *cepit* and *conquestum*). Non-classical and unusual spellings specifically noted by Hearne (often standardized and classicized by the later editors) have normally been restored to the text, especially if they are used more than once, as with the variations of *differre* and *deferre* (often confused in the Middle Ages), and the not infrequent use of *pre* for *pro*. Similarly, other minor unusual spellings copied 'silently' by Hearne and removed by later editors have been restored to the text on the reasonable assumption that

Hearne, normally an accurate transcriber, transcribed what he saw in the majority of cases. All these spelling variations appear to be well within the range we see in other fourteenth-century manuscripts. Many of them are the simple interchanges of vowels (e, i; *elegere*, *eligere*) and of consonants (d, t; c, s; c, t; *sed*, *set*; *obcessi*, *obsessi*; *amicicia*, *amicitia*) frequently found in other writers of the Middle Ages. Double consonants, especially *ll* and *mm*, are also often rendered singly. Otherwise, I have adhered to current Oxford Medieval Text usages in the matter of *i* and *j*, *u* and *v* and *U* and *V*.

Grammatical and other constructions specifically said by Hearne to be in West's manuscript have also normally been restored to the main text, unless they make manifest nonsense. I have not, however, restored to the text some odd usages where they are apparently those of the fourteenth-century scribe even if they are repeated in the text, as with *autem . . . aut* (pp. 32, 74), and *ad hoc* for *adhuc* (pp. 64, 76). I have normally left declensions and conjugations as the scribe used them and I have left singular verbs where a plural is grammatically correct in instances where this is understandable and likely to have been written by the scribe (for example, when the emphasis might be understood as being on one part of the subject with the other in silent parenthesis, as in 'the king, and his men, . . .'). However, where there are manifest errors and amendment is needed to make sense of the passage this has been made in the main text. I have noted in the critical apparatus variants of spelling, grammar, and construction suggested by previous editors.

Capitalization, punctuation, and paragraphing are modern. Rawlinson B. 180 shows that Hearne wrote his transcript as a continuous piece but marked the manuscript's paragraph marks. He also included a reasonable amount of punctuation in his original transcript, which may reflect that in the manuscript. Hearne then marked up his transcript for printing by adding many more commas and not infrequently changing the paragraphing. Stubbs and Denholm-Young made further changes to paragraphs. Those used here are mine.

ii. *Translation*

This translation is clearly indebted to that of N. Denholm-Young. In places where the Latin is very simple, there is little alternative to his phrasing; in other places it seemed difficult to better his choice of words. However, there are also a substantial number of changes.

Many are stylistic. The present translation retains more of the double verbs and the repetitions such as 'the said', 'the aforesaid' to reflect the style of the text; but to make the text easier on the modern ear, I have broken sentences, sometimes changed the word order, and at times used active rather than passive constructions. In a few places my amendments make significant shifts in sense. For example, in 1314 it seems clear that Gloucester was pinned beneath his horse, not weighed down by his body armour (pp. 90–1); in 1317 it seems from the previous and subsequent references in the text and by the use of 'curia' that Lancaster was ordered to come to the king's court, but not specifically to the court at the muster at Newcastle (pp. 136–7). And again, in 1319 the author mentions only two routes for the Scots to return home, and they return 'the other' way, that is through Lancaster's lines with his 'permission to pass' (pp. 166–7). This reading makes clear Lancaster's treasonous dealings with the Scots, already mentioned by the author.

In the translation personal names and surnames are given in the most usual modern form. Place names have all been modernized. Biblical quotations follow closely the Challoner revision of the Douai–Reims translation.

VITA EDWARDI SECVNDI

It is necessary to make clear the distinctions between the three levels of information which Hearne provided in his work. These are provided by He, MS, and R in the following sigla. In the apparatus criticus, where no mention is made of previous editors other than Hearne, this is because the subsequent editors have used the form given by Hearne in Rawlinson B 180 or the form specifically noted by Hearne as in the manuscript.

Den-Y   Denholm-Young, *Vita*, 1st cdn.

He   Hearne, *Trokelowe*. Hearne's suggestions and deliberate amendments for his printed text. These are also to be found in the marginal notes in R.

ML   Michael Lapidge

MW   Michael Winterbottom

MS   Hearne's specific references to particular readings he found in the lost MS belonging to James West.

R   Bodleian Library, Oxford: MS Rawlinson B. 180. This indicates readings in Hearne's transcript, which seem doubtful in spelling or meaning but to which Hearne drew no attention. These may be accurate copyings from the MS or may be spellings or errors introduced by Hearne himself. These also appear in the final printed text in *Trokelowe*. R has been retained for reference to the last page of Hearne's transcript, although this has now to be read through the printed version in *Trokelowe*.

St   Stubbs, *Chronicles*

VITA EDWARDI SECVNDI

1307 Edwardus post conquestum primus, anno regni sui quinto et tricensimo in die translacionis sancti Thome nature debitum soluens,[1] suscepit regnum filius eius Edwardus secundus, iuuenis et fortis robore, etatis sue annum agens circiter uicesimum tercium. Hic propositum patris sui nondum consumauit,[a] set in alia consilium mutauit. Petrum de Gaueston, qui nuper precepto patris regis terram Anglie abiurauerat, reuocauit.[2] Fuerat autem dictus Petrus, uiuente rege E⟨dwardo⟩[b] sene, iuuenis Edwardi, tunc principis Wallie, camerarius familiarissimus et ualde dilectus,[3] quod manifeste satis apparuit non multo post. Dominus enim rex iuuenis domino Petro, ab exilio reuerso, de consilio et assensu quorundam magnatum terre, uidelicet Henrici de Lacy comitis Lincolnie et aliorum, comitatum Cornubie contulit et donauit. Ipse etenim comes Henricus de Lacy, cum dubitaretur an rex predictum comitatum a iure quod cum corona habebat posset separare, proposuit regem posse, nam sic et alii reges bis antea fecerant.[4] Maior tamen pars baronum terre non consensit, tum quia Petrus alienigena erat a Vasconia oriundus, tum propter inuidiam. Inuidebant enim ei magnates terre, quia ipse solus haberet graciam in oculis regis et quasi secundus rex dominaretur, cui subessent omnes et par nullus. Inuidebat eciam illi quasi tota terra, maior et minor et senex,[5] et mala de eo predicabant; unde et nomen eius ualde diffamatum est. Nec tamen uoluntatem regis a Petro poterant separare, quin eciam quanto[c] plura audiret rex que graciam eius conarentur extinguere, tanto magis inualescebat amor et crescebat affectio regis erga Petrum. In tantum eciam ut ad partem Petri

---

[a] sic MS; consummauit St, Den-Y   [b] E. MS; Edwardo St, Den-Y   [c] quando MS; quanto Den-Y

---

[1] 7 July 1307.
[2] Gaveston had been in exile for just over two months. On 26 Feb. 1307 Edward I ordered him to leave three weeks after the next tournament, which was to be held two weeks after Easter. Gaveston should, therefore, have left about 30 Apr. (CCR 1302–7, pp. 526–7; Foed., i. 2. 1010).
[3] Camerarius simply means chamber officer, not necessarily chamberlain. There is no firm evidence then or when Piers returned that he was formally Edward's chamberlain. However, Chaplais quite convincingly suggests that the specific powers Piers wielded after Edward's accession, together with comments in both the Vita and the Annales Paulini, make it likely that he did de facto come to hold the position of king's chief chamberlain,

LIFE OF EDWARD THE SECOND

Edward, the first after the Conquest, died on the day of the translation 1307 of St Thomas in the thirty-fifth year of his reign,[1] and his son Edward II began his reign, a strong young man in about his twenty-third year. He did not fulfil his father's ambition, but turned his mind to other things. He recalled Piers Gaveston, who had recently abjured the realm of England at his father the king's command.[2] While the old king Edward was alive, the said Piers had been the closest and the very much loved chamber officer[3] of the young Edward, then prince of Wales. This appeared very clearly not long after. For the young lord king granted and gave to Lord Piers, on his return from exile, the earldom of Cornwall with the advice and assent of some of the great men of the kingdom, namely Henry Lacy, earl of Lincoln, and others. Indeed, when there was doubt as to whether the king could lawfully alienate the said earldom which he held with the crown, Earl Henry Lacy himself said that he could, as other kings had done so twice before.[4] The majority of the barons of the land did not, however, agree, not only because Piers was an alien of Gascon birth but also through envy. For the great men of the land hated him, because he alone found favour in the king's eyes and lorded it over them like a second king, to whom all were subject and none equal. Almost all the country hated him too, both the elder and younger men and the old,[5] and foretold ill of him, so that his name was reviled far and wide. However, they could not detach the king's affection from Piers, for the more the king heard as they tried to destroy his friendship, the more the king's love increased and his tenderness towards Piers grew. So much so, that, to strengthen Piers

probably with John Charlton acting for all practical purposes as his deputy (Chaplais, *Gaveston*, pp. 64–5, 101–6).

[4] The grant, dated 6 Aug. 1307, was witnessed by all the earls except Warwick and Oxford (*CChR 1300–26*, p. 108). Lincoln, at 55, was the oldest, most experienced, and wealthiest of Edward's earls, with lands worth about 10,000 marks (£6,666. 13s. 4d.) a year. His only child, Alice, married Thomas of Lancaster in 1294. Lincoln was normally a royalist and a moderating influence in politics, but was briefly angered enough to take the lead against Gaveston in 1308. He was also an Ordainer in 1310, but died on 5 Feb. 1311 before the completion of the ordinances (*HBC*, p. 470; Maddicott, *Lancaster*, pp. 3, 22, 74, 81, 102–4, 109–10; Davies, *Opposition*, app. no. 90). There had been three previous grants: briefly to Alan of Brittany in 1140, then to Reginald, illegitimate son of Henry I, also in 1140, and to Richard, brother of Henry III, in 1227 (*HBC*, p. 456). The author refers to the grant again below, pp. 8–9, 26–7, 28–9, 32–3, 64–5.   [5] Cf. Gen. 19: 31.

1307 fortificandam et amicis stipandam, filiam sororis sue, que fuit filia[a] quondam Gilberti comitis Gloucestrie, dominus rex dicto Petro collocauit ⟨in⟩[b] matrimonium.[6] Sane hec copulacio matrimonialis partem eius non modicum uallabat; fauorem namque amicorum sibi uehementer augebat et odium baronum refrenabat.

Interea conuocati sunt archiepiscopi, comites et ceteri terre magnates ad sepeliendum corpus regis nuper defuncti; et sepultus est dictus rex honorifice Londoniis apud Westmonasterium iuxta patrem suum Henricum tercium.[7] Post hec ad maiorem Petri famam augendam et nomen celebrandum, auxiliante et consulente domino rege, nomine domini Petri proclamatum est celebriter quoddam torneamentum in uilla uidelicet Walyngfordie, que est de dominico comitis Cornubie. Dies eciam prefigitur, dies scilicet sabbati proxima post festum sancti Andree.[8] Hoc itaque torneamentum comites et barones in odium Petri magis excitabat. Adueniente igitur die prefixo ex una parte coniuncti[c] sunt comites tres uel quatuor cum manu ualida, comes uidelicet Warennie, comes Herfordie, comes de Arundel, et barones non pauci;[9] ex parte domini Petri comes nullus erat nominatus expressus, set omnes fere milites iuniores et robustiores regni, qui prece uel precio poterant conduci, partem domini Petri iuuabant. Vnde et in illo torneamento pars eius superiorem manum habebat, ac optata reportabat, quamuis campus alteri parti remaneret.[10] Nam ipsius ludi lex esse dinoscitur, quod qui plus perdit et qui sepius ab equo deicitur, probior et forcior iudicatur.

Ex hiis et aliis in dies crescebat odium; erat enim Petrus homo ualde elatus et superbus in gestu. Nam omnes quos sibi pares regni consuetudo esse dictabat, humiles et abiectos, nec ipsum in probitate

---

[a] sic MS; uxor He   [b] om. MS; supplied He, St, Den-Y   [c] coniuti MS; coniuncti He, St, Den-Y

[6] Gaveston married Margaret de Clare on 1 Nov. 1307. She was the daughter of Joan of Acre, Edward II's sister, who married Gilbert de Clare, earl of Gloucester, in 1290. Joan had died on 23 Apr. 1307 (HBC, p. 38; Hamilton, Gaveston, p. 38 and note). It was clearly intended that this marriage into the royal family should protect Gaveston from overt hostility. The author certainly noted Gloucester's reluctance to take action against his brother-in-law in 1308 (below, pp. 10–11), and that the kinship with Gloucester ensured Gaveston a nobleman's death by beheading in 1312 (below, pp. 46–7). Margaret de Clare later inherited a third of the Gloucester estates after the death of her brother at Bannockburn (1314) and married Hugh Audley as her second husband in 1317.

[7] Edward I was interred in Westminster Abbey on 27 Oct. 1307.

[8] 2 Dec. 1307. Tournaments were popular, but tightly controlled because they brought dangerously large numbers of armed men together. They could also, as in this case,

and surround him with friends, the lord king married Piers to his 1307
sister's daughter, the daughter of the late Gilbert, earl of Gloucester.[6]
This marriage tie did indeed strengthen his position considerably; for
it greatly increased the goodwill of his friends and restrained the hatred
of the baronage.

Meanwhile the archbishops, the earls, and the other great men of
the land assembled to bury the body of the late king; and the said king
was interred honourably in London at Westminster next to his father,
Henry III.[7] Then, to further enhance Piers's reputation and honour
his name, with the king's support and counsel, a tournament was
ceremoniously proclaimed in Lord Piers's name, at Wallingford, a
town on the earl of Cornwall's demesne. A day was appointed, namely
the Saturday after the feast of St Andrew.[8] This tournament roused
the earls and barons to still greater hatred of Piers. Consequently,
when the appointed day came, on one side were three or four earls
together with a strong troop, namely Earl Warenne, the earl of
Hereford, the earl of Arundel, and not a few barons;[9] Lord Piers's
side could not raise an earl, but almost all the younger and harder
knights of the kingdom, whom persuasion or reward could bring
together, supported him. So it was that in this tournament his party
had the upper hand and carried off the spoils, although the other side
remained in possession of the field.[10] For it is a recognized rule in this
game that he who loses most and is most frequently unhorsed, is
judged the more valiant and the stronger.

From these and other incidents hatred grew day by day, for Piers
was a man very proud and haughty in bearing. He thought that all
those whom the custom of the realm deemed equal to him were lowly

increase hostility when the opposing companies formed along factional lines. The *Annales
Paulini* confirm the hatred engendered by the Wallingford tournament, explaining that
Gaveston proclaimed he would bring sixty men to fight but deceitfully brought 200 (J. R. V.
Barker, *The Tournament in England 1100–1400* (Woodbridge, 1986), pp. 49–50, 137–42;
Ann. Paul., pp. 258–9).

[9] The earls John of Warenne, earl of Surrey, 1306–47, Humphrey Bohun, earl of
Hereford, 1299–1322, Edmund fitz Alan, earl of Arundel, 1306–26, were all prominent in
the later action against Gaveston leading to his death in 1312 (*HBC*, pp. 449, 464, 484;
Maddicott, *Lancaster*, pp. 123–7). Thereafter their loyalties diverged: Warenne became a
moderate royal supporter; after a period of reconciliation, Hereford again went into open
rebellion and died at Boroughbridge in 1322; Arundel became a staunch royalist and was
executed by Isabella's forces in 1326.

[10] Normally the winners would both hold the field and win most booty, but this is not
the only case known where there was no clear-cut winner (Barker, *Tournament*, pp. 141–2).
The wry comment which follows suggests that the author of the *Vita* disapproved of
tournaments.

1307 quicquam attingere posse reputabat. Econtra comites et barones Anglie ipsum Petrum, quia alienigenam et humilem quondam armigerum, ad tantum decus et honorem prouectum, nec sui prioris status memorem, despiciebant. Vnde et apud omnes fere qui in regno erant pro ludibrio habebatur. Rex autem continuum amorem erga eum habebat, in tantum ut exiret a curia regis preceptum publicum ne quis eum nomine proprio uocaret, uidelicet dominum Petrum de Gauestone, set comitem Cornubie nominaret.[11]

1308   Deinde cum redissent nuncii qui ad dominum Philippum regem Francie missi fuerant pro matrimonio copulando inter filiam dicti regis Francie et regem Anglie, ac optata reportassent, dominus rex Anglie ad transfretandum se parauit et nauigio parato mare cum suis intrauit. Regnum autem in manu Petri in custodia deputatur. Mira res, qui nuper ab Anglia exul erat et eiectus, eiusdem terre iam factus est gubernator et custos. Celebratis itaque de more nupciis, rex Anglie cum coniuge sua letus in Angliam est reuersus.[12]

Post hec fiunt preparatoria coronacioni regis. Vocantur archiepiscopi, episcopi, comites et barones. Venerunt igitur omnes, set burgenses singularum ciuitatum aderant. Die sancti Mathie apostoli coronati et consecrati sunt rex et regina.[13] Episcopus Wyntoniensis[14] coronam capiti regis apposuit, set hoc de mandato et consensu archiepiscopi Cantuariensis, cum ad eius dignitatem et ecclesie sue noscatur pertinere, factum est, ipso archiepiscopo quominus adesset uel infirmitate prepedito uel nondum a transmarinis partibus in Angliam reuerso.[15] Finita igitur solempnitate et festiue celebrato conuiuio rediit unusquisque ad propria.

Nunc primum insurrexerunt contra Petrum de Gauestone omnes fere comites et barones Anglie, inuicemque iureiurando astricti sunt, a ceptis nunquam desistere donec Petrus terram Anglie euacuaret, et comitatum Cornubie dimitteret; nullusque magnatum partem Petri

---

[11] This statement may reflect the later terms of the first exile in June 1308, when Gaveston was forced to give up the lands he held as earl of Cornwall, but the king insisted that he keep the title (Hamilton, *Gaveston*, p. 53 and n.; Chaplais, *Gaveston*, pp. 45–9).

[12] Edward II was absent from England between 22 Jan. and 7 Feb. 1308. He married Isabella, Philip IV's daughter, at Boulogne on 25 Jan., and did homage to the king of France before the end of January (*HBC*, p. 39; *Foed.*, ii. 1. 30; Chaplais, 'Duché-Pairie', p. 143). Edward I had arranged this marriage, and his own second marriage to Margaret of France, as part of the reconciliation after the Anglo-French conflict 1294–8. The English possession of lands in Gascony, however, continued to cause problems over borders, jurisdictions, and homage.

[13] 25 Feb. 1308.

[14] Henry Woodlock, bishop of Winchester 1305–16 (*HBC*, p. 277).

and worthless, and that no one could equal him in valour. On the 1307 other hand the earls and barons of England looked down on Piers because he was a foreigner and formerly a mere squire raised to such splendour and eminence, nor was he mindful of his former rank. Thus he was an object of mockery to almost everyone in the kingdom. But the king had an unswerving love for him, so much so that a public edict issued from the king's court that no one should call him by his own name, that is Lord Piers Gaveston, but he should be styled earl of Cornwall.[11]

Then, when the ambassadors who had been sent to Philip, king of 1308 France, to contract the marriage between the said French king's daughter and the king of England had returned, bringing success, the lord king of England prepared to cross the Channel and, when the ship was ready, he set sail with his retinue. The kingdom was left in the hands and keeping of Piers. What an astonishing thing, he who was lately an exile and outcast from England has now been made governor and keeper of the same land! When the marriage had been duly celebrated the king of England returned joyfully to England with his wife.[12]

After this, preparations were made for the king's coronation. Archbishops, bishops, earls, and barons were summoned. All accordingly came, and burgesses from each city attended. The king and queen were crowned and consecrated on the feast of St Mathias the Apostle.[13] The bishop of Winchester[14] placed the crown on the king's head; but he did this at the command and with the assent of the archbishop of Canterbury, since [the privilege] is known to belong to his dignity and that of his church, and the archbishop himself was prevented from being present by illness or continued absence abroad.[15] At the conclusion of the ceremony and the joyful wedding feast everyone went home.

Now for the first time almost all the earls and barons of England rose against Piers Gaveston, and they were bound by a mutual oath never to cease from what they had begun until Piers had left the land of England and given up the earldom of Cornwall; and none of the

[15] Robert Winchelsey, archbishop of Canterbury 1293–1313, clashed with Edward I and at Edward's behest was suspended and summoned before the pope in 1306. (For his clash with Edward I, see below, pp. 70–3.) Winchelsey was reinstated on 22 Jan. 1308 but was still abroad at this time. The choice of the bishop of Winchester as his deputy at the coronation averted the threat to Canterbury's claim to precedence had York officiated (*HBC*, p. 277; Denton, *Winchelsey*, pp. 231, 245–7; *Ann. Paul.*, pp. 259–60).

1308 sustinuit excepto rege et Hugone le Dispenser.[16] Comes autem
Gloucestrie neutram partem promouit: cum Petro non fuit ne pares
suos offenderet; cum baronibus esse non potuit quia fratrem suum in
lege expungnare non decuit. Set et predictus Hugo de Spenser
omnibus baronibus exosus factus est, eo quod ipsos pro communi
utilitate regni laborantes deseruerat et, magis studio placendi et
cupiditate lucrandi quam ex alia iusta causa, parti Petri adheserat.
Ille uero qui Petrum prius fauore et amicicia pre ceteris excepto rege
fouerat et dilexerat, inter omnes barones maximus eius inimicus
factus est et persecutor. Hic erat Henricus de Lacy comes Lyncolnie,
et hec non ex uicio comitis set ex ingratitudine ipsius Petri noscitur
accidisse.

Hec sediciosa dissencio inter dominum regem et barones orta per
totam Angliam iam diuulgata est, set et tota terra pro tali tumultu
ualde desolata est; omne enim regnum in se diuisum desolabitur.[17]
Homines mediocres pacifici, pacis amatores, guerram et pacis exilium
ualde formidabant; predones uero qui predam captabant et ad aliena
manum extendere, bellum non pacem affectabant. Rex uero ciuitates
suas et castra muniri fecit et reparari, set magnates ex parte sua hoc
idem fecerunt. Per totam terram uero in comitatibus, hundredis,
ciuitatibus, burgis et uillis, conuocaciones et inprouisiones facte sunt,
et quibus quilibet armis, necessitate inueniente, uteretur ex debito
prouisum est et ordinatum. Certissime enim putabatur discencionem
iam ceptam sine magna ruina sedari non posse.

Post hec uidentes hii qui ex consilio regis erant, ex tali discordia
toti terre imminere discrimen, et precauentes in futurum, ne furor
adhuc recens radices suas ita extenderet, quod inueteratus de facili
extingui non possit, elaboratum est ab eisdem ut rex et barones sui in
amiciciam et concordiam reuocarentur. De communi igitur consilio
uocantur comites, barones et alii magnates terre tractaturi[a] de pace,
conueniuntque Londoniis non sine manu armata, prodicionem
metuentes; ubi rex eos expectabat.[18] Igitur cum diu res ipsa uoluta
et reuoluta esset nec tamen finem acciperet (multi enim, uolentes
utrique parti placere, uacillabant, ex quorum consilio et discrecione

---

[a] tractatus *MS*; tractaturi *He, St, Den-Y*

[16] This is the elder Despenser, a staunchly loyal administrator at Edward I's court who continued to serve Edward II (*CP*, iv. 262–3; Davies, *Opposition*, pp. 86–9; Chaplais, *Gaveston*, p. 48). The *Vita*'s author later shows particular dislike of the elder Despenser (below, pp. 52–3, 74–7), which may be why he mentions his role in central politics much sooner than most other chroniclers (but see *Ann. Paul.*, p. 264).

great men took Piers's part except the king and Hugh Despenser.[16] 1308
The earl of Gloucester, however, favoured neither party; he could not
side with Piers lest he offend his peers; nor could he go with the
barons because it was unseemly to fight against his brother-in-law.
And now the said Hugh Despenser became hateful to all the barons,
because he had deserted them as they worked for the common good of
the realm and had become a supporter of Piers more from a desire to
please and a lust for gain than for any creditable reason. But the one,
who, above all others except the king, had previously supported and
made much of Piers by his grace and friendship, had now, of all the
barons, become his greatest enemy and persecutor. This was Henry
Lacy, earl of Lincoln, and this is known to have happened through no
fault of the earl but through the ingratitude of Piers himself.

This treacherous quarrel, which had arisen between the lord king
and the barons, now spread far and wide through all England, and the
whole country was utterly devastated by such a disturbance: for every
kingdom divided against itself shall be brought to desolation.[17]
Ordinary peaceful men, peace-lovers, greatly feared war and the
banishment of peace; but robbers, who longed for booty and to lay
hands on the goods of others, desired war not peace. The king had his
towns and castles fortified and repaired, and the great men for their
part did the same. Throughout the whole land in shires, hundreds,
cities, boroughs, and vills, meetings were held and regulations made,
and it was duly provided and ordained what arms each should use in
the event of necessity. For it was thought most certain that the
quarrel once begun could not be settled without great destruction.

After this, those who were of the king's council, seeing that by such
discord the whole country could be put in danger, and thinking of the
future, in case the recent turmoil should spread its roots so that,
having become rooted, it could not easily be weeded out, formed a
plan by which the king and his barons might once more be brought
together in friendship and harmony. By common consent therefore
the earls, barons, and other great men of the land were summoned to
discuss peace, and they arrived at London with an armed force, as
they feared treachery; there the king was waiting for them.[18] Then,
when the matter had been discussed and rediscussed for a long time,
yet without a settlement (for many, on whose advice and judgement

---

[17] Luke 11: 17.
[18] Parliament (without commons) was summoned for 28 Apr. at Westminster (*HBC*,
p. 552).

1308 negocium dependebat), tandem post multos et uarios circuitus, cum in aliud consentire non possent, promissum est et concessum baronibus per regem quod Petrus de Gauestone terram Anglie egrederetur.[19] Per archiepiscopos eciam et episcopos sentencia[a] excommunicacionis in Petrum lata est si ultra terminum statutum in partibus Anglie moraretur. Terminus itaque positus est, dies uidelicet sancti Iohannis baptiste, quo et eodem festo per anni reuolucionem elapso idem Petrus eandem terram prius abiurauerat.[20] Adueniente igitur die prefixo, dominus rex et Petrus cum multo comitatu ad portum Bristollie sunt profecti; ibidemque post modicum a rege licenciatus Petrus cum multa familia in partes Hibernie se transtulit et recepit, totaque terra ex precepto domini regis Anglie sue dominacioni et potestati subdita est.[21]

Hiis itaque peractis nec adhuc uerus amor successit, nec uera concordia. Estimabant enim comites, in omnibus gestis adhuc se esse circumuentos, et priorem laborem inanem et cassum; propositum namque eorum exitum non sumpsit optatum. Voluissent certe comites quod Petrus Anglia recessisset, ita quod amplius in familiaritate regis non permansisset, nec terra diucius sumptibus suis sicut prius grauaretur; antecedebat enim fere regem in expensis. Defecit itaque propositum comitum: nam Petrus in Hibernia iam moram faciens, omnes redditus illius terre, qui ad regem Anglie pertinebant,[b] ex uoluntate regis et precepto, in suos usus sumpsit et consumpsit; sicque nouissimus error priore factus est peior.[22]

Interea Gilbertus comes Gloucestrie, filius quondam comitis Gilberti, filiam comitis de Holuestere duxit in uxorem. Ad nupcias conuenerunt multi magnates et nobiles, preposuerantque rotundam tabulam ibidem tenuisse; set pauor circumuencionis, timorque

---

[a] sentenciam MS; sentencia He, St, Den-Y   [b] pertinebat MS; pertinebant He, St, Den-Y

[19] The accusations against Gaveston read at this parliament were prefaced by a declaration that homage was made to the crown and not to the person of the king ('Articles against Gaveston presented by the earl of Lincoln to the king, March to April 1308', EHD, iii. 525–6). This is one of the clearest statements of political theory made during the reign and it is perhaps surprising that the author of the Vita, who shows much awareness of constitutional arguments, does not mention it. Of the chroniclers, the canon of Bridlington has the fullest description of these proceedings including a verbatim report of the first part of the document (Brid., pp. 33–4).
[20] The excommunication was issued on 24 May (Registrum Simonis de Gandavo, ed. C. T. Flower and M. C. B. Dawes, Canterbury and York Society, xl–xli (Oxford, 1934) i.

the matter hung, wished to please each side and so wavered), finally,   1308
after many and varied circumlocutions, since they could not agree on
anything else, the king promised and granted to the barons that Piers
Gaveston should leave England.[19] Furthermore, sentence of excommunication was pronounced upon Piers by the archbishops and
bishops if he should delay in England beyond the appointed term.
Accordingly, the term was fixed, namely St John the Baptist's day, on
which same feast a year before the same Piers had first forsworn the
same land.[20] When the appointed day arrived, therefore, the lord king
and Piers set out for Bristol with a great following; and there after a
little, having taken leave of the king, Piers crossed the sea with a large
household and took himself off to Ireland, and by command of the
lord king of England the whole country was subjected to his authority
and power.[21]

Even when these things had been carried out neither true love nor
true harmony resulted. The earls thought that they were still out-
witted in all their doings, their former effort vain and futile, for their
designs had not achieved the outcome they desired. The earls
undoubtedly wanted Piers to leave England, so that he should no
longer remain intimate with the king, nor the country be burdened
any longer as hitherto with his upkeep; for he almost outdid the king
in his spending. The earls' plan failed in this way: for now that Piers
was in Ireland, with the king's willing consent, he took for his own
use and squandered all the revenues of that land which belonged to
the king of England; and so the last straying from the path of
righteousness is made worse than the first.[22]

Meanwhile, Gilbert, earl of Gloucester, son of the late Earl Gilbert,
married the earl of Ulster's daughter. Many great and noble men
gathered at the wedding celebrations, and they had planned to hold a
Round Table there; but some of them were afraid of being trapped,

---

237–40. The sentence of exile, issued on 18 May, was for 24 June (*Ann. Lond.*, p. 154;
CPR 1307–13, p. 71); the exile in 1307 had been planned for about two months earlier in
the year (see n. 2 above).

[21] Gaveston was appointed royal lieutenant in Ireland on 16 Jun. 1308 and held the
office until June 1309. He appears to have found a good working relationship with Richard
de Burgh, earl of Ulster, who had been given lesser powers with the same title on 15 June.
He was remembered by Irish chroniclers as an effective lieutenant (Tout, *Ed. II*, p. 343;
Chaplais, *Gaveston*, pp. 49–61; Hamilton, *Gaveston*, pp. 55–66; J. Lydon, 'A land of war',
in A. Cosgrove (ed.), *A New History of Ireland*, ii: *Medieval Ireland 1169–1534* (Oxford,
1987), pp. 240–74, at pp. 262–3).

[22] Cf. Matt. 12: 45.

1308 prodicionis, quosdam inuasit fecitque quominus cepta procederent.[23]

Videns itaque rex barones suos quasi murum ex aduerso consis-
tere,[24] et propter hoc propositum suum non posse procedere, conatus
est fedus eorum rumpere, et potenciores ad se inclinare. Igitur
paterna et patria fretus[a] cautela, blandiuntur enim Anglici cum
uires oneri sufficere non uident, unum post alium donis, promissis
et blandiciis, ad suum nutum reduxit, in tantum ut uix unus ex
baronibus remaneret qui prius decreta et concessa defenderet. Solus
autem comes de Warewyk flecti non potuit. Dicebat enim sana
consciencia se a placitis recedere non posse, set cum omnes dissim-
ularent ipse solus stare non potuit. Nec tamen expresse consensit.
Interea multi tractatus et consilia habita sunt de defencione terre
Scocie et expugnacione Roberti de Brutz; cuius tamen effectus
fuerunt, nec in palam uenit neque de facto apparuit.[25]

1309 Dum hec ita agerentur et iam appropinquaret autumpnus, uider-
enturque barones cum rege unanimes, Petrus de Gauestone clam
propter insidias aduersariorum per partes Wallie ab Hibernia in
Angliam reuersus est. Sentencia uero que contra eum lata erat, si
amplius in Anglia moraretur, procurante rege, auctoritate apostolica
remissa est.[26]

Rex itaque, sciens Petrum iam rediisse, obuiam illi uenit ad
Cestriam,[27] ibique de reditu suo letus gratanter ualde eum tamquam
fratrem suum honorifice suscepit. Reuera fratrem suum semper
appellauerat.[28] Nullus autem baronum ausus est amplius uel contra
eum manum extendere, uel de reditu suo querelam deponere; claudi-
cabat enim cetus eorum, et pars eorum, in se diuisa, infirmata est. Sic
igitur qui bis antea dampnatus erat in exilium, iam exultat reuersus ad
solium. Comes autem Lincolnie, qui anno preterito inter omnes
barones exilium Petri maxime procurauerat, amicabilis compositor

---

[a] fetus MS; fretus He, St, Den-Y

[23] Gilbert de Clare, earl of Gloucester 1307–14, married Maud, daughter of Richard de
Burgh, earl of Ulster 1280–1326, on 29 Sept. 1308 at Waltham Abbey. His sister, Elizabeth
de Clare, married Richard's son, John de Burgh, on the following day (CP, v. 714; ibid. xii.
2. 178; Chaplais, Gaveston, p. 51). The 'Round Table', a tournament played out round the
Arthurian theme, was popular at this time (Barker, Tournament, pp. 88–95).
[24] Cf. Ezek. 13: 5.
[25] The author no doubt refers to the further parliaments which were summoned for 20
Oct. 1308, 28 Feb. 1309, and 27 Apr. 1309 (HBC, p. 552).
[26] The author's reference to autumn is misleading. The papal bull annulling the
sentence was read in London on 11 June. Its date of issue is generally accepted as 25

and dreaded treachery, so that they did not go ahead with their 1308
plans.[23]

When the king saw that his barons stood against him like a wall,[24]
and that because of this he could not carry out his intentions, he
tried to break up their alliance and draw the more powerful to his
side. Therefore, relying on native and traditional trickery—for the
English flatter when they see their strength is insufficient for a
task—he bent one after another to his will, with gifts, promises, and
blandishments, with such success that scarcely a baron remained to
defend what had previously been decided and agreed. Only the earl
of Warwick could not be swayed. He said that he could not with a
clean conscience go back upon what had been accepted, but when all
practised deceit he could not stand alone. On the other hand he did
not expressly give his consent. Meanwhile many consultations and
councils were held about the defence of the land of Scotland and the
defeat of Robert Bruce, but their outcomes did not become public
nor result in action.[25]

While these things were thus happening and autumn was now 1309
approaching, and the barons seemed to be at one with the king, Piers
Gaveston returned from Ireland to England through Wales secretly,
on account of the plots of his enemies. Even the sentence of
excommunication which had been pronounced against him, if he
stayed any longer in England, was remitted by papal authority at the
king's request.[26]

The king, therefore, knowing that Piers had returned, came to
meet him at Chester,[27] and there, delighted at his return, he very
joyfully received him with honour as his brother. Indeed he had
always called him his brother.[28] None of the barons now dared further
to raise a finger against him, or to lay any complaint about his return;
their ranks wavered, and their party, divided against itself, was
weakened. So he who had twice been condemned to exile exults,
having returned to high position. The earl of Lincoln, who the year
before had been the foremost of the barons in bringing about Piers's
exile, now became a friendly go-between and mediator; at his

Apr., but Chaplais argued for *c*.21 May, suggesting that Edward would want the sentence
known quickly and the delay between April and June would be unlikely. Gaveston was
back by 27 June (Hamilton, *Gaveston*, pp. 70, 73; Chaplais, *Gaveston*, pp. 58–9).

[27] Edward was at Chester from 27 June to 1 July (*Itin.*, p. 46).

[28] For discussion of this and other references in the *Vita* to Edward II's calling
Gaveston his brother, and the suggestion that the two were sworn brothers in arms, see
Chaplais, *Gaveston*, pp. 10–11 and *passim*.

1309 iam factus est et mediator; ad cuius preces solicitas et continuas comes de Warenna, qui, ab eo tempore quo torneamentum de Walyngford finem accepit, hillarem uultum Petro nunquam exhibuit, necessarius amicus iam factus est et fidelis adiutor. Ecce quam frequens et subita magnatum mutacio! Quibus sine fide*a* adhibemus in borea, contrarium reperimus in austro.*b* Amor magnatum quasi ludus in alea, et uota diuitum pennis*c* similima.[29]

Petrus uero ad pristinum statum iam reuersus deterius se cepit habere quam prius. Comites et barones despiciebat, et turpia cognomina similiter addebat.[30] Officia et potestates ab aliis auferebat, et suis familiaribus pro libito conferrebat. Vnde magnates terre ceperunt hec pro malo habere, et precipue comes Lancastrie, quia unus ex familiaribus suis procurante Petro eiectus erat ab officio suo.[31] Iccirco caue tibi, Petre, quia comes Lancastrie retribuet tibi simile.

Ipse igitur dominus rex de presencia Petri ualde gauisus est; quasi qui recepit amicum ex longa peregrinacione reuertentem, letos dies agitabat. Instante uero natiuitate Domini, dominus rex et Petrus ad locum quem rex ipse ualde dilexit cum tota familia iter direxit.*d* Locus autem ille Langeleye dicitur, qui iuxta uillam Sancti Albani situatur. In hoc igitur loco festa natalicia celebrarunt, cotidie colloquentes ac mutua conuersacione et diu affectata presencia priorem absenciam plene redimentes.

1310 Transacto natali solacio conueniunt Londoniis edicto regio barones uniuersi, qui cum ad locum consuetum parliamenti nostri uenire different,[32] et rex inconsuete more causam requireret, nunciis regis

---

a sic MS; sane fidem He; si fidem St; 'the text remains uncertain' Den-Y   *b* auster MS; austro He, St, Den-Y   *c* pernis R; pennis St, Den-Y   *d* sic MS; direxerunt He

[29] The barons received more than personal gifts. The author omits any reference to the parliaments at Westminster (27 Apr. 1309) and Stamford (27 Jul. 1309). At Stamford the barons had received solid concessions on problems dating back to Edward I's reign and beyond, notably on prise and purveyance. These concessions were almost certainly a condition for the return of Gaveston. For the parliaments and allied negotiations, see Hamilton, *Gaveston*, pp. 72–4 and Maddicott, *Lancaster*, pp. 97–105.

[30] Later the *Vita* notes that Warwick was called the 'Dog' (below, pp. 44–5). The longest list of names is in the *Brut* (pp. 206–7). There 'Robert' Earl of Gloucester is called 'Horessone'. Following Tout, Denholm-Young convincingly argued that it was Joan's second husband, Ralph Monthermer, known as earl of Gloucester by right of his wife, whom Gaveston so named. Gilbert, her son, who was Gaveston's new brother-in-law and (at least at first) one of Gaveston's supporters, is an unlikely recipient of such abuse (*Vita*, 1st edn., p. 8 n. 1).

[31] The instance referred to is not clear. It does not concern Nicholas Segrave, as

repeated and anxious requests the Earl Warenne who, ever since the 1309
conclusion of the Wallingford tournament, had never shown Piers a
welcoming face, became his inseparable friend and faithful helper.
See how often and abruptly great men change! Those whom we
regard as faithless in the North we find just the opposite in the South.
The love of great men is as a game of dice, and the desires of the rich
like feathers.[29]

Now that Piers had regained his former position he began to
behave worse than before. He looked down on the earls and barons
and gave them base nicknames.[30] He took offices and authority from
others, and granted these at his pleasure to members of his household.
The great men of the land began to resent this, and particularly the
earl of Lancaster, because one of his household had been thrown out
of office at Piers's instigation.[31] Therefore watch yourself, Piers, for
the earl of Lancaster will repay you like for like.

So then, the lord king himself was overjoyed at Piers's presence;
like one who receives a friend returning from a long pilgrimage, he
passed pleasing days with him. At Christmas the lord king and Piers
with the whole household travelled to a place of which the king was
very fond. That place is called Langley, which is situated near the
town of St Albans. There they passed the festive season, talking daily
and fully making up for the former absence by their long-desired
closeness and conversation together.

When the time of relaxation at Christmas was over, all the barons 1310
met at London by royal edict, but they put off coming to the normal
meeting place of our parliament,[32] and when the king enquired the

Denholm-Young suggested (*History and Heraldry 1254–1310: A Study of the Historical
Value of the Rolls of Arms* (Oxford, 1965), pp. 134, 141), since Segrave was still marshal in
1311. Maddicott suggested that it is more likely to be a reference to the appointment in
Sept. 1311 of Gaveston's associate Arnaud de Tilh as marshal of the exchequer, an office
which should have been in Nicholas Segrave's gift. An earlier instance which might fit the
author's chronology better is suggested by Chaplais. This was the dismissal of John
Segrave from the post of justice of the northern forest, a position he expected to hold for
life. Dislike between Lancaster and Gaveston also increased during the dispute in 1309
over the lordship of Powys between Lancaster's retainer, Griffin de la Pole, and Hawise,
wife of John Charlton, Gaveston's retainer (Maddicott, *Lancaster*, pp. 93, 117–18, 140–1;
Chaplais, *Gaveston*, pp. 70–1, 84).
[32] Parliament (without commons) was summoned for 8 Feb. 1310 at Westminster
(*HBC*, p. 552). The lords and bishops normally met in the White Chamber in the Palace of
Westminster (J. G. Edwards, *The Second Century of the English Parliament* (Oxford, 1979),
p. 4). This makes it plausible for them to say that they would not be safe there if Piers
Gaveston were to be in the king's chamber (nearby) at the same time. I am indebted to
Miss Barbara Harvey for pointing this out to me.

1310 tale dederunt responsum, dicentes quod ad mandatum regis et domini
naturalis uenire tenebantur ex debito, set dum capitalis inimicus
eorum, qui regnum turbauerat et ipsos, regio lateret in thalamo,
accessum eorum non fore securum, ac hoc, nec in hoc regis precepto
fore parendum, uno ore protestabantur, addentes quod, si se regio
conspectui representare oporteret omnimodo, non inermes ut facere
solebant, set armati copiam sui facere promiserunt. Nec ob hoc
offensam se regia maiestas sentiret aut lesam dum unusquisque
naturali uiam affectu tenetur eligere tuciorem.

Tandem rex de suorum consilio Petrum ad satis tuta loca
profectum*a* dimisit ad tempus, ut ceptum negocium uel finem caperet
optatum, uel saltem mora eius non faceret inperfectum. Extunc
conuenerunt comites et barones, causamque uocacionis audituri,
regem adierunt;[33] inter quos multa interlocutoria habita sunt, que
non in communem uenere noticiam. Set cum per multos dies
protelatum esset consilium, hoc demum ex parte baronum audiui
fuisse petitum, scilicet quod cum status regis et regni a tempore quo
bone memorie Edwardus rex senior diem clausit extremum ualde
declinasset in deuium, ac per hoc totum regnum lederetur non
modicum, petebant quod ex consensu et assensu domini regis et
suorum baronum eligerentur duodecim uiri discreti, bone opinionis et
potentes, quorum arbitrio et decreto status reformaretur et consoli-
daretur; et si quid in regni grauamen redundaret, eorum ordinacio
destrueret; si uel in aliquo casu regno esset prospectum,*b* eorum
discrecione plenarie foret consultum.[34]

Rex igitur, super hiis habita deliberacione, quia uidebantur sibi in
quibusdam suspecta, diucius differebat inexpedita; set barones unanimes uiriliter instabant multa allegantes, plurima minantes, ac demum
quasi uno ore in hiis residebant, dicentes quod, nisi rex petita
concederet, iam non ipsum pro rege haberent, nec fidelitatem iuratam
sibi seruarent maxime cum ipse iusiurandum in sua coronacione

---

a prefectum *MS*; *poss.* profecturum *He*; profectum *St, Den-Y*   *b* sic *MS*; *Den-Y*
suggested possibly prospectatum; *for* prospectus *ed.*

[33] The *Annales Londonienses* (pp. 167–8) wrongly gives 27 Feb. 1310 as the date of
parliament, but that date may, perhaps, be when barons and prelates now finally met the
king. The barons would already know in general terms the reason for the summons, which
was always mentioned briefly in the writ of summons. The reason was then formally
reiterated and developed by one of the king's chief ministers at the first full meeting of
parliament (Edwards, *Second Century of the English Parliament*, p. 3; *RP*, i. 350–1;
Parliamentary Texts, pp. 71, 83). Discussion continued through early March.
[34] The petition is recorded in *Annales Londonienses* (pp. 168–9) and the *Liber*

reason for the unusual delay, they answered the royal messengers 1310
thus, that it was their bounden duty to come at the command of their
king and natural lord, but as long as their chief enemy, who had set
the kingdom and themselves in an uproar, was skulking in the king's
chamber, their approach would not be safe, and this they declared
with one voice, that the king's mandate would not be obeyed in this;
in addition they vowed that if it was absolutely necessary to present
themselves before the king, they would make their appearance not
unarmed as they usually did, but in arms. His royal majesty should
not feel offended or injured by this, since by natural inclination
everyone is bound to choose the safer way.

At length on the advice of his friends the king sent Piers away for a
time to a very safe place, so that the business which had been started
should reach a conclusion, as desired, or at least should not be left
unfinished because of his delay. Thereupon the earls and barons met
together and approached the king to hear the reason for the
summons;[33] they held many deliberations amongst themselves, and
these were not made public. But when the council had dragged on for
many days, this at length, I heard, had been asked for by the barons:
namely that, as the state of the king and the kingdom had much
deteriorated since the death of the elder King Edward, of happy
memory, and the whole kingdom had been not a little injured by this,
they asked that, with the agreement and consent of the lord king and
his barons, twelve discreet and powerful men of good reputation
should be elected, by whose judgement and decree the situation
should be reformed and settled; and if anything should be found a
burden on the kingdom, their ordinance should destroy it; and if
there was to be provision for any deficiency in the kingdom, the
decision should be taken at their complete discretion.[34]

Having considered these proposals, the king was in no hurry to
expedite them, as they seemed to him suspect in certain particulars;
but the united barons strongly insisted, bringing forward many
points, making many threats, and at length as if with one voice
took their stand upon them, saying that unless the king granted their
requests they would not have him for king, nor keep the fealty that
they had sworn to him, especially since he himself was [not] keeping

Custumarum (pp. 198–9). It does not include a request for twelve men, but such a group
may have been suggested in discussions. A group of thirty-two barons promised that their
actions would not be prejudicial to the king, and there were finally twenty-one Ordainers
(see n. 38 below).

1310 prestitum ⟨non⟩^{a} seruaret,[35] cum in lege et naturali racione caueatur, quod 'frangenti fidem fides frangatur eidem'.[36] Hiis et aliis allegatis rex, arciori habito consilio, cum uideret rem iam in arto positam, nec sine discrimine uel scandalo necessitatem posse euitari, elecciones, ordinaciones et quicquid saluo honore regio pro communi utilitate regni crederent statuendum, expresse concessit, et scriptis sigillo suo roboratis confirmauit.[37]

Electi sunt igitur ordinatores de potencioribus et discrecioribus tocius regni, et tempus^b iurisdiccionis siue ordinacionis faciende et publicande limitatum est.[38] Quibus sub tali forma concessis et consilio finito secessit unusquisque ad propria.

Post paucos dies dominus rex de consilio suo Robertum de Brutz expugnare disposuit. Fecit enim edicto regio per totum regnum proclamari, quod uidelicet omnes qui regi^c exercitum ducenti ad bellum certum patrocinium ferre tenebantur, die sancti Iohannis baptiste apud Berewyk super Twede presto regi assisterent, debitum seruicium et auxilium ibidem impensuri.[39] Vnde uiri ecclesiastici, episcopi, abbates et priores, qui pro baroniis quas de rege tenebant in capite, et pro quibus ad diuersa seruicia domino regi ex fidelitate et homagio prestitis tenebantur^d astricti, pro talibus oneribus precipue^e compensabant non modicum thesaurum, set prout quisque conuenire poterat cum thesauro, regis infundentes errario.^{f} [40]

Quidam autem comitum et baronum huic precepto regis minime obtemperarunt. Comes enim Lincolnie^g custodiam terre a rege acceperat, iccirco uenire non poterat; comes de Warewyk et alii barones, circa ordinaciones predictas occupati, quominus adessent fuerant impediti; comes uero de Lancastre, comes de Penbrok, et

^{a} om. *MS*; *supplied He, St, Den-Y* ^{b} episcopis *R*; tempus *St, Den-Y* ^{c} regis *MS*; regi *He, St, Den-Y* ^{d} tenebatur *MS*; tenebantur *He, St, Den-Y* ^{e} precipuum *MS*; precipue *He, St, Den-Y* ^{f} *sic MS*; erario *St, Den-Y* ^{g} Lincolniensis *He, St*; Lincolnie *Den-Y*

[35] This and later threats against Edward's kingship, made in 1312 and 1321, are particularly interesting in the light of Edward's final deposition. However, here the threat is unlikely to be of deposition, but rather of withdrawal of obedience to make government impossible; see above, pp. lvi–lvii.

[36] This proverb is recorded by Walther, *Proverbia*, ii. 182, no. 9915.

[37] The king agreed to the appointment of the Ordainers on 16 Mar. 1310 (*CPR 1307–13*, p. 215).

[38] The Ordainers were elected and sworn on 20 Mar. 1310. The election was sophisticated: the bishops elected two earls, the earls elected two bishops, and these four elected two barons. The six then elected fifteen others, five bishops, six earls, and four

the oath which he had taken at his coronation;[35] since in law and 1310
common sense there is this reservation, that with the breaker of faith
faith may be broken.[36] After these and other matters had been aired,
the king, having taken fuller counsel, when he saw that the business
was now delicate and that the inevitable could not be avoided without
danger or scandal, expressly granted, and confirmed by his sealed
letters, the elections, ordinances, and (saving the royal honour)
whatever they believed should be established for the common good
of the kingdom.[37]

Ordainers were therefore elected from amongst the more powerful
and discreet men of the whole kingdom and a term was set by which
their decrees or ordinances were to be made and published.[38] When
these concessions had been duly made and the council had come to an
end, everyone went home.

A few days later the lord king of his own accord decided to attack
Robert Bruce. He had it proclaimed by royal edict throughout the
kingdom that all who were bound to bring a certain force to the king
when he led an army to battle should attend the king in a state of
readiness on St John the Baptist's day at Berwick-on-Tweed, there to
give him their due service and aid.[39] Consequently churchmen,
bishops, abbots, and priors, in return for the baronies which they
held from the king in chief, for which they were bound to the lord
king in various services by the fealty and homage that they had
performed, paid considerable sums specifically in exchange for such
burdens, pouring their money into the king's treasury, according to
what each had been able to agree with the treasury.[40]

Some of the earls and barons, however, did not comply with this
royal command. For the earl of Lincoln had been made keeper of the
realm by the king and therefore could not come; the earl of Warwick
and other barons, taken up with the said ordinances, were prevented
from being present; but the earl of Lancaster, the earl of Pembroke,

barons (*PW*, ii. 2. App., p. 27; Davies, *Opposition*, pp. 358–61). The term set was 29 Sept.
1311 (*Foed.*, ii. 1. 105; *CPR 1307–13*, p. 215).

[39] The author was mistaken about the date: the writ of summons to the feudal host was
issued on 18 Jun. 1310 to muster on the Nativity of the Virgin Mary (8 Sept.), not the
Nativity of St John the Baptist (24 June) (*PW*, ii. 2. 394–7). For the forces raised by the
seruitium debitum, see below, n. 168.

[40] The writer uses both *erarium* and *fiscus* in this work. In imperial Rome the first was
the public treasury and the second the emperor's treasury. It is possible that the author
makes a similar differentiation, equating *erarium* with the Exchequer (into which here
scutage is paid) and *fiscus* with chamber (later associated with gifts and confiscated lands)
(see below, pp. 134–5, 196–7; *Vita*, 1st edn., p. 11 n.).

1310 comes de Hereford, in odium Petri pre ceteris inuecti regem in
Scociam non sunt secuti. Profectus est igitur rex, a tribus comitibus
tantum comitatus, comite uidelicet Glouuernie, comite Warennie et
comite Cornubie, qui uocatur Petrus. Alii tamen barones et milites, et
peditum turba copiosa Walensium et Anglicorum, qui animum ad
questum habebant intentum, regem e uestigio sequebantur ad bellum.
Reuera, ut dicebatur, simulatum erat hoc regis opus et fictum; non
enim accessit rex finaliter in Scociam ut Robertum de Brutz
expugnaret, set ut mandatum regis Francie caute declinaret. Mandauerat enim rex Francie regi Anglie, ut pro terris quas in partibus
transmarinis ab ipso tenebat, ueniret sibi ut domino suo fidelitatem
facturus, ut^a pro eisdem terris debita et consueta seruicia similiter
impensurus.[41] Set timuit rex; coniciebat pro certo quod, si ad
mandatum regis Francie explendum accederet, Petro suo in Anglia
inter inimicos suos dimisso, mors, carcer, uel si quid deterius est,
forsan eueniret. Talia predicabantur in populo; si uera uel falsa sint
Deus scit,^{b} nescio.[42]

   Intrauit rex autem Scociam cum exercitu suo, nullusque ei
rebellus^c inuentus est, qui uel regi manum apponeret uel hominibus
regis insidias pararet, nisi forsan contingeret aliquos de exercitu causa
foragii uel prede capiende longius abscedere.[43] Tunc enim Robertus
de Brutz, qui in insidiis semper latebat, omne malum quod poterat eis
inferebat. Nam quadam die, dum sic quidam Anglorum et Walensium, qui parati sunt ad predam, causa depredacionis exissent,
necnon et equites quamplurimi simul cum eis pro tutela ab exercitu
discessissent, subito superuenerunt homines Roberti de Brutz, qui in
speluncis et locis nemorosis latuerant, ac grauem insultum nostris
hominibus dederunt. Videntes autem equites nostri quod eis^d succurrere non possent, horrendo clamore ad exercitum reuersi sunt;
statimque prosilierunt omnes ad arma et ad succurrendum suis, inter
hostes relictis, unanimiter properabant; set sera fuit defencio quam
nostrorum precessit occisio. Nam sero seram ponis stabulo post furta
latronis. Antequam enim milites nostri uenirent, trucidati sunt de

---

^{a} sic MS; et He, Den-Y ^{b} sit MS; scit He, St, Den-Y ^{c} sic MS; rebellis He, St,
Den-Y ^{d} ei MS; eis He, St, Den-Y

---

[41] The king of England's homage for his French lands had become a major diplomatic
problem since 1259 (G. P. Cuttino, *English Medieval Diplomacy* (Bloomington, Ind., 1985),
pp. 60–73). In this case, however, the author errs. Edward had done homage to Philip IV
in 1308 and was not called on to do it again. However, in 1311 meetings began at

and the earl of Hereford did not follow the king to Scotland because 1310
they hated Piers more than the others. So the king set out accompanied by only three earls, the earl of Gloucester, Earl Warenne, and
the earl of Cornwall, who is called Piers. However, other barons and
knights and a numerous crowd of Welsh and English infantry, who
were intent on gain, followed in the king's footsteps to war. This
indeed, it was said, was a mere pretext on the king's part; for the king
was not going at last to Scotland in order to fight Robert Bruce, but so
that he might prudently avoid the king of France's summons. For the
king of France had commanded the king of England to come and do
fealty to him, as to his lord, for the lands which he held of him
overseas, and also to perform the due and customary services for the
same lands.[41] But the king was afraid; he was convinced that if he
agreed to obey the king of France's summons and left Piers in
England in the midst of his enemies, death, imprisonment, or
worse would perhaps befall him. Such things were spoken of
openly; whether they are true or false God knows, I do not.[42]

   The king entered Scotland with his army, but not a rebel was
found to lay a hand upon him or to ambush his men, except that a
few from the army, out foraging or on a plundering raid, were cut
off.[43] For at those times Robert Bruce, who lurked continually in
hiding, did them all the harm that he could. One day, when some
English and Welsh, who were ready for plunder, had gone out on a
raid accompanied for protection by many horsemen from the army,
Robert Bruce's men, who had been concealed in caves and in the
woodlands, suddenly came upon and made a serious attack on our
men. Our horsemen, seeing that they could not help them, returned
to the army with terrible shouts, and immediately all sprang to arms
and hurried with one accord to the help of those who had been left
amongst the enemy; but assistance came too late to prevent the
slaughter of our men. For it is no use locking the stable door after
the robber's theft. Before our knights arrived, up to three hundred

---

Perigueux in an attempt to solve border and land disputes. Edward had expected to attend
and on 5 July 1311 Philip wrote to him regretting that because the Scots had broken the
truce he and Edward would not meet (*Foed.*, ii. 1. 110). See P. Chaplais, 'Règlement des
conflits internationaux franco-anglais au xive siècle (1293–1377)', in his *Essays in Medieval
Diplomacy and Administration* (London, 1981), ch. ix, at pp. 280–4.
   [42] 2 Cor. 12: 3.
   [43] The king entered Scotland on 16 Sept. 1310 (*Itin.*, p. 64). The most detailed accounts
of this rather desultory campaign, in which Gaveston was the most active earl, are those of
Hamilton, *Gaveston*, pp. 84–6, and McNamee, *Wars*, pp. 49–52.

1310 Walensibus et Anglicis usque ad trecentas[a] animas, hostesque reuersi sunt ad speluncas suas. Ex talibus insidiis frequenter inuenerunt homines nostri multa mala. Robertus enim de Brutz, sciens se tam ex uiribus quam ex fortuna sua regis Anglie imparem, decreuit sibi magis expedire contra regem nostrum arma latenter mouere quam in bello campestri de iure suo contendere. Reuera dominum Robertum de Brutz affectarem laudibus extollere nisi reatus homicidii et nota prodicionis cogerent me tacere; reatus autem excludit omnem honorem.[44]

Verumtamen quo iure regnum Scocie ad se pertinere contendit in breuibus apparebit. Post finem Alexandri regis Scocie, in dubium uenerat quis ei deberet succedere, erantque duo uel tres quorum quilibet se uerum et proximum heredem asseruit. Set ex decreto magnatum utriusque regni Iohannes[b] de Bailiol ut[c] proximus heres Alexandro successit, quem rex Anglie, debita seruicia negantem et fidem non seruantem, regno priuauit, receptisque fidelitatibus et homagiis a magnatibus illius terre regnum in breui totum occupauit.[45] Porro Iohanne de Bailiol[d] excluso, Robertus de Brutz comes de Carryk ius succedendi ad se deuolutum uisus est uendicare, ac diadema sibi imponens[46] contra regem et dominum suum cui fidelitatem prestiterat ceruicem cepit erigere, quem rex Edwardus cum exercitu suo diu persecutus est. Set capto Willelmo Waleys, Symon[e] Frysel, Iohanne de Arseles et aliis quampluribus,[47] hic solus euasit, et mediante probitate et industria sua, decreto regis nostri suo tempore subici non potuit. Hic alter Eneas, a captiuitate Troiana[f] solus effugiens, laudibus Enee, nisi crimina nota necarent, attolli meruit, set eas mala tot macularunt.[48]

1311 Perhendinauit itaque rex in Scocia per totam hiemem, et usque ad natiuitatem sancti Iohannis baptiste,[49] et castra sua ex omnibus necessariis muniri fecit et restaurari. Circuiuitque per ciuitates,

---

[a] trecentum *MS*; *for* tercentum *or* trecentas *He*   [b] Johannis *MS*; Iohannes *He, St,* Den-Y   [c] et *MS*; ut *He, St, Den-Y*   [d] Boiliol *MS*; Bailiol *He, St, Den-Y*   [e] sic *MS*; Symone *He, St, Den-Y*   [f] sic *MS*; Troie *St*

[44] *Cod.* iii. 24. 1, *Corpus Iuris Ciuilis,* ii. 130.

[45] Alexander died on 19 Mar. 1286; his granddaughter and heiress died on 26 Sept. 1290. John Balliol was accepted 17 Nov. 1292, but abdicated in the face of Edward I's demands on 10 July 1296 (*HBC,* p. 58). For Edward's actions towards Balliol and his subsequent attempt to conquer Scotland, see Prestwich, *Ed. I,* pp. 363–75, 469–516; Barrow, *Bruce,* pp. 39–76.

[46] Bruce took the throne on 25 Mar. 1306 (*HBC,* p. 59). For his early career, see Barrow, *Bruce,* pp. 20–6, 109–52.

Welsh and English souls were slaughtered, and the enemy returned 1310 to their lairs. From such ambushes our men often suffered heavy losses. For Robert Bruce, knowing himself unequal to the king of England in strength or fortune, decided that it would be better to make war against our king covertly rather than to assert his right in open battle. Indeed I might be tempted to honour Sir Robert Bruce with praises except that the guilt of homicide and the stain of treachery bid me keep silent; for criminal guilt involves the loss of all honour.[44]

Now the right by which he vigorously maintained that the kingdom of Scotland belonged to him will become apparent in a few words. After the death of Alexander king of Scotland, it was doubtful who should succeed him, and there were two or three, each of whom put himself forward as the true and nearest heir. But by decree of the great men of both kingdoms John Balliol succeeded Alexander as nearest heir. Because he refused his due service and did not keep faith, the king of England deprived him of his kingdom, and, having received the fealty and homage of the great men of that land, in a short time occupied the whole realm.[45] Then, when John Balliol had been removed, Robert Bruce, earl of Carrick, claimed that the right of succession had passed down to him and, placing the crown upon himself,[46] he began to set himself up against his king and lord to whom he had sworn fealty, and King Edward long pursued him with his army. And when William Wallace, Simon Fraser, John of Atholl, and many others were captured,[47] he alone escaped and, helped by his prowess and unremitting perseverance, he could not be subjected to our king's decree in his lifetime. Here was another Aeneas fleeing alone from the Trojan captivity, Aeneas's fame, but for his crimes, he might have won; by evil deeds his honour was undone.[48]

So the king stayed in Scotland throughout the winter and until the 1311 following feast of the nativity of St John the Baptist,[49] and had his castles put in a state of defence and restocked with all necessary

[47] Wallace was captured in Aug. 1305 and executed; Fraser was captured in Aug. 1306 and executed; John Strathbogie, earl of Atholl, was taken in Sept. and executed on 7 Nov. 1306 (Prestwich, *Ed. I*, pp. 501, 503, 507–8; *CP*, i. 306).

[48] The fall of Troy and Aeneas's flight into exile were well known in the Middle Ages. England, Ireland, and Scotland, as well as Rome and Merovingian France, claimed descendants of 'noble' Aeneas and his associates as their founders (Gransden, *Historical Writing*, i. 204 and n.; Patterson, *Chaucer*, pp. 90–3). For the author's interest in Troy, see above, pp. xxviii–xxix, and for Scotland's use of the legend, see below, pp. 224–5.

[49] 24 June 1311. Edward was at or near Berwick from 1 Nov. 1310 to 30 July 1311 (*Itin.*, pp. 66–75).

1311 uillas, et castra, et omnium optinuit municiones. Robertus autem de Brutz stetit a longe ut uideret finem,[50] non enim in tali uicinio uidebatur sibi locus esse securus, set semper appropinquante exercitu tenebat loca montana inuia aquosa, ad que non poterat talis exercitus faciliter peruenire. Et certe quamuis rex Anglie tam breui manu per septennium Scociam obsideret, Robertum[a] de Brutz suo carceri nequaquam manciparet. Verum occupatus erat rex circa duo, unum circa expungnacionem Roberti de Brutz, in quo remissus[b] agebat, pro eo quod maior pars baronum Anglie ad istud negocium non ferebat auxilium; aliud erat circa retencionem Petri de Gauestone, ad cuius expulsionem et exilium omnes fere barones Anglie unanimiter laborabant. In hiis duobus rex anxius et satis afflictus unum ob aliud non est consecutus. Versus:[c]

Nam qui binas lepores una sectabitur hora,
Vno quandoque, quandoque carebit utroque.[51]

Queret autem aliquis unde tantam indignacionem baronum mer-uerat Petrus; que causa odii, quid seminarium ire et inuidie extiterit, uehementer forsan admirabitur, cum in omnium fere magnatum domibus optentum sit hodie ut unus aliquis de familia dominice dileccionis gaudeat prerogatiua. Sane ut reprobacio unius alios instruat, et ruina reprobati ad aliorum cedat documentum, causas odii et inuidie pro posse meo curabo exprimere.

Hic Petrus a Wasconia oriundus filius fuit cuiusdam militis regis Edwardi senioris quondam familiaris.[52] Dum autem Edwardus iunior adhuc esset princeps Wallie, dictus Petrus armiger iuuenis in familiarem domus eius assumptus est, et grata exhibicione[d] obse-quiorem apud dominum suum summi fauoris apicem optinuit in breui. Et, ut paucis uerbis multa concludam, rex noster, cum mortuo patre suo regnum Anglie iam esset adeptus, Petrum de Gauestone comitem fecit Cornubie. Set Petrus iam comes Cornubie olim se fuisse Petrum et humilem armigerum noluit intelligere. Nullum suum comitem, nullum suum parem reputabat Petrus, nisi solum

---

[a] Roberto *MS*; Robertum *He, St, Den-Y*   [b] *sic MS*; remissius *He, St, Den-Y*
[c] Versus *inserted above the line by He in R*; Versus *prob. a marginal note in original MS, Den-Y*   [d] exhibucione *MS*; exhibicione *He, St, Den-Y*

---

[50] Matt. 26: 58.
[51] This proverb was widely known in European late medieval MSS (Walther, *Proverbia*, iv. 142, no. 23863).
[52] Piers's father was Arnaud de Gabaston, who held a respectable amount of land in

provisions. He went round the cities, towns, and castles, and obtained supplies of all things. But Robert Bruce stood afar off, that he might see the end,[50] for there seemed no safe place for him in such a neighbourhood, but always as the army approached he kept to the trackless boggy mountain places, into which such an army could not easily penetrate. And indeed even if the king of England were to lay siege to Scotland for seven years, being shorthanded as he was, he would never commit Robert Bruce to his prison. For the king was really occupied with two projects: one was the defeat of Robert Bruce, in which he acted feebly, because the greater part of the English baronage gave no help in the affair; the other was keeping Piers Gaveston with him, for whose expulsion and exile almost all the barons of England were working together. In these two matters the king, worried and very distressed, could not attain one on account of the other. A verse:

> For he who hunts two hares together,
> Will lose now one, and then the other.[51]

But if anyone asks how Piers had come to deserve such great baronial displeasure, what was the cause of the hatred, what was the seedbed of the anger and jealousy, perhaps he will be very surprised, since it happens in almost all noble houses today that some one of the lord's household enjoys a prerogative of affection. So, then, that the condemnation of one may instruct others, and the downfall of the one condemned become a lesson to others, I shall endeavour to explain the causes of this hatred and envy as best I can.

This Piers, originating from Gascony, was the son of a certain knight who had been a member of the elder King Edward's household.[52] While Edward the younger was still prince of Wales, the said Piers was received into his household as a young esquire, and by a pleasing attention to his duties he quickly found the very highest favour in his master's sight. And, to make a long story short, when he had obtained the kingdom of England on the death of his father, our king made Piers Gaveston earl of Cornwall. But Piers, now earl of Cornwall, was unwilling to remember that he had once been Piers the humble esquire. For Piers reckoned no one his fellow, no one his equal, except the king alone. In fact his countenance

---

Gascony but who became financially dependent on service to Edward I. He served in Wales, Scotland, and Gascony over a twenty-year period until his death in 1302 (Hamilton, *Gaveston*, pp. 21–8).

1311 regem. Reuera uultus eius maiorem reuerenciam exigebat quam regis.
Erat igitur baronibus fastus eius intollerabilis et prima causa odii
simul et rancoris. Nam uulgariter dicitur,

> Si tibi copia, si sapiencia, formaque detur,
> Sola superbia destruit*ᵃ* omnia si comitetur.[53]

Credo igitur et constanter teneo quia, si Petrus ab inicio
prudenter et humiliter erga magnates terre se gessisset,*ᵇ* nunquam
eorum aliquem sibi contrarium habuisset. Erat enim causa odii
secundaria hec, quod cum ab antiquo omnibus desiderabile*ᶜ* exsti-
terit habere graciam in oculis regum, solus Petrus graciam et uultum
hillarem regis habuit et fauorem, in tantum ut, si comes uel baro
colloquium habiturus cum rege cameram regis intraret, in presencia
Petri nulli rex uerba dirigebat, nulli faciem hillarem ostendebat, nisi
soli Petro. Et reuera ex talibus frequenter oriri solet inuidia. Sane
non memini me audisse unum alterum ita dilexisse. Ionathas dilexit
Dauid, Achilles Patroclum amauit; set illi modum*ᵈ* excessisse non
leguntur.[54] Modum autem dileccionis rex noster habere non potuit,
et propter eum sui oblitus esse diceretur, et ob hoc Petrus malificus
putaretur esse.

Causa autem quare a comitatu Cornubie nitebantur eum expellere
fuit hec. Dominus Edwardus rex senior uni ex filiis suis Thome uel
Edmundo comitatum Cornubie contulisse decreuerat; set mors amara
preueniens factum quod erat conueniens fecit inperfectum. Vnde
barones iunioris regis ingratitudinem uidentes, quia ignotum noto,
extraneum germano, et aduenam incole conebatur preferre, dominum
illegittimum, comitem superbum, uelle consilio preuium, nisi sunt
mittere in exterminium. Hiis maxime de causis excitata erat contra
Petrum indignacio baronum; et Petrus nihilominus magnanimus,
tumidus et elatus permansit. Set uereor ne superbia in ruinam et
precipicium ipsum deuoluat; scriptum est enim, ante ruinam exalta-
bitur cor;[55] ille qui in altis habitat et humilia respicit[56] superbiam
super omnia detestatur. Hec Luciferum mire claritudinis angelorum*ᵉ*

ᵃ sic *R*; distruet *St*   ᵇ gessisset *R*; gessisset *St, Den-Y*   ᶜ desiderabilem *MS*;
desiderabile *He, St, Den-Y*   ᵈ modus *MS*; modum *He, St, Den-Y*   ᵉ sic *MS*;
angelum *He, St, Den-Y*

---

[53] The verse is found in a variety of European late medieval MSS (Walther, *Carminum*,
p. 943, no. 17998).
[54] For Jonathan's love of David and defence of him even against his father, King Saul,
see 1 Kgs. (1 Sam.) 18: 1–4, 19: 1–7, 20: 1–42; 2 Kgs. (2 Sam.) 1: 12–27. The legend of

exacted greater deference than the king's. His arrogance was, then,
intolerable to the barons and the main cause of both the hatred and
the rancour. For it is commonly said,

> You may be rich and wise and handsome,
> But insolence could be your ruin.[53]

I therefore believe and firmly maintain that if Piers had behaved
discreetly and humbly towards the great men of the land from the
beginning, none of them would ever have opposed him. But there was
a secondary cause of their hatred, namely that, though of old it has
been desirable for all men to find favour in the eyes of kings, Piers
alone received the king's favour, welcome, and goodwill, to such an
extent that, if an earl or baron entered the king's chamber to speak
with the king, while Piers was there the king addressed no one, and
showed a friendly countenance to no one except Piers alone. And in
truth envy is accustomed frequently to spring from such behaviour.
Certainly I do not remember having heard that one man so loved
another. Jonathan cherished David, Achilles loved Patroclus; but we
do not read that they went beyond what was usual.[54] Our king,
however, was incapable of moderate affection, and on account of Piers
was said to forget himself, and so Piers was regarded as a sorcerer.

The reason, however, why they strove to expel him from the
earldom of Cornwall was this. The old lord king Edward had decided
that the earldom of Cornwall should be conferred upon one of his
sons, Thomas or Edmund; but his sad death, intervening, prevented
what was appropriate from being carried out. So, seeing the young
king's ingratitude, that he was trying to promote the unknown over
the known, the stranger over the brother, and the foreigner over the
native, the wish foreshadowing the plan, the barons strove to destroy
this unlawful lord, this insolent earl. These were the principal causes
which had aroused the anger of the barons against Piers; and Piers
nevertheless remained arrogant, haughty, and proud. But I fear that
his pride will bring about his ruin and headlong fall; for it is written,
'the heart will be lifted up before a fall';[55] 'He who dwelleth on high
and looketh down on the low things'[56] hates pride above all things.
This it was that hurled Lucifer, an angel of wonderful brightness,

Achilles' love for Patroclus, his grief at his death, and his revenge on Hector of Troy made
an apposite parallel for the friendship of Edward and Gaveston. See above, pp. xxviii–xxx
for the medieval interest in Greek history (mediated through Latin writers). For Achilles'
grief at Patroclus' death, see Homer, *Iliad*, esp. bk. xviii.

[55] Cf. Prov. 16: 18 (*ante ruinam exaltatur spiritus*).   [56] Ps. 112 (113): 5–6.

1311 ad yma deiecit;[57] hec reginam Vasti a solio regni similiter abiecit;[58] nec mirum si in superbia sua nec Deo nec homini foret acceptus. Nam in superbia et in abusione sublimes oculos distorquens in fastum, quadam pomposa et superciliosa facie despexit uniuersos, et omnia quasi pro imperio agens, magnates terre, quibus necessarius[a] esse non potuit quin eorum auxilio magis indigeret, uix aliquando et indignantissime respexit. Et certe in filio regis satis esset intollerabile supercilium quod pretendit. Publice tamen scitur quod non erat filius regis nec regalem prosapiam quicquid attingens.

Imminente[b] festiuitate sancti Iohannis baptiste, conueniunt Londoniis ordinatores,[59] quibus anno preterito commissa fuit potestas ordinandi, corrigendi et ad meliorem statum reducendi, si quid contra leges regni uel in commune dispendium fuisset attemptatum. Potestas enim eorum limitem habuit proximum futurum festum beati Michaelis. Vt ergo antequam exspiraret eorum iurediccio, statuta et ordinata per eos in publicum uenirent, uocauerunt dominum regem et alios magnates terre ut coram eis recitata uel infirmarentur uel approbarentur.[60] Quod enim omnes tangit ab omnibus debet approbari.[61] Recessit igitur rex a Scocia, et uenit Londonias,[62] et apud fratres predicatores hospicio se recepit. Cum quidam autem procerum moram facerent, sine quorum presencia res expediri non posset, dominus rex sacra loca uisitare Cantuariam proficiscitur, ac demum circa finem mensis Augusti reuertitur.[63]

Omnibus itaque quorum interesse uertebatur[c] adunatis, profertur in medium labor annalis, et capitula singillatim recitantur, et regis consiliariis copia porrigitur. Rex autem de consilio suo quedam sibi incommoda, quedam in odium suum adinuenta protestatur, et se hiis assensum prebere non teneri arguit et causatur, cum in commissione concessa regia magestas fuisset eccepta.[d] Sciebant tamen barones regis excusaciones friuolas esse et fictas et ad exquirendas dilaciones semper intentas; unde et ipsi uiriliter instabant, et cum omnium incomodo[e] regis magis commodum compensabant. Fuit autem inter ordinaciones illas una quedam que magis inter ceteras regem

---

[a] necessariis *MS*; necessarius *He, St, Den-Y*   [b] iminente *MS*; imminente *He, St, Den-Y*   [c] sic *MS*; poss.* uidebatur *He*   [d] sic *MS*; excepta *He, St, Den-Y*   [e] sic *MS*; incommodo *He, St, Den-Y*

[57] Cf. Isa. 14: 12–19.   [58] Cf. Esther 1: 9–22.   [59] 24 June 1311.
[60] For the powers of the Ordainers and the deadline of Michaelmas (29 Sept.), see above, pp. 20–1. Parliament was summoned for 8 Aug. 1311 in London; the first session ended on 9 Oct., and it met again in Nov. (*HBC*, p. 552).
[61] *Cod.* v. 59. 5 (2), *Corpus Iuris Civilis*, ii. 231.

down to the depths;[57] this likewise cast queen Vashti from the throne   1311
of her kingdom;[58] nor is it surprising if he in his pride should be
acceptable to neither God nor man. For, scornfully rolling his eyes
upwards in pride and in insult, he looked down upon all with
overbearing and disdainful countenance, and, carrying out everything
as if with supreme authority, he scarcely ever paid any heed, and then
most contemptuously, to the great men of the land, to whom he could
not be necessary, but whose help he needed rather more. And the
haughtiness which he affected would certainly have been unbearable
enough in a king's son. Yet it was universally known that he was not a
king's son, nor was he related to any royal stock whatsoever.

As the feast of St John the Baptist approached the Ordainers came
to London.[59] The year before they had been given the power of
ordaining, correcting, and reforming anything which had been done
against the laws of the realm or to the common loss. The term set to
their power was the following Michaelmas. Therefore, in order that
their decrees and ordinances should be made public before their
jurisdiction expired, they invited the lord king and the other great
men of the land to reject or confirm what was recited before them.[60]
For 'what touches all should be approved by all'.[61] So the king left
Scotland and came to London,[62] where he lodged with the Dominicans. When certain of the notables delayed, without whom the
business could not proceed, the lord king set out to visit the shrines
at Canterbury and at length returned towards the end of August.[63]

And so, when all those concerned had gathered together, the year's
work was produced and the chapters were recited one by one, and a
copy was made available to the king's counsellors. But the king and
his council protested that some things were disadvantageous to him,
some devised out of hatred, and he argued and pleaded that he was
not bound to give his consent to these, since in the commission
granted to them matters touching the king's sovereignty had been
excluded. The barons knew, however, that the king's excuses were
frivolous and invented and always meant to gain time; they therefore
firmly stood their ground, setting the common good above the king's
loss. There was, however, one of those Ordinances that distressed the
king more than the rest, namely the expulsion of Piers Gaveston and

---

[62] Edward left Berwick on 30 July; by 12 Aug. he was at St Albans, and the following
day his household was at Westminster (*Itin.*, pp. 75–6).
[63] The visit to Canterbury is not evident in the published itinerary, but is possible. The
king was certainly in London on 17 and 21 Aug. (*Itin.*, p. 76).

1311 affligebat, uidelicet expulsio Petri de Gauestone et eius exilium; set
rex ad hoc nullo sensu inclinari potuit uel induci. Vt tamen baronibus
satisfaceret hoc offerebat: 'quecunque', inquid, 'ordinata sunt, quecunque statuta, quantumcunque in meum priuatum incomodum
redundent, ad peticionem uestram ualeant atque perpetuo subsistant.
Verum a persecucione fratris mei Petri desistatis, et comitatum
Cornubie habere permittatis.' Hoc sepe et sepius petebat sic rex,
nunc illos blandiciis palpans, nunc autem minas adiciens; set barones
uiriliter instabant, plurima allegantes ut fideles regis regi consulentes,
ac demum, quasi uno animo et una uoce, hoc in calce sermonis
adiciebant, quod aut^a Petrus iuxta arbitrium ordinatorum exilium
subiret, aut unusquisque de capite proprio defendendo sibi consuleret. Videntes igitur hii qui de consilio regis erant quod, si dominus
rex ordinatorum decretis et placitis non acquiesceret, turbaretur
regnum et pacis sequeretur exilium; scientes eciam quod ciuile
bellum nunquam finem habuisset acceptum, de quo bellum de
Lewes manifestum reliquid exemplum et bellum de Euesham
eternam seruabat memoriam, in quo pro tempore iusticie nobilis
ille comes Leycestrie Symon occubuit;^{64} considerabant eciam quam
dura inter regem et barones suos et quam periculosa foret dissencio,
quod tocius terre sequeretur desolacio, quod inter dubios euentus uix
euitaretur regis capcio, et, sicut Roboam qui consilium seniorum
respuens consilio iuuenum adhesit, incaute solio forsan priuaretur et
regno;^{65} hec et hiis similia considerantes qui consulares regis esse
dicebantur, attencius instare ceperunt pro regno, pro populo, pro
semetipso^b regem interpellantes, quatinus suorum digneretur^c accep-
tare consilium, ineuitabile protestantes euenire periculum quod sibi et
suis perpetuum afferret obprobrium, nisi decretis baronum assentiret,
nisi ordinaciones eorum sine fraude concederet.

Rex igitur, suorum monitis et precibus inductus, ordinaciones,
prouisiones et statuta, quocunque nomine censeantur, pro se et suis
successoribus inuiolabiliter et imperpetuum rata teneri consentit.
Directa est igitur copia ordinacionum sub magno sigillo ad quemlibet comitatum, et ibidem publice proclamantur, et ab omnibus
proclamare precipiuntur. Quas hic ideo interserere nolui, quia

---

^{a} autem R; aut St, Den-Y ^{b} sic MS; semetipsis He ^{c} sic MS; dignaretur He,
St, Den-Y

^{64} During the Barons' Wars against Henry III the battle of Lewes took place on 14 May
1264 and the battle of Evesham on 4 Aug. 1265. At Lewes Henry III was captured, and at
Evesham Simon de Montfort, earl of Leicester, was killed.

his exile; to this the king could in no way be persuaded or brought to agree. Nevertheless, to satisfy the barons he offered these terms: 'whatever things have been ordained or decided upon', he said, 'however much they may redound to my private disadvantage, shall be established at your request and remain in force for ever. But you shall stop persecuting my brother Piers, and allow him to have the earldom of Cornwall.' The king sought this time and again, now coaxing them with flattery, now hurling threats; but the barons firmly stood their ground putting forward many arguments as the king's faithful subjects consulting the king's interests, and finally, as if with one mind and voice, they added at the end of their reply that either Piers should suffer exile according to the judgement of the Ordainers, or each man would consider how to defend his own life. The king's advisers, seeing that if the lord king would not agree to the decrees and resolutions of the Ordainers the kingdom would be in turmoil and peace would subsequently be driven out of the land; knowing also that civil war never yet had an acceptable end, of which the battle of Lewes remains an obvious example, and the battle of Evesham preserved an everlasting reminder, where that noble man Simon, earl of Leicester, died in the cause of justice;[64] considering also how harsh and dangerous the struggle between the king and his barons would be, that the suffering of the whole land would follow, that amidst the fluctuating events the king's capture would hardly be avoided, and like Rehoboam, who rejected the counsel of the elders and followed the advice of the young, he might perhaps through imprudence be deprived of his throne and of the kingdom;[65] considering these things and the like, those who were said to be the king's counsellors began to press more insistently, urging the king for the sake of the kingdom, the people, and himself to deign to accept their advice, showing that inescapable danger would arise, which would bring everlasting disgrace upon him and his, unless he agreed to the decrees of the barons and granted their Ordinances without deceit.

So the king, moved by their warnings and entreaties, agreed for himself and his successors that the Ordinances, provisions, and statutes, by whatever name they may be called, should be held inviolably valid for ever. A copy of the Ordinances was therefore sent under the great seal to every county, and there publicly proclaimed, and commanded to be proclaimed by all. Therefore I

---

[65] Cf. 3 Kgs. (1 Kgs.) 12: 8; 2 Chr. 10: 8. For comment on threats concerning the loss of the kingdom, see above, pp. lvi–lvii.

1311 seriem huius materie rescinderem[a] uel fastidium legentibus afferrem;[b] set, si quis eas sibi dixerit ignotas, inter alia statuta suo loco reperiet insertas.[66] Verum quia ordinacio illa que Petrum de Gauestone eiecit ab Anglia pluribusque[c] inter alias magis uidebatur accepta, inspicientes enim ordinaciones statim ad illam recursum habebant, cum tamen in ordine prima non esset, set decimum uel ulteriorem locum optineret, et ut ipsa ordinacione perlecta manifeste appareat ipsius exilii causa, iccirco in hac mee narracionis serie, quia multum concordat materie statutum illud, de uerbo ad uerbum, prout fuerat in audiencia publicatum, interserui sub forma que sequitur:—[67]

Quia notum est et per examinacionem prelatorum, comitum, baronum, militum et aliorum bonorum et legalium hominum regni repertum, quod Petrus de Gauestone dominum regem male duxit, domino regi male consuluit,[d] et ipsum ad male faciendum deceptorie et multiformiter induxit, contractando sibi totum thesaurum regis, quem eciam extra regnum elongauit; attrahendo sibi homines qui secum morarentur contra omnes gentes, et per thesaurum regis quem sic adquisiuit, de die in diem dominando supra statum regis et corone in destruccione regis et regni; specialiter elongando cor domini regis a suis legiis hominibus, consilia eorum despiciendo, bonos ministros legem facere non permittendo et bonos ministros amouendo; tales autem de sua familiaritate, tam alienigenas quam alios, constituendo, qui ad suum preceptum et uelle iusticiam offendunt ⟨et⟩[e] legem terre, acceptando terras et tenementa contra suum homagium de corona, nedum ante ordinaciones ad profectum regis et regni ab ordinatoribus concessas set eciam post, contra dictorum ordinatorum prouisiones et decreta.

Sustinet eciam predones et homicidas ipsisque cartas domini regis de pace adquirit, et sic aliis malefactoribus magis delinquendi prebet audaciam. Conducit regem in terram guerre sine communi consensu suorum baronum, in periculum regis et destruccionem regni; albas cartas sub magno sigillo regis facit consignari, in capcionem et exheredacionem regis et corone; et callide false et proditorie fecit[f] hec omnia predicta in magnum dedecus[g] et

---

[a] rescindere MS; rescinderem He, St, Den-Y   [b] auferem MS; afferrem He, St, Den-Y
[c] sic MS; poss. substitute pluribus or om. que He   [d] consiluit MS; consuluit He, St, Den-Y
[e] om. R; supplied St, Den-Y   [f] sic R; for facit, ed.   [g] dedicus MS; dedecus St, Den-Y

[66] The order to proclaim the Ordinances was issued on 11 Oct. 1311. The Ordinances consisted of forty-one clauses (six of which had been issued immediately in Mar. 1310 and were repeated). They covered a number of controversial political matters concerning finance, appointments, and war, and specified the expulsion from court of a number of individuals as well as Piers Gaveston. For the full text of th Ordinances see RP, i. 281–6; SR, i. 157–68; trans. in 'The New Ordinances, 1311', EHD, iii. 527–39. The author's phrasing suggests that he was writing for readers who would have access to the official

did not want to insert them here because I would break the flow of 1311
this narrative and prove tedious to readers: but if anyone should say
that he is unacquainted with them he will find them in their proper
place among the other statutes.[66] However, because the ordinance
which expelled Piers Gaveston from England seemed more welcome
to many than the rest, for when people examined the Ordinances they
at once turned to it although it did not come first in the list but was
tenth or later, and so that the cause of banishment may appear clearly
once this ordinance has been read through, I have therefore inserted
that decision in the course of my narrative as very relevant to my
theme, word for word as it was read out publicly, in the following
form:[67]

Because it is known and found by the examination of prelates, earls, barons,
knights, and other good and lawful men of the kingdom, that Piers Gaveston
has led the lord king astray, advised the lord king badly, and persuaded him
deceitfully and in many ways to do wrong; in gathering to himself all the
king's treasure which, moreover, he has exported from the country; in
attracting to himself men who would remain with him against all people, and
this by means of the king's treasure thus acquired from day to day; in lording
it over the state of the king and of the crown to the ruin of the king and
kingdom; more especially in estranging the lord king's heart from his liege
men; in despising their counsel, not permitting good ministers to enforce law
and removing good ministers; in appointing from his own circle, both
foreigners and others, such persons as, at his command and will, violate
justice and the law of the land; in receiving lands and tenements against his
homage to the crown, not only before the Ordinances ordained by the
Ordainers for the profit of the king and the kingdom, but also afterwards,
against the provisions and decrees of the said Ordainers.

   Also he maintains robbers and homicides and obtains the lord king's
pardons for them, and so encourages other evildoers to greater boldness in
crime. He takes the king into a country at war without the common consent
of his barons, to the danger of the king and the destruction of his kingdom;
he has blank charters sealed under the king's great seal to the deception and
disinheritance of the king and the crown; and all the aforesaid things he did
craftily, falsely, and treacherously to the great disgrace and damage of the

statute roll, or to a full collection of statutes copied and kept in a muniment room or
library of some size.
   [67] This is a close translation into Latin of clause 20 of the Ordinances (*RP*, i. 283; *SR*, i.
162a; 'The New Ordinances, 1311', *EHD*, iii. 532–3). The clause was in this position in
the rolls of parliament and in the official published version, and appeared even later in the
list in the Durham draft (M. Prestwich, 'A new version of the Ordinances of 1311', *BIHR*,
lvii (1984), 189–203, at 192, 201). The discrepancy in number may therefore be through
error, or an intermediate miscopying of .x. for .xx.

1311 dampnum regni, exheredacionem corone, in destruccionem populi multi-
mode.

Insuper habentes respectum ad facta nobilissimi regis patris domini nostri
regis qui nunc est, ⟨cuius⟩ᵃ edicto dictus Petrus regnum Anglie abiurauit et
exulauit, qui et uoluit quod dominus noster rex filius suus pro omni tempore
societatem illius abiurasset; inspicientes eciam quod postea communi assensu
tocius regni pariter et regis prospectum erat quod Petrus idem regnum
euacuaret, et euacuauit, et quod per communem assensum non rediit, set
duntaxat per consensum aliquorum, qui sub condicione, si post regressum
suum bene se gereret, ad hoc consenciebant; et nunc certissime repertus est
male gessisse; quamobrem et propter sua malefacta predicta, et propter alia
que uerisimiliter domino regi et populo contingere possent, et ad bonam
concordiam inter dominum regem et suos subditos nutriendam et multi-
modas discordias et pericula euitanda, nos ordinatores, ut ordinatores et
uirtute dicte commissionis regie, concessimus quod Petrus de Gauestone,
tanquam publicus hostis regis et regni, a regno penitus eiciatur et exuletur,
nedum ab Anglia set eciam Wallia, Scocia, Hibernia, Wasconia, et ab omni
terra tam ultra mare quam citra mare dominacioni regis Anglie subiecta, pro
omni die et sine reditu. Et quod citra festum omnium sanctorum proxime
futurum⁶⁸ regnum Anglie et omne ᵇregis dominiumᵇ relinquat et penitus
euacuet, et portum apud Douere sibi damus in forma predicta. Nec liceat sibi
alibi terram exire uel in alio sinu maris portum arripere. Et si dictus Petrus in
regno Anglie uel alibi in dominio regis nostri ultra statutum diem faciat
moram, extunc faciatᶜ de ipso tanquam de inimico regni, regis, et populi. Et
quicunque contra hanc ordinacionem uenerit, ad tardacionem dicti exilii, fiat
de ipsis prout uisum fuerit expedire cum super hoc fuerint conuicti.

Et Petri quidem exilium ex decreto ordinatorum sic erat.

Post festum omnium sanctorum, quia rex ordinacionibus baronum
stare iurauerat, Petrum in exilium ire disposuit, quia in breui satis
competenter sibi prouidere proposuit. Antequam tamen Petrus
terram Anglie egrederetur, de consilio quorundam qui parti sue
adherebant, litteras regis bone conuersacionis et fidelitatis testimo-
niales a rege impetrauit et optinuit; et hiis litteris rex sigillum suum
apposuit, et multi magnates similiter fecerunt, qui magis reprehen-
sione digni quam ex hoc facto laudandi fuerunt. Inter quos comes
Gloucestrie Gilbertus, iuuenis et precibus regis inductus, predictis
litteris testimonium prebuit. Nam et illas sigillo suo roborauit, set
postea saniori ductus consilio, et pretextu minoris etatis excusatus,

---

ᵃ om. R; supplied St, Den-Y   ᵇ⁻ᵇ regnum domu' MS; regni dominium He; regis
dominium St, Den-Y   ᶜ sic MS; poss. fiat He; fiat St, Den-Y

kingdom, the disinheritance of the crown, and the destruction of the people
in many ways.

Moreover, having regard to what was done by the most noble king, father
of our present lord king, by whose edict the said Piers abjured and was exiled
from the realm of England, and who wished that our lord king his son should
renounce the company of this person for all time; bearing in mind, further,
that afterwards by the common assent equally of the whole realm and of the
king it was decided that the said Piers should leave the realm, and he did
leave it, and that he did not return by common assent, but only by the
consent of some individuals, who consented to this on condition that after his
return he should behave well; and now it is found most certainly that he has
behaved badly; for which reason, and on account of his aforesaid wrongdoing, and on account of other things which are likely to happen to the lord
king and the people, and in order to foster good harmony between the lord
king and his subjects, and to avoid many kinds of discords and dangers, we,
the Ordainers, as Ordainers and by virtue of the said royal commission, have
decreed that Piers Gaveston, as a public enemy of the king and of the
kingdom, shall be utterly cast out and exiled from the kingdom, not only
from England, but from Wales, Scotland, Ireland, Gascony, and from every
land as well beyond the sea as on this side of the sea subject to the lordship of
the king of England, for ever and without return. And that before the feast of
All Saints next coming[68] he shall leave and completely depart from the
kingdom of England and every lordship of the king, and we assign to him in
the said form Dover harbour. Nor may he leave the land elsewhere nor from
another harbour. And if the said Piers stays in the kingdom of England or
elsewhere in the lordship of our king beyond the appointed day, he shall
thereafter be treated as an enemy of the kingdom, the king, and the people.
And let everyone who shall go against this Ordinance, to delay the said exile,
be dealt with as seems expedient when they have been found guilty of it.

And this was the manner of Piers's exile by decree of the Ordainers.

After the feast of All Saints, as the king had sworn to stand by the
Ordinances of the barons, he arranged for Piers to go into exile, because
he planned to provide for him very adequately soon. Before Piers left
England, however, on the advice of some who stuck to his side, he asked
for and obtained from the king letters testifying to his good character
and loyalty; and the king put his seal to these letters, and many great
men more worthy of reproof than praise for this deed did likewise.
Amongst these Gilbert, earl of Gloucester, a young man persuaded by
the king's entreaties, lent his testimony to these letters. For he
confirmed them with his seal, but afterwards, guided by wiser counsel

---

[68] That is 1 Nov. 1311. Several chroniclers noted that he left in fact after 1 Nov., and
the *Ann. Lond.* specified 4 Nov. (*in triduo post festum*, p. 202).

1311 errorem suum reuocauit, et impressionem sigilli sui a litteris illis extorsit.

Petrus igitur tali testimonio munitus clam propter aduersarios secessit in Flandriam, omni fere populo ignorante ad quas partes diuertisset.[69] Post hec comites iuxta ordinaciones domini regis ulterius disponere uolentes, complices et fautores Petri a curia regis sub pena incarceracionis recedere decreuerunt, ne et ipsi animum regis ad reuocandum Petrum de cetero instigarent.[70] Ad hec rex ultra modum commotus, quod nec unum familiarem iuxta proprium uotum retinere sibi liceret, set sicut prouidetur fatuo, tocius domus sue ordinacio ex alieno dependeret arbitrio, in odio comitum reuocauit Petrum, per animam Dei iurans ex solito quod libere proprio uteretur arbitrio.[71]

1312 Et Petrus quidem ad regis mandatum statim reuersus est in Angliam, quia regem Francie suspectum habebat, per Flandriam. Set quamuis periculosa sibi foret Francia, periculosior futura sibi fuit Anglia. Euenit enim sibi quod quidam ait,

Incidit in Scillam cupiens uitare Caribdim.[72]

Reuersus igitur Petrus caute ambulabat, et nunc in camera regis, nunc apud Walyngford, nunc in castello de Tyntagel latere putabatur. Cum autem appropinquaret natale Domini dominus rex et Petrus ad partes boriales sunt profecti, et apud Eboracum festa[a] natalicia celebrarunt.[73] Et dominus rex studiose in dies cum omni consilio suo de statu Petri et pace tractabat; et quia non erat Petro tutus locus in Anglia, Hibernia, Wallia, Wasconia nec Francia, de mora Petri tractare disposuit in Scocia, donec impetus baronum cessaret, uel Petro decencius et alibi prouideret; set inane studium uix habuit inicium. Cum enim Robertus de Brutz de fidelitate Petro seruanda et

---

[a] facta *R*; festa *St, Den-Y*

---

[69] There is no certain evidence for where Piers spent his short exile, but several of the chronicles record Flanders, which is likely (Hamilton, *Gaveston*, pp. 91–2; Chaplais, *Gaveston*, pp. 74–6).

[70] The supplementary ordinances survive in *Ann. Lond.*, pp. 198–202 and *Lib. Cust.*, ii. 2. 682–90, where they are said to be the work of the earls of Lancaster and Warwick.

[71] The king declared the Ordinances repealed on 9 or 16 Jan. 1312, but, faced with opposition to this, he again ordered their enforcement on 26 Jan., provided nothing was done to his prejudice or against the law. This proviso arguably excluded the enforcement of Gaveston's exile, which Edward had also separately declared unlawful on 18 Jan. (*Foed.*, ii. 1. 153–4; Chaplais, *Gaveston*, pp. 79–82; Maddicott, *Lancaster*, pp. 122–3). The

and excused on the grounds of his minority, he corrected his mistake   1311
and tore the impression of his seal from the letters.

Thus protected by such a testimonial Piers secretly, on account of
his enemies, departed to Flanders, almost everyone being ignorant of
his destination.[69] After this, the earls, wishing to make further
arrangements according to the lord king's Ordinances, declared that
Piers's friends and supporters should leave the king's court under
penalty of imprisonment, lest they should urge the king to recall Piers
once more.[70] At this the king, angered beyond measure that he was
not allowed to keep even one member of his household at his own
wish, but that, as is provided in the case of an idiot, the ordering of
his whole house should depend upon the decision of another, recalled
Piers out of hatred for the earls, swearing, as he was wont, on God's
soul that he would freely use his own judgement.[71]

And so Piers immediately returned to England at the king's   1312
command, by way of Flanders, because he mistrusted the king of
France. But though France might be dangerous for him, England was
going to be more dangerous. For it so turned out for him that, as is
commonly said,

> He falls into Scylla in trying to avoid Charybdis.[72]

When he returned, Piers proceeded cautiously, and was thought to be
skulking now in the king's apartments, now at Wallingford, now at
Tintagel Castle. As Christmas approached, however, the lord king
and Piers set out for the North, and celebrated the feast of the nativity
at York.[73] The lord king anxiously discussed day by day with his
whole council the question of Piers's position and the peace of the
realm; and because there was no safe place for Piers in England,
Ireland, Wales, Gascony, or France, he tried to arrange for Piers's
residence in Scotland, until the baronial attack should cease, or he
could provide more fittingly for Piers elsewhere; but this fatuous
scheme was scarcely even begun. For when Robert Bruce was

question of whether the king could revoke the exile on his own authority, without assent,
underlay the legal dispute after the murder of Gaveston.

[72] Walter of Châtillon, *Alexandreis*, v. 301 (*PL* ccix. 514). The phrase is proverbial after
his time (*Vita*, 1st edn., p. 21 n. 2).

[73] The *Annales Paulini* also mistakenly placed Edward at York for Christmas. He spent
it at Westminster, and arrived in York on 13 Jan. 1312 (*Itin.*, p. 81). He was by then
accompanied by Gaveston, who probably wished to be with his wife, who bore their first
child there in Jan. (Chaplais, *Gaveston*, pp. 78–9; Hamilton, *Gaveston*, pp. 92–3). The king
declared Gaveston's exile unlawful on 18 Jan., and restored his estates on 20 Jan. (*Foed.*, ii.
1. 153–4; *CCR 1307–13*, pp. 448–9).

1312 condicione pacis requir⟨er⟩etur*a* et inuitaretur; cum eciam sibi multa
offerentur ac demum ipsum regnum*b* Scocie tranquille et imperpe-
tuo domino Roberto promitteretur, hoc modo regis mandato fertur
respondisse, 'Quomodo rex Anglie pactum michi seruaret, qui legiis
suis hominibus, quorum fidelitatem et homagia recepit, quibus
eciam mutuo fidem seruare tenetur, promissa eciam iuramento
uallata non custodit? Non est adhibenda fides homini tam uario;
non me decipiet sua promissio.' Sic cassata spes regia, sic eluduntur
regis promissa.

Audientes autem comites et pro certo iam scientes quod rediisset
Petrus, uidentes autem quod non procederet ordinacio quam
statuerant circa eum, congregati sunt cum primato*c* suo Roberto
Cantuariensi archiepiscopo. Et primas quid⟨em⟩,*d* sicut erat spiritu
feruens et pacem regni zelans, gladium suum arripuit et Petrum
anathemate percussit, ut sic lata sentencia euacuaretur gracia;[74] nam
qui iuste ligatur raro efficaciter operatur. Et barones ex parte sua
non minus laborant ad querendum remedia, fueruntque ad defen-
cionem ordinacionum principaliter intenti et inuicem iureiurando
similiter astricti comites subscripti: Thomas comes Lancastrie,
Adolmarus comes Penbroke, Humfridus comes Herfordie, Edmundus comes Darundel, et Guydo comes Warewyke. Hii quinque
comites armis strenui, genere preclari, et copiosa armatorum multitudine uallati, circa capcionem Petri unanimiter consultant. Quid
autem in illo consilio fuerit decretum, uel quibus insidiis molirentur
in Petrum, diu quidem latuit; set quid ibidem actum fuerit ex post
factis satis apparuit; et caute quidem et prouide actum, ut ita lateret
eorum propositum, ne diuulgata intencio immunem prestaret in
uicio.*e* Secesserunt igitur comites ab inuicem unusquisque in uiam
suam, et comes Glouuernie, quamuis in hoc proposito socius non
esset, ratum tamen habere promisit quicquid comites facerent,
quicquid in hac expedicione disponerent. Comes autem Lancastrie
ad partes boriales se transtulit, et ceteri comites, ne ex uisu armorum
terreretur prouincia, fecerunt per diuersa loca proclamari tornea-
menta, ut sub tali pretextu colligerent quos sibi necessarios esse,*f* et

a requiretur R; requireretur St, Den-Y   *b* regem MS; poss. fore understood He;
regnum St, Den-Y   *c* sic MS; primate He, St, Den-Y   *d* quid MS; quidem He, St,
Den-Y   *e* He read innicio in MS and suggested inicio; in uicio St, Den-Y   *f* sic MS;
poss. existimarunt understood He

[74] Winchelsey and the bishops met the magnates in London on 13 Mar. 1312. No
record of Gaveston's excommunication survives, but at the provincial council in May a

sounded out and asked about keeping faith with Piers and the terms   1312
of peace; when, too, many offers were made to him, and finally the
kingdom of Scotland itself was offered to Lord Robert freely and for
ever, he is said to have replied to the king's message in this manner:
'How shall the king of England keep faith with me, since he does not
keep the sworn promises made to his liege men, whose homage and
fealty he has received, and with whom he is bound in return to keep
faith? No trust can be put in such a fickle man: his promise will not
deceive me.' Thus was the king's hope shattered, thus the king's
promises were mocked.

When the earls had heard and knew for certain that Piers had
returned, realizing that the ordinance which they had made concerning him would not be enforced, they met together with their primate
Robert, archbishop of Canterbury. And the primate, as he was
passionate in spirit and eager for the peace of the realm, seized his
sword and struck Piers with anathema, so that with the sentence
having been made public he should be excluded from grace;[74] for he
who is bound in due form is seldom effective in action. And the
barons for their part worked no less to find a remedy; they were
chiefly concerned with the defence of the Ordinances, and the
following earls were likewise bound by a mutual oath: Thomas, earl
of Lancaster, Aymer, earl of Pembroke, Humphrey, earl of Hereford,
Edmund, earl of Arundel, and Guy, earl of Warwick. These five earls,
active soldiers, of famous families, and surrounded by a strong force
of men-at-arms, took counsel together about the capture of Piers.
What, however, was decreed in that council or what traps they laid for
Piers was long kept secret; but what had been done there later became
clear; and, indeed, that their plan was thus kept concealed was done
shrewdly and with foresight, lest knowledge of their intentions should
keep him safe in his crime. So the earls separated from one another,
each going his own way, and the earl of Gloucester, although he was
not a partner in this plan, nevertheless promised that he would
approve whatever the earls did, whatever they should arrange in this
enterprise. The earl of Lancaster betook himself to the North, and the
other earls, lest the country should be terrified by the sight of arms,
had tournaments proclaimed in different places, so that under cover
of such a pretext they might gather those who were necessary to

decision was made to issue a general excommunication of all those who disturbed the peace
of the realm (Denton, *Winchelsey*, pp. 265–7; Wright, *Reynolds*, p. 350). Gaveston would
have been covered by this.

1312 sic mouerunt se de loco ad locum donec transirent Eboracum, et comes Lancastrie circa solis occasum aggressus est iter suum. Sic Thomas de nocte uolat, sub luce moratur, ut lateat, modicum cursum ne fama loquatur; et hac cautela nisus^a ad Nouum Castrum subito uenit et inprouisus,[75] ubi^b dextrarii et magni caballi ipsius Petri uel uerius domini regis morabantur. Erat eciam ibidem copiosa multitudo armorum, in quibus erat fiducia^c Petri defendendi et resistendi se. Set hec omnia cepit comes, et custodibus eiectis suis hominibus et hec omnia custodienda mandauit, ut^d regis erant, fideliter restituerentur et regi.

Accidit itaque modicum post hec ut dominus rex et Petrus ab inuicem separarentur; unus apud Scardeburghe, alter apud Knaresbrugg morabatur.[76] Quod cum perpendisset comes Lancastrie, disposuit se in medio esse, ne unus ad alterum posset habere regressum, et ceteri comitum interim obsiderent Petrum. Cum igitur uideret Petrus obsidionem iam ceptam, auxilium regis interceptum, castrum uictualibus destitutum et socios minus sufficientes ad bellum, misit ad comitem Penbrokie se reddere uolens sub condicione; et erat condicio hec uidelicet quod dictus comes Petrum usque ad gulam Augusti seruaret illesum, et, si placeret ei quod interim comites disponerent, bene quidem; sin autem, restitueretur in pristinum statum, scilicet ad castrum unde exierat et ad sororem quam prius relinquerat.^e [77]

Comes autem de hac capcione gauisus, sociis inconsultis, immo ex proprio capite sumpto consilio, cepit Petrum, et placuit condicio, et ad Petrum seruandum sub forma predicta obligauit regi terras et tenementa.[78] Nam et huius rex conscius erat, quia de consilio regis res ipsa prodierat; sperauit enim ante predictum terminum sufficiens prestare Petro subsidium: quia si Petrus exspectasset Augustum, ad libitum, ut dicitur, rediisset arbitrium. Nam papa et rex Francie ordinassent remedium, quia rex Anglie donasset Wasconiam eis in feodum.

Comes igitur Adolmarus cum uinculato suo Petro recessit a borea,

^a uisus R; nisus St, Den-Y   ^b nisi R; ubi St, Den-Y   ^c fudicia MS; fiducia He, St, Den-Y   ^d sic MS; que supplied after ut Den-Y   ^e sic MS; reliquerat He, St, Den-Y

[75] He arrived on 4 May 1312 (Maddicott, Lancaster, p. 343).
[76] Edward had arrived at Scarborough by sea on 10 May (Brid., p. 42); by 14 May he was at Knaresborough and by 19 May at York (Itin., p. 85). By 17 May the siege of Scarborough had begun (CCR 1307–13, p. 460).
[77] Probably Amy de Gabaston, who stayed in England to serve first Queen Isabella, then Edward III's wife, Queen Phillippa (Hamilton, Gaveston, p. 102).

them; and thus they moved from place to place until they passed York, and about sunset the earl of Lancaster set out on his way. Thus Thomas flies by night and hides by day so as to remain unknown, lest rumour divulge his slow progress; and relying on this cautious procedure he came suddenly and unexpectedly to Newcastle,[75] where the war-horses and great riding-horses of the said Piers, or rather of the lord king, were stabled. There was also a large supply of arms there, in which lay Piers's confidence that he could resist and defend himself. But the earl took all these, and, having thrown out the guards, ordered his own men to guard all these things, since they belonged to the king and should be faithfully restored to the king.

Shortly after this it happened that the lord king and Piers were separated from one another; one stayed at Scarborough, the other at Knaresborough.[76] When the earl of Lancaster had considered this carefully, he took up his position in between them, so that the one could not fall back upon the other, and meanwhile the other earls should besiege Piers. When Piers saw that the siege had begun, help from the king was cut off, the castle was without food, and his supporters were too few to give battle, he sent to the earl of Pembroke, wishing to surrender conditionally; the condition was this, namely that the said earl should keep Piers unharmed till the first of August, and if he agreed to what the earls in the meantime decided, well and good; if not he should be restored to his former state, namely to the castle from which he had moved out, and to the sister whom he had previously left.[77]

The earl was delighted by this capture and without consulting his fellows, on the contrary on his own initiative, he took Piers and accepted the condition, and pledged his lands and tenements to the king under the said form for Piers's safety.[78] Now the king knew of this, because the suggestion had been put forward at the king's instigation; for he hoped to give Piers adequate support before the said deadline: because if Piers could have held out until August, he would have recovered, it is said, his personal freedom. For the pope and the king of France would have arranged a remedy, because the king of England would have given them Gascony in fee.

Therefore Earl Aymer left the North with Piers as his prisoner,

[78] Piers surrendered on 19 May 1312. The deadline of 1 Aug. and the pledge of property are accurately reported. Pembroke's biographer thinks it unlikely that Pembroke failed to inform the other lords (Phillips, *Pembroke*, pp. 33 and n., 34).

1312 ad Anglie*a* tendens interiora, et cum circiter quinque dietas uel amplius peregisset, tandem in comitatum*b* Northamtoniensem deueniens, uocato Petro dixit, 'Fatigatus es ex itinere, et opus esset tibi recreacione; est autem hic iuxta uilla modica, locus amenus et ampla edificia. Ego uero quedam*c* negocia ad tempus recedam; ibidem morare donec ueniam.' Et Petrus quod comes optulit gratanter accepit; et misit eum ad dictam uillam cum custodia;[79] set non uidit comes Petrum amplius in Anglia.

Cum autem didicisset comes Warewykye omnia que agebantur circa Petrum, accepta manu ualida, accita eciam tota patria, clam tendit ad locum ubi cognouit esse Petrum, et ualde mane una sabbatorum[80] ueniens ad uillam intrauit portam curie et circumdedit cameram. Exclamauit autem comes uoce magna, 'Surge proditor, captus es'. Et Petrus audiens comitem, uidens eciam manum comitis superiorem et custodiam cui deputatus ⟨erat⟩*d* non resistentem, induens uestimenta sua descendit de camera. Capitur igitur Petrus et non sicut comes, immo sicut latro, producitur; et qui solebat palfridos ascendere iam pedes cogitur ire.

Cum autem transissent a uilla ad modicum, iussit comes preberi Petro iumentum ut eo uelocius maturaret iter suum. Et*e* Petrum sequebantur cornua tonancia, populus clamans et uox horrida. Iam Petrus deposuit cingulum milicie, sicut fur et proditor tendit Warewykye, et ibidem ueniens mittitur in carcerem. Modo suis uinculis Petrum subiugauit quem canem Warewyk Petrus appellauit.[81]

Et Petrus quidem seruabatur in carcere, oracio autem fiebat sine dilacione ab Adolmaro comite ad barones pro eo.[82] Statim enim ut cognouit captum esse Petrum, accessit ad comitem Glouernie plorans et orans quatinus iniuriam sibi illatam uindicaret, et Petrum omnimodo sibi restitueret. Addidit eciam quod, nisi comes succurreret, obprobrium sempiternum subiret, et terras quas obligauerat amitteret. Et comes Glouernie ita fertur respondisse, 'Domine comes, iniuria tibi illata comiti Guydoni non est imputanda. Quod enim fecit, consilio et auxilio nostro fecit; et si, ut tu dicis, terras tuas obligasti, ipsas utique perdidisti. Nichil ergo ulterioris restat consilii nisi ut

a Angliam *MS*; Anglie *He, St, Den-Y*   *b* comitatu *MS*; comitatum *He, St, Den-Y* *c* circa *supplied before* quedam *He, St, Den-Y*   *d* deputatus *R*; deputatur *Den-Y*; erat *supplied ed.*   *e* et et *MS*; et *om. He, St, Den-Y*

[79] Piers was lodged at Deddington, Oxfordshire, while Pembroke went to his manor at Bampton, Oxfordshire, to visit his wife (*Ann. Lond.*, p. 206).

and made for the heart of England, and when he had gone about five 1312
days' journey or more, coming at length to the county of Northampton, he sent for Piers and said, 'You are tired from the journey,
and need rest; there is a small village near here, a pleasant place with
ample lodgings. I am going off on certain business for a time; stay
there till I come.' Piers gratefully accepted the earl's offer; and he sent
him to the said village under guard;[79] but the earl never saw Piers
again in England.

When the earl of Warwick had learned all that was happening
about Piers, he took a strong force, raised the whole countryside, and
secretly approached the place where he knew Piers to be. Coming to
the village very early in the morning one Saturday[80] he entered the
gate of the courtyard and surrounded the chamber. Then the earl
called out in a loud voice: 'Arise traitor, thou art taken.' And Piers,
hearing the earl, also seeing the earl's superior force and that the
guard to which he had been allotted was not resisting, putting on his
clothes came down from the chamber. In this fashion Piers is taken
and is led forth not as an earl but as a thief; and he who used to ride
palfreys is now forced to go on foot.

When they had left the village a little behind, the earl ordered Piers
to be given a mare so that their journey might proceed more quickly.
Blaring trumpets, yelling people, and savage shouting followed Piers.
Now Piers has laid aside his belt of knighthood, he travels to Warwick
like a thief and a traitor, and coming there he is thrown into prison.
He whom Piers called Warwick the Dog[81] has now bound Piers with
his chains.

Piers therefore was kept in prison, but prayer was made without
delay by Earl Aymer unto the barons for him.[82] For as soon as he
knew that Piers had been captured he approached the earl of
Gloucester, beseeching him with tears to vindicate the wrong that
had been done to him, and at all costs to restore Piers to him. He also
added that, unless the earl would help, he would suffer eternal
disgrace, and lose the lands which he had pledged. The earl of
Gloucester is said to have replied thus: 'My lord earl, the wrong done
to you is not to be blamed on Earl Guy. For he did what he did with
our support and counsel; and if, as you say, you have pledged your
lands, you have lost them anyhow. It only remains to advise you to

[80] Cf. Mark 16: 2; Piers was seized on Saturday 10 June 1311 (*Ann. Lond.*, p. 206).
[81] For Piers's nicknames for the barons, see above, pp. 16–17.
[82] Cf. Acts 12: 5.

1312 discas alias cautius negociari.' Comes autem, ut uidit preces suas sic esse repulsas, confusus abcessit*a* et uenit apud Oxoniam. Congregate uniuersitati clericorum ostendit causam suam, et transcriptum obligacionis legi fecit coram omnibus clericis et burgensibus similiter adunatis. Deposuit querelam suam coram eis, ut uel sic ad recuperandum Petrum consilium communicarent et auxilium, uel ut iusticiam suam ostenderet ne quis forsan de se aliter presumeret. Habebatur enim apud quosdam suspectus, quasi in capcione Petri tam durum peccatum dolo confirmasset, ut Petrum facilius morti traderet quem longa obsidione forsan non cepisset. Set nec clerici nec burgenses rem ad se non pertinentem tractare uel attemptare curabant.[83]

Altera autem die non longe post capcionem Petri, reliqui comites Warewykye conueniunt, et de morte Petri tractantes sic tandem diffiniunt, quod propter affinitatem comitis Glouernie nec ut fur suspenderetur nec ut proditor protraheretur, set sicut nobilis et ciuis Romanus capitalem penam pateretur.[84] Comes autem Warewykye acutum nuncium emisit ad Petrum, mandans ei ut consuleret anime sue, quia hec foret dies ultima quam uisurus esset in terra. Et nuncius accelerans mandatum statim accessit ad Petrum: 'Consule,' inquid, 'tibi, domine, quia morte morieris hac die.'[85] Et Petrus, ubi nomen mortis audiuit, modicum suspirans ingemuit:*b* 'O,' inquit, 'ubi sunt dona mea quibus tot familiares amicos acquisiueram,*c* et quibus potestatem sufficientem habuisse putaueram? Vbi sunt amici mei, in quibus erat fiducia*d* mea,[86] corporis tutela et tota salutis substancia; quorum iuuentus ualida, probitas inuicta et uirtus ad ardua semper accensa; qui eciam in bello pro me stare, carcerem intrare, et mortem promiserant non uitare? Certe superbia mea, elacio quam nutriuit eorum una promissio, regis fauor et regis curia, duxerunt me in hec tedia. Non habeo subsidium, uacat omne remedium, fiat uoluntas comitum.'[87]

---

a sic R; abscessit St, Den-Y   *b* ingenuit R; ingemuit St, Den-Y   *c* acquisieram R; acquisiueram ed.   *d* fudicia MS; fiducia He, St, Den-Y

[83] This is the fullest description of Pembroke's distress at Gaveston's seizure; he promptly and unequivocally returned to support the king (Phillips, *Pembroke*, pp. 36–7).

[84] To a Roman citizen capital punishment meant simply death, or the civil death of loss of citizenship, but that the author of the *Vita* is implying beheading is plain from his reference to nobility, and the contrast with hanging and drawing. The relationship of these three is made clear later at the execution of Lancaster (below, pp. 212–13), where *protrahere* and *suspendere* are clearly contrasted with *capite truncare*. Whether the author believed that the execution method for Roman citizens was beheading (as it had been for

learn another time to negotiate more cautiously.' When the earl saw that his prayers were thus rejected, he departed in confusion and came to Oxford. He explained his cause to the assembled university of clerks, and had a copy of his pledge read out before all the clerks and burgesses similarly meeting together. He laid his plea before them, either so that they might lend their aid and counsel in recovering Piers, or so that he might show the justice of his cause in case anyone perhaps should think otherwise. For he was suspected by some, in taking Piers, of having deceitfully abetted so harsh a crime in order to hand Piers over to death more easily, when perhaps he would not have captured him by a lengthy siege. But neither the clerks nor the burgesses cared to take up or discuss a matter that did not concern them.[83]

On a day not long after the capture of Piers, the remaining earls met at Warwick, and after discussing Piers's death they finally decided that on account of his kinship with the earl of Gloucester he should not be hanged as a thief nor drawn as a traitor, but should suffer capital punishment as a nobleman and a Roman citizen would.[84] The earl of Warwick sent a sharp-tongued messenger to Piers, telling him to look to his soul, because this was the last day that he would see on earth. And the messenger, hastening with his message, immediately he reached Piers, said: 'Look to yourself, my lord, for this day you shall die the death.'[85] And Piers when he heard the word death, sighing a little, groaned: 'Oh!', he said, 'where are my gifts through which I had acquired so many close friends, and with which I had thought to have sufficient power? Where are my friends, in whom was my trust,[86] the protection of my body, and my whole hope of safety; whose vigorous youth, unbeaten valour, and courage was always on fire for hard tasks; who had promised, furthermore, to stand by me in war, to suffer imprisonment, and not to shun death? Assuredly, my pride, the arrogance that one single promise of theirs has nourished, the king's favour and the king's court have brought me to this loathsome position. I have no help, every remedy is vain, let the earls' will be done.'[87]

St Paul), or was enjoying a moment of wordplay around *capitalis*, is unclear. He appears to play with the word *caput* in *capitolium* later (see below, pp. 214–15). I am indebted to Mr Ian Moxon for a discussion on this passage.

[85] Exod. 21: 17; Matt. 15: 4.   [86] Cf. Deut. 32: 37.

[87] This echoes the words of the Lord's Prayer, *fiat uoluntas tua* (Legg, *Sarum Missal*, p. 216).

1312   Circa hora terciam[88] educitur Petrus de carcere; et comes de
Warewyk Petrum uinculatum reliquid comiti Lancastrie, et Petrus,
ut comitem illum uidit, procidens in terram orauit dicens, 'Generose
comes, miserere mei.' Et comes, 'Tolle,' inquid, 'tolle eum, per
Deum perducetur.' Et qui uiderunt lacrimas continere non potuerunt. Quis enim continere se posset cum uideret Petrum, nuper
gloriose[a] militantem, nunc autem misericordiam in tam flebili fine
petentem? Eductus Petrus de castro properauit ad locum ubi passurus
erat supplicium; et ceteri comites sequebantur a longe ut uiderent
finem,[89] nisi quod comes Guydo remansit in castro suo.

Cum autem uenissent ad locum qui Blakelowe dicitur,[90] pertinens
ad comitem Lancastrie, missus quidam a comitis latere iussit Petrum
in predicto loco remanere; et statim iussu comitis traditus est
Walensibus duobus, de quibus transfodit[b] hic corpus, amputauit
ille[c] caput. Et nunciatum est comiti quod res sic se haberet.[d] Ille
autem non credidit donec caput ipse uideret; et post rem sic
consummatam reuersi sunt comites in uiam suam. Fratres autem
Iacobini[91] collegerunt[e] Petrum, et caput corpori consuentes detulerunt
illud Oxoniam; set quia innodatus erat sentencia, non sunt ausi sepelire
corpus in ecclesia. Exitus hic Petri qui, dum conscendit in altum,

> labitur in nichilum qui fuit ante nichil.[92]

Ecce Petrus nuper in aula regis ceteris nobilior, nunc propter
inportunitatem sui gestus iussu comitis Lancastrie iacet decolatus.[f]
Videant amodo curiales Anglici ne, de regio fauore confisi, barones
despiciant. Sunt enim membrum regis principale,[93] sine quo nil
grande poterit rex aggredi uel consummare. Ergo qui barones
paruipendunt, regem utique contempnunt et lese magestatis se reos
ostendunt.

Set quare iussu comitis Lancastrie occiditur Petrus magis quam
aliorum comitum, dubitabit aliquis in posterum. Sciat autem in

---

[a] gloriosa MS; gloriose He, St, Den-Y   [b] sic MS; poss. confodit He   [c] illos MS;
ille He, St, Den-Y   [d] habere MS; haberet He, St, Den-Y   [e] colligerunt MS;
collegerunt He, St, Den-Y   [f] sic MS; decollatus He, St

[88] On 19 June 1312 (HBC, p. 456).
[89] Matt. 26: 58.
[90] This is Blacklow Hill, about two miles north of Warwick Castle towards Kenilworth.
A memorial, 'Gaveston's Cross', stands at OS SP 289 675.
[91] The Dominicans were known as Jacobins from the name of their first house in Paris,
the Hospital of St Jacques (St James) (Du Cange, Glossarium, under 'Jacobini').
[92] This sentence cannot be traced through PL, the Vulgate, or Walther's Initia and

About the third hour[88] Piers was led out from prison; and the earl 1312
of Warwick handed Piers over bound to the earl of Lancaster, and
Piers, when he saw the earl, cast himself on the ground and pleaded,
saying, 'Noble earl, have mercy on me.' And the earl said 'Lift him
up, lift him up. In God's name let him be taken away.' And the
onlookers could not hold back their tears. For who could contain
himself on seeing Piers, lately in his martial glory, now seeking mercy
in such lamentable straits. Piers was led out from the castle and went
quickly to the place where he was to suffer the last penalty; and the
other earls followed afar off that they might see the end,[89] except that
Earl Guy remained in his castle.

When they had come to a place called Blacklow,[90] which belonged
to the earl of Lancaster, an envoy from the earl ordered that Piers
should stay there; and immediately by the earl's command he was
handed over to two Welshmen, one of whom ran him through the
body and the other cut off his head. It was announced to the earl that
thus it had been done. He, however, did not believe it until he had
seen the head himself; and after the business had been thus
dispatched the earls again went their ways. The Dominican
Friars,[91] however, gathered up Piers, and, sewing the head to the
body, they carried it to Oxford; but because he was excommunicate
they dared not bury the body in church. Such Piers's end, who,
climbing up too high,

> Crashed into nothingness from whence he came.[92]

See how Piers, recently more celebrated than the rest in the king's
hall, now for his insolent behaviour lies beheaded by order of the earl
of Lancaster. Let English courtiers henceforth beware lest, trusting in
the royal favour, they look down upon the barons. For they are the
king's chief member,[93] without which the king cannot attempt or
accomplish anything of importance. Therefore those who belittle the
barons without doubt despise the king and show themselves guilty of
treason.

But someone in future will be unsure why Piers was killed by order
of the earl of Lancaster rather than of the other earls. However, he

Proverbia, but it is also used by Murimuth (about the abortive popular crusade of 1320):
'vertitur in nihilum, quod fuit ante nihil' (_Murimuth_, p. 32).
[93] The image of the body politic with the king as the head and various groups as the
organs and limbs of the body was well developed at this time. A full elaboration of the
image is found in John of Salisbury's _Policraticus_, v–vi.

1312 occisione Petri comites Anglie arduum negocium assumpsisse, nec diebus nostris aliquando simile contigisse. Occiderunt enim magnum comitem quem rex adoptauerat in fratrem, quem rex dilexit ut filium, quem rex habuit in socium et amicum. Opus ergo erat ut ille magnus esset qui tale factum defenderet. Vnde Thomas comes Lancastrie, sicut omnibus generosior, ita et ceteris potencior, periculum huius rei in se assumpsit, et Petrum post tria exilia, quasi post tres moniciones legittimas, non obtemperantem, occidi mandauit.

Hic comes Thomas dominum regem in secundo gradu consanguinitatis contingebat, utpote qui ex duobus fratribus qui primum faciunt gradum descendebant, ex rege scilicet Edwardo seniore et fratre eius Edmundo comite Lancastrie. Mater eius erat regina Nauarie, et soror eius regina Francie, et filia sororis sue regina nunc est Anglie.[94] Sic utroque parente regios habens natales generosior apparet quam ceteri comites. Per uires patrimonii potenciam eius attendere potes. Habebat enim quinque comitatus in Anglia, uidelicet comitatum Lancastrie, Leycestrie, et comitatum de Ferers ex parte patris; comitatum Lyncolnie et Saresburie ex parte uxoris. Ecce dominacio tot comitatuum olim nobilium redigitur in unum. Potest nunc solus Thomas quod aliquando comes Edmundus, dominus de Longespeye, dominus de Lacy, et dominus de Ferers singillatim potuerunt.[95] Nec credo ducem uel comitem, sub imperio Romano militantem, de terrarum prouentibus tantum facere posse quantum Thomas comes Lancastrie.

Post consummacionem Petri, cum uox publica mortem eius auribus singulorum inculcasset, letata est terra, gauisi sunt omnes habitantes in ea. Confidenter dicam mortem unius hominis, nisi grauasset rem publicam, nunquam antea tot et tantis gratanter acceptam. Gaudet terra, gaudent incole, Petro mortuo pacem inuenisse: soli familiares eius, et maxime quos ipse promouerat, mortem domini sui egre ferebant. Nam multa multis contulit, de stabulo ad cameram quosdam ascendere fecit, de quibus quidam militant qui

---

[94] His mother, Blanche, married first Henry, king of Navarre, then Edmund of Lancaster, Thomas's father. Joan, Blanche's daughter by the first marriage and thus Thomas's half-sister, married Philip IV of France. Their daughter Isabella, Thomas's niece, married Edward II (Maddicott, *Lancaster*, pp. 2–3).

[95] Earl Edmund was Edmund 'Crouchback', youngest son of King Henry III, earl of Leicester 1265–96 and earl of Lancaster 1267–96 (and thus Thomas's father) (*HBC*, pp. 468–9). William Longespée, illegitimate son of Henry II, married Isabel, heiress to the earldom of Salisbury, and was styled earl of Salisbury (1197–1226). Neither his son William II (d. 1249) nor his grandson William III (d. 1257) inherited the title of earl of Salisbury as Isabel outlived them both, and they were known as Lords Longespée. The

should understand that in killing Piers the earls of England had
undertaken a difficult task, unlike anything that has ever happened in
our time. For they put to death a great earl, whom the king had
adopted as a brother, whom the king cherished as son, whom the king
regarded as a companion and friend. Therefore it was necessary for
the one who should prosecute such a deed to be great. Hence
Thomas, earl of Lancaster, being of higher birth than all the others
and so more powerful than the rest, took upon himself the risk of this
business, and ordered Piers, after three terms of exile, as one
disobedient to three lawful warnings, to be put to death.

This Earl Thomas was related to the lord king in the second degree
of kinship, for they were descended from two brothers in the first
degree, namely from the elder King Edward and his brother
Edmund, earl of Lancaster. His mother was queen of Navarre, his
sister queen of France, and his sister's daughter is now queen of
England.[94] As each parent was of royal birth he is clearly of nobler
descent than the other earls. You may assess his power by the size of
his patrimony. For he had five earldoms in England, namely the
earldoms of Lancaster, Leicester, and Ferrers from his father, and the
earldoms of Lincoln and Salisbury from his wife. See how the
lordship of so many noble earldoms is now reduced to one. Now
Thomas alone can do as much as formerly Earl Edmund, Lord
Longespée, Lord Lacy, and Lord Ferrers, each singly, could do.[95] I
do not believe that any militarily active duke or count under the
Roman empire could do as much from the profits of his lands as
Thomas earl of Lancaster.

After Piers's end, when the voice of the people had dinned his
death into everyone's ears, the country rejoiced, and all its
inhabitants were glad. I may say with confidence that the death of
one man, unless he had oppressed the state, had never before been
accepted with joy by so many. The land rejoices, its inhabitants
rejoice that they have found peace in Piers's death: only his
household, and particularly those whom he had promoted, bore
the death of their lord with grief. For many owed much to him; he

Salisbury title and lands were brought to the Lacy family by William III's only daughter
and heiress, who married Henry Lacy in 1256 and inherited the title on the death of her
great-grandmother Isabel in 1261 (*CP*, xi. 375–85; *HBC*, p. 481). Lord Lacy was this same
Henry Lacy, earl of Lincoln 1272–1311, Thomas's father-in-law (*HBC*, p. 470). Lord
Ferrers was Robert Ferrers, the last of the Ferrers earls of Derby, 1260–6; he forfeited his
lands and title in 1266 for opposing Henry III; the title and lands were given to Edmund of
Lancaster, Thomas's father (*HBC*, p. 458).

1312 nunquam militasse decreuerant; et ut paucis multa concludam, de causa Petri gaudent omnes inimici, atque dolent pauci nisi qui sunt eius amici.

Post tres pluresue dies conueniunt Wygornie predicti comites,[96] ut de predictis tractarent et aduersus futura consulerent. Sciebant enim quod, cum res in regis ueniret noticiam, tanquam ob illatam sibi iniuriam, si liceret ei, procederet ad uindictam. Iccirco caute et prouide inter eos prospectum est, quod, si processum eorum iure tenere[a] non possent, saltem se et sua armorum suffragiis unanimiter defenderent. Nam uim ui repellere lege permittitur, et quod quis ob tutelam sui fecerit, iure fecisse uidetur.[97]

Postquam notificatum est autem regi quod mortuus est Petrus, contristatus ualde condoluit, et post modicum astantibus dixit: 'Per animam Dei, ut fatuus egit. Nam de consilio meo ad manus comitum nunquam peruenit. Hoc[b] est quod semper inhibui. Nam et que nunc facta sunt prius quam fierent excogitaui. Quid sibi fuit de comite de Warewyk, quem constat Petrum nunquam dilexisse? Sciebam certe quod, si eum apprehenderet, de manibus eius nunquam euaderet.' Hoc uerbum regis leniter[c] prolatum, cum tandem deueniret in publicum, plures excitauit ⟨ad⟩[d] risum. Set certus sum regem ita doluisse de Petro, sicut aliquando dolet pater de filio. Nam quanto magis procedit dileccio, tanto magis dolet infortunio. In planctu[e] Dauid super Ionatan amor ostenditur, quem dicitur super amorem mulierum dilexisse.[98] Fatetur et sic rex noster; superaddit quod[f] mortem Petri uindicare disposuit. Nam accitis consiliariis suis querit consilium quid super istis foret agendum, ratum tamen habens propositum illos destruere qui occiderunt Petrum.[g] Et erat cum rege comes Penbrokye, cuius intererat[h] comites debellare, et dominus Hugo de[i] Despenser apud regem latuit,[99] qui plus quam Petrus forte demeruit. Henricus de Beaumount adhuc est in curia, qui

---

[a] teneri *MS*; tueri *or* tenere *He*; tueri *St, Den-Y*   [b] hec *MS*; hoc *He, St, Den-Y*
[c] sic *R*; leuiter *St, Den-Y*   [d] om. *MS*; ad risum *or* pluribus excitauit risum *He*; ad risum *St, Den-Y*   [e] plactu *MS*; planctu *He, St, Den-Y*   [f] dum *MS*; for quod *MW*
[g] Rex proponit uindictam *marginal note in R*   [h] intereat *R*; intererat *He, St, Den-Y*
[i] sic *R*; le *St, Den-Y*

[96] On 20 July Edward prohibited assemblies at Worcester, where opposition might be discussed and where obligations might be entered into 'to come and die together'; the prohibition was extended to other places on 24 July (*CPR 1307–13*, p. 481; *CCR 1307–13*, p. 540; *Foed.*, ii. 1. 172).
[97] *Dig.* ix. 2. 4, ix. 2. 45 (4), *Corpus Iuris Civilis*, i. 125, 130. The Roman law doctrine of self-defence was well known in the Middle Ages through development by canon lawyers,

promoted some from the stable to the chamber, of whom some serve
as knights who had never thought to have done so; and, to sum up
briefly, all enemies rejoice at Piers's end, and few there are to grieve
except his friends.

After three or more days the aforesaid earls met at Worcester,[96] to
discuss what had happened and make plans for the future. For they
knew that when the matter came to the king's notice, he would, if he
could, proceed to take revenge as though for a wrong done to himself.
Therefore, they carefully and cautiously made provision among
themselves, that if they could not defend their proceedings in law,
they could at least, together, entrust themselves and theirs to the
judgement of arms. For it is permitted by law to meet force with
force, and what anyone may do for his own protection he is deemed to
have done lawfully.[97]

When the king was informed that Piers was dead, he was
saddened and he grieved very much indeed and after a little while
he said to the bystanders: 'By God's soul, he has acted like a fool. If
he had taken my advice he would never have fallen into the hands of
the earls. This is what I always told him not to do. For I guessed
that what has now happened would occur. What was he doing with
the earl of Warwick, who was known never to have liked Piers? I
knew for certain that if the earl caught him, Piers would never
escape from his hands.' When this moderate utterance of the king
became public it moved many to derision. But I am certain the king
grieved for Piers as a father at any time grieves for his son. For the
greater the love, the greater the sorrow. In the lament of David upon
Jonathan, love is depicted which is said to have surpassed the love of
women.[98] Our king also spoke like that; and he added that he
planned to avenge the death of Piers. For, having summoned his
counsellors, he enquired from them what should be done about
these things, although he had already decided to destroy those who
killed Piers. With the king was the earl of Pembroke, whose interest
it was to vanquish the earls; and Sir Hugh Despenser,[99] who was
perhaps even less deserving than Piers, lurked with the king. Henry
Beaumont is still at court, though according to the Ordinances he

not only for private defence but as one of the causes of a just war; see F. H. Russell, *The
Just War in the Middle Ages* (Cambridge, 1975), pp. 41–4, 95–8.

[98] 2 Kgs. (2 Sam.) 1: 26.

[99] Hugh Despenser the elder became an increasingly important figure in domestic and
foreign affairs after 1312, when Pembroke became dominant (Davies, *Opposition*, pp. 87–8;
Phillips, *Pembroke*, p. 52).

1312 iuxta ordinaciones recedere debuisset ab illa;[100] Edmundus de
Maulee[101] et alii milites qui nuper fuerant Petri familiares. Hii
siquidem regem instigabant ut ex fidelibus suis exercitum colligeret,
et aduersarios suos audacter impeteret. Nam triumphum secure
reportaret ex quo pro iure suo legittime tractaret. Addunt eciam
infideles uincere non posse, quos constat domino suo fidem non
seruare; protestantes a seculo inauditum simile delictum in aliquem
regem esse commissum, et cum pro quouis *crimine minori* possit
satisfieri, crimen lese magestatis non poterit purgari. Alii uero sanioris
consilii, bene scientes futura metiri,*b* nullo sensu prebebant assensum,
ut rex cum baronibus iniret conflictum. Nam si rex caperetur hoc foret
absurdum; nec regi proficeret distruccio*c* comitum, maxime cum
Robertus de Brutz iam totam Scociam occupauerat, et terram Northumbrorum ad tributum compulerit;[102] plus expediret terram defendere
quam terre defensores uelle destruere. Placuit tamen regi prius
consilium, quia magis accessit*d* ad uotum suum; quod enim iuxta
uelle consulitur, frequenter apud homines magis acceptatur. Ad hoc
eciam naturaliter regem inducebat indignacio quam contra comites pro
morte Petri conceperat; magnanimitas in paucis experta, et suggestio
malorum hominum nimis assidua. Nam hii qui post mortem Petri ad
regem confugerant, guerram magis quam pacem procurabant. Timebant enim quod, si rex placitis baronum adquiesceret, hoc in dampnum
eorum forsan redundaret. Semper enim trepidat qui sibi conscius
exstat.

Certe adulatorum figmenta milites decipiunt et ad finem desper-
atum frequenter perducunt. Bene cum magnatibus ageretur, si uerum
a falso discernerent, si simulaciones a uero iudicio separarent. Set
nescio qua deprauacione nature aures diuitum delicate gracius
acceptant mendacis lingue blandicias quam aperte testimonium
ueritatis. Nam iuxta poetam,

a–a crimior' *MS*; crimine *He*; crimine minori *St, Den-Y*   *b* meturi *MS*; metiri *He*,
St, Den-Y   *c* sic *MS*; destruccio *St, Den-Y*   *d* secessit *MS*; *poss.* se gessit *He*;
accessit *ed.*

[100] Henry Beaumont, part of a well-connected French family making its way in
England, was a staunch royal supporter until the last years of the reign. Through his
wife, Alice Comyn (m. 1310), he claimed substantial lands in Scotland, and he was briefly
granted the kingdom of Man in 1310 and 1312 (*HBC*, pp. 65, 502). In 1311 he and his
sister, Isabella de Vescy, were banished from court and Isabella had to give up Bamburgh
Castle (Ordinances, caps. 22, 23; see *SE*, i. 163b, trans. in 'The New Ordinances of 1311',
EHD, iii. 533–4). Henry, however, remained frequently at court, and their brother, Louis,
became bishop of Durham with the support of Queen Isabella. They were the children of

should have left it;[100] [as are] Edmund Mauley,[101] and other knights 1312
who had been lately in Piers's household. These men urged the king to
collect an army from his faithful supporters and boldly attack his
enemies. He would surely triumph because he was lawfully striving for
his rights. They add that faithless men, who are known not to have kept
faith with their lord, cannot be victorious; protesting that for such a
crime to have been committed against any king was utterly unheard of,
and though satisfaction could be made for any lesser crime, the crime of
treason could not be purged. Others, however, of wiser counsel,
knowing well how to assess what would happen, would have nothing
to do with the proposal that the king should engage in a struggle with
the barons. For, if the king was taken captive, this would be absurd; nor
would the destruction of the earls benefit the king, particularly since
Robert Bruce had now occupied the whole of Scotland, and will have
forced all Northumbria to pay tribute;[102] it would be better to defend
the land rather than to try to destroy its defenders. The king however,
preferred the former counsel, because it was more in accord with his
desires; indeed it is frequently more acceptable to advise a man to
follow his wishes. Also the anger which he had conceived against the
earls on account of Piers's death naturally inclined the king to this
view; few people are magnanimous and the suggestions of evil men are
ever with us. For those who had fled to the king on Piers's death were
looking for war rather than peace. For they feared that if the king
agreed to the baronial pleas, this might perhaps redound to their loss.
He is always fearful who is thinking of himself.

In truth, the imaginings of flatterers deceive soldiers and frequently
lead them to a hopeless end. It would go well with great men if they
could distinguish truth from falsehood, if they could separate pretence
from sound judgement. But I do not know by what perversion of
nature the tender ears of the rich more readily receive the flatteries of a
lying tongue than the candid testimony of truth. As the poet says,

Louis de Brienne, vicomte of Beaumont in Maine, grandchildren of Jean de Brienne, who
had been king of Jerusalem and Latin emperor of Constantinople (*CP*, ii. 59–60).

[101] Edmund Mauley was a constant royal supporter, and not unacceptable to the
baronial opposition since he was given grants with their approval in the early period of the
Ordinances (*Ann. Lond.*, p. 198). He was steward of the household *c.*28 Dec. 1310 until his
death at Bannockburn, 24 June 1314, apart from three months in the winter of 1312–13,
when he had to answer accusations of forgery (Tout, *Ed. II*, p. 314).

[102] The tribute paid on several occasions in this period by the inhabitants of Northumberland was the price of a truce with the Scots; the Lanercost chronicler notes at least
three tributes paid between 1311 and 1314 (McNamee, *Wars*, pp. 131–2). The *Vita* refers
to the system again below, pp. 82–3, 176–7.

1312
        Cum quis adulator facilem placauerit[a] aurem,[103]
        Continuo cunctos superat cum uera loquentur.

Huius pestis detestanda frequencia hodie nimis regnat in curia.

Rex igitur noster in ulcionem Petri quosdam de baronibus inpugnare proponit; nam comitem Warewyk aut capite priuabit aut bonis confiscatis perpetuo deportabit. Milites uocat ad arma, milites conducit in castra, forestarios et sagittarios congregat, pedites in expedicionem pugne uenire procurat.

Interim autem barones et comites ad parliamentum suum publico citauit edicto.[104] Ipsi uero, proprie salutis non inmemores, ad parendum regis mandato hoc modo se preparant. Comes Lancastrie mille loricatos, mille et quingentos pedites secum adduxit. Comitiua comitis Herfordie turba Wallensium uallata, siluestris et fera, non erat uilis nec modica. Comes Warewykye homines suos de Arderne animosos ualde preparanter[b] mandauit adesse, et ceteri barones qui erant ex parte comitum, unusquisque pro posse suo communem uallauit exercitum, et sic profecti sunt ad parliamentum. Venientes autem[c] Londonias non statim accesserunt ad regem, set nuncios suos prouide miserunt, qui aduentum eorum domino regi nunciarent et causam uocacionis humiliter inquirerent.

Cum ergo didicisset rex aduentum comitum et formam aduentus eorum, consilium suum conuocat ut instans negocium consulte disponat; uolens eciam inquirere an cum comitibus expediret congredi, uincere sperarent necne.[d] Quidam uero, quibus de uiribus utriusque partis iam liquide constabat, conflictum ad presens penitus dissuadebant. Nam quicquid de rege accideret, pars regis sine dubio periret, cum regis[e] exercitum pars aduersa in duplo superaret; et hoc forsitan ad terrorem dicebant, quia pacem bello preferre uolebant. Et erant eodem tempore cum rege Lodowycus frater regis Francie et quidam cardinalis qui secum uenerat de partibus transmarinis.[105] Hii omnem opem et operam concordiam formandi cotidie inhibebant.[f]

---

    [a] placuerit *MS*; placauerit *He, St, Den-Y*   [b] sic *R*; properanter *St, Den-Y*   [c] *He read* sunt *(poss. reading* sut *for* aut*) and suggested deletion*; autem *St, Den-Y*   [d] *He read* unde .c. *and noted* .c. *as redundant*; necne *St, Den-Y*   [e] rege *MS*; regis *He, St, Den-Y*   [f] sic *R*; *poss. for* adhibebant *Den-Y*

---

    [103] Cf. Juv. *Sat.* iii. 122 (*nam cum facilem stillauit in aurem*) for the first line of the verse. The quotation also appears in John of Salisbury's *Policraticus* (*PL* cxcix. 486c); and in Peter of Blois, *Ep.* lix (*PL* ccvii. 178) together with the second line found here (*continuo cunctos adigit, qui uera loquuntur*). I am grateful to Dr J. Binns for the reference to Peter of Blois.
    [104] Parliament was summoned for 23 July at Lincoln. It is not clear what force *publico edicto* might have: the lords were called by individual writ as usual (*PW*, ii. 2, 72–6). The difficulties

When a flatterer soothes the attentive ear[103]
At once he conquers all who speak the truth.

This pest predominates at court with deplorable frequency today.

Thus our king proposes to attack certain of the barons out of revenge for Piers; for he will either have the earl of Warwick's head, or having confiscated his goods he will banish him for ever. He summons the knights to arms, garrisons his castles, gathers his foresters and archers, sends for infantry ready to campaign.

Meanwhile he called the earls and barons to his parliament by public edict.[104] They in truth, not unmindful of their own safety, prepared to obey the king's command in this way. The earl of Lancaster brought with him a thousand men-at-arms and fifteen hundred foot. The retinue of the earl of Hereford, strengthened by a crowd of Welsh, wild men from the woodlands, was neither poor nor mean. The earl of Warwick summoned his stout-hearted men from Arden to come in all readiness, and the other barons who were on the side of the earls, each according to his means, contributed to the common army, and so they set out for parliament. When they reached London, however, they did not immediately approach the king, but wisely sent their messengers, who announced their arrival to the lord king and humbly enquired the cause of summons.

Consequently, when the king learned of the arrival of the earls and the way in which they had come, he called together his council so as to dispatch the immediate business by their advice; he also wished to enquire whether it was practical for him to attack the earls; did they expect him to win, or not? Some, indeed, who knew clearly the strength of either side, advised strongly against fighting at present. For whatever happened to the king, the king's party would undoubtedly be destroyed, since his adversaries had an army double the size of his; they said this, perhaps, to cause alarm, because they preferred peace to war. At that same time there were with the king, Louis, brother of the king of France, and a certain cardinal who had come with him from abroad.[105] These used all their strength and effort every day to bring about an agreement.

of the period are reflected in the postponement of the parliament to 20 Aug. at Westminster; then in the first dismissal of the commons on 28 Aug; their resummoning for 30 Sept.; and their final dismissal on 16 Dec. (*HBC*, p. 553). The author explains the essence of the arguments on both sides very well, but gives little sense of the complex chronology of meetings and negotiations. These are clearly set out in Maddicott, *Lancaster*, pp. 135–51.

[105] Louis of Evreux, brother of Philip IV of France and the queen's uncle, arrived in London on 13 Sept. 1312 (*Ann. Paul.*, p. 272). There were two cardinals in England in the

1312   Comes autem Gloucestrie mediatoris partes sustinuit, et regem de pace et concordia erga barones suos habenda frequenter conuenit: 'Amici tui sunt,' inquid comes, 'quos inimicos uocas. Amici tui sunt quos inprudenter expugnas. In commodum tuum cedit quicquid faciunt. Pro commodo tuo multa satis expendunt. Rex, si barones tuos destruis, honorem tuum certe contempnis. Nec tamen hoc pati tenentur, nec in aliquo delinquunt si propria iura tuentur.' Et rex comiti sic respondit: 'Non est qui uicem meam doleat;[106] non est qui pro iure meo aduersus istos contendat. Tu uero, nepos meus et dux meus et notus meus, auunculum tuum deseris, et aduersariis eius amicum te facis. Protestor amicos meos non esse qui res meas et ius meum nituntur expungnare. Si michi iure regio sicut aliis regibus uti liceret, non hominem exulatum ex quacunque causa de regia potestate ad pacem possem reuocare? Hoc iure propria sua auctoritate me priuarunt, nam cui pacem concesseram crudeliter necarunt. Et comes Lancastrie michi proximus agnatus, cui possent sufficere quinque comitatus licet aliena non raperet, apud Nouum Castrum homines meos inuasit et quedam[a] mei iuris secum asportauit; quod si minor aliquis fecisset, furti posset argui, et ui bonorum raptorum iudicio recte condempnari. Et comites ad parliamentum uocati in dedecus regis cum magno exercitu ueniunt armati. Vnde cum mea rapuerint et homines meos occiderint, satis est uerisimile quod michi nolunt deferre, set coronam rapere et alium sibi regem preficere.' Et comes, 'Domine, si quid ⟨in⟩[b] iniuriam tuam comites presumpserint, decet emendari; et si[c] satisfacere fuerint parati, merito debent reconciliari. Est enim sentencia uulgaris[d] ut nemo in admittenda satisfacione sit difficilis.[e] Expedit igitur comites prius conueniri et amicabiliter de grauaminibus per eos uobis illatis interpellari, ut ex responsione eorum appareat an iure uel iniuria res finem acceperit.[f] Est enim apud omnes consuetudo ut lenia premittantur,[g] que si non proficiant aspera subsequantur.'[107]

Et annuit rex. Accessit ergo comes ille mediator ad comites, et

---

[a] que R; quedam St, Den-Y   [b] om. MS; supplied He, St, Den-Y   [c] sibi MS; tibi He; si St, Den-Y   [d] uulgare MS; uulgaris He, St, Den-Y   [e] dificilis MS; difficilis He, St, Den-Y   [f] acceperat MS; acceperit He, St, Den-Y   [g] permittantur R; premittantur Den-Y

autumn of 1312, Arnald Nouvel, abbot of Fontfroide (Languedoc) and cardinal priest of Santa Prisca, and Arnald d'Aux, bishop of Poitiers and cardinal bishop of Albano (Eubel, *Hier. Cath.*, i. 13, 14, 35, 49). They were appointed by the pope on 14 May 1312 as mediators to foster peace in England (*CPL 1305–42*, pp. 104–8). Nouvel was in London by 29 Aug. (*Ann. Paul.*, pp. 271–2), and the bishop of Poitiers was at court by 6 Sept. 1312

The earl of Gloucester took the part of mediator and frequently 1312
met the king about how to produce a state of peace and harmony with
the barons. 'Those whom you call enemies,' said the earl, 'are your
friends. Those you rashly attack are your friends. Whatever they do is
for your benefit. They are paying out much for your advantage. King,
if you destroy your barons, you indeed make light of your own
honour. And they are not bound to suffer this, nor do they commit
any offence if they protect their own rights.' And the king replied
thus to the earl: 'There is not one that pitieth my case:[106] none who
fights for my right against them. Even you, my nephew, my military
commander, and my friend, desert your uncle, and make friends with
his adversaries. I declare that those who strive to attack my property
and my rights are not my friends. If I may use my royal prerogative as
other kings do, may I not, by royal power, recall to my peace a man
exiled for any reason whatever? They deprived me of this right by
their own authority, for they cruelly put to death the man to whom I
had granted peace. And the earl of Lancaster, my first cousin, who
might have been content with five earldoms without seizing others,
attacked my men at Newcastle and carried off some of my property; if
any lesser man had done it, he could be found guilty of theft and
rightly condemned by a verdict of robbery with violence. And the
earls summoned to parliament come, to the king's shame, armed and
with a large army. In this, since they have seized my goods and killed
my men, it is very likely that they do not wish to be subject to me, but
to seize the crown and set up for themselves another king.' And the
earl replied, 'Sire, if the earls have presumed to do you wrong, it must
be put right; and if they are prepared to offer amends, they ought in
justice to be reconciled. For there is a common saying that no one
should make difficulties about receiving satisfaction. Therefore it is
advisable that the earls should first be assembled and questioned in a
friendly way about the injuries done by them to you, so that from
their answer it may be known whether the matter has been rightly or
wrongly judged. For everywhere it is usual for leniency to be tried
first, and if it is profitless harsh measures may follow.'[107]

The king agreed. So the earl as mediator approached the earls, and

---

(Maddicott, *Lancaster*, p. 134 n.). The cardinals worked through the year and were present
at the agreement finally reached in Oct. 1313; see below, pp. 74–5.

[106] 1 Kgs. (1 Sam.) 22: 8.

[107] The same sentiment is expressed below, pp. 160–1, which refers more clearly to
Deut. 20: 10–12.

1312 querelam regis ac causas iniuriarum seriatim exposuit. Ipsi uero super hiis consulti ita responderunt: 'Nos domini regis nostri Anglie barones, et secundum possibilitatem humane condicionis per omnia fideles, in priuacionem iuris regalis nichil presumpsimus, nichil attemptauimus, nec in preiudicium uel incommodum eius unquam aliquid excogitauimus. Verum est quod proditorem quendam exulantem, et post exilii decretum in terra latitantem, occidi mandauimus, et hoc non in dedecus regis nec contra pacem eius; nec propria auctoritate hoc fecimus, set iuxta ordinaciones legittimas, assensu regis et suorum baronum editas et promulgatas, processimus, quas nec rex sola uoluntate sua reuocare potuit uel immutare. Nichil enim sine consilio et communi assensu domini regis et suorum baronum potest statui; igitur eadem racione nec dissolui. Nam secundum leges ciuiles nichil tam naturale quam unumquodque dissolui eo genere quo ligatur,[108] et alibi omnes*a* res per quascunque causas nascitur per easdem dissoluitur. Patet igitur quod pax regia ipsi proditori concessa non ualuit, quia rex ipsam pacem contra ordinaciones concessit, quas solo et proprio arbitrio tollere non potuit.'

Comes de Lancastre ad obiecta sibi per regem respondit quod in predam uel rapinam nunquam concessit;*b* homines regis non inuasit; bona regis nequaquam asportauit, set apud Nouum Castrum ueniens multa, que ad regem pertinere cognouit, quasi pro derelicto habita, et occupare uolentibus exposita, ut*c* dominum regem conseruaret indempnem,*d* occupauit et ad opus regis, inuentorio de omnibus confecto, custodiendo*e* mandauit.[109]

Ita reponderunt omnes unanimiter quod non in contemptum regis, set propter quosdam sibi suspectos ad parliamentum muniti uenerunt, cum iuxta consilium sapientis nec nudi deberemus*f* contendere nec inhermes nos inimicis opponere. Ex hiis dictis*g* satis apparere in coronam regiam se nichil deliquisse; protestantes eis in mentem nunquam euenisse alium regem sibi preficere uoluisse.[110] Et in

---

a sic MS; omnis He, St, Den-Y   *b* sic R; poss. for consensit Den-Y   *c* ad R; ut St, Den-Y   *d* sic MS; poss. indempnia He   *e* sic MS; custodienda He, Den-Y *f* debere MS; debemus He; poss. deberemus or debeamus MW   *g* a verb is possibly omitted; perhaps exposuerunt or similar, ed.

[108] Dig. l. 17. 35, Corpus Iuris Civilis, i. 869.

[109] The issue of Gaveston's jewels and horses was an important one. The jewels included gifts from the royal treasury and were extremely valuable, and their detention was symbolic of Lancaster's powerful opposition. The negotiators agreed that they should be returned by 13 Jan. at St Albans, but Lancaster detained them until 23 Feb. (Maddicott, Lancaster, pp. 137, 139–40, 146–7; R. A. Roberts, 'Edward II, the Lords Ordainer, and Piers Gaveston's jewels and horses' (Camden Miscellany, xv, Camden Society 3rd ser., xli (1929), 3, 5–7).

explained the king's complaint and the reasons for his grievances one by 1312
one. When they had taken counsel in the matter, they replied thus: 'We,
as barons of our lord king of England, and faithful in all things so far as is
humanly possible, have not presumed to diminish the royal prerogative
in anything, we have sought nothing nor ever devised anything to his
prejudice or disadvantage. It is true that we ordered a certain exiled
traitor, who hid in the land after exile had been decreed, to be killed, but
this was not to the king's dishonour nor against his peace; nor did we do
this on our own authority, but we acted according to lawful ordinances
put forth and published with the assent of the king and his barons,
which the king by his will alone cannot revoke or change. For nothing
can be decreed without the counsel and common consent of the lord
king and his barons; therefore for the same reason nothing can be
annulled. For according to the civil law nothing is so natural as that
everything is loosened in the same way that it is bound,[108] and,
elsewhere, every obligation is dissolved by those same processes from
which it arises. It is therefore evident that the king's peace granted to
that traitor was not valid, because the king granted that peace against
the Ordinances, which by his own mere will he could not annul.'

The earl of Lancaster replied to the king's accusations against him,
that he had never acquiesced in plunder or booty; he had not attacked
the king's men; he had never carried off the king's goods, but coming
to Newcastle he seized many things, which he knew belonged to the
king, which were regarded as abandoned and open to any who wished
to take them, so that he might save the lord king from harm, and,
having made an inventory of everything, he ordered them to be kept
to the king's use.[109]

All replied unanimously in this wise: that they had not come
armed to parliament in contempt of the king, but on account of
some who were suspect to them, since according to the counsel of
the wise we should not engage in conflict stripped of our armour
nor oppose our enemies unarmed. From these remarks [they
maintained] it was quite clear that they had committed no crime
against the royal crown; protesting that it had never entered their
heads to wish to set up another as king.[110] And at the end of this

[110] Threats made to the king in 1310–11 (as in 1321) refer to withdrawal of fealty rather
than replacement of the king, and the author believed that captivity and restraint rather
than replacement were the aims of Lancaster and the others (see below, pp. 76–7). The
actions of the opposition may have led to rumours that they wished to replace the king and,
indeed, the king in his previous speech accused them of planning this (above, pp. 58–9).
For comment on threats to Edward, see above, pp. lvi–lvii.

1312 calce sermonis hec simul adiciunt; 'Manifeste,' inquiunt, 'iam liquet quia dominus rex occasiones querit aduersus nos. Cum enim iam per quinquennium et amplius, pro confirmacione regni, pro augmentacione honoris regii, satis ultra uires expenderimus, satis tamen incassum laborauimus, quia dominus rex omnia in dedecus eius excogitata, omnia in odium eius adinuenta conqueritur. Vtinam dominus noster quid*a* bonum est in oculis faciat; unum autem sciat, quod cum homines eius simus, fidem ei seruabimus; set quamuis a nobis fidelitatem receperit et homagium, equum et ipse nichilominus iuramentum seruare tenetur illesum. Et si forsan ab hoc pacto uellet recedere, nos absque fidei lesione nequaquam teneremur acquiescere. Roboam filius regis Salamonis, quamuis regnum iure hereditario sibi competeret, quia tamen barones suos iusta petentes non admisit, decima parte regni contentus, reliquam partem penitus amisit.[111] Igitur si dominus rex affeccione qua decet comites et barones suos tractauerit, si rancorem quem contra nos sine causa concepit benigne remiserit, et proditores a curia sua dimiserit, sibi ut regi parebimus, sibi ut domino seruiemus.'

Sub tanto rerum strepitu, dum uarii rumores hinc inde uolarent, dum unus pacem, alter guerram predicaret, natus est regi filius formosus et dudum affectatus. Impositum est autem ei nomen patris eius, nomen Edwardus; et natus puer iste in festo sancti Bricii,[112] quod annuatim celebratur post festum sancti Martini. Hec adoptata natiuitas tempore accepto nobis aduenit,[113] quia duos effectus Deo disponente feliciter impleuit. Dolorem namque regis quem ex morte Petri conceperat ualde mitigauit, et certum heredem regno prouidit. Nam, si rex decessisset sine prole, pro certo mansisset corona sub lite. Viuat igitur iuuenis Edwardus, et, auitis patribus assimilatus, quod singulos ditabat solus optineat. Regis Henrici secundi sectetur industriam, regis Ricardi notam probitatem, ad regis Henrici proueniat*b* etatem, regis Edwardi recolat sapienciam, uiribus et specie referat cum corpore patrem.

Audiens igitur rex responsiones comitum, prudentes allegaciones et probabiles excusaciones eorum, aduertens eciam manum ualidam ex parte baronum, et per hoc suum impediri propositum,*c* simulatam affeccionem pretendit, et uotis eorum parere promisit. Vnde ne nil

___

a sic *MS*; quod *He, St, Den-Y*   *b* sic *MS*; perueniat *He*   *c* prepositum *MS*; propositum *He, St, Den-Y*

[111] Cf. 3 Kgs. (1 Kgs.) 12: 1–24.   [112] 13 Nov. 1312.   [113] 2 Cor. 6: 2.

speech they also added: 'It is abundantly clear that the lord king is
looking for pretexts against us. Though for five years and more we
have exhausted our strength to support the realm and to increase
the king's honour, we have laboured in vain, because the lord king
complains that everything has been designed to put him to shame,
everything has been contrived out of hatred for him. Let our lord
do what is good in his eyes. But let him know one thing, that as we
are his men, we will keep faith with him; but, although he has
received fealty and homage from us, he is no less bound to keep his
oath intact. And if perhaps he wishes to withdraw from this
contract, we without breach of faith are in no way bound to
agree. Although the realm belonged to him by hereditary right,
Rehoboam, son of King Solomon, however, because he did not
admit the just claims of his barons, had to be content with the
tenth part of his kingdom and lost the rest utterly.[111] Therefore, if
the lord king treats his earls and barons with the regard that is
their due, if he freely gives up the bitterness that he has conceived
against us without cause, and sends the traitors away from his
court, we will obey him as king, we will serve him as lord.'

Amidst this uproar, while various rumours flew this way and
that, while one man foretold peace, and the other war, a handsome
and long-desired son was born to the king. He was christened
Edward, his father's name; and the boy was born on St Brice's
Day,[112] which is celebrated each year after the feast of St Martin.
This longed-for birth was timely for us,[113] because by God's will it
fortunately had two consequences. For it greatly lessened the grief
which the king had experienced on Piers's death, and it provided a
known heir to the realm. For if the king had died without issue,
the crown would certainly have remained in dispute. Long live,
therefore, the young Edward, and may he himself embody the
virtues that enriched each of his forefathers separately. May he
follow the industry of King Henry II, the well-known valour of
King Richard, may he reach the age of King Henry, revive the
wisdom of King Edward, and remind us of the physical strength
and comeliness of his father.

On hearing the answers of the earls, their astute justifications and
plausible excuses, and having regard to the armed strength of the
barons, by which his plans might be hindered, the king showed a
feigned regard for them and promised to comply with their wishes.
Whereupon, in case he should seem to have done nothing, he

1312 uideretur egisse, mandat baronibus sub forma concordie ut peticiones eorum exponerent, et quicquid dictaret racio indubitanter reportarent. At illi dixerunt se nichil aliud petere uelle nisi ut rex ordinaciones, quarum effectus in magna sui parte iam erat suspensus, sicut autem*a* promiserat, confirmaret, et mortem Petri proditoris suis fidelibus et legiis hominibus benigne remitteret.[114]

Et dominus rex sic ad petita respondit: 'Excepto fiscali priuilegio ordinaciones concessi,[115] et adhuc*b* concedo; mortem Petri comitibus remitto, set proditorem nequaquam appello.' Et comites hanc regis indulgenciam parui momenti fore dixerunt; 'nam, si rex mortem Petri remittit, suam sectam tamen non remittit, set uxori aut filiis accusacionem non tollit. At si proditoris mencionem faceret, nulli ulterius secta competeret. Et si rex comitatum Cornubie aliquo colore intendit repetere, profecto requiritur ut Petrus tanquam proditor obiisse dicatur. Nam extra hunc casum non poterit rex comitatum acquirere, nisi per Petrum uel si decessisset sine prole: set neutra condicio potest proficere, quia Petrus moritur prole superstite.[116] Igitur, nisi proditor Petrus habeatur, ordinacionibus multum derogatur, nec comitatum Cornubie poterit rex de iure repetere.'

Set rex baronibus ita respondit: 'Regi,' inquit, 'uariare non conuenit, nec sine causa reuocare quod prius indulgetur.*c* Omne crimen per nos fuit Petro*d* remissum, ergo proditorem eum reputare non possum, quia beneficium principis decet esse mansurum. Petant igitur barones quicquid petendum iuste putauerint; obsequar in omnibus eorum arbitrio, set Petro prodicionem nullatenus imputabo.' Et sic hac uice sub hiis finibus contencio recedit, set neutra parcium optata reportauit. Reuera omne studium regis erat ut negocium protelaret,*e* ut sic laboribus et expensis barones afficeret. Vnde et

a sic R; ante St, Den-Y   *b* ad hoc MS; adhuc Den-Y; the copyist uses the same form below (p. 76) ed.   *c* indulcitur MS; indulgetur He, St, Den-Y   *d* Petrum MS; Petro He, St, Den-Y   *e* procelaret MS; protelaret He, St, Den-Y

[114] The emphasis in this passage on the Ordinances as well as on Piers as traitor reflects strongly the terms in the 'Prima Tractatio' of early Sept. However, the placing of the passage after the birth of the king's son suggests chronologically that it may refer to the later 'Rationes'. These also strongly emphasize that Piers was a traitor, but make less reference to the Ordinances (Ann. Lond., pp. 210–11; Roberts, 'Piers Gaveston's jewels', pp. 15–16; Maddicott, Lancaster, pp. 145–6).

[115] It is not clear what the author means by this. Edward II accepted the Ordinances unconditionally on 27 Sept. 1311. However, the terms of reference of the Ordainers had provided that any ordinances were to be 'to our honour and profit and the profit of our people according to right and reason and our coronation oath'; the barons had sworn that the Ordinances would not be prejudicial to the king; and on 12 Jan. 1312 Edward had for

commanded the barons to draw up a list of their requests as a basis for agreement, and they would undoubtedly obtain whatever reason dictated. But they said that they wished to ask for nothing else than that the king should, as he had indeed promised, confirm the Ordinances, which were now largely in abeyance, and that he should freely pardon his faithful and liege men for the death of Piers the traitor.[114]

The lord king replied thus to the petitions: 'I granted the Ordinances, except the fiscal privilege,[115] and these I still grant. I pardon the earls for the death of Piers, but I will never call him traitor.' The earls said that this royal forgiveness would be of little value; 'for if the king pardons the death of Piers, but nevertheless he does not give up his right of prosecution, he does not deprive the wife or children of their right of accusation. But if he should make mention of a traitor, no further suit would be permissible. And if the king proposes to reacquire the earldom of Cornwall under any pretext, then it is necessary that Piers should be said to have died as a traitor. For, if this charge is not allowed, the king could not acquire the earldom, except through Piers or if he had died without issue; but neither condition can be fulfilled because Piers died leaving issue.[116] Therefore, unless Piers is held to be a traitor, the Ordinances are much diminished, and the king will not be able lawfully to reacquire the earldom of Cornwall.'

But the king replied thus to the barons: 'It is not fitting', he said, 'for the king to change or revoke without cause what he has previously granted. We pardoned Piers of every crime, therefore I cannot regard him as a traitor, because royal favours should be lasting. Therefore let the barons seek whatever they think may justly be sought; I will comply with their judgement in all things, but I will in no wise charge Piers with treason.' And so on this occasion the dispute died down to some extent, but neither party obtained what it had sought. Indeed the king's whole purpose was to drag out the business, in order to wear down the barons with their exertions and expenses. Shortly afterwards the king left

the first time emphasized that the Ordinances were to be observed only in so far as they were not prejudicial to the Crown (*CCR 1307–13*, pp. 215, 253, 449). The clauses on finance and the barons' later prohibition of the king's appointment of Langton as treasurer could certainly be seen as prejudicial to royal rights (Davies, *Opposition*, pp. 389–92), but there is no evidence that Edward had specifically reserved any fiscal rights.

[116] Gaveston's only child, Joan, was born *c*.12 Jan. 1312 and died 13 Jan. 1325 (Chaplais, *Gaveston*, pp. 78–9; Hamilton, *Gaveston*, pp. 101–2; *CMI 1307–49*, no. 1290, pp. 325–6).

1312 citro post rex a Londoniis recessit, et uersus Wyndulsore iter arripuit ut reginam uisitaret que nuper peperit.[117]

1313   Effluxerunt itaque dies anni usque ad Quadragesimam, et circa festum annunciacionis beate Marie sperabatur rex colloquium cum baronibus Londoniis habiturus, et habita concordia regni negocia cum comitibus dispositurus. Set[a] rex morbo ut putabatur ficto detentus ad diem non uenit; unde nec ipsa dissencio adhuc finem accepit.[118] Post Pascha misit rex Francie uiros magnos et honoratos nuncios in Angliam,[b] qui regem Anglie inuitarent ad conuiuium quod parauerat filio suo in festo Pentecostes.[c] Voluit enim rex Francie filio suo regi Nauarie uel cingulum milicie tradere ⟨uel⟩[d] regni diadema capiti eius imponere.[119] Vnde rex noster statim de suo itinere disposuit et necessaria prouideri mandauit. Miserunt comites ad eum, consulentes ei ne regnum suum periculo exponeret, ne ita inconsulte mare transiret, maxime cum terra ipsa esset quasi in se diuisa, et hostis opugnaret ciuitates et castra. Robertus enim de Brutz Eboracum[e] iam eciam appropinquauit, et Londonias adire disposuit; nec uidetur inpossible, ex quo non est qui uelit resistere.[120] Verumptamen rex a proposito suo non recessit, set in breui transfretare disposuit. Vnde nepotem suum comitem Glouernie custodem regni constituit,[121] et aliis comitibus sub hoc tenore rescripsit, mandans et rogans quatinus una cum dicto comite ad regni[f] curam intenderent, et quicquid ius dictaret aut racio in reditu suo certissime reportarent. Vnde et festum translacionis beati Thome terminum prefixit[122] in quo Deo dante redire disposuit, et tunc presentibus eis plenarie compleret quod promisit.

    Hiis itaque peractis, rex et regina, cum ceteris electis nauem ascendentes, tendunt in Franciam, et ibidem uenientes in maximo

---

[a] si *MS*; set *He, St, Den-Y*   [b] Anglia *MS*; Angliam *He, St, Den-Y*
[c] Pentecosten *MS*; Pentecostes *He, St, Den-Y*   [d] om. *MS*; supplied *He, St, Den-Y*
[e] Eboracen' *MS*; Eboracum *He, St, Den-Y*   [f] regi *MS*; regni *He, St, Den-Y*

[117] The king spent much of the winter at Windsor. He left it to be at Westminster only 12–16 Dec., 29 Jan.–3 Feb., and 18–20 Feb. (*Itin.*, pp. 93–6).

[118] The date given (25 Mar.) is approximately correct. Parliament was summoned (with commons) for 18 Mar. 1313, adjourned on 7 Apr., and reassembled on 6 May (*HBC*, p. 553).

[119] In 1313 Easter Sunday was on 15 Apr. and Whit Sunday on 3 June. Philip IV's eldest son, Louis, inherited the Navarrese throne through his mother, Jeanne, queen of Navarre and wife of Philip IV. (She had died in 1305.) The Navarrese throne remained annexed to the French throne until the death of Philip's last son, Charles IV of France, in 1328, when it reverted to Louis's daughter. This French meeting was a considerable

London, and made his way to Windsor to visit the queen, who had 1312
lately given birth.[117]

So the days rolled by until Lent, and about the feast of the 1313
Annunciation it was hoped that the king would hold a meeting
with his barons at London and, with harmony restored, would deal
with the business of the realm with the earls. But the king did not
come at the appointed day, detained, as it was thought, by a feigned
illness; because of which this same quarrel still did not come to an
end.[118] After Easter the king of France sent great and distinguished
men as envoys to England, to invite the king of England to the
banquet which he had prepared for his son at Whitsuntide. For the
French king wished to knight or to crown his son, the king of
Navarre.[119] Whereupon our king at once arranged for his journey and
ordered the necessary supplies to be prepared. The earls sent to him,
advising him not to put his kingdom in danger nor to go abroad so
unadvisedly, particularly as the land was divided against itself, and an
enemy might besiege his towns and castles. For Robert Bruce was
already in the neighbourhood of York, and proposed to march on
London; nor did it seem impossible, since there was none who would
resist him.[120] The king, however, did not change his mind, but
proposed to cross the Channel shortly. He appointed his nephew, the
earl of Gloucester, as keeper of the realm,[121] and he wrote to the other
earls in this sense, charging and requesting them to look to the
interests of the kingdom together with the said earl, and most
certainly they would obtain whatever right or reason dictated on
his return. He named the feast of the translation of the Blessed
Thomas[122] as the day on which, God willing, he would return, and
then he would fulfil to those present all that he had promised.

When this had been done, the king and queen, going aboard ship
with the others chosen to go with them, set out for France, where on

success. Ceremonies included the knighting of Philip's sons, a banquet for Charles of
Valois, and both kings took the cross. Philip finally remitted all penalties due from Edward
and his men for offences in Gascony (Phillips, *Pembroke*, pp. 63–4).

[120] There were fears of a Scottish invasion at this time but the rumours were false.
Bruce was in the Isle of Man in May and June 1313 (Barrow, *Bruce*, p. 193; McNamee,
Wars, pp. 56–7).

[121] The author errs here. The regent was John Droxford, bishop of Bath and Wells
(*HBC*, p. 39). Gloucester was, however, one of four men appointed on 1 July 1313 to open
parliament because of the king's delayed return (*CPR 1307–13*, p. 594). He had earlier
been keeper of the realm during Edward's absence on the Scottish campaign in 1311 (ibid.
333).

[122] 7 July 1313.

1313 honore suscipiuntur per totam patriam.[123] Regem nostrum et reginam saluos reducat Deus in Angliam, illos autem destruat qui regnum peruertunt et regiam familiam.

Ecce nunc rex noster Edwardus sex annis complete regnauit, nec aliquid laudabile uel dignum memoria hucusque patrauit, nisi quod regaliter nupsit et prolem elegantem regni heredem sibi suscitauit. Alia fuerunt[a] inicia regis Ricardi, qui nondum elapso triennio regni sui probitatis sue radios longe lateque dispersit; nam Messanas ciuitatem[b] Sisilie[c] uno die uiriliter subiecit, et terram Cypri in quindecim diebus potenter subiugauit. Deinde apud Acon et in aliis partibus transmarinis ⟨quomodo⟩[d] se habuerit, historia Latino et Gallico sermone digesta luculenter percurrit. O si rex noster Edwardus inicio regni sui bene se habuisset, et consilio malorum hominum non aduenisset,[e] ex antecessoribus suis nobilior illo nequaquam fuisset. Ditauerat enim Deus ipsum omnium uirtutum dotibus, parem immo excellentiorem fecerat aliis regibus. Nam si quis ea que regem nostrum nobilitant[f] uellet describere, parem in terra non poterit inuenire. Generositatem eius auiti patres ostendunt, quorum successiones se iam ad decem gradus extendunt. Diuicias habuit in principio regni sui, terram locupletem[g] et fauorem populi. Gener factus est regi Francie, proximus cognatus regis Hispannie.[124] Si adhesisset baronum consilio Scotos humiliasset pro nichilo. O si armorum usibus se exercitaret, regis Ricardi probitatem precederet. Hoc enim deposcit materia habilis, cum statura longus sit, et fortis uiribus, formosus homo decora facie. Set quid moror ipsum describere? Si tantam dedisset armis operam quantam impendit[h] circa rem rusticam,[125] multum excellens fuisset Anglia; nomen eius sonuisset in terra. O qualis sperabatur adhuc princeps Wallie! Tota spes euanuit dum factus est rex Anglie. Petrus de Gauestone regem duxit in deuium, terram turbauit, consumpsit thesaurum, tribus uicibus exilium subiit, et postea rediens caput perdidit. Set adhuc remanent in regis curia de familiaribus Petri et

---

    [a] fuerint *MS*; fuerunt *He, St, Den-Y*   [b] comitatem *MS*; comitatum *or* ciuitatem *He*; ciuitatem *St, Den-Y*   [c] *sic MS*; Sicilie *He, St, Den-Y*   [d] *om. MS; supplied He, St, Den-Y*   [e] *sic R*; adquieuisset *St, Den-Y*   [f] nobilitauit *MS*; nobilitant *He, St, Den-Y*   [g] locuplete *MS*; locupletem *He, St, Den-Y*   [h] impendidit *R*

    [123] The king and queen were absent from 23 May to 16 July 1313 (*HBC*, p. 39).

    [124] Edward's mother, Eleanor of Castile, was sister to Alfonso VIII of Castile. In 1313 Edward was first cousin twice removed to the reigning king, Alfonso XI, great-grandson of Alfonso VIII.

    [125] If this passage was written in 1313, it is one of the earliest voiced criticisms of

arrival they were received with the greatest honour all through the 1313
country.[123] May God bring back our king and queen safe to England,
and destroy those who lead astray the kingdom and the royal
household.

Behold, our King Edward has now reigned six full years and up
until now he has achieved nothing praiseworthy or memorable,
except that he has made a splendid marriage and has produced a
handsome son and heir to the kingdom. How different were the
beginnings of the reign of King Richard, who, before the end of the
third year of his reign, scattered far and wide the rays of his valour. In
one day he courageously took Messina, a city of Sicily, and ably
subjugated the land of Cyprus in a fortnight. Then, how he bore
himself at Acre and in other foreign parts history vividly relates in
both the Latin and French tongues. Oh! If our King Edward had
borne himself as well at the outset of his reign, and not accepted the
counsels of wicked men, not one of his predecessors would have been
more renowned than he. For God had endowed him with gifts of
every virtue, and had made him equal to or indeed more excellent
than other kings. Certainly if anyone cared to describe those qualities
which ennoble our king, he could not find his like in the land. His
ancestry, reaching back to the tenth generation, shows his nobility. At
the beginning of his reign he had wealth, a land of abundance, and the
goodwill of his people. He became the son-in-law of the king of
France, and was closest kin to the king of Spain.[124] If he had followed
the advice of the barons, he would have humbled the Scots with ease.
Oh! If he had practised the use of arms, he would have exceeded the
prowess of King Richard. Physically this would have been inevitable,
for he was tall and strong, a handsome man with a fine figure. But
why linger over this description of him? If only he had given to arms
the attention that he expended on rustic pursuits,[125] he would have
raised England on high; his name would have resounded through the
land. Oh! What hopes he raised as prince of Wales! All hope vanished
when he became king of England. Piers Gaveston led the king astray,
threw the country into confusion, consumed its treasure, was exiled
three times, and then returning lost his head. But there still remain at
the king's court those from Piers's intimates and members of his

Edward's pastimes. Otherwise the earliest recorded reference is in the Crown's prosecution
in 1315 of Robert le Messager, who in an unguarded moment in July 1314 blamed the loss
at Bannockburn on Edward's interest in rustic pursuits (H. Johnstone, 'The eccentricities
of Edward II', *EHR*, xlviii (1933), 264–7).

1313 eius familia, qui perturbant pacem tocius patrie et regem inducunt uindictam querere. Da pacem, Domine, diebus nostris,[126] et rex cum baronibus fiat unanimis.[a]

Hiis temporibus mortuus est Robertus de Wynchelse Cantuarie antistes,[127] cuius memoria in benediccione est, qui templum Domini in uita sua roborauit, et in diebus suis ecclesiam protexit. De ipso enim specialiter dici potest, non est inuentus similis illi qui conseruaret legem Excelsi.[128] Ascendit namque ex aduerso et opposuit se murum pro clero.[129] Exiit aliquando edictum ab Edwardo Cesare[130] ut taxarentur fructus ecclesie, et sicut talliabatur populus, ad tallagium compelleretur et clerus. Porro Robertus primas Anglie preceptum regis non est passus procedere. Dicebat enim omni iuri fore contrarium, ut[b] in bonis clericorum haberet rex imperium, quos eciam lex imperialis multis priuilegiis insigniuit et ab omni exaccione liberos esse statuit. Hoc eciam uolunt statuta canonum;[131] et ipsi ethnici manifestum nobis reliquerunt exemplum: quando Egipcii pre magnitudine famis seruituti regie se subiecerunt, pontifices et ceteri templorum ministri liberi remanserunt.[132] Set rex exasperatus, et aduersus primatem et tocius Anglie clerum uehementer commotus, publica uoce promisit curialibus ut in nullo penitus defferrent[c] clericis, set, siue religiosis seu secularibus obuiarent, ipsos ab equis protinus deicerent et in usum proprium equos assumerent, et indistincte nullis parcerent nisi regia proteccione gauderent. Verumptamen Cantuarie archiepiscopus magis cepit esse tumidus et securus, unde in sarculum suum percussit,[133] et in grassantes ulterius processit, et omnes regiam proteccionem impetrantes excommunicauit. In tantum autem excreuit laicorum audacia ut nec ulli parcerent in archipresulis curia, quin eciam ipsum archipresulem ab equo deicerent, et omnem suppellectilem diriperent, unde archiepiscopus pacienter ferrens[d] iniuriam pedes coactus est ire per patriam.

---

[a] unanime *MS*; unanimis *He, St, Den-Y*   [b] uel *MS*; ut *He, St, Den-Y*   [c] sic *MS*; deferrent *He, St, Den-Y*   [d] ferre *MS*; ferens *He, Den-Y*; ferrens *ed.*

[126] From the liturgy: prayer at Matins and Vespers (Legg, *Sarum Missal*, p. 225).
[127] Winchelsey died on 11 May 1313 (*HBC*, p. 233).
[128] Ecclus. 44: 20, with *conseruauit* for the *Vita*'s *conseruaret*.
[129] Ezek. 13: 5.   [130] Luke 2: 1.
[131] Edward I imposed a direct tax of half their income on the clergy in 1294, and another tenth in 1295. The clergy paid (although reluctantly), because canon law followed Roman law in allowing such payments to the ruler in the case of urgent necessity for the common good; this normally included war. However, Boniface VIII's papal bull *Clericis laicos*, issued in Feb. 1296 and received in England in Nov. 1296, forbade payments to lay

household, who disturb the peace of the whole country and persuade 1313
the king to seek vengeance. Give peace in our time, O Lord,[126] and
may the king be at one with his barons!

At this time died Robert Winchelsey, archbishop of Canterbury,[127]
of blessed memory, who in his lifetime strengthened the temple of the
Lord, and during his time of office protected the church. Of him
especially it can be said, 'There was not found the like to him, who
kept the law of the most High'.[128] For he 'went up to face the enemy'
and 'set himself up as a wall' for the clergy.[129] There once went out a
decree from Caesar Edward,[130] that the fruits of the church should be
taxed and just as the people were tallaged, so also the clergy were to
be forced to pay tallage. But Robert as primate of England did not
allow the king's decree to take effect. He said that it would be
contrary to all law for the king to have authority over the goods of
churchmen, whom the imperial law also marked out with many
privileges and ordered to be free from every exaction. Canon law
intends this too;[131] and the heathen themselves have bequeathed us a
manifest example: when the Egyptians for their great hunger put
themselves under the royal yoke, the priests and other servants of the
temples remained free.[132] But the king being wrathful and strongly
roused to anger against the primate and the clergy of all England,
publicly announced to his officials that they should have no con-
sideration at all for clerks, but, when they met regulars or secular
clergy, should at once have them off their horses and take the horses
for their own use, and, without discrimination, they should spare no
one unless they enjoyed royal protection. However, the archbishop of
Canterbury became more incensed and self-confident, and he smote
with his rake,[133] and, proceeding further against the thieves, excommunicated all those obtaining royal protection. The presumption of
the laymen increased to such an extent that they spared no one in the
archbishop's court, even pulling the archbishop himself off his horse,

rulers without papal licence. This provided Winchelsey with firm canon law grounds for
his opposition to Edward's further exactions in 1296. Boniface qualified *Clericis laicos* in
1297 by permitting payment without papal licence in cases of great necessity, of which the
king would be judge. At the convocation of 1317 this qualified position is clearly stated by
the prelates; see below, pp. 132–3. For the doctrine of necessity see G. L. Harriss, *King,
Parliament and Public Finance in Medieval England to 1369* (Oxford, 1975), pp. 17–24, 51–
2, 59–60; for Winchelsey's actions, see Denton, *Winchelsey*, pp. 89–135.

[132] Cf. Gen. 47: 20–2, 26.

[133] Cf. Isa. 7: 25. The phrase is possibly incomplete, but the allusion to Isaiah seems
clear, with the implication that the archbishop was cutting out the thorns and briars from
good land.

1313 Denique rex ad penitenciam reductus, et grauiter se peccasse confessus, curialium repressit audaciam et liberam manere iussit ecclesiam.[134] Iterum orta dissencione inter regem et archipresulem, procurante rege uocatus est ad curiam Romanam, et ibi per biennium fere remansit, et fructus suos biennales confiscatos amisit. Deinde mortuo rege in Angliam rediit, et ecclesiam suam pacifice usque huc gubernauit.[135] Nunc autem nature debita persoluens, celestem migrauit ad patriam, Cantuariensem ut creditur ornaturus ecclesiam.

Anno igitur septimo regis intrante, in festo translacionis beate Thome[136] conueniunt Londoniis comites et barones iuxta promissum regis aduentum exspectantes, ibidemque fere per quindenam commorantes, neque regis copiam habuerunt, neque de regis reditu certos nuncios acceperunt. Vnde comites, laboribus et expensis satis fatigati, sine die ad propria sunt reuersi. Circa gulam Augusti rediit dominus rex,[137] et quasi de recessu comitum molestus, scripsit comitibus rogans quatinus moram suam excusatam haberent, et in festo sancti Mathei[138] si placeret ad parliamentum redirent, et tunc communi consilio quicquid faciendum, quicquid corrigendum esse prospicerent, communiter repararet.

Set quid prosunt regi procrastinaciones assidue? Dicunt quidam, ut aduersarios suos cogat expendere, uel mortem comitis forsan exspectat[a] quem alias superare non sperat. Sane peccat qui hoc audet asserere, immo non apparet uerisimile ut rex ipse tam necessarii mortem affectaret amici. Quis magis regi succurreret in summa necessitate, quam cognatus eius Thomas Lancastrie? Certe non socius eius ipse rex Francie, nec Petrus, si uiueret, comes Cornubie. Reuera quicquid dolose actum est in curia regis processit ex

---

[a] sic MS; expectet He

[134] Edward's quarrel with Winchelsey over the king's attempt to tax the clergy is well covered by Denton, *Winchelsey*, pp. 100–76, and more briefly by Prestwich, *Ed. I*, pp. 414–18, 420. On 12 Feb. 1297 the king ordered the confiscation of all the clergy's lay fees and the goods and chattels on them unless the clergy purchased protection, the fines for which approached the level of the proposed tax itself. Several chronicles mention Edward's confiscation of horses at this time (they constituted valuable army supplies) and Winchelsey's horses were confiscated at Maidstone in early March as he was travelling from Canterbury to meet the king at Salisbury (Denton, *Winchelsey*, pp. 108, 119). Edward was not formally reconciled with Winchelsey until 11 July 1297.

[135] The later quarrel began in 1305 when Edward promoted a series of lawsuits against Winchelsey, and attempted to have him removed. Clement V, favourably disposed towards Edward, suspended Winchelsey in a bull of 12 Feb. 1306, and Winchelsey left England for Rome 19 May 1306 (Denton, *Winchelsey*, pp. 213–24, 231–6, 247; S. Menache, *Clement V* (Cambridge, 1998), pp. 58–60). Winchelsey did not return until 24 Mar. 1308, after Edward II's coronation; see above, n. 15.

and plundering all his goods, so that the archbishop, bearing the 1313
wrong patiently, was forced to go about the countryside on foot. At
length the king repented, and, confessing that he had gravely sinned,
restrained the presumption of his courtiers and gave orders for the
church to remain free.[134] When the quarrel broke out again between
the king and the archbishop, the latter was summoned to the court of
Rome at the king's request, and he remained there for almost two
years, losing his revenues for two years by confiscation. Then on the
king's death he returned to England and ruled his church in peace
until the present time.[135] But now, going the way of all flesh, he has
departed to heaven, to be an ornament, it is thought, to the church of
Canterbury.

At the beginning of the seventh year of the king's reign, on the
feast of the translation of the Blessed Thomas,[136] the earls and barons
met at London, awaiting the king's promised arrival, and stayed there
almost a fortnight, having neither access to the king, nor any certain
news of the king's return. So the earls, weary enough of the trouble
and expense to which they had been put, went home indefinitely. The
lord king returned about the first of August,[137] and as if upset by the
departure of the earls, wrote to them asking them to excuse his delay
and please to return to parliament on the feast of St Matthew,[138] and
then by common counsel he would make good with them whatever
they thought should be done or reformed.

But of what use to the king are these constant delays? Some say
that he is forcing his opponents to waste their resources, or is perhaps
waiting for the death of an earl whom he does not hope otherwise to
overcome. But whoever dares to assert this is wrong, for it is clearly
unlikely that the king would desire the death of so necessary a friend.
Who could help the king more in his greatest need than his cousin
Thomas of Lancaster? Certainly not his ally the king of France, nor,
had he lived, Piers, earl of Cornwall. Indeed whatever wickedness was
perpetrated in the king's court proceeded from his counsellors, but

---

[136] 7 July 1313. Parliament (with commons) had been summoned for 8 July, the day
after that on which Edward had indicated he would return from France (*HBC*, p. 553).
The *Vita* appears to show either sympathy with the opposition baronage or ignorance, as
Gloucester, Richmond, and two others had been appointed on 1 July to open parliament
and keep it in session until the king returned. See above, n. 121.

[137] Edward reached England again on 15 July and was in London by 23 July at the latest
and possibly a day or two earlier (*Itin.*, p. 102).

[138] 21 Sept. Writs were sent out on 26 July summoning parliament (with commons) for
23 Sept. at Westminster. The parliament lasted until 15 Nov. (*HBC*, p. 553).

1313 consiliariis eius, set consilium eorum est inefficax et machinacio peritura. Maledictus furor*a* eorum quia pertinax, et indignacio eorum[139] quia diuidentur tandem a curia et dispergentur in ignominia. Iustum est enim ut suos auctores teneant peccata,[140] ne maleficia remaneant impunita.

Ad festum sancti Mathei conueniunt Londoniis comites predicti, et manserunt in eodem loco per aliquod tempus, nec regi mittentes, nec mandatum a rege recipientes. Vt autem per eos non staret quominus concordia fieret, miserunt ad dominum regem petentes quatinus sepe promissa consummaret, et baronibus suis sub fide non ficta rancorem remitteret. Rex uero non statim annuit, set pocius ex solito negocium protelauit. Tandem quia uox publica testimonium prebuit, et rex ipse per exploratores suos manifeste cognouit, quia aut*b* peticioni comitum satisfieret, aut sibi suisque tucius esse ante tempus occurrere quam post uulneratam causam remedium querere; multa eciam instancia cardinalis et domini Lodowicy*c* precibus inductus,[141] mandauit comitibus et baronibus quatinus, omni suspicione reiecta et securitate quam uellent petita et optenta, ad presenciam suam accederent, et beniuolenciam eius multociens requisitam pro libito reportarent.

Comites igitur in crastinum dominum regem adierunt, ipsumque flexis genibus sicut decuit salutarunt. Quos ipse benigne suscipiens protinus erexit, et singillatim singulos in osculo suscepit, ab omni delicto prius eis imposito penitus absoluit, racionabiliter petita et in posterum petenda similiter concessit, et hec omnia iureiurando et scripto, magno sigillo confirmatis, roborauit.[142] Rex eciam ad maioris federis signum comites inuitauit ad prandium; ipse uero altera die in mensa comitis Lancastrie.*d* Hic etenim mos inoleuit in Anglia ut pax confirmetur ad communia.*e* Sic ergo mors Petri remittitur, et comes de Penbroke reconciliatur, et de ceteris amicis regis factum est sicut rex uoluit; set Hugo Despenser graciam habere non potuit. Caueat sibi de comite Lancastrie, et terram euacuet si uelit euadere. Tota terra uersa est in eius odium; pauci lugerent eius infortunium. Multis

---

a fauor R; furor Den-Y; furor *is the correct Vulgate wording and improves the sense, ed.*
b autem MS; aut He, St, Den-Y   *c* sic R; Lodowici St, Den-Y   *d* *a verb omitted here* MW, *possibly* cenauit *ed.*   *e* sic R; conuiuia St, Den-Y

---

[139] Gen. 49: 7.
[140] Cod. ix. 47. 22 (2), Corpus Iuris Civilis, ii. 392.
[141] Two cardinals and Louis of Evreux had been in England as mediators since the autumn of 1312; see above, pp. 56–7 and n. 105.

LIFE OF EDWARD THE SECOND 75

their advice is futile and their plots will fail. Cursed be their anger, 1313
because it is stubborn, and their wrath,[139] because they shall at length
be separated from the court and scattered in disgrace. For it is right
that sins should bind those who commit them,[140] so that evildoing
may not go unpunished.

At the feast of St Matthew the said earls met in London, and
remained there for some time, neither sending to the king, nor
receiving any command from him. But so that the lack of agreement
might not be laid at their door, they sent to the lord king asking him
to fulfil what he had so often promised, and give up his grudge
towards his barons in genuine good faith. The king did not
immediately agree, but rather dragged out the business as usual.
However, because it was at length being publicly said, as the king
clearly knew through his spies, that he must satisfy the earls' petition,
and that it would be safer for him and his supporters to make answer
too soon rather than to seek redress once his case had been damaged;
also persuaded by the great earnestness of the cardinal and the prayers
of lord Louis,[141] the king told the earls and barons that, having put
aside all suspicion and having sought and obtained the security that
they wanted, they should come before him, and freely obtain the
goodwill for which they had so often asked.

On the next day, therefore, the earls approached the lord king and
greeted him, as was proper, on bended knee. Receiving them
graciously he at once raised them and kissed them one by one,
wholly absolved them of every crime of which they were accused,
granted what they reasonably sought or should seek hereafter, and
confirmed all these things by oath and in writing under the great
seal.[142] The better to celebrate the treaty, the king also invited the
earls to dinner, dining himself next day with the earl of Lancaster.
For the custom is growing in England for a reconciliation to be
confirmed at banquets. So then Piers's death is pardoned and the earl
of Pembroke is reconciled, and as for the other friends of the king
matters were arranged as the king willed; but Hugh Despenser could
find no favour. Let him beware of the earl of Lancaster and leave the
country if he wishes to escape. The whole land has turned to hatred of
him. Few would mourn his downfall. He has harmed many unjustly

[142] The pardon was agreed in parliament on 15 Oct. 1313 and proclaimed on 16 Oct. for
Lancaster, Hereford, Warwick, Percy, Clifford, and 467 of their supporters (*CPR 1313–17*,
pp. 21–6). The matter had been settled broadly on Edward's terms, since there was no
reference to the Ordinances nor to Gaveston being a traitor (see Maddicott, *Lancaster*,
pp. 150–3).

1313 in officio suo iniuste nocuit; plures magnates et uiros diuites
exheredauit; et utinam amitteret quod sic adquisiuit ut puniretur in
quo deliquit.[143] Summe Deus, auctor iusticie, falsos et perfidos a rege
remoue; inter regem et barones hoc fedus initum, Te protegente,
seruetur in posterum.

Queret forsan aliquis quid comites fecissent si regem in promissis
difficilem inuenissent. Credo constanter quod regem captum sub
custodia posuissent, donec eos auctores discordie penitus destrux-
issent. Nonne sic comes Symon de Mountefort regem Henricum
tenuit et filium eius Edwardum carceri mancipauit? Set non est tutum
contra regem ceruicem erigere, quia tristes exitus frequenter solet
afferre. Nam Symon ille comes Leycestrie[a] tandem apud Euesham
occubuit in acie; comes de Ferrers terras perdidit; comiti Marescallie
rex ipse successit; quilibet istorum regi restitit, et quilibet istorum in
fine succubuit.[144]

Sic igitur rege et baronibus suis sub forma predicta in amiciciam
reuocatis, comites et ceteri magnates terre dederunt regi in subsidium
guerre sue uicesimum denarium tocius Anglie, cetera autem ordi-
nanda in futurum distulerunt ad proximum parliamentum;[145] et
comes Herfordie remansit de regis familia; ceteri uero comites reuersi
sunt ad propria.

Quia prius mencionem feci de morte Cantuariensis archiepiscopi,
nunc de eius successore, et quomodo successit, aduerto.[b] Mortuo
namque archipresule, prior ecclesie Christi Cantuariensis, et eiusdem loci conuentus, processerunt ad eleccionem, unanimi consensu
elegerunt magistrum Thomam de Cobham uirum nobilem, diuini et
humani iuris professorem; qui statim iter arripiens mare transiit et
iuri suo prosequendo operam dedit.[146] Due tamen cause impediebant
eum. Adhuc[c] enim languente primate miserat papa bullam suam
qua[d] reseruauit sibi disposicionem archiepiscopatus et eleccionem

---

[a] Lancastrie *MS*; *recte* Leycestrie *He, St, Den-Y*   [b] aduerte *R;* aduerto *ML*   [c] ad
hoc *MS*; adhuc *He, St, Den-Y*; *the copyist uses the same form above (p. 64) ed.*   [d] quam
MS; qua *He, St, Den-Y*

[143] Despenser was justice and keeper of the forest south of the Trent, which the author
mentions again below (pp. 194–5). Despenser held the office under Edward I (1297–1307),
was reappointed by Edward II at pleasure on 16 Mar. 1308, and for life on 28 Aug 1309.
He lost the office temporarily in 1311–12; but was reappointed in 1312–15 (Tout, *Ed. II*,
pp. 320–1). An investigation into complaints against his abuse of office began on 13 July
1315. John Walwayn sat on one of the investigating commissions (*CPR 1313–17*, pp. 407–
8), and the author's keen awareness of Despenser's role as forester may support the
suggestion that he was Walwayn.
[144] For the losses of Ferrers and the Earl Marshal after the battle of Evesham in 1265,

through his office; he has disinherited many great men and rich men; 1313
would that he might lose what he has thus acquired, that he might be
punished in his crime.[143] All-Highest God, author of justice, remove
false men and traitors from the king; may this treaty entered into by
king and barons, under Thy protection, be kept hereafter.

Perhaps someone may ask what the earls would have done if they
had found the king slow to make promises. I firmly believe that they
would have kept the king under restraint, until they had utterly
destroyed the creators of discord. Did not Earl Simon de Montfort
thus hold King Henry and imprison his son Edward? But it is not safe
to rise up against the king, because the outcome is often likely to be
unfortunate. For even Simon, earl of Leicester, was at last laid low in
battle at Evesham; the Earl Ferrers lost his estates; the king himself
succeeded the Earl Marshal; each of these resisted the king, and each
of them in the end succumbed.[144]

Thus, the king and his barons being reunited in friendship in this
way, the earls and other great men of the land gave to the king as a
war subsidy the twentieth penny of all England, but they put off the
other matters to be settled to the future at the next parliament;[145] and
the earl of Hereford remained at court; the other earls went home.

Because I made mention above of the archbishop of Canterbury's
death, I turn now to his successor and the manner of his succession.
On the death of the primate, the prior and convent of Christ Church
Canterbury proceeded to an election, and by a unanimous agreement
chose Master Thomas Cobham, a nobleman, and a doctor of canon
and civil law, who, setting out at once, crossed the sea to undertake
the prosecution of his cause.[146] However, he was hindered by two
circumstances. While the primate was still on his sickbed the pope
had sent his bull reserving for himself the arrangements for the

see K. B. McFarlane, 'Had Edward I a "policy" towards the earls?', *History*, l (1965),
reprinted in his *The Nobility of Later Medieval England* (Oxford, 1973) pp. 248–67, at
pp. 254–6, 262.

[145] The author mentions only two of Edward's seven parliamentary taxes, this one and
the one in 1319 (below, pp. 160–1). In both he states that the lords alone approved the tax,
ignoring the role of the commons. In both he also ignores the differential tax on towns.
This grant was for one-twentieth on the countryside and one-fifteenth on the towns; it
brought in £38, 453. 15*s.* 3 1/2*d.* (*Lay Taxes*, p. 31; Willard, *Parliamentary Taxes*, p. 344).

[146] Cobham was elected on 28 May 1313. A royal clerk who had given Edward II good
service in diplomatic affairs, particularly with France in 1309–13, he had every reason to
expect royal support, but the election was quashed 1 Oct. in favour of Walter Reynolds.
Cobham subsequently became bishop of Worcester, 1317–27 (*HBC*, pp. 233, 279; *BRUO*,
i. 450–1). For Cobham's diocesan work, see E. H. Pearce, *Thomas de Cobham, Bishop of
Worcester 1317–1327* (London, 1923).

1313 futuri pontificis. Misit et rex Anglie summo pontifici, orans ut clericum suum Wygorniensem episcopum ad sedem archiepiscopalem duceret^a promouendum.[147] Hiis de causis impediebatur electus, nec eligencium sibi proficere potuit assensus, quin rege^b instante et multa ut creditur pecunia interueniente, dominus papa archiepiscopatum conferret, et dictum episcopum ecclesie Anglicane proficeret.[148]

O quanta inter electum et prefectum erat differencia! Nam electus ipse flos Cancie, nobilis generis, rexerat in artibus,^c in decretis, et magister erat theologus,^d sedi Cantuariensis ecclesie satis ydoneus. Dictus uero episcopus nuper erat simplex clericus et minus competenter litteratus, set in ludis theatralibus principatum tenuit, et per hoc regis fauorem optinuit. Vnde in familia^e regis assumptus post modicum tempus factus est regis thesaurarius, et de thesauraria Wygorniensis episcopus, postmodum cancellarii gessit officium et ecce, nunc promotus est in archiepiscopum. Mirantur quidam de uiri fortuna, set ego magis miror de domino papa, cur tam excellentem personam respueret, et inydoneum scienter assumeret, cum de utriusque meritis patenter sibi constaret. Set domina pecunia omne negocium consummat in curia. Consuetudinem et mores Romane curie, si forsan ignorans, aduerte. Amat causas, lites, iurgia, quia expediri non possunt sine pecunia; et causa que curiam semel ingreditur pene inmortalis efficitur; et hec fuit causa quare, omisso quolibet medio, licuit ad papam appellare. Quilibet eciam sola contentus esse debet ecclesia, sicut cauit capitulum *de multa*[149] excipiuntur tamen sublimes persone, dispensacionem accipiunt indistincte, sic^f omnes qui pecuniam dare sufficiunt. Hec miranda uanitas, hec curie detestanda cupiditas, totum orbem in sui scandalum excitauit. Multis retro temporibus exstitit inauditum, ut citramontanus eligeretur in papam; post hec nunquam eueniat ut

---

^a ducet *MS*; duceret *He, St, Den-Y*   ^b regem *MS*; rege *He, St, Den-Y*
^c arcubus *R*; artibus *St, Den-Y*   ^d sic *MS*; theologie *He, St*; *the copyist uses the same form below (p. 178) ed.*   ^e sic *MS*; *poss.* familiam *He*   ^f set *R*; sic *ed.*

---

[147] In a bull dated 27 Apr. 1313 the pope had reserved the right to appoint Winchelsey's successor, but he ordered his nuncios not to deliver it until July, by which time Cobham had been elected. Walter Reynolds, bishop of Worcester since Nov. 1307, treasurer from Aug. 1307 to July 1310, and chancellor from July 1310 to Sept. 1314, was provided to Canterbury on 1 Oct. 1313 and Cobham's election was quashed. Reynolds's character has been treated harshly by historians following the unflattering pictures in the *Flores* and *Vita*, but some chroniclers were more sympathetic, and the pope saw him as a suitable candidate

archbishopric and the choice of the next bishop. Also the king of 1313 England sent to the pope, begging him to see fit to promote his clerk the bishop of Worcester to the archiepiscopal see.[147] For these reasons the archbishop-elect was frustrated, nor could the assent of the electors help him, for, at the king's instance and, it is believed, after much money had changed hands, the lord pope conferred the archbishopric and set the said bishop over the English church.[148]

Oh! What a difference there was between the elect and the one appointed! For the elect was the very flower of Kent, of noble stock; he had lectured in arts and on canon law, and was a master of theology; a man eminently fitted for the see of Canterbury. The said bishop, on the other hand, had recently been a mere clerk and was scarcely literate, but he excelled in theatrical presentations, and through this obtained the king's favour. For this he was taken into the king's household, and soon became the king's treasurer, and from the treasury became bishop of Worcester; later he took on the office of chancellor, and see! now he is made archbishop. Some are surprised at the man's good luck, but I am more surprised at the lord pope, at why he should reject so excellent a person, and deliberately adopt an unsuitable one, when the merits of each were clearly known to him. But My Lady Money transacts all business in the Curia. If perhaps you do not know the custom and practices of the Roman Curia pay attention to this. It loves causes, lawsuits, disputes, because they cannot be cleared up without money; and a case once entered upon at the Curia becomes almost immortal; and this was the reason why, disregarding any mediator, an appeal to the pope was allowed. Anyone ought to be content with one church only, as the chapter *de multa*[149] decrees, but people of high position are excepted, they receive dispensations indiscriminately, and so it is for all who have sufficient means to give money. This astonishing deceitfulness, this detestable greed of the Curia, has brought scandal on it throughout the whole world. For a long time past it has been unheard of for a non-Italian to be elected pope; after this may it never happen [again]

who could work in cooperation with the king (Menache, *Clement V*, pp. 63–4; Wright, *Reynolds*, pp. 243–62).

[148] The allegation of a substantial bribe is without confirmation, and it is probable that no more money passed hands than was usual at the beginning of an episcopate (Wright, *Reynolds*, p. 245 and n.).

[149] This is canon 29 of the Fourth Lateran Council, 1215: *Decretal. Gregor. IX*, L. 3 t. 5 c. 28 (*Corpus Iuris Canonici*, ii. col. 477). An English translation is readily available in 'Canons of the Fourth Lateran Council, 1215', *EHD*, iii. 643–76, at 657–8.

1313 tam uicinus homo cathedram papalem ascendat.[150] Octo annis et
amplius papa Clemens quintus uniuersalem rexit ecclesiam, set
quicquid profuit homini euasit memoriam. Apud Vienniam consilium congregauit, et Templarios disposuit, indulgencias pro Terra
Sancta concessit, infinitam pecuniam congessit, set Terre Sancte
nichil omnino profuit.[151] Regibus concessit decimas, pauperum
spoliauit ecclesias. Melius esset rectoribus papam non habere
quam tot exaccionibus in dies subiacere. Set an hoc possit facere[a]
non est meum discutere, quia instar sacrilegii est de potestate
principis disputare.[152] Inter omnes mundi prouincias sola Anglia
dominum papam[b] sentit onerosum;[153] nam ex plenitudine potestatis
multa presumit, nec princeps nec populus sibi contradicit; omnes
pingues redditus sibi reseruat,[154] atque rebellantes statim excommu-
nicat; ueniunt legati et terram spoliant;[155] ueniunt bullati et prebendas uendicant. Omnes decanatus alienigenis contulit ubi lex
indigenas[c] preferri statuit. Residencia decanorum iam nunc aboletur,
et canonicorum numerus ualde desolatur.[156] Nonne[d] sicut papa[e]

[a] sic MS; poss. fieri He   [b] ipsam MS; papam He, St, Den-Y   [c] idiginas MS;
indigenas St, Den-Y   [d] nomen MS; nonne He, St, Den-Y   [e] papam MS; papa He,
St, Den-Y

[150] Clement V, elected on 5 June 1305, was Bertrand de Got, bishop of Bordeaux from
1299, who had worked as a royal clerk in Gascony and was well disposed to the English
kings (J. H. Denton, 'Pope Clement V's early career as a royal clerk', EHR, lxxxiii (1968),
303–14). The next Gascon pope was Benedict XII, elected in 1334.
[151] The Council of Vienne opened on 16 Oct. 1311. In Mar. 1312 at the end of its first
session, it approved the bull Vox in excelso suppressing the Order of the Templars. In its
second session, which opened on 3 Apr. 1312, and after informal negotiations, Clement V
announced the imposition of a sexennial tenth for the crusade on all ecclesiastical
provinces, but no decision was reached about the crusade itself. Only one year's tenth
was ever levied in England. For the Council's decrees, of which a substantial number were
later incorporated in the decretal collection known as the Clementines, see N. Tanner
(ed.), Decrees of the Ecumenical Councils (2 vols., London, 1990), pp. 336–401; for the
sexennial tenth, Lunt, Financial Relations, pp. 395–8. I am indebted to Miss Barbara
Harvey for this note on the Council of Vienne.
[152] Cod. ix. 29. 2, Corpus Iuris Civilis, ii. 385.
[153] Despite the author's complaint, papal demands on England do not seem to be out of
line with those made elsewhere; see, for instance, the level of papal provisions in France
and England (Menache, Clement V, pp. 54–100).
[154] The fat rents were undoubtedly a reference to annates, payments of a proportion of
the first year's income by new incumbents of benefices. They were levied for the first time
as a papal tax in England in 1306–9, and caused immediate resentment. They were
prohibited at the parliament of Carlisle in 1307, but the king revoked the prohibition. The
total sum collected over the three years has been estimated at £18,838. It was attractive
enough for Pope John XXII to repeat the imposition in 1316–19 (Lunt, Financial Relations,
pp. 486–94; W. E. Lunt, 'William Testa and the parliament of Carlisle', EHR, xli (1926),
332–57, at 339, 343–5).

that a man so near to us ascends the papal throne.[150] For eight years 1313
and more Pope Clement V has ruled the church universal, but how it
has profited any man escapes my memory. He has gathered together a
council at Vienne, and disposed of the Templars, he has granted
indulgences for the Holy Land, collected a vast amount of money, but
it has profited the Holy Land not at all.[151] He has granted tenths to
kings, he has plundered the churches of the poor. It would be better
for rectors not to have a pope than to be subject to so many daily
exactions. But whether this can be done is not for me to discuss,
because it is the equivalent of sacrilege to dispute the prince's
power.[152] Amongst all the provinces of the world England alone
feels the lord pope a burden;[153] for he presumes much on his *plenitudo
potestatis*; neither the prince nor the people refuses him; he reserves
all fat rents for himself,[154] and immediately excommunicates the
rebellious; legates come and plunder the land;[155] men come with bulls
and claim prebends. He has bestowed all deaneries on foreigners
although the law has decreed that natives should be preferred. The
residence of deans is now already destroyed, and the number of
canons is greatly diminished.[156] As pope does he not rule over

[155] Of the legates sent to England before 1313, only William Testa, papal tax-collector
1305–13, received a large number of benefices and could be said to have 'plundered the
land'. Peter of Spain, Arnald d'Aux, and Arnald Nouvel received only modest gifts,
although other cardinals, resident abroad, held deaneries and prebends at this time
(Wright, *Reynolds*, pp. 286, 289–90, 292, 298–9, 305, 306–7).

[156] Direct papal provision to church benefices was increasing throughout Europe. The
number of provisions made in England was not high compared with those made later
but the practice already caused strong resentment (Denton, *Winchelsey*, pp. 242–4;
Wright, *Reynolds*, pp. 29 and n., 275). Attacks on the provision of non-resident
foreigners were made in the parliament at Carlisle in 1307 and repeated at Stamford
in 1309 (*RP*, i. 207a–208a, 220b–221a; *Councils and Synods with Other Documents Relating
to the English Church*, ed. F. M. Powicke and C. R. Cheney (Oxford, 1964), ii. 1236–40;
CPR 1307–13, p. 180; *Foed.*, ii. 1. 84). Cathedral offices without cure of souls were
especially attractive for foreigners, since licences for non-residence were easier to obtain.
The effect can be seen at York, where up to one-third of cathedral offices were held by
foreigners (R. B. Dobson, 'The later Middle Ages, 1215–1500', in Aylmer and Cant,
York Minster, pp. 79–80). The author's indignation may have been fired by three recent
high-profile disputes over provisions to the archdeaconry of Richmond, the deaconry of
St Paul's, and a prebend at York (Menache, *Clement V*, pp. 68–9). The law to which the
author refers is unclear. The statute of Carlisle dealt only with money sent abroad from
abbeys. However, the barons at Stamford in 1309 clearly believed they could appeal to
law: their petition, explicit in its dislike of foreign incumbents, stated that 'according to
the law of the land' any use made of church possessions which was not in line with the
intentions of the donors would lead to revocation of the original grant and return of the
property to the donors or their heirs (*SR*, i. 150–2; *Councils and Synods*, ed. Powicke and
Cheney, ii. 1236–40).

1313 spiritualia moderatur, et sic*a* princeps imperatorum*b* in temporalibus dominatur? Cur igitur papa magis presumit in clericis, quam ipsa magestas et dominacio imperialis in laicis? Imperator enim sine causa a nullo quicquam exigit; dominus papa passim cum uult mutat, confert et repetit. Domine Iesu, uel papam tolle de medio, uel potestatem minue quam presumit in populo, quia priuilegium meretur amittere qui concessa sibi abutitur potestate.[157] Quid dicam de clericis qui hiis diebus accedunt ad curiam, et multa refusa pecunia tanquam in foro uenali dignitates emunt et prebendas? Si dicamus simoniam committi, ipse papa non poterit excusari, quia simonia ultro citroque est obligatoria; sicut enim ementem ligat sic et uendentem condempnat.[158] Set forsan dicet papa se supra leges esse et per consequens legibus ligari non posse. Set non debet*c* facere quod necesse habet alios prohibere, ne inde nascantur iniurie, unde iura debent procedere.[159] Ego tamen ad presens dominum papam excuso; nec ipsum excedere credamus in aliquo, quia uel honoris gracia datur, uel ad elimosinam pape redigitur quicquid ex hac causa confertur; unde liberalitas domini pape sic excitatur, set uendicio nusquam contrahitur. Nam si quis honoris gracia in auditorio quicquam tribuit, non tamen propter hoc ipsum conducit; alioquin non ex mandato set ex conducto competeret accio.[160] Prebet*d* autem se ipsum homo et secum diligenter deliberet, an sibi*e* impetrare uel non impetrare magis expediat, quia gehenne ignis exspectat incendium qui*f* lesa consciencia tendit ad iudicium.

Interea Robertus de Brutz partes Northumbrorum uiolenter inuasit, uillas et burgos succendit, homines occidit, animalia eorum abegit, et multos ad tributum coegit. Nam ciues et incole, uidentes se sui regis defensione carere, et seuiciam Roberti de Brutz non posse sufferre, fecerunt pacem cum eo quam poterant, de termino ad terminum soluendo certum tributum. Erat autem tributum quod modico tempore sic extorserat, quasi quadraginta milia librarum.[161]

---

a sic MS; sicut Den-Y   *b* sic MS; poss. imperator He   *c* debere MS; debet He, St, Den-Y   *d* sic R; probet St, Den-Y   *e* si R; sibi Den-Y   *f* quia R; qui St, Den-Y

[157] Decretum C. 11 q.3 c.63, Corpus Iuris Canonici, col. 660.
[158] Decretum C. 1 q.1 c.6, Corpus Iuris Canonici, col. 359.
[159] Dig. viii. 5. 15, Corpus Iuris Civilis, i. 121.
[160] These were both actions for breach of contract in Roman law. But whereas mandatum was a contract of support and service entered into freely and honourably without money changing hands, conductum was a hiring or renting contract for cash. The

spiritualities, just as the prince of emperors governs in temporalities? 1313
Why therefore does the pope take more from clerks than the imperial
majesty and dominion itself does from laymen? For the emperor
demands nothing from anyone without cause; the lord pope far and
wide at will changes, bestows, and withdraws. Lord Jesus! Either take
away the pope from our midst or lessen the power that he presumes to
exercise over the people, for he who abuses the power granted to him
deserves to lose his privilege.[157] What shall I say of the clerks who
beset the Curia these days, and buy dignities and prebends with a
great profusion of cash as if in the marketplace? If we say that simony
is committed, the pope himself cannot be excused, because simony is
mutually binding; for just as it binds the purchaser so also it
condemns the seller.[158] But perhaps the pope will say that he is
above the laws and consequently cannot be bound by the laws. But he
ought not to do what of necessity he must prohibit others from doing,
lest wrongs arise from that from which rights should proceed.[159]
Nevertheless, at present I myself excuse the lord pope; we should not
believe that he oversteps the limit in any way, because whatever is
contributed for this reason is either given as a mark of respect, or is
paid in to the pope's charitable relief; by this the lord pope's
generosity is aroused in return, but a sale is nowhere contracted.
For if anyone pays anything at an audience as a mark of respect, he
does not bribe the pope by this; otherwise an action would lie not *ex
mandato* but *ex conducto*.[160] But let each man examine himself and
carefully weigh in his mind whether it is better for him to obtain or
not to obtain, for he who proffers a troubled conscience at the day of
judgement awaits the blaze of hellfire.

Meanwhile Robert Bruce violently attacked Northumbria, burned
vills and towns, killed men, drove off their cattle, and forced many to
pay tribute. For the citizens and inhabitants, seeing that their king did
not defend them, and being unable to bear the savagery of Robert
Bruce, made such peace with him as they could, paying a fixed tribute
from term to term. The tribute which he thus extorted in a short time
was of the order of forty thousand pounds.[161] He utterly destroyed, too,

technicalities of the actions therefore differed. The *actio mandati* was familiar at this time
as part of the decretalists' discussions of a vassal's obligation to his lord in war (Russell,
Just War, pp. 150–2).

[161] This is a reference to the truce from 24 June 1313 to 29 Sept. 1314 bought by
Northumberland from Robert Bruce and recorded by the Lanercost chronicler. It was
raised by a levy resembling the normal kind, and, if similar in scale to other recent
payments, amounted to £2,000 (McNamee, *Wars*, pp. 131–2). The suggestion that

1313 Muros eciam uillarum et castrorum in Scocia funditus destruxit, ne
1314 superuenienti genti Anglorum municioni forent in posterum. Cepit
autem duo castra regis Anglie munitissima, Edenburghe scilicet et
Rokesburghe; unum per prodicionem cuiusdam Vasconis qui erat
cognatus Petri de Gauestone, cui rex noster custodiam castri
tradiderat. Ipse periurus et proditor adhesit Roberto de Brutz et
castrum prodidit.*[162] Alterum castrum captum erat per industriam
Iacobi Dugelas, qui erat ex parte Scotorum.[163] Nam ipse Iacobus
quadam nocte clam ad castellum accessit, et scalas latenter allatas ad
murum apposuit; et sic per eas murum ascendit, et custodibus
dormientibus uel incautis socios introduxit; et quos reperiebat inuasit
et castrum cepit, et eodem modo castrum de Berewyke cepisset nisi
quidam canis uigiles excitasset.

Deinde Robertus de Brutz ad obsidendum castrum de Stryuelyn se
conuertit. Hoc quidem castrum dominus Edwardus rex Anglie senior
cum toto exercitu suo per tres menses et amplius obsedit antequam
capere posset. Videns igitur custos castri obsidionem iam ceptam,
uictum eorum insufficientem, Robertum et Scotos in[b] insidiis semper
latentes,[c] treugas accepit sub hoc pacto, quod aut procuraret regem
Anglie ad defendendum castrum uenire, aut, si regem ad hoc
inducere non posset, castrum indilate relinqueret; et hoc petitum
sic initum fide media confirmatur, et dies natiuitatis sancti Iohannis
baptiste pro termino assignatur.[164]

Circa principium Quadragesime[165] uenerunt nuncii ad regem
narrantes municipiorum Scocie destruccionem, castrorum capcionem
et murorum in circuitu dirupcionem. Venit et constabularius de
Stryuelyn indicans regi quale petitum necessitate compulsus inierat;
procurauit regem exercitum in Scociam ducere, castrum suum et
terram defendere.

* perdidit MS; prodidit He, St, Den-Y   b et MS; in He, St, Den-Y   c latentem
MS; latentes He, St, Den-Y

£40,000 was raised from Northumberland is clearly an exaggeration, but the total tribute
taken by Bruce was high. Harclay's treaty with Bruce in 1323 envisaged compensation of
40,000 marks (£26,666. 13s. 4d.), and Isabella's treaty in 1328 £20,000 (Stones, Anglo-
Scottish Relations, pp. 312, 336).

[162] These castles had been the spoils, along with Berwick and Stirling, of Edward I's
great campaign in 1296. Edinburgh was taken on 14 Mar. 1314 by Thomas Randolph, earl
of Moray. Edinburgh's commander was Pierre Lubaud, who joined Bruce after the castle's
capture (Barrow, Bruce, pp. 195–6; The Bruce, x. 327–8: pp. 396–9).

[163] Roxburgh was taken on the night of 19–20 Feb. by James Douglas. Douglas was a
member of a well-established but minor Lanarkshire military family, whose father died in
captivity in the Tower of London. Knighted by Bruce after Bannockburn, he took part in

the walls of the castles and towns in Scotland, lest they should later ₁₃₁₃ serve to protect the advancing English. He took two of the king of ₁₃₁₄ England's strongest fortresses, namely Edinburgh and Roxburgh; one through the treachery of a certain Gascon, who was Piers Gaveston's cousin, to whom our king had given the custody of the castle. This perjurer and traitor supported Robert Bruce and betrayed the castle.[162] The other castle was taken through the efforts of James Douglas, who was on the side of the Scots.[163] For this James came secretly to the fort one night, brought up ladders stealthily and placed them against the wall; and by this means he climbed up the wall, and led his companions upon the sleeping or careless guards; and he attacked those he found and took the castle, and he would have taken Berwick Castle in the same way except that a dog roused the watchmen.

Then Robert Bruce turned to the siege of Stirling Castle. The elder lord Edward, king of England, besieged this castle with his whole army for three months and more before he could take it. When the keeper of the castle saw that the siege had already begun, that their stores were insufficient, that Robert and the Scots lay continually in ambush, he agreed to a truce on this condition, that he would either get the king of England to come to defend the castle, or, if he could not persuade the king to do this, he would give up the castle without delay. This arrangement, entered into as described, was ratified by pledge of faith, and the day of the nativity of St John the Baptist was appointed as the deadline.[164]

About the beginning of Lent[165] messengers came to the king with news of the destruction of the Scottish towns, the capture of the castles, and the breaching of the surrounding walls. The constable of Stirling came, too, and revealed to the king what sort of deal he had been forced by necessity to enter into. He persuaded the king to lead an army to Scotland, to defend his castle and the country.

almost every military engagement thereafter, and led many of the raids into England. He became one of Bruce's most active and trusted commanders. He died 25 Aug. 1330 fighting the Muslims in Spain, bearing Bruce's embalmed heart to fulfil Bruce's vow to fight on crusade (Barrow, *Bruce*, pp. 236–40, 323–4; M. Brown, *The Black Douglases* (Lancaster, 1998), pp. 14–28; see also *DNB*, 'Douglas').

[164] 24 June 1314. Stirling castle had first fallen into English hands in 1296; the Scots retook it in 1299, and Edward I had taken it back after a siege lasting from Apr. to July 1304 (Prestwich, *Ed. I*, pp. 473, 484, 501–2). The castellan was Philip Mowbray, a Scot, who had served Edward I loyally, and had fought alongside the earl of Pembroke at Methven, 1306. He had been keeper of Stirling Castle since at least 1311 (*CDS*, no. 424).

[165] Ash Wednesday was 20 Feb. 1314; it would have been some time after that when news came of the fall of the castles.

1314 Audiens hec rex uehementer doluit, et pro castrorum capcione lacrimas continere uix potuit. Mandauit igitur comitibus et baronibus quatinus in auxilium suum uenirent, et proditorem qui se regem facit expungnarent.[166] Responderunt comites melius fore ad parliamentum omnes conuenire et ibidem unanimiter diffinire quid in hoc negocio oportet agere, quam si ita inconsulte procederent; nam et ordinaciones hoc uolunt. Dixit autem rex instans negocium magna acceleracione indigere, et ideo parliamentum exspectare non posse. Dixerunt comites ad pugnam sine parliamento uenire nolle, ne contingeret eos ordinaciones offendere. Consiliarii uero et domestici regis quidam consuluerunt regi, ut debita seruicia ab omnibus exigeret, et audacter in Scociam tenderet. Certum esse quod tot in auxilium uenirent quibus nec Robertus Brutz nec Scoti resisterent. Quid comes Gloucestrie, quid comes de Penbroke, quid comes de Herford, Robertus de Clifford,[167] Hugo de Spenser et regis familia et ceteri barones qui sunt in Anglia? Omnes hii uenient cum suis militibus: non est magna cura de reliquis comitibus. Rex igitur debita seruicia ab omnibus exegit, et commeatui necessaria prouideri mandauit.[168] Premisit quoque comitem de Penbrok cum manu militari, qui insidias Scotorum diligenter exploraret, et uiam regis in Scociam prepararet.

Omnibus itaque necessariis collectis, rex et alii magnates terre cum magna multitudine curuum[a] et quadrigarum profecti sunt in Scociam. Cumque dominus rex ad Berewyk peruenisset,[169] aliquantulum moram fecit ut uenturum exercitum exspectaret. Comes autem Lancastrie, comes Warennie, comes de Arundel et comes de Warewik

---

[a] sic MS; curruum He, St, Den-Y

[166] This chronology is not strictly correct. A campaign had already been planned before the losses of Edinburgh and Roxburgh and the attack on Stirling. A summons had been issued on 23 Dec. 1313 to muster at Berwick on 10 June 1314 (CCR 1313–17, p. 86; PW, ii. 2. 421–3).

[167] Clifford became of baronial status when he combined his Clifford inheritance in the Welsh Marches with half the Vipont estates in the north-west, inherited from his mother in 1291. This also shifted his major interest to the northern counties. He was first summoned to parliament in 1299 (CP, iii. 290–1). He was among the open critics of the king and Gaveston: he was associated with the Boulogne agreement in 1308 (for which he was dismissed from the constableship of Nottingham castle); he guaranteed that the Ordinances would not be to the prejudice of the king; and he associated himself with Gaveston's death, for which he was pardoned in Oct. 1313 (CPR 1313–17, pp. 25–6). Nonetheless, like Hereford, he joined the king at Bannockburn, without appealing to the Ordinances. His son Roger was to join Hereford and Lancaster in 1322.

[168] The service of the feudal host cum equis et armis et toto seruicio quod nobis debetis (PW, ii. 2. 421) would provide about 400 heavy cavalry. The Ordainers who refused to serve

When the king heard the news he was very much grieved, and for 1314
the capture of his castles could hardly restrain his tears. He therefore
summoned the earls and barons to come to his help and overcome
the traitor who pretends to be king.[166] The earls replied that it
would be better for all to meet in parliament and there unanimously
to decide what ought to be done in this matter, rather than to
proceed thus without consultation; moreover the Ordinances
demand this. But the king said that the present business required
the utmost speed and he could not therefore wait for parliament.
The earls said that they would not come to fight without parliament,
in case they infringed the Ordinances. Some of the king's counsellors and household officials in fact advised the king to demand their
due service from all, and to set out boldly for Scotland. It was
certain that so many would come to his help that neither Robert
Bruce nor the Scots would resist. What of the earl of Gloucester, the
earl of Pembroke, the earl of Hereford, Robert Clifford,[167] Hugh
Despenser, and the king's household and the other barons in
England? All these would come with their knights: there is no
need to worry about the other earls. The king therefore demanded
their due service from all, and ordered the necessary supplies to be
provided.[168] He sent the earl of Pembroke ahead with a force of
knights, to reconnoitre carefully for Scottish ambushes, and prepare
the king's route into Scotland.

When all the necessary supplies had been collected, the king and
the other great men of the land with a great multitude of carts and
baggage wagons set out for Scotland. When the lord king had reached
Berwick,[169] he made a short halt there to await the arrival of the army.
However, the earl of Lancaster, Earl Warenne, the earl of Arundel,

personally did so because the king had issued the summons without baronial consent to the
war, taken in parliament, as demanded by clause 9 of the Ordinances. They nonetheless
provided the minimum service (the due service) they owed. Extra cavalry forces were
raised by appealing to the fealty of tenants in chief and asking them to send additional
forces. Hereford, Gloucester, Pembroke, and many barons willingly served in 1314, and
the cavalry probably amounted to 2,000–2,500 horse. Orders to muster 21,000 infantry
were issued, although not all may have served. Willing service could be increased by offers
of reward as in 1319 (below, pp. 162–3). For Edward's forces at Bannockburn see
M. Prestwich, 'Cavalry service in early fourteenth-century England', in J. Gillingham
and J. C. Holt (eds.), *War and Government in the Middle Ages: Essays in Honour of J. O.
Prestwich* (Woodbridge, 1984), pp. 147–58, at pp. 148–52; Maddicott, *Lancaster*, pp. 157–
8; Barrow, *Bruce*, pp. 204–8; McNamee, *Wars*, pp. 125–6. Edward clearly had adequate
men and supplies at Bannockburn, as the author emphasizes again in the following
paragraph.
[169] Probably by 11 June, when the privy seal was used there (*Itin.*, p. 115).

1314 non uenerunt, set milites instructos qui debita seruicia pro eis impenderent ad exercitum premiserunt. Instante iam festo sancti Iohannis baptiste, sexto uel septimo die precedente,[170] rex noster cum uniuerso exercitu suo a Berewyk exiuit, et uersus Stryuelyn iter arripuit. Erant autem armatorum amplius quam duo milia excepta peditum turba copiosa. Fuerunt in societate illa satis sufficientes[a] ad penetrandum totam Scociam, et iudicio aliquorum, si tota Scocia collecta fuisset in unum, non exspectaret regis exercitum. Reuera hoc fatebatur tota comitiua, quod tempore nostro talis exercitus non exiuit ab Anglia. Multitudo quadrigarum, si seriatim extensa fuisset in longum, occupasset spacium uiginti leucarum.

Rex igitur, de tanta et tam clara multitudine confisus et animosus effectus, de die in diem festinanter ad locum prefixum est profectus, non tanquam exercitum ducturus ad bellum set magis profecturus ad Sanctum Iacobum.[171] Breuis erat mora capiendi sompnum, set breuior erat mora sumendi cibum; unde equi, equites et pedites, labore et fame fatigati, si minus bene rem gererent non erant culpandi.

Comes autem Gloucestrie et comes Herfordie primam aciem regebant. Die itaque Dominica, que erat beati Iohannis uigilia,[172] cum iam quandam siluam preteriissent et castrum de Stryuelyn iam appropinquarent, ecce Scoti quasi fugientes errabant sub nemore,[b] quos miles quidam Henricus de Boun[c] cum Walensibus persecutus est usque ad introitum nemoris.[173] Gestabat enim in animo quod, si Robertum de Brutz ibidem inueniret, uel morti traderet uel secum captum adduceret. Cum autem eo peruenisset, Robertus ipse a latebris silue statim exiuit;[d] uidensque predictus Henricus quod multitudini Scotorum resistere non posset, redire uolens ad socios equum retorsit; set Robertus ei restitit et securi quam manu gerebat caput ipsius contriuit. Armiger autem eius, dum dominum suum tueri uel uindicare conatur, a Scotis opprimitur.

Inicium malorum hoc! ipso eodem die satis acre bellum geritur, in

[a] sufficienter *MS*; sufficientes *He, St, Den-Y*   [b] more *MS*; nemore *He, St, Den-Y*
[c] Doun *R*; Boun *Den-Y*; *He also read, or his MS provided,* Danastre *for* Banastre, *see below*
[d] exibit *MS*; exibat *He, St*; exiuit *Den-Y*

[170] That is 17 or 18 June 1314.
[171] Santiago de Compostela in Galicia, north-west Spain, was one of the great pilgrimage centres of the period. Edward thus was acting as if hastening to a peaceful destination.
[172] That is 23 June 1314.
[173] The wood was Torwood, south of Stirling Castle, and the clash with Henry Boun

and the earl of Warwick did not come, but sent knights equipped to 1314
do their due service for them in the army. On the sixth or seventh day
before the feast of St John the Baptist,[170] our king with his whole
army left Berwick and made his way towards Stirling. The men-at-
arms numbered more than two thousand, without counting a very
large troop of foot soldiers. There were in that company quite
sufficient to penetrate the whole of Scotland, and some thought
that if the whole strength of Scotland had been gathered together,
they would not have stayed to face the king's army. Indeed all who
were present agreed that never in our time has such an army marched
out from England. The great number of wagons, if they had been
placed end to end, would have stretched for twenty leagues.

The king therefore took confidence and courage from so great and
fine an army and hurried day after day to the appointed place, not as if
he was leading an army to battle but rather as if he were going to
Santiago.[171] Short were the halts for sleep, shorter still were those for
food; hence horses, horsemen, and infantry were worn out with toil and
hunger, and if they did not bear themselves well it was not their fault.

The earl of Gloucester and the earl of Hereford commanded the
first line. On Sunday, which was the day before St John's day,[172]
when they had passed a certain wood and were approaching Stirling
Castle, the Scots were seen straggling under the trees as if in flight,
and a certain knight, Henry Boun, pursued them with the Welsh to
the edge of the wood.[173] For he had in mind that if he found Robert
Bruce there he would either kill him or carry him off captive. But
when he had come there, Robert himself came suddenly out of his
hiding place in the wood, and the said Henry seeing that he could not
resist the crowd of Scots, turned his horse intending to return to his
companions; but Robert opposed him and struck him on the head
with an axe that he carried in his hand. His squire, trying to protect or
rescue his lord, was overwhelmed by the Scots.

This is the beginning of their troubles! On the same day a sharp

(or Bohun) took place at its northern end at New Park (Barrow, *Bruce*, pp. 209–13, 218).
Henry Bohun was among the group which left Edward I's army prematurely in 1306 to
attend a tournament and which was pardoned in 1307; he was possibly a nephew of the earl
of Hereford (*CCR 1302–7*, p. 482; *The Bruce*, xii. 25–59: pp. 448–51). Hearne read (or his
manuscript gave) Doun, and Tout noted that Doun was a well-known Welsh name (*Ed. II*,
p. 339). However, in the light of Hearne's reading (or the manuscript's provision) of
Danastre for Banastre later, and of the clear record of Henry Bohun in the lists of those
dead at Bannockburn (*The Bruce*, as above; *Ann. Lond.*, p. 231; *Cont. Trivet*, p. 14), it is
certain that we should read Boun.

1314 quo comes Gloucestrie ab equo deicitur, in quo Robertus de Clifford turpiter in fugam conuertitur, set et homines nostri diu Scotos persequentur,[a] multi ex utraque parte perimuntur. Quia uero inclinata erat iam dies conuenit totus exercitus ad locum ubi ipsa nocte reclinaret. Set nulla erat quies; totam enim illam duxerunt insompnem; putabant namque Scotos pocius insultum dare de nocte quam bellum expectare de die. Mane[174] autem facto certo cercius compertum est Scotos paratos ad prelium cum magna multitudine armatorum. Vnde homines nostri, milites scilicet ueterani, et hii qui magis erant experti, consilium dederunt ipso die non esse pungnaturum,[b] set diem crastinum magis expectandum, tum propter solempne festum, tum propter laborem preteritum. Vtile quidem et honestum erat consilium apud iuuenes reprobatum, inhers et ignauum[c] reputatum.

Comes autem Gloucestrie consuluit[d] regi ne ipso die in bellum prodiret, set propter festum pocius uacaret, et exercitum suum ualde recrearet. Set rex consilium comitis spreuit, et prodicionem et preuaricacionem sibi imponens in ipsum uehementer excanduit.[e] 'Hodie,' inquid comes, 'erit liquidum quod nec proditor nec preuaricator sum', et statim parauit se ad pungnandum. Interim Robertus de Brutz socios monuit et instruxit, panem et uinum prebuit, et modo quo potuit confortauit; ubi uero didicit acies Anglorum in campum deuenisse totum exercitum suum eduxit de nemore. Circiter quadraginta milia hominum secum produxit, ipsosque in tres turmas diuisit; et nullus eorum equm ascendit, set erat unusquisque eorum leui armatura munitus, quam non faciliter penetraret gladius. Securim habebant ad latus et lanceas ferebant in manibus. Ibant eciam quasi sepes densa conserti,[f] nec leuiter potuit talis turma penetrari.[175] Cum autem ad hoc uentum esset ut congredi simul oporteret, Iacobus Douglas, qui prime turme Scotorum preerat, aciem comitis Gloucestrie acriter inuasit. Et comes ipsum uiriliter[g] excepit, semel et iterum cuneum penetrauit, et triumphum utique reportasset si fideles socios habuisset. Set ecce, subito irruentibus Scotis equus comitis occiditur et comes in terram labitur. Ipse eciam defensore carens et mole corporis nimis oneratus faciliter exsurgere

---

[a] sic MS; persequuntur He, St, Den-Y   [b] sic R; for pungnandum MW
[c] ignarum R; ignauum St, Den-Y   [d] consiluit MS; consuluit He, Den-Y
[e] excandauit MS; excanduit He, St, Den-Y   [f] sic MS; poss. conferti He
[g] ipsum repeated after uiriliter MS; om. He, St, Den-Y

[174] That is on 24 June 1314.

action takes place, in which the earl of Gloucester is thrown from his 1314
horse, and Robert Clifford is disgracefully put to flight, and though
our men long pursue the Scots, many are killed on each side. Because
now the day was over, the whole army gathered at the place where it
was to rest that night. But there was no rest; for they spent the whole
night sleepless, expecting the Scots rather to attack by night than to
wait for battle by day. At daybreak[174] it was abundantly clear that the
Scots were ready for the conflict with a great force of armed men.
Therefore our men, that is the veteran knights and those who were
more experienced, advised that we should not fight that day, but
rather wait for the next day, both on account of the importance of the
feast and their previous exertion. This practical and honourable
advice was rejected by the younger men as lethargic and cowardly.

The earl of Gloucester, on the other hand, counselled the king not
to go forth to battle that day, but rather to rest on account of the feast,
and let his army recuperate as much as possible. But the king scorned
the earl's advice, and grew very heated with him, charging him with
treachery and deceit. 'Today,' said the earl, 'it will be clear that I am
neither a traitor nor a liar', and at once prepared himself for battle.
Meanwhile Robert Bruce briefed his company and drew them up in
battle array, gave them bread and wine, and heartened them as best he
could; when he learned that the English line had reached the field he
led his whole army out from the wood. He brought about forty
thousand men with him, and split them into three divisions; and not
one of them was on horseback, but each was furnished with light
armour, which a sword would not easily penetrate. They had axes at
their sides and carried lances in their hands. They advanced like a
thick-set hedge, and such a troop could not easily be broken.[175]
When, however, it had come to the point that the two sides must
meet, James Douglas, who commanded the first division of the Scots,
vigorously attacked the earl of Gloucester's line. The earl withstood
him manfully, time and again he penetrated their wedge, and would
without doubt have been victorious if he had had faithful companions. But look! At a sudden rush of Scots, the earl's horse is killed
and the earl falls to the ground. Furthermore, without a defender and
burdened by the weight of its body he could not easily rise, and of the

---

[175] The number is a clear exaggeration. Bruce probably had about 500 cavalry and 5–
6,000 infantry (Barrow, *Bruce*, p. 209). The tight-packed Scottish schiltrom or wedge
formation was difficult to overcome, and is frequently mentioned by English chroniclers.
For its use at Bannockburn see Barrow, *Bruce*, pp. 220–1.

1314 non potuit, set inter quingentos armatorum quos suis sumptibus
duxerat ad bellum, ipse fere solum occubuit. Cum enim uiderent
dominum suum ab equo deiectum, stabant quasi attoniti non ferentes
auxilium. Maledicta milicia^a cuius summa necessarie^b perit audacia.
Heu! uiginti milites armati satis subuenissent comiti, set inter
quingentos fere non profuit unus. Confundat eos Dominus!

Alii dixerunt comitem Gloucestrie ex incauto processu subito
periisse. Certabant enim inter se ipse et comes Herfordie quis in acie
alterum deberet procedere,^c et comes Herfordie dicebat hoc sibi de iure
competere eo quod constabularius sit Anglie. Alius dicebat progenitores suos semper in acie primos exstitisse, et hoc ideo ad se pertinere de
consuetudine. Porro dum in hunc modum uterque certaret, et acies
Scotorum acriter appropinquaret,^d prosiluit comes Gilbertus inordinate uolens de primo congressu triumphum reportare; set ecce
irruentibus Scotis comes excipitur et equus eius statim occiditur;
quia defensore caruit ab equo deiectus, et multis uulneribus confossus,^e
turpiter occubuit. Heu! uiginti milites armati satis subuenissent comiti,
set inter quingentos fere non profuit unus. Confundat eos Dominus!

Egidius de Argentym, miles strenuus^f et in re militari multum
expertus, dum frenum regis regeret et casum comitis aspiceret,¹⁷⁶ acer
et anxius illuc properauit subuenire comiti, nec potuit. Fecit tamen
quod potuit, et cum comite simul occubuit, honestius arbitrans cum
tanto uiro subcumbere^g quam fugiendo mortem euadere; nam qui in
acie pro re publica perimuntur semper per gloriam uiuere intelli-
guntur. Eodem die Robertus de Clifford, Paganus Typetot, Willelmus Mareschal, milites preclari, potentes et strenui, a Scotos
oppresi^h ibidem occumbunt.¹⁷⁷

Videntes hii qui cum rege nostro erant aciem comitis contritam et
socios eius paratos ad fugam, dixerunt, periculosum est diucius

---

^a malicia R; milicia St, Den-Y   ^b necessarie R; necessitate St, Den-Y   ^c sic MS;
precedere He, St, Den-Y   ^d apropinquaret MS; appropinquaret He, St, Den-Y
^e confessus MS; confossus He, St, Den-Y   ^f strenuis MS; He changed his first reading of
strenuus to strenuis without comment; strenuus St, Den-Y; the copyist used strenuis again
below (p. 210) ed.   ^g sic R; succumbere St, Den-Y   ^j sic R; oppressi St, Den-Y

---

¹⁷⁶ Argentein was an active soldier, who fought in Scotland, on the Continent, and as a
crusader in the east. He was also a keen tourneyer. He left Edward I's campaigns in 1302
and 1306 to attend tournaments, was at the Dunstable tournament in 1309, and was a
leading figure as 'king of the green wood' at the following tournament in Stepney (Barker,
Tournament, pp. 127–8; H. Johnstone, Edward of Caernarvon: 1284–1307 (Manchester,
1946), pp. 116–17 and nn.). To be in charge of the king's rein was the equivalent of being
his personal bodyguard. Barbour's Bruce notes both Pembroke and Argentein as appointed
to hold the king's rein (The Bruce, xi. 180–4, xiii. 295–8: pp. 415, 495).

five hundred men-at-arms whom he had led to battle at his own 1314
expense, almost only he was killed. For when they saw their lord
thrown from his horse, they stood stunned and did not help him.
Cursed be the knighthood whose courage fails in the hour of greatest
need!

Alas! Twenty armed knights might have saved the earl, but among
some five hundred, not one was of any use. May the Lord confound
them! Some said that the earl of Gloucester had perished suddenly by
reason of his rash attack. For there was rivalry between him and the
earl of Hereford, over who should take precedence over the other in
the line, and the earl of Hereford said that this was lawfully his by
right, because he was constable of England. The other replied that his
forbears had always led the van, and therefore this was his by custom.
Then, while they argued in this fashion, and the Scottish forces were
approaching rapidly, Earl Gilbert dashed forward in disorder, seeking
to carry off the glory of the first clash; but see! the earl is met by the
onrushing Scots and his horse immediately killed; because there was
no one to defend him when he was thrown from his horse, he was
pierced by many wounds, and was shamefully killed. Alas! Twenty
armed knights might have saved the earl, but among some five
hundred not one was of any use. May the Lord confound them!

While he was in command of the king's rein, Giles Argentein, an
active knight and very experienced in the art of war,[176] saw the earl's
misfortune and rushed there, eager and anxious to help the earl, but
he could not. Yet he did what he could, and fell together with the earl,
thinking it more honourable to perish with so great a man than to
escape death by flight; for those who fall in battle for their country are
known to live in everlasting glory. On the same day Robert Clifford,
Payn Tibetot, William Marshal, famous, powerful, and active
knights, overcome by the Scots, died there.[177]

When those who were with our king saw that the earl's line was
broken and his men ready to run, they said that it would be dangerous

---

[177] Here the author probably reflects a contemporary newsletter which listed the dead.
These three names are also the first and in the same order in the long list cited in *Ann.
Lond.* (p. 231), and apart from Gloucester are, together with Argentein and Mauley, the
ones most frequently cited in contemporary chronicles. For Clifford see n. 167 above.
Tibtoft was a notable soldier and tourneyer, but also active in politics, and held the offices
of justice of the forest south of the Trent, and of justice of Chester for certain periods.
Like Clifford, he put his name to the Boulogne agreement and guaranteed the Ordinances
(Johnstone, *Ed. of Caernarvon*, pp. 116–17 and nn.; Tout, *Ed. II*, pp. 320, 337; Phillips,
Pembroke, p. 316). Marshal was an Ordainer, but clearly did not make upholding the
Ordinances an excuse not to serve at Bannockburn.

1314 morari set tucius fore regem reuerti. Ad quorum dicta rex campum reliquit et uersus castrum properauit. Porro dum uexillum regis abire conspicitur, totus exercitus cito dispergitur. Ducenti milites et amplius, qui nec gladium eduxerant nec ictum quidem protulerant, in fugam conuersi sunt.

O gens inclita multis retro temporibus inuicta, cur fugis pedites que uincere solebas equites? Apud Berewyke, Dounbar et Fou- kyrk, triumphum reportasti,[178] nunc Scotis peditibus terga dedisti. Set quicquid dicant alii, non erat tecum manus Domini. Sic Benedab fortissimus rex Syrie fugatur per pedissecos[a] principum Samarie.[179]

Dum igitur gens nostra fugeret, dum uestigia regis arriperet, ecce quedam fossa multos absorbuit, magna pars nostrorum in ipsa periit.[180] Veniens namque rex ad castrum et credens ibidem habere refugium, tanquam hostis repellitur; pons attrahitur et porta claudi- tur. Vnde custos castri a plerisque prodicionis expers non esse credebatur, et tamen in acie armatus quasi pro rege pungnaturus ipso die uidebatur.[181] Verum nec custodem absoluo, nec prodicionis accuso, set consilio Dei fateor euenisse regem Anglie castrum non intrasse, quia si tunc admissus fuisset sine capcione nequaquam euasisset.

Cum rex sic se repulsum uidisset, nec aliud refugium iam super- esset, uersus Dounbar iter arripuit, et ibidem ueniens nauem ascendit, ad portum de Berewyke cum suis applicuit. Alii uero nauem non habentes per terram ueniunt. Milites arma exuunt et nudi fugiunt; Scoti semper persequuntur[b] a tergo; quinquaginta miliaribus durauit persecucio. Multi quidem ex nostris perimuntur, et multi similiter capiuntur. Nam incole terre, qui prius pacem finxerant, nunc homines nostros passim trucidabant, quia[c] proclama- tum erat per dominum Robertum de Brutz captiuos ducere et capientes lucrum sentire. Vnde Scoti satagebant ualde magnates capere ut multam pecuniam possent extorquere. Capti sunt itaque

---

[a] pedissetos *MS*; pedissequos *He, St, Den-Y*; pedissecos *ed.*   [b] persequentur *MS*;
persequuntur *He, St, Den-Y*   [c] sic *R*; quare *Den-Y*

[178] These were the famous victories of Edward I. Berwick was captured and the battle of Dunbar won in 1296, Falkirk was won in 1298.
[179] Cf. 3 Kgs. (1 Kgs.) 20: 13–21.
[180] This is Bannock Burn, which here had steep sides (Barrow, *Bruce*, p. 229).
[181] After the English defeat, the castellan, Philip Mowbray, was obliged to surrender

to remain longer and safer for the king to retreat. On their advice the
king left the battlefield, and hurried towards the castle. Then, when
the royal standard was seen to depart, the whole army quickly
scattered. Two hundred knights and more, who had neither drawn
their swords nor even struck a blow, were reduced to flight.

Oh! Famous race unconquered through the ages, why do you, who
used to conquer knights, flee from foot soldiers? At Berwick, Dunbar,
and Falkirk you carried off the victory,[178] and now you have turned
your backs to Scottish infantry. But whatever others may say, the
hand of the Lord was not with you. Thus was Ben-hadad, a most
powerful king of Syria, put to flight by the foot soldiers of the princes
of Samaria.[179]

Then, while our people fled, following in the king's footsteps, see! a
certain ditch entrapped many of them, and a great part of our army
perished in it.[180] The king, coming to the castle and expecting to find
refuge there, was driven off as if he were an enemy; the drawbridge
was raised and the gate closed. Because of this the castellan was
thought by many to be not innocent of treason, and yet that very day
he was seen in armour in the battle line as if he was going to fight for
the king.[181] Truly I neither absolve the castellan nor accuse him of
treachery, but I think it was God's doing that the king of England did
not enter the castle, for if he had been admitted then he would never
have escaped capture.

When the king saw that he was repulsed in this way and that no
other refuge now remained to him, he set out towards Dunbar, and
coming there took ship, [and] landed with his following at the port of
Berwick. Others having no ship came by land. The knights threw
down their arms and fled without them; the Scots continually
harassed their rear; the pursuit lasted fifty miles. Many of our men
perished and many, too, were taken prisoner. For the inhabitants of
the countryside, who had previously feigned peace, now butchered
our men everywhere; whereupon it was proclaimed by Lord Robert
Bruce that they should take prisoners and hold them to ransom. So
the Scots busied themselves with taking prisoner the great men in
order to extort large sums from them. Accordingly there were

Stirling castle to the Scots, as previously agreed. Although he behaved wholly correctly at
this time, his loyalty to Edward II became suspect because he then stayed with Bruce and
later fought with Edward Bruce in Ireland. He was acknowledged as a brave soldier and
was twice praised by Barbour as a good man in a tight corner (see above, n. 164; Barrow,
Bruce, pp. 195, 217, 231; *The Bruce*, x. 812, xiv. 26: pp. 403, 521).

1314 comes de Herforde, Iohannes Gyffard,[182] Iohannes de Wylyntone,[183] Iohannes de Segraue,[184] Mauricius de Be⟨r⟩kelee,[185] barones certe magne potencie, et multi alii quos non oportet numerare, quorum multi de redempcione conueniunt, et pecuniam soluentes absoluti sunt. Non profuit ibidem cognicio, quia difficilior erat redempcio. Quingenti et amplius putabantur mortui qui captiui ducti sunt et postea redempti. Porro inter omnia aduersa hoc quidem exercitui nostro prospere contigit, quod, dum gens nostra fuge presidium quereret, magna pars Scotorum ad spolia diripienda se conuertit; quia si omnes Scoti pariter persecucioni nostrorum intendissent, pauci ex nostris Scotos euasissent. Vnde dum Robertus de Brutz cum suis quadrigas nostras inuasit, plurima pars Anglorum ad Berewyke salua peruenit. Siquidem a seculo recordor inauditum talem exercitum coram peditibus tam subito dispersum, nisi cum flos Francie coram Flandrensibus apud Coutray cecidit, ubi nobilis ille comes Artagensis Robertus occubuit.[186]

O dies ulcionis et infortunii, dies perdicionis et opprobrii, dies mala et execranda, nec in anni circulo computanda; que famam Anglorum maculauit, et spoliauit Anglicos, et Scotos ditauit, in qua preciosa supellex nostrorum dirripitur, que ducentarum milium librarum estimatur! Tot boni proceres, iuuentus ualida, tot equi nobiles, tot arma bellica, preciose uestes et uasa aurea, dies dura et breuis hora abstulit hec omnia.

Queret forsan et dicet aliquis quare percussit nos hodie Dominus, quare subcubuimus coram Scotis, cum uiginti annis preteritis semper

---

[182] John Giffard of Brimpsfield (Glos) was a rich and well-connected Marcher, at first entirely loyal to Edward. He became a royal retainer in 1316, was often at court, and was one of the additional members of the standing council appointed in 1318 (*CP*, v. 644–6; Phillips, *Pembroke*, app. 3; Cole, *Docs. Illus.*, p. 12). His Marcher lands, however, later brought conflict with the Despensers and he joined the rebellion against him. He was tried at Gloucester (*CPR 1321–4*, p. 149) and executed in 1322.

[183] John Willington, who held lands in Wiltshire, Devon, and Somerset, had a modest military and administrative career. He had been a conservator of the peace in 1308, at the Dunstable tournament in 1309, and served in the siege of Bristol in 1316. Like Giffard and Berkeley he became a contrariant, and for that he was heavily fined. His brother Henry, also a contrariant, was executed at Bristol. Both had been associates of the Berkeleys (Fryde, *Tyranny*, p. 72).

[184] John Segrave, a Lancastrian retainer, came from Leicestershire. He was the eldest brother of Nicholas and Henry, and father of Stephen, all of whom had strong Lancastrian connections (Maddicott, *Lancaster*, pp. 59, 116). He was to become a member of the original standing council nominated after the treaty of Leake, 1318 (*PW*, ii. 1. 184–5). See above, n. 31.

[185] Three Berkeleys were captured: Thomas senior, Lord Berkeley, by this time aged about 69, and his grandsons, Thomas and Maurice, sons of Maurice senior. Maurice

captured the earl of Hereford, John Giffard,[182] John Willington,[183] 1314
John Segrave,[184] Maurice Berkeley,[185] undoubtedly barons of great
power, and many others whom it is not necessary to specify, of whom
many agreed ransoms and, paying the money, were set free. Being
well known was no advantage there, because the ransom was then
more difficult to agree. More than five hundred were thought to be
dead, but were taken captive and later ransomed. In fact, amongst all
their misfortunes this one thing at least turned to the advantage of our
army, that, while our people sought safety in flight, a great part of the
Scottish army turned to plunder; because, if all the Scots had been
equally intent on the pursuit of our men, few of our men would have
escaped the Scots. So while Robert Bruce with his men attacked our
baggage train, the greater part of the English came safe to Berwick.
Indeed I think it is unheard of in our time for such an army to be
scattered so suddenly by infantry, unless when the flower of France
fell before the Flemings at Courtrai, where the noble Count Robert of
Artois was killed.[186]

Oh! day of vengeance and misfortune, day of ruin and dishonour,
evil and accursed day, not to be reckoned in our calendar, that stained
the reputation of the English, and robbed the English and enriched
the Scots, in which our men's costly belongings, valued at two
hundred thousand pounds, were snatched away! So many fine noble-
men, [and] strong young men, so many noble horses, so much
military equipment, costly garments, and gold plate—all lost in one
harsh day, one fleeting hour.

Perhaps some one will enquire and ask why the Lord smote us this
day, why we succumbed to the Scots, when for the last twenty years

senior, first son and heir of Thomas senior, escaped. The Berkeleys were one of the most
important southern Marcher families and long-standing retainers of Pembroke. Maurice
senior was becoming a major political figure at this period. He was made keeper of Berwick
1315 and justice of South Wales 1316, probably through Pembroke's influence. The
relationship was to break down in 1318. The Berkeleys transferred their allegiance to
Mortimer and were drawn into the Marcher rebellion against Despenser (*CP*, ii. 127–9;
Phillips, *Pembroke*, pp. 75 n., 261–7; W. J. Smith, 'The rise of the Berkeleys: an account of
the Berkeleys of Berkeley castle 1243–1361', *TBGAS*, lxx (1951), pp. 64–80). For the
possible relationship of the Berkeleys with John Walwayn, see Denholm-Young, 'Authorship', pp. 275–8.

[186] The battle of Courtrai took place in 1302. The defeat of cavalry and the subsequent
slaughter of knights shocked the military classes. An English political song of the time
notes how the Count of Artois tried to yield to a free man in chivalric mode, 'that y ne
have no shame ne no vylte', only to have his head cut off by a Flemish butcher who
resented paying for prisoners' food (T. Wright, *The Political Songs of England from the
Reign of John to that of Edward II*, Camden Society 1st ser. (1839), repr. with new
introduction by P. Coss (Cambridge, 1996) p. 192).

1314 uictoriam habuerimus; reuera casus antiquorum exemplum prebent, et actus Hebreorum manifeste respondent. Medorum rex Serseles potentissimus dum Grecis bellum indiceret in classe numerosa et multitudine contumaci, uix licuit uicto sola cum naue reuerti.[187] Israel dum Beniamyn expungnaret propter scelus commissum in Gabaa, de numero et fortitudine confidens, bis in prelio ceditur, bis coram Beniamyn in fugam *a* conuertitur.[188] Sic homines nostri, qui in superbia et abusione uenerunt, in ignominia et confusione redierunt. Certe superba nostrorum presumpcio *b* Scotos fecit gaudere triumpho.

De superbia modernorum, et quis fructus inde proueniat, modicum si placet lector aduertat. Hodie pauper et tenuis, qui nec obolum habet in bonis, maiorem se contempnit, et maledictum pro maledicto referre non metuit. Set ex rusticitate forsan hoc accidit. Veniamus igitur ad eos qui se putant eruditos. Quis putas maiori rixa in alium excandescit *c* quam curialis? Dum forte rancore tumescit inferiorem non respicit, parem fastidit, maiori par fieri semper intendit. Nam armiger militem, miles baronem, baro comitem, comes regem, in omni fere cultu antecedere nititur et laborat. Porro dum sumptus deficit, quia patrimonium non sufficit, ad predam se conuertunt, uicinos spoliant, subditos *d* expilant, et in ipsos Dei ministros infamem questum exercent. Hinc est quod magnates terre uel cadunt in bello, uel moriuntur sine filio, aut sexus femineus hereditatem diuidit, et nomen patris imperpetuum euanescit.

Post hec rex de consilio suorum relicta Berewike sub custodia tendit Eboracum,[189] et ibidem cum comite Lancastrie et ceteris magnatibus habuit consilium, et de suis infortuniis querit remedium.[190] Dixerunt comites ordinaciones obseruatas non esse, et iccirco regi deterius accidisse; tum quia rex ordinacionibus stare iurauerat, tum quia archiepiscopus omnes contrauenientes excommunicauerat. Vnde nichil bene posse fieri protestantur, nisi ordinaciones plenius obseruentur. Rex uero ad omnia pro communi utilitate

---

a sic R; fuga St, Den-Y   *b* sic MS; poss. et presumpcio He   *c* excadescit MS; excandescit He, St, Den-Y   *d* subitos MS; subditos He, St, Den-Y

[187] Xerxes, king of the Persians and Medes, son of Darius I, succeeded his father in 486 BC. He attacked the Greeks in 480 BC to avenge his father's defeat at the battle of Marathon (490 BC). After initial success at the battle of Thermopolae and in sacking Athens, he was defeated at the naval battle of Salamis. Information on Greek history was readily available in the Middle Ages through Roman writers (see above, pp. xxviii–xxx). For Xerxes in Greece, see Herodotus, *The Histories*, books vii–viii.

[188] Cf. Judg. 20: 21–5.

we have always been victorious; indeed antiquity offers an example, 1314
and the actions of the Hebrews clearly provide a parallel. Xerxes,
most powerful king of the Medes, when he waged war upon the
Greeks with a numerous fleet and steadfast army, was scarcely
allowed in defeat to escape with a single ship.[187] Israel when it
fought Benjamin for the crime committed in Gibeah, trusting in
numbers and courage, was twice defeated in battle, twice put to flight
before Benjamin.[188] Thus our men, who came in pride and insolence,
returned in shame and rout. Without doubt the proud arrogance of
our men made the Scots rejoice in triumph.

I shall turn for a moment, if it please the reader, to the pride of
present-day men and the fruit which it bears. Today the poor and
needy man, who has not a halfpenny to his name, despises his betters,
and is not afraid to exchange a curse for a curse. But perhaps this
arises from rusticity. Let us come therefore to those who think
themselves educated. Who do you think is inflamed with greater
malice against another than the courtier? While he is greatly puffed
up with bitter ill-feeling he ignores his inferiors, despises his equals,
is always striving to equal his betters. For in almost every aspect of
life the squire strains and strives to outdo the knight, the knight the
baron, the baron the earl, the earl the king. Moreover when they
cannot afford their expenses, because their inheritance is insufficient,
they turn to pillage, they plunder their neighbours, fleece their
tenants, and practise nefarious extortions upon the servants of God.
Hence it is that the great men of the land either fall in battle, or die
without a son, or the female sex divides the inheritance, and the name
of their father disappears for ever.

After this the king on the advice of his friends left a garrison in
Berwick and moved to York,[189] and there took counsel with the earl of
Lancaster and the other great men, and sought a remedy for his
misfortunes.[190] The earls said that the Ordinances had not been
observed, and for that reason events had turned out worse for the
king; both because the king had sworn to stand by the Ordinances and
because the archbishop had excommunicated all who opposed them.
Therefore they declared that nothing could be well done unless the
Ordinances were more fully observed. The king indeed said that he

---

[189] Edward left Berwick on 13 July 1314, and was at York by 17 July, where he stayed
until 9–10 Oct. (*Itin.*, pp. 116–19).
[190] Parliament (with commons) was summoned to York for 9 Sept. 1314 and lasted until
27–8 Sept. (*HBC*, p. 553).

1314 ordinata paratum se dixit, et se ordinaciones obseruare in bona fide promisit. Dixerunt comites nil uideri actum dum aliquid superesset [a] agendum,[191] set ⟨si⟩[b] ordinaciones debeant obseruari oportet eas execucioni demandari. Rex execucionem concessit; nichil[c] comitibus denegauit. Igitur cancellarius, thesaurarius, uicecomites et alii officiarii remouentur, et iuxta tenorem ordinacionum noui subrogantur.[192] Voluerunt eciam comites quod Hugo Despenser, Henricus de Beaumount et quidam alii curiam regis euacuarent, donec ad sibi obicienda responderent interrogatis,[d] et super obiectis satisfaccionem prestarent conuicti; set hoc ad instanciam regis differtur. Hugo tamen Despenser latitare compellitur.

De expungnacione Roberti de Brutz et recuperacione Scocie ad proximum parliamentum distulerunt, quia comes Herfordie et alii barones in uinculis detenti nondum redierunt. Lugebat autem soror regis maritum suum comitem Herfordie,[193] et dominus rex dedit ei omnes captiuos Scocie. Nam tempore regis Edwardi senioris quidam capti fuerant qui usque ad presens tempus sub carcere remanserant; inter quos erat uxor Roberti de Brutz, episcopus de Glascou', et quidam comes iuuenis, et alii milites Scotorum quindecim et amplius. Elaboratum est interim ut comes postliminio[e] rediret, set ⟨non⟩[f] promittitur, nisi multa conferret; et multa quidem offeruntur, set plura satis et que uires eius excederent exiguntur. Tandem post uarios circuitus sic actum est, ut Robertus de Brutz uxorem suam et ceteros captiuos Scotorum reciperet,[g][194] et comitem Herfordie sine mora restitueret; et hac permutacione sic facta rediit comes noster ad propria.

Post natale Domini paucis euolutis diebus dominus rex corpus Petri de Gauestone, sui quondam specialis amici, ab Oxonia ad Langeleye fecit transferri. Iam enim de capitacione ipsius biennium transiuit et amplius, et usque nunc apud fratres Oxonie iacuit

---

[a] superesse *MS*; superesset *He, St, Den-Y*   [b] *om. R*; *supplied St, Den-Y*   [c] *sic R*; nihil *St*   [d] *sic R*; interrogati *Den-Y*   [e] postlimino *MS*; postliminio *He, St, Den-Y*   [f] *om. R*; *supplied Den-Y*   [g] reciperit *MS*; reciperet *He, St, Den-Y*

[191] Lucan, *De bello civili*, ii. 657.

[192] The insistence on the Ordinances and a purge of the administration and household led in Nov. to John Sandall replacing Reynolds as chancellor and Walter Norwich replacing Sandall as treasurer. Ingelard Warley and John Ockham (who had been named in the supplementary ordinances of 1311) were dismissed at this time, but were back at the Exchequer by 1316 and 1317 respectively. The majority of sheriffs was also changed (*HBC*, pp. 86, 104; Tout, *Ed. II*, pp. 305–7; Maddicott, *Lancaster*, pp. 164–5; *List of Sheriffs, passim*).

[193] The king's sister, Elizabeth, had married the earl of Hereford on 14 Nov. 1302, after the death of her first husband John, count of Holland. She died *c*.5 May 1316 (*HBC*, p. 38).

was prepared to do everything ordained for the common good, and 1314
promised that he would observe the Ordinances in good faith. The
earls said that nothing seemed to have been done as long as anything
remained undone,[191] and if the Ordinances ought to be observed, it
was proper to ask for their execution. The king granted their
execution; he refused nothing to the earls. Therefore the chancellor,
the treasurer, the sheriffs, and other officials were removed and new
ones were put in their place according to the text of the Ordinances.[192] The earls also wanted Hugh Despenser, Henry Beaumont,
and certain others to leave the king's court, until they should answer
certain matters put to them, and if convicted give satisfaction in the
matters raised; but at the king's request this was put off. Nevertheless
Hugh Despenser was forced to keep out of the way.

They postponed discussion of the struggle against Robert Bruce
and the recovery of Scotland until the next parliament, because the
earl of Hereford and other barons held captive had not yet returned.
However, the king's sister lamented for her husband, the earl of
Hereford,[193] and the lord king gave to her all the Scottish captives.
For in the time of the elder King Edward some had been captured
who had remained in prison until the present time; among them was
the wife of Robert Bruce, the bishop of Glasgow, a certain young earl,
and fifteen or more other Scottish knights. Meanwhile it was worked
out how the earl might return home, but this was only promised if a
large amount was paid; much indeed was offered, but even more was
demanded, beyond his ability to pay. At length after various toings
and froings it was decided that Robert Bruce should receive back his
wife and the other Scottish captives,[194] and he should restore the earl
of Hereford without delay; and when this exchange had been made
our earl returned home.

A few days after Christmas, the lord king had the body of Piers
Gaveston, once his intimate friend, brought from Oxford to Langley.
For now two years and more had gone by since he was beheaded, and
until now he had lain unburied with the friars at Oxford. For, it is

---

[194] Elizabeth de Burgh, daughter of Richard de Burgh, earl of Ulster, was Bruce's
second wife. She was captured in 1306 after the battle of Dail Righ, along with his sister
Mary and his daughter Marjorie. Robert Wishart, bishop of Glasgow (1273–1316), was
captured earlier the same year at Coupar. The earl was Donald of Mar, who was also
captured in 1306 after the battle either of Methven or of Dail Righ (Barrow, *Bruce*,
pp. 153, 160–1, 274). They were sent to Carlisle on 2 Oct. to be exchanged for
Hereford, but Mar elected to stay with Edward (*CPR 1313–17*, p. 183; Barrow, *Bruce*,
p. 274).

1314 inhumatus. Proposuerat namque rex, ut dicitur, prius mortem Petri
uindicasse, deinde corpus eius sepulture tradidisse. Set iam reuocati
1315 in amiciciam sunt ex quibus uidebatur rex petere uindictam. Rex
apud Langeleye, ubi fratribus predicatoribus iam pridem domum
construxit, corpus sui Petri honorifice sepeliuit.

Deinde ad purificacionem beate Marie[195] conueniunt Londoniis
comites et barones uniuersi, de statu regis et regni et de expungnacione Scotorum tractaturi.[196] Et in primis eiecerunt a consilio regis
Hugonem Despenser, et Walterum de Langetone episcopum Cestrie,
olim thesaurarium domini regis Anglie.[197] Postea remouerunt a curia
regis familiam superfluam, regi et terre nimis onerosam, ut dicebatur.
Ex illa remocione expense regis cotidiane in decem libris sunt
diminute.[198] Cepit igitur parliamentum pacifice tractari et usque ad
finem Quadragesime fere protelari.[199]

In hoc parliamento, quia negociatores in uendendis[a] uictualibus
per patriam transeuntibus modum excesserunt, comites et barones,
rei publice prospicientes, huic morbo medelam apposuerunt; unde in
bobus, porcis et ouibus, in auibus, pulcinis et columbis, et in ceteris
communibus uictualibus certum precium statuerunt. Prouisum est
eciam et concessum ut Vascones uina sua ad portus Anglie transue-
herent, et ibidem tonellum secundum precium in parliamento
taxatum uenderent, nec Anglici ulterius tanquam forstallarii ad
querenda uina transfretarent. Hec omnia per terram sic diuulgantur
et in comitatibus ⟨et⟩[b] burgis publice proclamantur.[200]

---

[a] uendidis MS; uenditis or uendendis He; uendendis St, Den-Y   [b] om. MS; ac He; et St, Den-Y

[195] 2 Feb. 1315.
[196] Parliament (with commons) was summoned to Westminster for 20 Jan., and the commons were dismissed 9 Mar. (HBC, p. 553).
[197] The elder Despenser was removed as keeper of the forest south of the Trent on 19 Feb. 1315 and investigations into complaints took place in Feb. and July (CFR 1307–19, p. 230; CPR 1313–17, pp. 309, 407–8). Langton had been treasurer from Sept. 1295 to Aug. 1307, and also briefly from Jan. to May 1312 without baronial assent. He held the bishopric of Coventry and Lichfield, which was still frequently known as the bishopric of Chester, from 1296 to his death on 9 Nov. 1321 (HBC, pp. 104, 253).
[198] The lack of household accounts before Dec. 1314 and the general difficulty of interpreting the surviving accounts make estimates difficult. Edward's household expenses ran at about £30 a day in 1314–16, and even rose gently to £33 a day in 1316–17. They then steadily fell and by 1318–19 were £10 less at c. £23 a day. Later household pruning thus seems to have had more effect than the earlier strictures. Edward's expenses do not seem grossly extravagant. At £8,311 in 1318–19 royal expenses were less than double the household expenses of Lancaster (Tout, Ed. II, p. 93; Tout, Chapters, vi. 84–5; Maddicott, Lancaster, p. 27).
[199] Counsellors were reconvened for 13 Apr. to deal with unfinished business, such as

said, the king had proposed first to avenge Piers's death and then to 1314
lay his body in the grave. But already those from whom the king
seemed to seek vengeance have been readmitted to friendship. The 1315
king buried Piers's body with honour at Langley, where he had long
since built the Dominicans a house.

Then at the purification of the Blessed Mary[195] the earls and all the
barons met at London, to discuss the state of the king and the realm,
and the conquest of the Scots.[196] And first they removed Hugh
Despenser from the king's council, and Walter Langton, bishop of
Chester, formerly treasurer of the lord king of England.[197] Next they
removed from the king's court the unnecessary members of his
household, exceedingly burdensome to the king and to the country,
it was said. By that move the king's daily expenses were reduced by
ten pounds.[198] Parliament therefore began to discuss matters peaceably and it dragged on almost to the end of Lent.[199]

In this parliament, because merchants going about the country
selling victuals charged excessive prices, the earls and barons, looking
to the welfare of the state, applied a remedy to this affliction; they
established a fixed price for oxen, pigs, and sheep, for fowls, chickens,
and pigeons, and for other common foods. It was also provided and
granted that the Gascons should transport their wines to English
ports, and sell them there by the cask according to the price assigned
in parliament, and that Englishmen should not in future cross the sea
seeking wine, as forestallers so to speak. These matters were
published thus throughout the land, and publicly proclaimed in
shire courts and boroughs.[200]

petitions, which had been delayed by the main business of reform and Scotland. This
continuation was still in session 30 Apr. 1315 (*HBC*, p. 553).

[200] The ordinance on prices was issued on 13 Mar. 1315. Different prices were fixed for
London and the countryside (*CCR 1313–18*, pp. 160–1; *RP*, i. 295; *Lib. Cust.*, p. 678).
This concern with prices (other than of grain) came before the famine years, and rising
prices were probably largely due to monetary inflation (M. Mate, 'High prices in early
fourteenth-century England: causes and consequences', *EcHR*, 2nd ser., xxviii (1975), 1–
16; for a good brief survey of the problem and its historiography, see M. Allen, 'The
volume of English currency, 1158–1470', *EcHR*, 2nd ser., liv (2001), 595–611). The
ordinance was repealed in 1316 (below, pp. 120–1 and n. 235). The concern with wine
prices was shown with an order on 10 Apr. against forestalling, the practice of buying
goods before they reached the open market in order to create scarcity and drive up prices.
This was followed on 30 May by a separate ordinance fixing retail wine prices at 3 pence
the gallon (*CCR 1313–18*, pp. 182, 227). Gascon merchants and London retailers objected
to the fixing of wine prices, and in Oct. 1315 it was agreed that wines imported before the
ordinance might be sold at 'reasonable' prices. Prices were allowed to rise to 5 pence a
gallon in 1316 (M. K. James, *Studies in the Medieval Wine Trade* (Oxford, 1971), pp. 11–
12; *Let. Bk. E*, pp. 44, 72).

1315   Mauricius de Berkelee curam et custodiam uille de Berewik accepit,[201] unde ad eam tuendam sine dilacione iter arripuit. Est autem Berewyke uilla fortis et bene murata in inicio Scocie super mare posita, mercatoribus in tempore pacis satis accommoda;[a] que si prodicione non fraudetur nunquam Scocie subicietur; obsidionem non formidat, dum tamen Anglia sibi succurrat. Naues enim Anglicane totam terram circuerunt,[b] et in arte nauigandi et in conflictu nauali principatum gerunt; unde si tota Scocia Berewyk inuaderet, a parte maris timeri non oportet.

Exiit preterea a curia regis preceptum publicum, ne quis arma uel bladum uel aliquod genus uictualium ad Scotos transferret; si quis autem huius precepti transgressor inueniretur, tanquam proditor et hostis publicus puniretur. Vnde Iohannes Bodecourtus[c] [202] cum manu armata ex parte una, et alii magnates ex altera, meatus marinos obseruabant, et ne quid in subsidium hostium differretur[d] summo opere procurabant. Itaque opere et opera eorum in breui sic actum est ut tanta esset apud Scotos bladi penuria quod pro centum solidis uenderetur quarterium frumenti in Scocia. Missi sunt eciam ad partes Northumbrorum comes de Penbrok et Bartholomeus de Bades-mere[e] [203] cum quingentis armatis ad fines illos tuendos et ad frequentes insultus Scotorum propulsandos, ut sic uirtus eorum undique lacessita, et machinacio eorum pro parte refrenata, minus proficeret ad singula.

Dum hec aguntur in Anglia, Robertus de Brutz de aliis negociis deliberat in Scocia. Nam exercitum copiosum adunauit, et ciuitatem de Cardoil obsedit.[204] Sane hec urbs Scotis semper erat odiosa, hec urbs Scotis semper formidanda, incursus eorum frequenter excepit et

---

[a] acomoda *MS*; accommoda *He, St, Den-Y*   [b] sic *R*; circueunt *St, Den-Y*   [c] sic *R*; Bodetourtus *St, Den-Y*   [d] sic *MS*; or deferretur *He*   [e] sic *R*; Badlesmere *St, Den-Y*

---

[201] For his indenture, dated 18 Apr. 1315, see Davies, *Opposition*, app., no. 46.

[202] Botetourt was appointed admiral of the northern fleet on 15 Mar. 1315, while William Cray was put in command of a combined Welsh, Irish, and Cinque Port fleet (presumably operating off the west coast) on 29 May 1315 (*HBC*, p. 136). Botetourt, an East Anglian landowner, was one of Edward I's bannerets by 1298, but not, as has been suggested, his illegitimate son (Prestwich, *Ed. I*, pp. 131–2). He served in Gascony and Scotland and had considerable administrative and judicial experience. He was one of the Boulogne group in 1308, one of the guarantors that the Ordinances would not be prejudicial to the king in 1310, and supported the execution of Gaveston, but he associated himself with Hereford and Clifford rather than Warwick and Lancaster (Maddicott, *Lancaster*, p. 152). Thereafter he served the king loyally, becoming a royal indentured retainer from 1316–17 until shortly before his death in 1324 (Phillips, *Pembroke*, pp. 149, 314).

Maurice Berkeley received the keeping and custody of the town of 1315 Berwick,[201] and he at once set out to defend it. Berwick is a strong and well-walled town situated on the coast on the borders of Scotland, very convenient for merchants in time of peace, a town which will never be subject to Scotland unless it is cheated out of us by treachery. It fears no siege while England supports it. For English ships sail round the whole land, and both in the art of navigation and naval warfare they are supreme; so that if the whole of Scotland attacked Berwick, nothing would be feared from the sea.

Besides all this a public edict went out from the king's court that no one should carry arms or grain or any kind of food to the Scots; if anyone should be found breaking this edict, he would be punished as a traitor and public enemy. So John Botetourt[202] with an armed squadron on the one side, and some other great men on the other, kept a watch on the maritime approaches, and did their utmost to ensure that nothing was carried over to help the enemy. Consequently their labour and care resulted in a short space of time in the Scots being so short of grain that a quarter of wheat was sold for a hundred shillings in Scotland. Furthermore the earl of Pembroke and Bartholomew Badlesmere[203] were sent to Northumbria with five hundred men-at-arms to protect the borders and repel the frequent attacks of the Scots, so that with their strength challenged on all sides and their plots to some extent held in check, they would profit less on each occasion.

While these things were happening in England Robert Bruce was considering other things in Scotland. For he collected a large force and laid siege to the city of Carlisle.[204] This city was indeed always hateful to the Scots; it was always feared by them, for it frequently intercepted

---

[203] Badlesmere, from a Kent family, was a member of Gloucester's household. He served on the council while Gloucester was keeper of the realm in 1311, accompanied Gloucester and the queen to Paris in 1314, and transferred to the royal household after Gloucester's death, with terms of indenture similar to those of the earl of Hereford. He worked closely with Pembroke and was on the king's council from 1316. He was made an additional member of the standing council and a member of the reforming committee in the York parliament, 1318. He was steward of the household 20 Oct. 1318–14 June 1321. Why he swung towards the Marchers in 1321 is unclear. His treason was greater for being committed while he still held the stewardship, and for this his head was spiked on the city gate of Canterbury (Phillips, *Pembroke*, pp. 143–5; Davies, *Opposition*, pp. 427–9, 209 n.; *HBC*, p. 76).

[204] Carlisle was blockaded by 14 July; the full siege was under way by 22 July and lasted until 1 Aug. 1315 (H. Summerson, *Medieval Carlisle: The City and the Borders from the Late-Eleventh to the Mid-Sixteenth Century*, Cumberland and Westmorland Antiquary and Archaeological Society, extra ser., xxv (1994), i. 216–19).

1315 uolatus eorum multociens impediuit. Hanc igitur si capere posset, usque ad Nouum Castrum nullus sibi resisteret. Premiserat*a* quoque fratrem suum Edwardum cum electa manu militum in Hiberniam, qui gentem illam aduersus regem Anglie excitaret, et terram si posset sue dominacioni subiceret.[205] Et erat rumor quod, si ibidem ad uotum proficeret, statim ad partes Wallie se transferret, et Walenses similiter contra regem nostrum procuraret. Hec enim duo genera faciliter in rebellionem excitantur, et iugum seruitutis egre ferentes dominacionem Anglorum execrantur.

Iusticiarius autem Hibernie, Edmundus Botiler nomine,[206] audiens Scotos in terram de Huluestre appulisse, de fidelibus regis congregauit exercitum, et Scotis eorumque fautoribus fecit insultum. In primo autem congressu fugati sunt Scoti ad montana quasi greges ouium dispersi per pascua. Habitant siquidem in montanis et nemoribus illius terre Hibernienses siluestres, terras non colunt, set de animalibus et eorum lacticiniis uiuunt; et, si quandoque panibus indigeant, ad uillas Anglorum super maritima descendunt; uendunt autem animalia et comparant sibi frumenta. Hos et eorum regulos associauit sibi Edwardus contra Anglicos. Si comes de Huluestre fuerit fidelis, non est enim timendum ab eorum insidiis.[207]

Exiuit interim falsus rumor per totam Angliam quod exercitus noster de Hibernia Scotos disperserat, quod Edwardus de Brutz perierat, quod uix unus ex Scotis uiuus remanserat. Vnde Robertus de Brutz tum propter rumores desperatos, tum quia audiuit comitem Penbrokye cum multis armatis nouiter aduenire, obsidionem reliquit, et uersus Scociam iter arripuit. Videntes hii qui erant infra ciuitatem quod exercitus Scotorum recederet,*b* ⟨exierunt⟩*c* post eos, diu persequentes*d* a tergo. Vnde in illa persecucione multi ex Scotis perierunt, plures uero lesi, et quidam remanserunt captiui.

Mirabitur forsan aliquis in posterum quomodo gens Scotorum audaciam resistendi concepit, et cur sic repente uirtus Anglorum

a promiserat *MS*; premiserat *He, St, Den-Y*   *b* resideret *R*; recederet *St, Den-Y*   *c* om. *R*; supplied *St, Den-Y*   *d* sic *MS*; poss. persequebantur *He*

[205] Edward Bruce arrived in Larne on 26 May 1315 (Lydon, 'Impact', p. 282).

[206] Butler was justiciar from 4 Jan. 1315 until 6 May 1318, at first alone then from 23 Nov. 1316 under Roger Mortimer, the king's lieutenant. He had also served as deputy justiciar in 1304–5 and 1312–14. He had collected an army against Bruce by July 1315, but he and the earl of Ulster failed to coordinate, and the Scots beat Ulster at the battle of Connor on 20 Sept. 1315. Butler was cleared of suspicion of collusion with the Scots in 1320 (*HBC*, p. 162; Lydon, 'Impact', pp. 286–94, 295). This statement of an early government success against the Scots cannot be substantiated. Either the author is

their raids and many times hindered their flight. If, therefore, he could 1315
take this place there would be no one to resist him as far as Newcastle.
He had also sent his brother Edward to Ireland with a picked force of
knights, to stir up that people against the king of England, and subject
the country, if he could, to his authority.[205] And there was a rumour
that, if he gained his desire there, he would at once cross to Wales, and
raise the Welsh likewise against our king. For these two races are easily
roused to rebellion; they bear the yoke of slavery reluctantly, and curse
the lordship of the English.

The justiciar of Ireland, however, Edmund Butler by name,[206]
hearing that the Scots had landed in Ulster, assembled an army of the
king's loyal men, and attacked the Scots and those who helped them.
At the first clash the Scots were driven to the hills like flocks of sheep
scattered over the pastures. Since the Irish are woodland people and
dwell in the mountains and forests of their country, they do not
cultivate the land, but live on their livestock and the dairy produce
from them; and if from time to time they need bread, they come down
to the English towns on the coast; they sell livestock and buy grain.
With these people and their kinglets Edward allied himself against the
English. If the earl of Ulster is loyal there is nothing to be feared from
their plots.[207]

A false report meanwhile spread throughout England that our
army in Ireland had scattered the Scots, that Edward Bruce had
perished, and that hardly one of the Scots had remained alive. Hence
Robert Bruce, both on account of these wild stories and because he
heard that the earl of Pembroke had recently arrived with many men-
at-arms, gave up the siege and set out towards Scotland. When those
who were within the city saw that the Scots were leaving, they moved
out after them, pursuing them for a long time. Many of the Scots
perished in that pursuit, very many were wounded, and some were
left behind as prisoners.

Someone hereafter may perhaps wonder how the Scottish race had
the boldness to resist, and why the courage of the English should have

repeating the rumour mentioned immediately below (which he clearly knows to be wrong)
or 'Scotos' is possibly written in error.
[207] Richard de Burgh, earl of Ulster, was closely linked to England through the Clare
family by marriages of his daughter Maud to Gilbert, earl of Gloucester, and of his son John
to Gilbert's sister Elizabeth (see above, n. 23). This link was broken by the deaths of John in
June 1313 and of Gilbert at Bannockburn in 1314, but Ulster remained loyal to England.
Nevertheless, because another daughter had married Robert Bruce, rumours of Ulster's
collusion with his son-in-law were frequently recorded (Lydon, 'Impact', pp. 116–19).

1315 defecerit. Reuera populus sine duce facile dispergitur, et membra
deficiunt cum caput deprimitur. Olim reges Anglie, dum contra
hostes erigerent uexillum, quindecim comites et plures sequebantur
ad bellum. Nunc autem quinque uel sex tantum regi nostro ferunt
auxilium. Comitatus Cornubie, Marescallie et Cestrie in manu regis
sunt hodie. Comes Lyncolnie nuper obiit, comes Glouernie in bello
cecidit, et comes Warewykye infirmus occubuit.[208]

De comite Gloucestrie censeo[a] dolendum quia tam potens et
iuuenis tam premature decessit, quod heredem de corpore suo non
reliquit, et tamen uxor eius comitissa per annum iam et amplius
expectatur paritura; et licet nunc pareret non uideo quo iure puer
hereditatem uendicaret, quia iure cauetur quod, si posthumus ultra
undecimum mensem natus fuerit, hereditatem defuncti uendicare
non poterit.[209] Igitur si hereditas comitis ad sorores descendat, tres
partes fieri continget, et scutum quod semper fuit integrum iam erit
tripertitum. Set comes Warewykye ⟨si⟩ in uiuis[b] ⟨fuisset⟩[c] fuisset, tota
patria pro eo: consilio eius ⟨et⟩[d] ingenio ordinaciones prodierunt, et
ceteri comites eo audito multa fecerunt; in prudencia et consilio non
habuit similem. Heredem reliquit set ualde iuuenem. Credo constanter quod hec uindicta Dei, hec mutacio dextere Excelsi,[210] propter
peccata et scelera nostra duces nostros preripiat, et populus terre
indefensus intereat.

Temeritatis quidem argui possem si patriam meam, si proprium
genus, infamarem; set, si uera loqui licet aut conuenit, gens Anglorum
pre ceteris nacionibus in tribus excedit, in superbia, in dolo et in
periurio. Modernos homines et maxime iuuenes reputo superbos quia
contumaces, et cum superbia inicium sit omnium malorum, abierunt
hodie de uicio[e] in uicium, de superbia in dolum et periurium. In omni
regno circa mare Grecum reperies multos de genere Anglorum, et
uulgo dicitur et fama nunciat quod in hiis pre ceteris dolus habitat.
Est et species doli maxima et quidem frequens in Anglia; de hiis
loquor qui mutuum accipiunt et statutis diebus debitum non soluunt.

---

[a] senseo *MS*; censeo *He, St, Den-Y*   [b] uicinius *MS*; si in uiuis *He, Den-Y*;
unianimis *St*   [c] *om. MS*; *supplied to accompany* si in uiuis *He, Den-Y*   [d] *om. MS*;
supplied He, St, Den-Y   [e] de *om. R*; de *supplied before* uicio *St, Den-Y*

[208] Lincoln died on 5 Feb. 1311; Gloucester died at Bannockburn on 24 June 1314;
Warwick died on 12 Aug. 1315 (*HBC*, pp. 470, 463, 486).
[209] It is not clear what law the author had in mind. Bracton does not specify eleven
months, simply writing of one born 'so long after' his father's death that it is impossible

so suddenly failed them. In truth, a leaderless people is easily 1315
scattered and the limbs fail when the head is removed. Formerly
fifteen earls and more followed the kings of England to war, when
they raised their standard against the enemy. Now, however, only five
or six bring aid to our king. The earldoms of Cornwall, of the
Marshal, and of Chester are today in the king's hand. The earl of
Lincoln recently died, the earl of Gloucester fell in battle, and the earl
of Warwick lay ill.[208]

I think we must grieve for the earl of Gloucester, because so
powerful and youthful a man died so early that he left no heir of his
body, and yet the countess his wife has been expected to give birth for
a year or more; and if she should now give birth, I do not see by what
right the boy could claim the inheritance, because it is decreed by law
that if a posthumous child is born after the eleventh month, it cannot
claim the inheritance of the deceased.[209] Thus, if the earl's inheritance
descends to sisters, it will fall into three parts and the shield that was
always whole will thenceforth be in three parts. But if the earl of
Warwick had been alive, the whole country would have been behind
him: the Ordinances came from his advice and skill, and other earls
did many things only after listening to him; in wisdom and counsel he
had no like. He left an heir, but very young. I firmly believe that this
judgement of God, this change of the right hand of the Most High,[210]
carries off our leaders for our sins and crimes, and leaves the people of
the land defenceless.

I could indeed be accused of irresponsibility if I attacked the good
reputation of my country, my own people; but, if it is right and
proper to speak the truth, the English race excel other nations in three
qualities, in pride, in deceit, and in perjury. Present-day men,
especially young ones, I regard as proud because they are insolent
and, since pride is the beginning of all evils, they have gone today
from vice to vice, from pride to deceit and perjury. In every kingdom
bordering the Mediterranean you will find many of the English race;
it is commonly said and rumour relates that deceit resides in them
above all others. There is indeed a very great kind of deceit that is
common in England; I speak of those who accept a loan and fail to pay
the debt on the appointed days. Indeed, he who withholds what he

that the child is legitimate (Bracton, *De Legibus*, iv. 299, 304). The *Digest* does not
appear to consider very late posthumous birth (*Dig.* xxxvii. 9. 1 (14), *Corpus Iuris Civilis*,
i. 556).
[210] Ps. 76: 11 (77: 10).

1315 Iam^a dolo facit qui detinet quod enim^b restituere oportet.[211] Omne
malicie potest obuiari, set mali debitores non possunt castigari. Si non
mutuo, inimicus ero; si repeto, amicicias perdo. Quid ergo melius est,
non mutuando inimicum habere, quam^c mutuum perdere et inimicitias
nichilominus incurrere? Merlinus de nobis^d ait ue genti periure,[212]
ostendens propter periurum^e aliquod excidium nobis euenire.

Omnes fere lites et placita que agitantur in regis curia per assisas
terminantur in patria. Porro cum ad assisam uentum fuerit, qui plus
dare sufficit proculdubio optinebit. Heu omnis religio, omnis dignitas, et omnis potestas cedit precio. Hinc quidam festiue ait,

> Manus ferens munera pium facit impium;
> Nummus iungit federa dat^f nummus consilium.
> Nummus in prelatis est pro iure satis,
> Vos qui iudicatis nummo locum datis.[213]

Per alia quedam signa apparet manus Dei contra nos extenta. Nam
anno preterito tanta fuit habundancia pluuie quod uix licuit hominibus frumenta colligere uel horreo^g salua recondere. Anno uero
presenti deterius euenit. Nam inundacio pluuiarum omne fere
semen consumpsit, in tantum ut^h uaticinium Ysaye iam uideretur
expletum esse; ait enim decem iugera uinearum faciunt lagunculam
unam, et triginta modii sementis faciunt modios tres.[214] Et in
pluribusque locis fenum tam diu sub aquis latuit quod nec falcari
nec colligi potuit. Oues autem communiter perierunt et alia animalia
subita peste ceciderunt.[215] Valde autem nobis timendum est ne, si

---

^a sic R; nam St   ^b sic R; eum St   ^c quasi MS; quam He, St, Den-Y   ^d uobis
R; nobis Den-Y   ^e sic MS; periurium He, St, Den-Y   ^f dati MS; datus He; dat St,
Den-Y   ^g horeo MS; horreo He, St, Den-Y   ^h uel MS; ut He, St, Den-Y

---

[211] *Dig.* xvii. 1. 8 (9), *Corpus Iuris Civilis*, i. 215. The reference to the English around the
Mediterranean is interesting but difficult to explain. English merchants rarely went so far
at this time, but the reference may be to churchmen, lawyers, pilgrims, or to those who
had joined later crusades.

[212] *Geoff. Mon.*, vii. 4, *Ve periure genti, quia urbe inclyta propter eam ruet.* Merlin's
prophecies in Geoffrey of Monmouth's *Historia Regum Britanniae* are largely unintelligi-
ble, but they were clearly intended to show that Welsh resistance to the Anglo–Saxons
would eventually be successful (*The Historia Regum Britanniae of Geoffrey of Monmouth*,
ed. A. Griscom (London and New York, 1929), pp. 383–97; a modern translation is found
in Geoffrey of Monmouth, *The History of the Kings of Britain*, ed. L. Thorpe (Harmonds-
worth, 1966), pp. 170–85). For a discussion of the sources for Merlin and his prophecies,
see J. Tatlock, *The Legendary History of Britain: Geoffrey of Monmouth's Historia Regum
Britanniae and its Early Vernacular Versions* (Berkeley and Los Angeles, 1950), pp. 171–6,
403–21. Because Geoffrey's history provided the basis for the early sections of the French
prose Brut chronicle, very popular in the late 13th and 14th cc., Merlin's prophecies

truly ought to restore is employing deceit.[211] All ill-will can be 1315
resisted but bad debtors cannot be subdued. If I do not lend I shall
be an enemy, if I seek repayment I lose friendships. Which, therefore,
is the better: by not lending to make an enemy, or to lose the loan and
none the less incur enmity? Merlin says of us, 'Woe to a perjured
race',[212] showing that for perjury some destruction will befall us.

Almost all the lawsuits and pleas started in the king's court are
brought to an end by assizes in the provinces. Then when it comes to
an assize, he who can give more will certainly win. Alas! every
religious institution, every high office, every authority has its price.
Hence someone says in jest:

> Some men bring us presents, changing right to wrong;
> Money seals our treaties, money sings its song.
> Money for the prelacy surely will suffice,
> You who sit in judgment are paid for your advice.[213]

By certain other portents the hand of God appears to be raised
against us. For in the past year there was such plentiful rain that men
could scarcely harvest the wheat or store it safely in the barn. In the
present year worse has happened. For the floods of rain have rotted
almost all the seed, to such an extent that the prophecy of Isaiah
might seem now to be fulfilled, for he says that ten acres of vineyard
shall yield one little measure and thirty bushels of seed shall yield
three bushels.[214] And in many places the hay lay so long under water
that it could neither be mown or gathered. Sheep commonly died and
other animals were killed by a sudden pestilence.[215] It is greatly to be

became even better known—but in a different form. In the French prose Brut they were
rewritten to reflect more clearly the reigns of Henry III, Edward I, and Edward II, and
their significance was specifically explained after each of these reigns (*Brut*, pp. 72–6, 177–
8, 203–4, 243–7). For interest in political prophecies in Edward II's reign, see J. R.
S. Phillips, 'Edward II and the Prophets', in W. M. Ormrod (ed.), *England in the
Fourteenth Century* (Woodbridge, 1986), pp. 196–201; R. M. Haines, *King Edward II: His
Life, his Reign, and its Aftermath, 1284–1330* (Montreal and London, 2003), pp. 23–35.

[213] This verse was very widely known in the Middle Ages (Walther, *Carminum*, p. 543,
no. 10661); a full text can be found in *The Latin Poems Commonly Attributed to Walter
Mapes*, ed. T. Wright, Camden Society, xvii (1841), pp. 226–8.

[214] Isa. 5: 10.

[215] This was the beginning of a catastrophic famine in England. The bad harvest in 1314
could be weathered, but the subsequent bad harvests in 1315 and 1316 brought famine
conditions. The problem covered most of northern Europe so that supplies could not easily
be imported and some were sought from Spain and the Mediterranean (*CPR 1313–17*,
pp. 466, 624; *CCR 1313–18*, pp. 425, 452). The death rate in England is unknown, but in
Ypres (Flanders) it was nearly 10 per cent in the summer of 1316. The improved harvest
of 1317 and the good harvest of 1318 at last brought the prices down, but there were

1315 Dominus post hec flagella incorrigibiles nos inueniat, homines et
pecora simul disperdat; et constanter credo quod, nisi intercederet
Anglicana religio, dispersi fuissemus elapso tempore multo.

Accidit interea ut quidam miles, Adam de Banastre[a] nomine, de
domo et familia comitis Lancastrie, perpetrasset homicidium, et de
uenia desperans ac peccatum suum augmentans, insurgere cepit contra
dominum suum. Credidit enim regi placere si comitem infestaret, qui
tociens regi restiterat, qui tociens regem initum[b] coegerat[c] mutare
consilium. Vnde terras comitis cepit inuadere et precipue comitatum
Lancastrie, et, secundum relatum aliquorum, quasi a rege iussus,
baneriam regis erexit, et sub hoc colore multos auxiliarios secum
assumpsit, castella comitis latenter intrauit, arma in exercitum Scotorum preparata et multam pecuniam simul asportauit.[216]

Erant autem quasi octingenti uiri in auxilium eius procurati,
quidam precio conducti, quidam mortis timore compulsi, quos uel
oportuit patriam relinquere uel secum in arma concurrere. Audiens
ergo comes proditoris insaniam, et considerans rem esse periculosam,
statim precepit militibus suis ut infidelem illum prudenter inuesti-
garent, et inuentum prudenter inuaderent. Ibant ergo armatorum
quasi sexcenti in mortem Ade de Banastre[d] omnes accensi. Et cum
uenissent prope locum ubi congregauerat Adam exercitum suum,
diuiserunt se in duas turmas ut prima ueniens hostes inuaderet, que si
non sufficeret, altera superueniens negocium consummaret. Hoc
postquam Adam de Banastre[e] cognouit, cum fautoribus et complicibus suis primam turmam acriter excepit, et ipsam sine dubio penitus
dissipasset, nisi secunda turma recenter aduenisset. Adam uero et sui
sequaces aduersarios accrescere uidentes, et multo plures adesse
putantes, iam uacillare ceperunt, et post modicum, aduersariorum
impetum non ferentes, fugam inierunt.[217] Set fugientes passim
ceduntur a tergo. Porro persequencium tota fuit intencio, ceterorum

    [a] Danastre R; Banastre St, Den-Y   [b] sic MS; poss. inuitum He   [c] cogerat MS;
coegerat He, St, Den-Y   [d] see above, n. a   [e] see above, n. a

continued hardships with livestock diseases and with another bad harvest in 1321. For the
scale and significance of the famine, see I. Kershaw, 'The great famine and agrarian crisis
in England, 1315–22', Past and Present, lix (1973), pp. 3–50, esp. at pp. 6–15; for the
famine in Europe, see W. C. Jordan, The Great Famine (Princeton, 1996), passim. For the
author's comments on English prices, see below, pp. 120–1.

[216] The revolt began on 8 Oct. 1315 and the rebels were active in the area between
Warrington and Preston (Lancashire). Banaster had been a faithful Lancastrian retainer since
1305, and part of the cause of the revolt may have been rivalry with the Holand family, who
were also Lancastrian retainers. Lancaster's letter to Edward II after the revolt, in which he

feared that if the Lord finds us incorrigible after these scourges, he
will destroy at once both men and beasts; and I firmly believe that if
the English church had not interceded for us, we should have
perished long ago.

Meanwhile it happened that a certain knight, named Adam
Banaster, in the household and retinue of the earl of Lancaster,
committed homicide and, without hope of pardon, yet aggravating his
crime, he took it upon himself to rise up against his lord. For he
believed that it would please the king if he attacked the earl who had
so often opposed the king and so often forced the king to change plans
already under way. Therefore this knight began to attack the earl's
estates, especially the earldom of Lancaster, and according to some
accounts he raised the royal standard, as if on the king's orders, and
under this colour he drew to himself many helpers, entered the earl's
castles by stealth, and carried off equipment prepared for the army
against the Scots together with a large sum of money.[216]

Some eight hundred men were persuaded to help him, some
bought for a price, some forced by fear of death, who had either to
leave the area or join him in arms. The earl, hearing of the traitor's
madness, and considering the situation dangerous, at once ordered his
knights to make a careful search for this faithless man, and to attack
him with well-considered tactics when they found him. So hundreds
and hundreds of men-at-arms went forth all fired up for Adam
Banaster's death. When they had come near the place where Adam
had assembled his army, they split up into two troops, so that the first
one should come up and attack the enemy, and, if this was not
enough, the other should come up too and finish off the business.
When Adam Banaster realized this, with his accomplices and
supporters he took on the first troop fiercely, and would doubtless
have completely defeated it, if the second troop had not arrived in
time. When Adam and his followers saw that their opponents grew in
numbers, and thinking that many more were nearby, they began to
waver, and after a little while, unable to withstand their opponents'
attack, they took flight.[217] But as they fled they were everywhere cut
down from behind. Now the whole intention of the pursuers was to

accepts that Edward had not encouraged Banaster, appears to confirm the *Vita*'s comment
that Banaster claimed to be acting in the king's interest (Maddicott, *Lancaster*, pp. 175–7).
For a detailed chronology of the revolt, see G. H. Tupling (ed.), *South Lancashire in the Reign
of Edward II* (Chetham Society, 3rd ser., i. 1949), pp. xlii–xlvi, 42–6).

[217] Banaster's defeat was on 4 Nov. at Deepdale near Preston (Tupling, *South
Lancashire*, pp. 39, 45–6).

1315 signiferum Adam comprehendere, et uiuum si possent comiti pre-
sentare. Fugerat *a* autem in quoddam horreum, et ibidem latitabat, set
modicum; non enim diu latitare potuit qui totam patriam uelud *b*
hostis publicus debellauit. Aduersarii eius domum obsederunt et
ipsum ad dedicionem sepius monuerunt; set ipse, delicti sui conscius
et quocumque *c* se uerteret de morte securus, audaciam ex desper-
acione concepit et se aduersariis audacter opposuit; quosdam eorum
occidit et plures ex eis male uulnerauit. Tandem, quia sine magno
periculo uiuum capere non poterant, inpressionem *d* in eum facientes
ipsum occiderunt, et caput eius auferentes comiti detulerunt.²¹⁸ Sic
Ciba filius Botri dominum suum Dauid regem expungnauit, quem
Ioab princeps milicie fugientem in Abbella capite priuauit.²¹⁹

Paganus de Torboruile curam terre de Glamorgan acceperat a
rege, unde ministrales *e* prius constitutos nouis subrogatis cepit
amouere;²²⁰ quamobrem Leulinus Bren *f* commotus est, nec poterat
Pagano quicquam loqui pacifice. Erat autem Leulinus ille Walensis
uir magnus et potens in partibus suis.²²¹ Hic uiuente comite
Gloucestrie magnum officium sub ipso gerebat, et nunc preposito
Pagano potestatem sibi sublatam egre ferebat. Vnde Paganum
contumeliis frequenter aggreditur, et pluribus audientibus in has
minas inuehitur: 'Venient,' inquid, 'dies, et cessare faciam superbiam Pagani, reddam sibi uices quas impendit michi.' Propter quod
accusatus est Leulinus apud regem quod sediciosus esset, quod
occasiones rebellandi quereret, et, nisi rex diligenter precaueret,
Leulinus de nouo Walenses excitaret. Audiens Leulinus condicionem suam sic apud regem deterioratam, de consilio amicorum
accessit ad curiam, uolens si posset se ipsum excusare, aut saltem
iniuriam suam caute palliare. Spreuit eum rex, iurans et protestans

---

a fugeat *MS*; fugerat *He, St, Den-Y*   *b* sic *R*; uelut *St, Den-Y*   *c* sic *R*;
quocunque *St, Den-Y*   *d* sic *R* (corrected without comment from impressionem);
impressionem *St*; inpressionem *Den-Y*   *e* minstrales *or* ministrales *MS* (*He leaves
reading unclear, ed.*); ministrales *St, Den-Y*   *f* Breu *R, He*; Bren *St, Den-Y*

²¹⁸ Again the author's details are sketchy. In the legal records Banaster is said to have
fled to the moors, but was betrayed when he asked for refuge in Charnock Richard on 11
Nov. He was executed on 12 Nov. (Tupling, *South Lancashire*, pp. xlvii, 38, 46).
²¹⁹ Cf. 2 Kgs. (2 Sam.) 20: 21–2.
²²⁰ Turberville, from an Anglo-Norman family which had been settled in Coety since
the 12th c., was keeper of the Gloucester lands in Glamorgan from July 1315 to Apr. 1316.
It was possibly his lack of sympathy with the Welsh, his changing of officials, and his
financial pressures which encouraged Bren's rebellion (*CPR 1313–17*, pp. 362, 370, 432,
433; *CCR 1313–18*, pp. 253, 263, 275–6; J. Beverley Smith, 'The rebellion of Llewellyn
Bren', in T. B. Pugh (ed.), *Glamorgan County History*, iii: *The Middle Ages* (Cardiff, 1971),

capture Adam, the ringleader of the others, and take him to the earl 1315
alive if they could. He, however, had escaped to a certain barn and lay
hidden there, but only for a while; for the man who had brought war
to the whole countryside like a public enemy could not hide for long.
His opponents laid siege to the building and urged him again and
again to surrender; but he, aware of his guilt and certain of death
whichever way he turned, took courage from despair and faced his
enemies boldly; he killed some of them and seriously wounded many
of them. At length, because they could not take him alive without
great danger, they made a rush upon him and killed him, and cutting
off his head took it to the earl.[218] So likewise Seba son of Bochri
fought against his lord king David, and Joab captain of the soldiery
beheaded him as he fled to Abela.[219]

Payn Turberville had received the administration of the land of
Glamorgan from the king, and began to replace the previously
appointed officials by new ones;[220] this angered Llywelyn Bren, so
that he could not speak peaceably to Payn. Now, that Llywelyn was a
Welshman, a great and powerful man in his own country.[221] While
the earl of Gloucester was alive he had held high office under him,
and now with Payn in charge he bore it hardly that his authority was
taken from him. Hence he frequently attacked Payn with insults, and
in the hearing of many uttered these threats: 'The day will come', he
said, 'when I will put an end to Payn's arrogance and give him in turn
as good as he gives me.' For this, Llywelyn was accused before the
king of sedition, and of seeking an excuse for rebellion; and unless the
king took great care Llywelyn would rouse the Welsh afresh.
Llywelyn hearing that his position with the king had been made
worse, came to court on the advice of his friends, wishing to excuse
himself if he could, or at least carefully to cover up his crime. But the

pp. 75–82). His accounts for the lordship, rendered by his widow, are on the pipe roll for
10 Ed. II (*Vita*, 1st edn., p. 66 n.).

[221] Llywelyn Bren was the son of Gruffud ap Rhys, the last independent ruler of
Senghennydd, South Wales, whose lands had been brought under the lordship of the earls
of Gloucester in the 1260s. The *modus vivendi* which had been reached was overturned
with the death of Gilbert in 1314, when royal administrators in his lordship, particularly
those from old Marcher families such as Turberville, showed little sympathy with the
Welsh. The administrators may also have been tightening control in 1315–16, fearing that
Bruce's invasion of Ireland might spread to Wales. The parliament of 1316 received
complaints of oppression from all over Wales. Bren surrendered by 26 Mar. 1316 and was
sent to the Tower. Despenser later had him executed in Cardiff (R. R. Davies, *Conquest,
Coexistence and Change: Wales 1063–1415*, History of Wales, ii (Oxford, 1987), pp. 281–2,
388; Smith, 'Rebellion of Llewellyn Bren', pp. 74–86; *CPR 1313–17*, pp. 433–4; *CCR
1313–18*, pp. 274–5; *RP*, iii. 364; *Stats.*, i. 183).

1315 quod filius mortis esset,[222] si crimen ei obiectum manifestum foret. Habuitque in mandatis ad Lyncolniam uenire, et ibidem super hiis responsum expectare.[223]

1316 Leulinus ergo, accepto tali mandato, clam et festinanter ad partes suas rediit, et quod ante proposuerat statim patefecit. Prius quidem fecerat*a* uerba maliuola, set iam de uerbis peruentum est ad uerbera. Nam quadam die, dum custos de Kaerfili extra castrum curiam teneret, superuenit Leulinus cum filiis et fautoribus suis ad constabularium, captum secum abduxit, quibusdam ministris cesis et pluribus qui ad curiam illam conuenerant male uulneratis. Castrum quoque statim inuasit, set custodibus resistentibus intrare non potuit, ulteriorem uero custodiam totam incendit.[224] Iam palam facte sunt inimicitie. Leulinus minatus ⟨est⟩*b* Paganum occidere. Paganus declinauit eius insidias donec accresceret uires suas.

Interim Leulinus ipse terras sub tuicione Pagani constitutas uiolenter aggreditur: cedit, incendit, et depredatur. Associauerat sibi enim in auxilium quasi decem milia Walensium. Omnia bona sua, boues, uaccas et cetera uictualia ad montes transtulerant; nam in cauernis montium et in latebris nemorum erat eorum refugium. Hiis et aliis malis perpetratis ac domino regi notificatis, precepit rex seruis suis dicens, 'Ite uelociter, et persequimini proditorem illum, ne forte ex mora deterius eueniat, et tota Wallia contra nos insurgat.' Committiturque negocium comiti Herfordie, nam res ipsa precipue uidebatur ipsum tangere; terra*c* enim de Breynok que ad comitem pertinet terram de Glamorgam collateralem habet, et iuxta poetam,

Tunc tua res agitur paries dum proximus ardet.[225]

Abiit ergo comes in terram suam ut persequeretur Leulinum, et uterque Rogerus de Mortimer ferebat auxilium.[226] Willelmus de

---

a fecerit *MS*; fecerat *He, St, Den-Y*   *b* minatur *R*; minatus ⟨est⟩ *ed.*   *c* terram *R*; terra *St, Den-Y*

[222] 1 Kgs. (1 Sam.) 20: 31 (that is: he would die).

[223] Parliament (with commons) was summoned to Lincoln for 27 Jan. 1316 (*HBC*, p. 553).

[224] Caerffili castle was a symbol of English overlordship. It was begun in 1267 by the earl of Gloucester to control the newly subdued land of Senghennydd (Davies, *Wales 1063–1415*, pp. 281–2).

[225] Horace, *Ep.* i. 18. 84. Hereford was appointed to overall command of the campaign on 11 Feb. 1316 (*CPR 1313–17*, p. 432).

[226] Roger Mortimer of Wigmore and Roger Mortimer of Chirk were important Marcher barons. Roger Mortimer of Wigmore, earl of March 1328–30, was heir to the family lands

king rejected him, swearing and asserting that he was the son of   1315
death[222] if the crime charged against him was proved. He was ordered
to come to Lincoln, and there await a reply on these matters.[223]

Then, having received such an order, Llywelyn returned secretly   1316
and in haste to his own country and at once made clear what he had
previously had in mind. He had formerly uttered words of disaffec-
tion, but now it went beyond words to blows. For on a certain day,
while the keeper of Caerffili was outside the castle holding his court,
Llywelyn with his sons and accomplices fell upon the constable and
led him away captive; some of the servants were killed, and many who
had come to the court were badly wounded. Llywelyn also at once
attacked the castle, but because of the resistance of the guards he was
unable to enter; nevertheless he burnt the whole of the outer ward.[224]
Hostilities now became open. Llywelyn threatened to kill Payn. Payn
avoided his plots until he should increase his forces.

Meanwhile Llywelyn himself violently attacked the lands under
Payn's protection: he killed, burned, and plundered. He had attracted
to himself the help of some ten thousand Welshmen. These had carried
off all Payn's goods to the mountains, oxen, cows, and other victuals;
for their refuge was in mountain caves and wooded hiding places.
When these and other wrongs which had been committed had been
reported to the lord king, the king gave orders to his servants saying,
'Go quickly, and pursue that traitor, lest perhaps worse should happen
through delay and all Wales should rise against us.' And the affair was
committed to the earl of Hereford, as the situation itself seemed to
affect him particularly; for the land of Brecon, which belongs to the
earl, has land adjoining Glamorgan, and according to the poet,

Have a care for your eaves, if your neighbour's dwelling burns.[225]

The earl therefore went off to his lands to pursue Llywelyn, and
both the lords Roger Mortimer helped him.[226] William Montague,

in the Marches and in Ireland. He was knighted at the same time as Prince Edward in
1306, and until 1321 served loyally in Scotland, the Welsh Marches, and in Ireland. He
was king's lieutenant and keeper of Ireland 1316–18 and justiciar of Ireland 1319–21. His
opposition to the Despensers in 1321–2 brought imprisonment and exile. His later liaison
with Queen Isabella brought him the earldom of March (*CP*, viii. 433–42; Tout, *Ed. II*,
pp. 343–4). Roger Mortimer of Chirk, third son of Roger Mortimer of Wigmore (d. 1282),
was the uncle of this Roger Mortimer of Wigmore. As a younger son he had had to make a
career for himself: he served Edward I loyally and rose to prominence under Edward II,
serving as justice of North and South Wales in 1308–15, 1316, and 1317–22. However, like
his nephew, he opposed Despenser in 1321–2, and was imprisoned in the Tower, where he
died on 3 Aug. 1326 (*CP*, ix. 251–4; Tout, *Ed. II*, p. 336).

1316 Monte Acuto prefectus*ᵃ* milicie regis ex parte una, Iohannes Gyffard
et qui cum eo erant ex altera uenerunt.²²⁷ Henricus de Lancastria²²⁸ et
alii barones et milites, terras in uicinio habentes, opem tulerunt, ut sic
Walenses undique obsessi*ᵇ* nullatenus haberent locum diffugii.
Videns ergo Leulinus quod male errasset, quod ad resistendum non
sufficeret, Walenses*ᶜ* enim bis uel ter Anglicos predanter*ᵈ* acceperant,
set semper ubique deterius reportauerant, obtulit se comiti sub
condicione, ut scilicet uitam*ᵉ* et membra, terras et cetera bona mobilia
salua liceret habere, et pro satisfaccione delicti optulit magnam
summam argenti; set noluit comes eum admittere, nisi simpliciter
se uellet reddere. Tandem cum exercitus noster apropinquasset et
excubias Walensium iam didicisset, Leulinus suos homines sic cepit
alloqui: 'Non est,' inquit, 'tutum cum Anglis congredi. Ego dedi
causam negocio. Ego me tradam pro toto populo. Melius est enim ut
unus moriatur quam tota gens exulet uel gladio perimatur.'²²⁹

Descendens*ᶠ* ergo Leulinus de montibus reddidit se comiti,
subiciens se penitus regie uoluntati; misitque eum comes ad regem
ut misericordiam expectaret aut legem. Hec est consuetudo Walensium ut uetus*ᵍ* insania. Si quieuerint per decennium statim respirant
ad prelium, et quod multo tempore congesserint uadit in exterminium.*ʰ* Leulinus ap Griffyth et frater eius Dauid poterant in pace
uixisse, set rebellantes uitam perdiderunt et principatum Wallie.²³⁰
Verum si consuete rebellionis causam *ⁱ*uelis perscrutari,*ⁱ* hoc pro
racione poterit assignari. Walenses, prius dicti Britones, olim dicti*ʲ*
quidem erant nobiles et tocius Anglie regnum possidentes; set super-
uenientibus Saxonibus eiecti fuerunt, et regnum ⟨et⟩*ᵏ* nomen simul
amiserunt. Terra fertilis et plana cessit Saxonibus; terra sterilis et
montuosa remansit Walensibus. Porro ex dictis Merlini prophete,
sperant adhuc Angliam recuperare.²³¹ Hinc est quod frequenter

ᵃ profectus *MS*; prefectus *He, St, Den-Y*   *ᵇ* obcessi *MS*; obsessi *He, St, Den-Y*
ᶜ Walensis *MS*; Walenses *He, St, Den-Y*   *ᵈ* sic *R*; predantes *Den-Y*   *ᵉ* uita *MS*;
uitam *He, St, Den-Y*   *ᶠ* ascendens *R*; descendens *Den-Y*   *ᵍ* sic *R*; *perhaps* uel pocius
Den-Y   *ʰ* exterminum *MS*; exterminium *He, St, Den-Y*   *ⁱ⁻ⁱ* uel perscrutar *MS*;
uelis perscrutari *He, St, Den-Y*   *ʲ* sic *R*; *om. Den-Y*   *ᵏ* *om. MS*; nomenque *He*; et
supplied *St, Den-Y*

²²⁷ Montague was a household knight from a rising west country family. His active
military service began in 1301, and he served also as diplomat and courtier. By 1316–17, he
was a prominent courtier along with Amory, Audley, and the two Despensers. With
Audley and others he acted against Bren, and left a report of his action (*CPR 1313–17*,
p. 384; *CChW*, i. 437–9). He rose to become steward of the household in Nov. 1316 to
Nov. 1318, after which he was appointed seneschal of Gascony on 20 Nov. 1318. He was
dead by 6 Nov. 1319 (*CP*, ix. 80–2; Maddicott, *Lancaster*, pp. 194–5; *HBC*, p. 76; Tout,

commander of the king's forces, came from one side, and John 1316
Giffard and those who were with him came from the other.[227]
Henry of Lancaster[228] and the other barons and knights who had
lands in the neighbourhood brought help, so that the Welsh, hemmed
in on all sides, had no place of refuge at all. Therefore, seeing that he
had made a bad mistake and that he did not have a sufficient force to
resist, for the Welsh had two or three times met the English on
plundering raids but had always everywhere come off worse,
Llywelyn offered to submit to the earl on condition, namely that he
should have safety of life and limb, lands, and other moveable goods,
and in satisfaction of his crime he offered a great sum of money; but
the earl would not receive him unless he would surrender unconditionally. At length when our army had drawn near and had already
recognized the Welsh guards, Llywelyn began to address his men
thus: 'It is not safe', he said, 'to engage the English. I provoked this
business. I will hand myself over for the whole people. For it is better
that one man should die than that the whole race should be exiled or
perish by the sword.'[229]

Coming down from the hills therefore Llywelyn gave himself up to
the earl, submitting himself utterly to the king's will; and the earl sent
him to the king to await his mercy or judgement. This habit of the
Welsh is a long-standing madness. They keep quiet for ten years and
then, in an instant, are ready again for battle, and what they have
achieved over a long period is quickly destroyed. Llywelyn ap
Gruffudd and Daffyd his brother could have lived in peace, but
they lost their lives and the principality of Wales in rebellion.[230] And
if you wish to trace the roots of this rebellious habit, this may be given
as a reason. The Welsh, formerly called the Britons, were once noble
and owned the whole realm of England; but they were expelled by the
incoming Saxons and lost both name and kingdom. The fertile
lowlands went to the Saxons; the barren and mountainous districts
were left to the Welsh. But because of the sayings of the prophet
Merlin they still hope to recover England.[231] Hence it is that the

Ed. II., p. 350). His son continued in royal service and was created earl of Salisbury in
1337. For Giffard see above, n. 182.
[228] Henry was the younger brother of Thomas of Lancaster. [229] Cf. John 11: 50.
[230] These were the last princes of Gwynedd. Their rebellion in 1282 provoked Edward
I's final conquest of Wales. Llywelyn was killed in battle 11 Dec. 1282, and Daffyd, his
younger brother, was executed 3 Oct. 1283 (*HBC*, pp. 51–2; Davies, *Wales 1063–1415*,
pp. 348–54; Prestwich, *Ed. I*, pp. 193–6, 202–3).
[231] For Merlin's prophecies, see above n. 212.

1316 insurgunt Walenses, effectum uaticinii implere uolentes; set quia
debitum tempus ignorant, sepe decipiuntur et in uanum laborant.
Dominus rex apud Lyncolniam barones conuocauerat,[232] set
propter guerram Leulini Bren,[a] de paucis consuluerat.[b] Perambulacio
tamen forestarum ibidem conceditur, et comes Lancastrie principalis
consiliarius regis efficitur.[233] Ordinaciones super uictualibus prius
facte penitus dissoluuntur.[234] Itinerantes enim per patriam multum
grauabantur, nam ex quo processit illud statutum, nichil uel modicum
in foro reperiebatur expositum, cum tamen prius habundaret forum
uenalibus, licet cara uiderentur transeuntibus. Porro melius est emere
care quam nichil emendum ad opus inuenire. Nam licet raritas
annonam facit cariorem, habundancia subsequens reddet meliorem.
    Transeunte solempnitate Paschali cepit caristia bladi uehementer
augeri. Non est uisa temporibus nostris in Anglia nec audita centum
⟨annis⟩[c] retroactis tanta caristia. Nam Londoniis et locis uicinis
uendebatur modius tritici pro quadraginta denariis, et aliis partibus
terre ubi minor erat concursus hominum triginta denarii erat
commune precium.[235] Porro durante penuria creuit et fames ualida,
et post famem dura pestilencia, ex qua moriuntur in diuersis locis
plus quam milia. A quibusdam eciam audiui relatum, quod in
partibus Northumbrorum canes et equi et alia immunda sumebantur
ad esum. Hii enim propter frequentes incursus Scotorum maiori tedio
laborabant, quos maledicti Scoti suis uictualibus cotidie spoliabant.
Heu terra Anglie! que olim ex tua fertilitate aliis terris solebas
subuenire, nunc pauper et indigens cogeris mendicare. Terra fructi-
fera uertitur in salsuginem;[236] aeris intemperies deuorat pinguedinem;

---

[a] Bru R, He; Bren St, Den-Y   [b] consulerat MS; consuluerat He, St, Den-Y
[c] om. R; supplied St, Den-Y

[232] Parliament (with commons) was summoned for 27 Jan. 1316 and ended on 20 Feb.
(HBC, p. 553).
[233] The perambulation of the forests and Lancaster's appointment were both agreed on
17 Feb. 1316 (RP, i. 351). The fullest description of the business in this parliament is in
Davies, Opposition, pp. 408–15. This marks the highest point of Lancaster's activity in
government. The experiment did not work well, but this was not entirely due to
Lancaster's own failures (Maddicott, Lancaster, pp. 180–9). The standing council which
was set up in 1318 no longer had Lancaster as a member (see below, n. 299).
[234] For the ordinance see above, pp. 102–3. The repeal was agreed on 14 Feb. 1316;
writs went out on 20 Feb. (RP, i. 351; CCR 1313–17, p. 325).
[235] Easter fell on 11 Apr. in 1316. The string of bad harvests had begun in 1314 and
brought severe famine conditions in 1315–17 (see above, pp. 110–11). The author was
correct in stating that the price levels reached were unheard of; they have been called
'quite unparalleled in English history' (Kershaw, 'Agrarian crisis', p. 13). Normally prices
ranged between 6s. and 8s. a quarter in the early 14th c.; the modius was almost certainly a

Welsh frequently rebel, hoping to give effect to the prophecy; but 1316
because they do not know the appointed time, they are often deceived
and their effort is in vain.

The lord king had summoned the barons to Lincoln,[232] but on
account of the war of Llywelyn Bren he had dealt with few matters.
However, the perambulation of the forests was granted there, and the
earl of Lancaster was made the king's chief counsellor.[233] The
regulations formerly made about food were completely abolished.[234]
In fact, those who travelled about the country were suffering much
hardship, for, as a result of that statute, little or nothing was exposed
for sale in the markets, whereas formerly the market had been full of
goods, even though they seemed dear to travellers. But it is better to
buy dear than to find there is nothing to buy when you need it. For
although scarcity makes produce dearer, subsequent plenty brings
back a better time.

After the celebration of Easter the dearth of grain began to increase
greatly. Such a scarcity has not been seen in our time in England, nor
heard of for a hundred years. For the bushel of wheat was sold in
London and its vicinity for forty pence, and in other less thickly
populated parts of the country thirty pence was a common price.[235]
Indeed during this time of scarcity a great famine appeared, and after
the famine came a severe pestilence, from which many thousands died
in different places. I have even heard it said by some, that in Northumbria dogs and horses and other unclean things were consumed as
food. There, indeed, on account of the frequent raids of the Scots,
people are afflicted with greater hardship as the accursed Scots rob
them daily of their food. Alas, land of England! You who out of your
abundance once helped other lands, now, poor and needy, are forced to
beg. A fruitful land is turned into barrenness;[236] the inclemency of the

bushel and therefore, at eight bushels to the quarter, the author of the *Vita* is reporting
prices of 20s. to 26s. 8d. a quarter. Manorial and market prices of wheat at over 25s. a
quarter were not uncommon, and in the worst-hit areas chroniclers reported wheat prices
at 40s. the quarter. For prices, see D. L. Farmer, 'Prices and wages', in H. E. Hallam (ed.),
Agrarian History of England and Wales, iii: *1042–1350* (Cambridge, 1988), fig. 7.4,
pp. 736–7.
[236] Ps. 106 (107): 34. Excessive rain was mentioned by nearly all chroniclers as the main
cause of the grain shortage. Sea storms and coastal flooding also caused recurrent problems
for the low-lying areas on the east coast in the late 13th and first half of the 14th cc.,
although the famine years themselves did not see as many recorded inundations as the
1280s or the subsequent years of the 1330s and 1340s (M. Bailey, 'Per impetum maris:
natural disaster and economic decline in eastern England', in B. M. S. Campbell (ed.),
Before the Black Death: Studies in the 'Crisis' of the Early Fourteenth Century (Manchester,
1991), pp. 184–208, at pp. 187–96.

1316 seritur frumentum et procreatur lollium. Eueniunt autem omnia a
malicia habitancium in ea.[237] Parce, Domine, parce populo tuo.[238]
Subsannant et derident nos qui sunt in circuitu nostro.[239] Dicunt
tamen sapientes astrologie has celi tempestates naturaliter euenisse;
Saturnus enim securus et frigidus asperitates procreat inutiles
seminibus; triennio iam regnans cursum consummauit, et sibi mitis
Iubiter ordine successit. Porro Ioue regnante cessabunt pluuiales
unde, ualles habundabunt frumento[a] et campi replebuntur uber-
tate;[240] etenim Dominus dabit benignitatem, et terra nostra dabit
fructum suum,[241] et cetera.

Iampridem orta fuit dissencio in uilla Bristollie super consuetudinibus in portu maris et in foro, super priuilegiis et aliis rebus, in
quibus quatuordecim de maioribus eiusdem uille uidebantur pre-
rogatiuam habere.[242] Obstitit[b] communitas, asserens burgenses omnes
unius condicionis esse et hoc in libertatibus et priuilegiis pares
existere. Super huiuscemodi rebus frequentes inter se habuerunt
altercaciones, donec in curia regis impetrarent iudices qui de causa
cognoscerent et ipsam debite terminarent. Porro quatuordecim illi
predicti procurauerant in inquisicione forenses associari. Credebantur
insuper et ipsi conducti et ad partem illorum quatuordecim totaliter
inclinati. Allegauit communitas libertatibus uille fore contrarium
causas intrinsecas uentilari[c] iudicio forensium; set iustitiarii tales
allegaciones friuolas reputabant, unde nec libertatibus nec[d] priuilegiis
eorum in hoc deferebant. Videntes ergo maiores communitatis
excepciones suas repelli, ius eorum fauore potius quam racione
confundi, conturbati nimirum exierunt ab aula ubi de consuetudine
tractantur iudicia, nunciaueruntque plebi dicentes, 'Venerunt iudices
aduersariis nostris fauentes, et in preiudicium nostrum forenses
admittunt, unde et iura nostra sine fine peribunt.' Ad hec uerba
uulgus insipiens in sedicionem uertitur, et totus populus pre tumultu
timore concutitur.[e] Redeuntes denuo cum multo comitatu uenerunt
in aulam ubi ius eorum iam uertent[f] in iniuriam. Nam pungnis et

[a] ferro R; frumento St, Den-Y   [b] abstitit MS; obstitit He, St, Den-Y   [c] uentelari
MS; uentilari He, St, Den-Y   [d] in MS; nec He, St, Den-Y   [e] concucitur MS;
concutitur He, St, Den-Y   [f] sic MS; uerterunt or uertunt He; uertunt St

[237] Ps. 106 (107): 34; and see also Jer. 12: 4.
[238] From the liturgy: in the Litany or prayer of general supplication (Legg, *Sarum
Missal*, pp. 54, 151).
[239] Ps. 43 (44): 14.   [240] Ps. 64 (65): 14, 12.   [241] Ps. 84 (85): 13.
[242] Some initial discontent was felt over Badlesmere's farm of the town in 1309 for £210

weather destroys the fatness of the land; wheat is sown and tares are 1316
brought forth. All this comes from the wickedness of them that dwell
therein.[237] Spare, O Lord, spare thy people![238] They scoff and deride
us, that are round about us.[239] Yet those who are wise in astrology say
that these storms in the heavens have happened naturally; for Saturn,
heedless and cold, brings rough weather that is useless to the seed; in
the ascendant now for three years he has completed his course, and
kindly Jupiter has in turn succeeded him. Henceforth, under Jupiter
these floods of rain will cease, the vales shall abound with corn, and the
fields shall be filled with plenty;[240] for the Lord will give goodness and
our earth shall yield her fruit,[241] etc.

A long time ago discontent arose in the town of Bristol, over the
customs in the harbour and the market, over privileges and other
matters in which fourteen of the greater townsmen appeared to take
precedence.[242] The community opposed them, maintaining that all
the burgesses were of one rank and therefore equal in liberties and
privileges. Over such matters they had frequent disputes among
themselves, until they asked the king's court to provide judges to take
cognizance of the case and duly bring it to a conclusion. Now those
said fourteen had arranged for outsiders to be on the panel of jurors.
And, moreover, these men were believed to have been won over and
to be entirely favourably disposed to the side of those fourteen. The
community alleged that it would be against the liberties of the town
for domestic issues to be subject to the judgment of outsiders; but the
justices regarded such allegations as frivolous, and would not allow
them their liberties or privileges in this. The leaders of the community, seeing that their liberties were rejected, that their rights were
upset rather by favour than by reason, in much distress left the hall
where judgments are customarily given, and spoke to the people
saying, 'Judges favourable to our opponents have come, and to our
prejudice they admit outsiders, by which our rights will be lost for
ever.' At these words the foolish crowd turned to rioting, and the
whole populace trembled from fear of the disorder. Returning once
more with a large following, they entered the hall, where they turned
their right to wrong. For with fists and sticks they began to attack the

p. a. This was compounded by internal disputes and open violence between the townsmen,
led by John Taverner on one side and William Randolph on the other. Further opposition
to the Crown came in the refusal to pay the tallage of 16 Dec. 1312, and by 10 Nov. 1313
the town was taken into the king's hands. It took nearly three more years to resolve the
problems (E. A. Fuller, 'The tallage of 6 Edward II and the Bristol rebellion', *TBGAS*, xix
(1894–5), pp. 173–83).

1316 fustibus obuiam sibi turbam inuadere ceperunt, et ipsa die subito fere
uiginti homines fatue peremerunt.ᵃ Timor namque non uanus nobiles
et ignobiles tantus inuasit ut plures per fenestras de summo solarii in
plateam exilierunt, et crura uel tibias in terram decidentes enormiter
leserunt.ᵇ Timebant et iudices, humiliter petentes in pace recedere,
quos maior uille, plebis insaniam uix tandem compescens, illesos fecit
abire.

Indictati fuerunt super hoc quasi octoginta uiri, et habita inquisicione diligenter coram iustitiariis regiis apud Gloucestriam condempnati,ᶜ postea de comitatu exiguntur, et non uenientes neque parentes
exules fieri precipiuntur. Ipsi uero bene muniti continuerunt se intra
uillam suam; non parebunt regis mandato nisi per manum ualidam.

Quatuordecim illi predicti, qui aduersabantur communitati, domos
et redditus relinquentes a uilla recesserunt; nam sub tali tempestate
morari cum aduersariis inutile censuerunt. Per duos annos et amplius
durauit ista rebellio communitatis Bristollie, et tamen ex parte regis
pluries sunt moniti ad pacem uenire. Maluit enim rex penam grass-
ancium si uellent mitigare, quam plenam uindictam expetendo bonam
uillam destruere. Perstiterunt autem ipsi semper rebelles, mandatum
et preceptum regis semper contempnentes. Non uenerunt uocati, non
paruerunt moniti, causantes omnem processum contra eos habitum
iniustum, quia priuilegiis et libertatibus eorum omnino contrarium.

Nolensᵈ ergo rex malicie eorum ulterius satisfacere, milites et
maiores de comitatu Glouernie uocantur Londonias, quibus iniunxit
in uirtute sacramenti ibidem prestiti causam Bristollie et cuius esset
iniuria patenter edicere. Qui omnes dixerunt communitatem Bristollie partem sinistram fouere, et octoginta uiros auctores iniurie. Misit
ergo Bristollie Adolmarum comitem de Penbrok,²⁴³ qui uocatis
maioribus communitatis dixit eis ex parte regis: 'Dominus rex,'
inquit, 'caussamᵉ uestram uentilans, uos reos inuenit, et ut iuri
pareatis uos monet et precipit. Homicidas et reos illos tradite, et
uos et uilla uestra in pace manete. Promitto quod, si sic feceritis,
dominum regem erga uos satis placibilem et misericordem inuenietis.'
Respondit communitas: 'Nos iniurie auctores non fuimus; nos in

---

ᵃ sic R; perhaps for perierunt MW; or perempti sunt ed.   ᵇ lederunt MS; leserunt He,
St, Den-Y   ᶜ condempnari MS; condempnati St, Den-Y   ᵈ nolentes MS; nolens
He, St, Den-Y   ᵉ sic R; causam St, Den-Y

²⁴³ Pembroke, William Inge, John de Lisle, and John Musard were appointed on 20
June 1316 to investigate and to force the Bristol townsmen back to obedience (CPR 1313–
17, p. 489; Phillips, Pembroke, pp. 102–3; Fuller, 'Bristol rebellion', pp. 185–6).

crowd opposed to them, and suddenly that day nearly twenty men
lost their lives for nothing. A very natural fear seized noble and
commoner, so great that many leapt out of the top-storey windows
into the street, and seriously injured their legs or thighs as they fell to
the ground. The judges too were afraid, humbly begging to leave in
peace, and the mayor of the town, with difficulty at last restraining
the frenzy of the populace, got them away safely.

About eighty men were indicted for this, and after a searching
enquiry before the royal justices at Gloucester, were condemned,
then the county was ordered to produce them. As they neither came
nor obeyed, they were ordered to be exiled. In truth, well protected,
they stayed within their town; they will not obey the king's command
unless they are forced to.

Those said fourteen who were opposing the commons, abandoning
their houses and rents, left the town, for they judged it useless to
remain with their opponents during such a commotion. This
rebellion of the community of Bristol lasted for two years and
more, though they were many times warned by the king to make
their peace. For the king preferred a penalty from the rioters if they
would comply, than to destroy a good town by demanding full
vengeance. However, they always persisted in their rebellion at all
times, constantly disregarding the king's command and order. They
did not come when they were summoned; they did not appear when
they were instructed, pleading that the whole process against them
was unjust, because it was entirely contrary to their privileges and
liberties.

Unwilling, therefore, to put up any longer with their wickedness,
the king summoned the knights and the more important men of
Gloucestershire to London, and enjoined them by virtue of an oath
taken there to make a clear pronouncement on the case of Bristol and
who had suffered wrong. And they all said that the Bristol community
had favoured the wrong cause and that the eighty men were the
authors of the wrongdoing. So the king sent to Bristol Aymer, earl of
Pembroke,[243] who called together the leaders of the community and
spoke to them on the king's behalf: 'The lord king,' he said, 'on
hearing your cause has found you guilty, and he warns and commands
you to obey the law. Hand over the killers and the guilty, and you and
your town shall remain in peace. I promise that if you do this you will
find the lord king lenient and merciful enough towards you.' The
community replied: 'We were not the authors of this wrongdoing; we

1316 dominum regem nichil deliquimus. Quidam nitebantur iura nostra tollere, et nos sicut decuit e contra defendere. Iccirco, si dominus rex ea que nobis inponuntur remiserit, si uitam et membra, redditus et predia nobis concesserit, sibi ut domino parebimus, et omnia quecunque uoluerit faciemus; alioquin persistemus ut cepimus, et libertates et priuilegia nostra usque ad mortem defendemus.'

Audiens rex contumaciam eorum, et considerans rem esse mali exempli, iussit uillam obsederi,[a] et non recedere donec caperentur obsessi. Et statim obsessa est uilla, municiones contra eam et propungnacula facta. Mauricus de Berkele obseruabat uiam maris. Aderat Iohannes de Cherltone regis camerarius,[244] Rogerus de Mortimer, Iohannes de Wylinthone, et alii barones et milites quam plurimi, et Bartholomeus de Badesmere procurator tocius negocii.[245] Erant eciam in castro quod est uille contiguum uiri cum petrariis et aliis machinis facientes assultum. Per aliquot[b] dies obsessi nitebantur uillam defendere, quia sperabant exteriores non longam moram facere, tum quia comes Gloucestrie dudum prius sic uillam obsesserat, set infecto negocio tandem recesserat, quia tum[c] sciebant regem in Scociam tendere, et suorum procerum auxilio indigere. Fefellit eos spes uacua; non recedent nec uilla subiecta. Nam[d] petraria castri uehemencius acta conquassabat muros et edificia. Quod uidentes opidani turbati sunt, et timore concussi [e]mittunt totam uillam in dedicionem,[e] et maiores capti missi sunt in carcerem.[246] Puniri non potuit tota multitudo, set multis grassantibus opus est exemplo.

Iam sciunt Bristollienses se male errasse, et rebellionem suam nichil perficisse.[f] Si condicionem pacis oblatam prius acceptassent, tota fere communitas et bona eorum tuto remansissent, set quia malo sunt usi consilio relicti sunt omnes regis iudicio. Inutile quidem fuit

_____

[a] sic MS; obsideri He, St   [b] aliquod MS; aliquot He, St, Den-Y   [c] sic R; tum quia St, Den-Y   [d] non MS; nam He, St, Den-Y   [e-e] timentes totam uillam in dedicionem MS; tradidere or similar verb to be supplied He; tradunt supplied St; timentes totam uillam in ⟨destructionem ire; ita consensere in⟩ dedicionem conjectured Den-Y; it is possible that timentes, which simply repeats the previous ideas of turbati sunt and timore concussi, is itself a corruption of a verb, perhaps mittunt. I am indebted to Mr Ian Moxon for this suggestion, ed.   [f] sic MS; profecisse He, St; perfecisse Den-Y

[244] Charlton had been one of Gaveston's yeomen. He was royal chamberlain in 1310–18, and possibly from 1308. If Gaveston was Edward's chamberlain (see above, n. 3) then Charlton may have acted as deputy chamberlain in the early years. His presence at court was opposed by the baronage in the supplementary ordinances in Oct. 1311, but without effect (Hamilton, Gaveston, p. 43 and n. 52; Tout, Ed. II, p. 315; Ann. Lond., p. 20; Chaplais, Gaveston, p. 65).
[245] This was Mortimer of Wigmore (Phillips, Pembroke, p. 103). For Mortimer and

have done nothing wrong towards the lord king. Certain men strove 1316 to take away our rights, and we, as was proper, strove to defend them. Therefore if the lord king will remit the penalties placed upon us, if he will grant us life and limb and rents and property, we will obey him as lord and do whatever he wishes; otherwise we shall continue as we have begun, and defend our liberties and privileges to the death.'

The king hearing of their stubbornness, and thinking that this was a bad example, ordered the town to be besieged, and not left until those besieged had been taken. And immediately the town was besieged, fortifications and siegeworks were prepared against it. Maurice Berkeley guarded the approach by sea. Present were John Charlton, the king's chamberlain,[244] Roger Mortimer, John Willington, and very many other barons and knights, and Bartholomew Badlesmere, in charge of the whole business.[245] In the castle, which adjoins the town, there were also men assaulting it with mangonels and other engines. For some days the besieged struggled to defend the town, hoping that those outside would not stay long, both because the earl of Gloucester had long ago besieged the town but had at length departed without taking it, and also because they knew that the king was going to Scotland and needed the help of his great men. This vain hope deceived them; they [the besiegers] will not depart until the town is taken. Moreover, one of the castle's mangonels, handled more forcefully, shattered the walls and buildings. When the townsmen saw this they were thrown into confusion and, stricken with fear, they surrendered the whole town, and the leading men, having been seized, were sent to prison.[246] The whole crowd could not be punished, but when there are many lawbreakers an example is needed.

The Bristollians now know that they have made a bad mistake, and that their rebellion has achieved nothing. If they had accepted the condition of peace offered earlier, almost the entire community and their goods would have remained safe, but because they have followed bad advice they are all left at the king's mercy. The advice indeed was

Willington, see above, nn. 183, 226. Badlesmere (for whose career see above, n. 203) had a long-standing interest in Bristol as constable of the castle from 1307 to 1320, with only a short break in 1312 (*CFR 1307–19*, pp. 2, 122, 147; ibid. *1319–27*, p. 33). He inevitably became drawn into internal town conflicts, as one side looked for government (i.e. the constable's) support.

[246] The siege took place between 19 and 26 July 1316; by 18 Dec. most of the guilty had bought their pardons and Bristol's liberties had been restored (Phillips, *Pembroke*, p. 103; Fuller, 'Bristol rebellion', pp. 186–7).

1316 consilium dum utilitas priuatorum transit*ᵃ* in commune dispendium. Sane meminisse debuerant obsessorum apud Bedeford finem desolatum, et eorum pariter qui apud Kenelesworthe contra regem tenuerunt castrum: illi quidem capti et omnes fere suspensi; isti uero uel in carcerem detrusi uel in exilium deportati.²⁴⁷

Quid est regi resistere nisi propriam uitam contempnere et omnia bona pariter amittere? Nam si insulanus*ᵇ* contra regem insulanum rebellat, proinde ac si uinculatus cum magistro carceris contendat. Per huiusmodi dissenciones deterioratur patria, et multipliciter leduntur indigene; quas,*ᶜ* si rex manum rigidam et correctricem apponeret, sedaret facillime. Set hodie frequenter accidit quod, licet aliquem deliquisse constiterit, pro muneribus iustificatur; fouetur impius, et ⟨in⟩*ᵈ* innocentem culpa retorquetur. Ex hoc quippe crescit audacia nocendi. Nam facilitas uenie incentiuum prebet delinquendi. Et si queratur cuius auctoritate fiant talia, dici potest quod tota iniquitas originaliter exiit a curia. Auaricia enim curialium uotis subsequitur singulorum. Hii sunt de quibus loquitur Dauid in Psalmis: Dextera eorum repleta est muneribus.²⁴⁸ Iccirco nil magis utile ⟨et⟩*ᵉ* necessarium foret in curia, quam ut rex tales collaterales haberet in camera, qui pro loco et tempore regem excessibus*ᶠ* suppliciter corriperent et impiorum satillitum cum uiderint expedire facta suggerent.*ᵍ* Propter quod uir quidam religiosus et note auctoritatis confessori domini regis misit litteras sub hiis uerbis:²⁴⁹

Cum rex a regendo dicatur,²⁵⁰ utpote qui populum legibus gubernare et gladio debeat ab inimicis defendere, dum bene regit conuenienter rex

---

ᵃ *sic MS; for* transiit *He*   ᵇ insulamus *MS;* insulanus *He, St, Den-Y*   ᶜ quam *MS; poss.* patriam *to be understood, otherwise* quas *to refer to* dissenciones *He*   ᵈ *om. MS; supplied He, St, Den-Y*   ᵉ *om. MS; supplied He, Den-Y*   ᶠ *sic R; perhaps* de excessibus *MW*   ᵍ suggerentur *MS;* suggererent *He, St;* suggerent *Den-Y*

²⁴⁷ At the fall of Bedford in 1224 William de Bréauté and over eighty of the garrison, which had rejected the offer of surrender and mercy, were executed for breach of fealty (D. A. Carpenter, *The Minority of Henry III* (London, 1990), pp. 366–7). The garrison of Kenilworth was allowed to go home when it finally capitulated on 14 Dec. 1266, but the siege had lasted nearly five months, and had already caused immense hardship (F. M. Powicke, *Henry III and the Lord Edward* (Oxford, 1947), ii. 539).

²⁴⁸ Ps. 25 (26): 10.

²⁴⁹ Both Stubbs and Denholm-Young noted the similarity of the beginning of this letter to the *Speculum Regis Edwardi III.* The *Speculum* survives in two recensions, which Leonard Boyle has convincingly argued should be seen as two separate works; a letter (*Epistola*) to the king written at the beginning of 1331 (Recension A in Moisant's edition) was followed up in 1332 by the *Speculum* proper (Recension B in Moisant's edition). Both were almost certainly written by William de Pagula, vicar of Winkfield in Windsor Forest. Both bitterly criticized

useless since the advantage of individual citizens turned into common 1316
loss. They ought, indeed, to have remembered the tragic fate of the
besieged at Bedford, and equally of those who held the castle of
Kenilworth against the king; the former were captured and almost all
hanged; the latter were cast into prison or sent into exile.[247]

What does it serve, to resist the king, except to throw away one's
life and lose all one's goods as well? For an islander to rebel against an
island king is as if a chained man were to try his strength with the
warder of his prison. By such quarrels the country is weakened, and
the inhabitants are injured in many ways; if the king applied a firm
correcting hand he would very easily settle them. But it often happens
today that, although someone is known to have done wrong, he clears
himself by gifts; the wicked man is encouraged, and guilt is fastened
upon the innocent. Because of this the boldness of the wrongdoer
certainly increases. For ease of pardon is a stimulus to crime. And if
anyone should ask by whose authority such things are done, it could
be said that the whole evil originally proceeds from the court. For the
courtiers' greed pursues the offerings of individuals. These are they
of whom David speaks in the Psalms: Their right hand is filled with
gifts.[248] Therefore nothing would be more useful and necessary at
court, than that the king should have such companions in his
chamber, who, at the right time and place, would restrain the
king's excesses by their entreaties and point out the doings of
wicked dependants as they saw it necessary. On this subject a certain
member of a religious order of acknowledged authority sent a letter to
the lord king's confessor in these words:[249]

since a king is so styled from the fact of ruling,[250] as one who should rule
his people with laws, and defend them with his sword from their enemies,
he is fittingly called king while he rules well; when he robs his people he is

---

the king's use of prise (L. E. Boyle, OP, 'William of Pagula and the *Speculum Regis Edwardi
III*', *Mediaeval Studies*, xxxiii (1970), 32–6; J. Moisant, *De Speculo Regis Edwardi III* (Paris,
1891), *passim*). This passage reflects more closely Recension A than Recension B, but there is
not necessarily any direct connection between Pagula's work and the *Vita* apart from a
common concern with the overuse of prise. This was a burning issue in the last years of
Edward I and throughout the reign of Edward II.

[250] This definition of kingship was widely used and paraphrased in the Middle Ages; for
an extensive list of early usages, see R. Maltby, *Lexicon of Ancient Latin Etymologies*
(Leeds, 1991) under *rex*; for further examples, see Kingsford, *Song of Lewes*, pp. 104–6.
Similar phrasing was used by Bracton, writing close to this period: *dicitur enim rex a bene
regendo et non a regnando, quia rex est dum bene regit, tyrannus dum populum sibi creditum
violenta opprimit dominacione*; Bracton, *De Legibus*, ii. 305. For full statements of the
lawyers' views of kingship, see ibid. 33, 304–6; *Fleta*, ii. 35.

1316 appellatur; dum populum spoliat tyrannus magis esse iudicatur. Sane rex noster transiens per patriam bona hominum capit et nil uel modicum aut male soluit. Set et hii frequenter, quibus ex tali causa aliquid debetur, ut labores euitent, de quota remittenda faciunt pactum, ut eo cicius soluatur residuum. Olim quidem gaudebant incole regis aduentantis uultum aspicere, nunc uero, quia in aduentu regis populus leditur, recessum eius ualde prestolantur et abeuntem*a* inprecantur*b* ut nunquam reuertatur. Rex eciam religiosis domibus nimis . . .

[*Bina folia, siue quatuor pagine, infortunio plane dolendo interciderunt. Hearne*]

. . . ueniret.

Reuera anno preterito ordinatum erat quod dominus rex sine consilio comitum et procerum nichil graue, nichil arduum inchoaret, et comitem*c* Lancastrie de consilio suo principaliter retineret.[251] Set quicquid placet domino regi domestici*d* comitis nituntur euertere; et quicquid placet comiti domestici*e* regis dicunt proditorium esse; et ita ad suggestionem seminatoris zizannie*f* interponunt se utriusque familiares, et dominos suos, per quos deberet terra defendi, non sinunt esse concordes. Siquidem Robertus de Brutz iam per multos annos, cum uastaret terras in Marchia, predia comitis semper dimisit intacta. Sperat enim, ut creditur, procurante comite penam diu comminatam euadere, et regnum *g*ante uendicatum*g* sub aliquo colore pacis retinere. Timet forsan et comes ne rex aliquando, memor iniurie quam exercuit comes in Petrum, ulcionem exspectat*h* cum uiderit*i* oportunum. Iccirco, ut dicitur, nititur comes Robertum de Brutz in regno Scocie solidare, ut, si forsan solus contra regem non possit resistere, saltem Roberti de Brutz fretus auxilio minas regias compellat arescere; set in hiis an fidei transgressor, an lese magestatis reus, comes habeatur, iudicio maiorum relinquatur: nam iure naturali saluti proprie per fas et nefas*j* licet consulere. Sic Dauid, fugiens a facie domini sui regis Saul, sibi prouidit, et ad regem Ghet cum suis omnibus prudenter conuolauit.[252]

Interea mandauerat*a* archiepiscopus Cantuariensis in ecclesia

---

a habentem *R*; abeuntem *St, Den-Y*   *b* sic *R*; imprecantur *St*   *c* comite *MS*; comitem *He, St, Den-Y*   *d* domesticis *MS*; domestici *He, St, Den-Y*   *e* domesticis *MS*; domestici *He, St, Den-Y*   *f* sic *R*; zizanie *St, Den-Y*   *g-g* autem uendicat *R*; ante uendicatum *St, Den-Y*   *h* sic *MS*; expectet *He, St, Den-Y*   *i* uideris *MS*; uiderit *He, St, Den-Y*   *j* nefa *MS*; nefas *He, St, Den-Y*

---

[251] This refers to the agreements made in the Lincoln parliament in Jan. 1316 (1315 by the medieval calendar); see above, pp. 120–1.

rather adjudged to be a tyrant. Indeed our king, passing through the country, 1316 takes men's goods and pays little or nothing or badly. In fact, those to whom something is owed from such a cause, in order to save trouble, often make an agreement to remit a percentage, so that the balance may be paid more quickly. Formerly, indeed, the inhabitants rejoiced to see the face of the king when he came, but now, because the people are injured by the king's arrival, they look forward greatly to his departure and as he leaves they pray that he may never return. The king moreover too often ⟨visits⟩ religious houses . . .

[Two leaves or four pages by a lamentable misfortune have wholly perished. Hearne]

. . . came.

In fact it had been decreed the year before that the lord king should initiate nothing weighty or important without the advice of the earls and great men, and should keep the earl of Lancaster at the head of his council.[251] But whatever pleases the lord king the earl's servants try to upset; and whatever pleases the earl the king's servants call treachery; and so at the prompting of the Devil the followers of each interfere, and do not allow their lords, by whom the land ought to be defended, to come to agreement. Indeed for many years past Robert Bruce, when he was laying waste to lands in the March, always left the earl's estates untouched. For he hopes, so it is believed, that with the earl's help he will escape the long-threatened penalty, and with some show of peace keep the kingdom which he has claimed. The earl also fears perhaps that the king, mindful of the wrong that the earl did to Piers, is waiting for revenge when he sees the opportunity. Therefore, it is said, the earl is trying to strengthen Robert Bruce in the kingdom of Scotland, so that, if by chance he cannot hold out alone against the king, with the help of Robert Bruce he may at least force the royal threats to cease; but whether in these matters the earl should be considered in breach of fealty or guilty of treason may be left to the verdict of more important persons: for by natural law it is proper to provide for one's own safety by any means, lawful and unlawful. Thus David, fleeing from the face of his lord king Saul, saved himself, and with all his men wisely took refuge with the king of Gath.[252]

[252] Cf. 1 Kgs. (1 Sam.) 21: 10. This appears to be the earliest reference to rumours that Lancaster was in contact with the Scots with treasonous intent. The author's concerns with treason and with its definition are evident here. For a discussion of his attitudes to resistance see above, pp. liii–lvii, and for a fuller discussion see Childs, 'Resistance and treason', pp. 179–91.

1316 sancti Pauli Londoniis tocius Anglie clerum conueniri;[253] petiitque idem archiepiscopus, cum ceteris episcopis ab aula electis, de media uel tertia parte bonorum ecclesiasticorum domino regi subueniri. Videntes illi pauci episcopi, qui ab ecclesia erant assumpti, primatem suum cum maiori parti coepiscoporum in partem domini regis inclinatum, iam in unam et eandem sentenciam conuenerunt, et peticionem archipresulis racionabilem fieri decreuerunt; set communitas cleri pluribus racionibus ab huiusmodi prestacione nitebatur absolui; *tum quia* sine auctoritate apostolica speciali non debet laicis de bonis ecclesiasticis aliqua porcio concedi, tum quia annona cara et annus sterilis, porcioneque regis et necessariis reseruatis, non haberent rectores quid erogarent* pauperibus. Responderunt prelati auctoritatem apostolicam in hoc casu non debere requiri, quia, cum rex infra regni sui terminos expungnatur, regi tanquam commune negocium gerenti communiter debet subueniri. Similiter ⟨per⟩* sterilitatem anni non oportet prestacionem tam necessariam impediri,* nam mediante archiepiscopo diebus oportunis fiet solucio. Tandem procuratores cleri, importunitate petencium uicti, decimam ecclesie domino regi concesserunt, et diem Purificacionis proxime sequentem, et eundem anno reuoluto iterum uenientem, dies solucionis acceperunt.[254]

Sane timendum est ne huiusmodi collecta, que grauat ecclesiam, domino regi cedat in ruinam. Nam bona ecclesie sunt bona pauperum. Nunquam pauperum, nunquam ecclesie spolia prosperum habuerunt auspicium. Certe sub Pharaone, cum ex principali decreto omnes ad solucionem quinte partis generaliter urgerentur, sacerdotes tamen fuerunt ab obseruancia et onere illius constitucionis immunes.[255] In libro eciam Numeri, ad figuram perpetue libertatis precepit Leuiticam tribum ab omni publica funccione liberam esse, *summi pontificis* duntaxat arbitrio subiacere.[256] Quid aliud potest aut debet exigere princeps a pontificibus uel a clero, quam ⟨ut⟩* incessanter fiat oracio ab ecclesia ad Deum pro eo? Omnis enim pontifex ex hominibus assumptus pro hominibus constituitur in hiis

---

a mandauerit *MS*; mandauerat *He, St, Den-Y*   *b–b* quia tamen *MS*; tum quia *He, St, Den-Y*   *c* errogarent *R*; erogarent *St, Den-Y*   *d* om. *MS*; poss. sterilitas *He*; per supplied *St, Den-Y*   *e* sic *MS*; poss. impedire with sterilitas *He*   *f–f* summus pontifex *MS*; summi pontificis *He, St, Den-Y*   *g* om. *MS*; supplied *He, St, Den-Y*

[253] The southern province was summoned for 11 Oct. 1316. The northern province met between 26 Oct. and 23 Nov. (*HBC*, p. 594).

[254] The payments were to be made on 2 Feb. 1317 and 1318. The reference to papal

Meanwhile the archbishop of Canterbury had ordered the clergy of 1316 all England to meet in the church of St Paul's, London;[253] and the same archbishop, together with the other bishops chosen by the court, asked for a half or a third of ecclesiastical goods to be given in aid to the lord king. Those few bishops chosen by the church, seeing that their primate with the majority of their fellow-bishops inclined towards the lord king's side, now came over to one and the same conclusion, and decided that the archbishop's reasonable request should be granted; but the community of the clergy urged on many grounds that they should be quit of this kind of payment; both because no part of ecclesiastical goods ought to be granted to laymen without special papal authority, and also because, by reason of the high price of grain and the poor year, when the king's share and other necessaries had been put aside, rectors would not have anything to give to the poor. The prelates replied that papal authority need not be sought in this case; because, since the king was being attacked within the borders of his kingdom, he should be supported by the community as one who was undertaking a matter of common concern. Likewise so necessary a contribution ought not to be hindered by the unfruitfulness of the year, for through the mediation of the archbishop payment would be made at convenient times. At length the proctors of the clergy, overcome by the persistence of the petitioners, granted an ecclesiastical tenth to the lord king and agreed to the feast of the Purification next following, and the same again the year after, as the days for payment.[254]

It is indeed to be feared lest this kind of contribution, which burdens the church, should bring about the lord king's ruin. For the goods of the church are the goods of the poor. Robbing the poor or the church has never been a good omen. Certainly under Pharaoh, when by the princely decree all in general were exhorted to pay the fifth, the priests were nevertheless exempt from the observance of this burdensome order.[255] Further, in the book of Numbers, as a symbol of perpetual liberty He ordered that the priestly tribe should be free from every public office, though subject to the judgement of the high priest.[256] What else can or should the prince demand from the bishops or clergy, than that prayer should continually be offered to God by the church for him? For every high priest taken from among

licence refers to the bull *Clericis laicos* (1296). For the church's view on clerical taxation to support the lay ruler, see above, n. 131.
[255] Cf. Gen. 47: 26.   [256] Cf. Num. 1: 47–53, 3: 5–10, 32, 18: 2–3.

1316 que sunt ad Deum, ut offerat dona et sacrificia[257] pro rege et populo,
et, si iratus est Dominus, sacerdos medius intercedat, et in tempore
iracundie factus[a] est reconciliacio.[258] Iratus Dominus populum suum
Israel delere decreuerat, stetitque Moises in confraccione[b] in conspectu eius,[259] et motum diuine indignacionis oracione placuit.[c] Item
flamma[d] diuina animauersacionis[e] deseuiente in populo, Aaron
arrepto[f] turibilo[g] medius inter uiuos et mortuos se flamme obiecit,
et cessauit quassacio.[260] Moise orante et manus erigente, Hebrei
uicerunt. Et sacerdotibus uociferantibus ad Dominum muri Ierico
corruerunt.[261] Hec est uis oracionis et sacrificii; aduersus non
preualebunt uectes inferi.[h 262] Recolat utinam dominus rex non ad
oppressionem set ad tuicionem ecclesie se[i] potestatem gladii ab
ecclesia suscepisse. Set et locum et officium in quo posuit eum
Dominus agnoscat, nec de thesauris ecclesie, que debentur pauperibus, set de [j]fiscali erario[j] bellum inferat inimicis.[263]

1317   Instante iam uerno tempore misit rex nuncios ad curiam Romanam, qui cum uenissent petierunt ex parte regis Anglie quatinus
dominus papa dictum regem ab obseruacione[k] quarundam ordinacionum, quibus idem rex iuramento tenebatur astrictus, digneretur[l]
absoluere. Asserebant enim predictas ordinaciones, licet de communi
assensu procerum editas et confirmatas, in perniciem regni et
ecclesie Anglicane periculose nimis redundare. Petierunt eciam
sentenciam excommunicacionis in Robertum de Brutz et omnes
sibi adherentes fulminari, et terram Scotorum interdicto supponi,
donec idem Robertus super commissis erga regem Anglie se
reformaret, et regnum Scocie, quod iniuste occupare dinoscitur,
penitus relinqueret. Supplicarunt insuper domino pape quatinus
domino regi, qui totum thesaurum suum pro defencione regni sui
et ⟨ecclesie impenderat⟩[m] per aliquod tempus dignaretur subuenire,

---

    [a] sic MS; facta He, St; factus Den-Y (which conforms with the Vulgate reading, ed.)
  [b] confirmacione R; confraccione St, Den-Y (which conforms with the Vulgate reading, ed.)
  [c] sic MS; placauit He, St, Den-Y   [d] flamam MS; flamma He, St, Den-Y   [e] sic MS;
animaduersionis He, St, Den-Y   [f] arepto MS; arrepto He, St, Den-Y   [g] sic MS;
thuribulo He, St; turibulo Den-Y   [h] inferri MS; inferi He, St, Den-Y   [i] set MS; se
He, St, Den-Y   [j-j] sic R; fisco uel erario suggested by Den-Y   [k] ad obseruacionem
MS; ab obseruacione He, St, Den-Y   [l] sic MS; dignaretur He, St, Den-Y   [m] om.
MS; impenderat conjectured He, St; ecclesie inpenderat supplied Den-Y

    [257] Heb. 5: 1.
    [258] Ecclus. 44: 17.
    [259] Ps. 105 (106): 23.

men is appointed for men in the things that pertain to God, so that 1316
he may offer up gifts and sacrifices[257] for the king and the people,
and if the Lord is angered, the priest may intercede as a mediator,
and in the time of wrath he was made a reconciliation.[258] The Lord
in his wrath had decided to destroy his people Israel, and Moses
stood before him in the breach,[259] and appeased by prayer the
mounting anger of the Lord. Also, the fire of divine punishment
going out upon the people, Aaron took up his censer and stood
against the flame between the dead and the living, and the plague
ceased.[260] As Moses prayed and lifted up his hands, the Hebrews
conquered. And as the priests cried to the Lord the walls of Jericho
fell down.[261] This is the power of prayer and sacrifice; and the gates
of hell shall not prevail against it.[262] Would that the lord king
remembered that he has received the power of the sword from the
church not for the oppression but for the protection of the church.
Let him, further, acknowledge both the place and office in which the
Lord has placed him, and wage war upon his enemies not from the
wealth of the church which should be for the poor, but from the
royal treasury.[263]

When spring came round the king sent an embassy to the court of 1317
Rome; when they had arrived, these asked on behalf of the king of
England that the lord pope should regard it as fitting to absolve the
said king from the observance of certain Ordinances to which the
same king was closely bound by oath. They maintained that the said
Ordinances, though published and confirmed by the common
consent of the great men, were contributing extremely dangerously
towards the destruction of the kingdom and the English church.
They also asked for sentence of excommunication to be promulgated
against Robert Bruce and all his supporters, and for the land of the
Scots to be put under an interdict, until the same Robert should
make good the wrongs committed by him against the king of
England, and should utterly give up the kingdom of Scotland,
which he is known to have seized wrongfully. They also begged
the lord pope to see fit to help for a time the lord king, who [had
expended] all his treasure for the defence of his realm and [the
church]; adding that the king was determined, when he had made

---

[260] Num. 16: 46, 48; Ps. 105 (106): 30.
[261] Cf. Josh. 6: 20.
[262] Matt. 16: 18.
[263] For the author's use of *fiscus* and *erarium* see above, n. 40.

1317 adicientes regem intentum, pacificato regno suo, si competeret facultas, summa deuocione contra paganos transfretare.²⁶⁴

Ad hec respondit papa regem Anglie ab obseruacione predictarum ordinacionum absolui non debere, cum, sicut acceperat, fidedignorum studio fuissent confecte, quos non erat uerisimile in preiudicium regni uel ecclesie aliquid ordinasse. Decreuit eciam dominus papa regnum Scotorum interdicto non esse supponendum donec constaret de iure parcium. Denique ecclesiam uel decimas ecclesie noluit dominus papa potestati laicorum submittere, set sueᵃ tantum ordinacioni reseruaret, et, si regem Anglie in subsidium Terre Sancte armari contingeret,ᵇ de fructibus ecclesie, si necesse foret, sumptus habundanter ministraret.²⁶⁵ Promisit insuper dominus papa legatos in Angliam mittere, qui de hiis diligenter inquirerent et auctoritate apostolica omnes controuersias fine debito terminarent.²⁶⁶

Interim adueniente tempore quo solent reges ad bella procedere,²⁶⁷ uocauit rex proceres ad parliamentum ut iuxta tenorem ordinacionum, antequam procederetur ad bellum, in communi parliamento deliberaretur quid esset agendum; set die statuto adueniente non uenit comes Lancastrie. Interim sub fidelitate et homagio monetur esse parliamento; set, nec sic ueniens, sub forisfactura omnium que possidebat in Anglia, copiam sui facere iubetur in curia. Tunc misit comes nuncios qui excusarent eum coram rege et allegarent similiter causas absencie;²⁶⁸ qui statim iussa complentes accesserunt ad regem dicentes: 'Domine, si placet, offendi uel mirari non debetis, si comes Lancastrie ad parliamentum non uenit, timet enim quorundam insidias capitales quos curia regia tuetur et nutrit.

ᵃ sine *MS*; sue *He, St, Den-Y*   ᵇ contigeret *MS*; contingeret *He, St, Den-Y*
ᶜ inueniente *MS*; ueniente *or* adueniente *He*; ueniente *St, Den-Y*

---

²⁶⁴ Letters empowering the bishops of Ely and Norwich, the earl of Pembroke, and Bartholomew Badlesmere to treat in Avignon were issued in Dec. 1316. Their clear tasks were to renegotiate the loan from Clement V, and to obtain support against Scotland, a delay to Edward's vow to go on crusade, and a grant of clerical taxation. This is a unique reference to the attempt to annul the Ordinances at this time, but as the author is accurate about the other matters, he may be equally so about this. Edward was acutely aware of the Ordinances at this time because of the various negotiations with Lancaster. An annulment was possibly part of verbal instructions. In a letter of 18 Jan. 1317 the pope was asked to give credence to what the ambassadors should tell him about a private matter close to Edward's heart. This could certainly describe the Ordinances (*Foed.*, ii. 1. 302–29; Phillips, *Pembroke*, pp. 107–8; Maddicott, *Lancaster*, p. 199).
²⁶⁵ John XXII had just imposed a second levy of papal annates (first fruits) to run for three years from Dec. 1316. He granted half the first year's revenue to the king (Lunt, *Financial Relations*, pp. 494–501); for the first levy, see above, n. 154.
²⁶⁶ By Mar. 1317 two legates had been duly appointed. They were Gaucelin d'Euse, the

peace in his realm, if the opportunity occurred, to cross the sea 1317
against the pagans with the utmost dedication.[264]

To this the pope replied that the king of England ought not to be
absolved from the observance of the said Ordinances since they had
been drawn up, as he had been informed, through the endeavour of
trustworthy persons, and it was not likely that they had ordained
anything to the prejudice of the kingdom or the church. The lord pope
also decreed that the kingdom of Scotland was not to be put under an
interdict until the rights of both sides had been established. Finally, the
lord pope refused to put the church or the tenths of the church into the
control of laymen, but would keep such things at his own disposal, and
if it happened that the king of England took up arms to help the Holy
Land, he would if necessary abundantly provide expenses from the
fruits of the church.[265] The lord pope also promised to send legates to
England, to make careful enquiry about these matters, and, by
apostolic authority, put a due end to all controversies.[266]

Meanwhile, as the time approached when kings go forth to war,[267]
the king summoned the nobles to parliament so that, according to the
tenor of the Ordinances, before proceeding to war they should
consider in common parliament what was to be done; but when the
appointed day arrived the earl of Lancaster did not come. He was
warned in the meantime to attend parliament by reason of his fealty
and homage; but, as he did not so come, he was ordered on pain of
forfeiting all that he possessed in England, to make his appearance at
court. Then the earl sent messengers to excuse him before the king
and likewise to put forward the reasons for his absence.[268] They at
once approached the king in fulfilment of their orders, saying: 'My
Lord, if it please you, you ought not to be offended or surprised if the
earl of Lancaster does not come to parliament, for he fears the deadly
plots of certain men whom the royal court protects and fosters. Their

pope's nephew, appointed cardinal priest of SS Marcellino and Pietro in 1316 and (later)
cardinal bishop of Albano in 1327, and Luca dei Fieschi, kinsman of King Jaime II of
Aragon, appointed cardinal deacon of Santa Maria in Via Lata in 1300 and of SS Cosma e
Damiano in 1306 (Eubel, *Hier. Cath.*, i. 13, 15, 35, 44, 49; *Foed.*, ii. 1. 317, 318). They
were in England by 1 July (*CCR 1313–18*, p. 482).

[267] 2 Kgs. (2 Sam.) 11: 1.

[268] Clause 9 of the Ordinances demanded the assent of the baronage in parliament for
war. The author's use of the word parliament for the meetings in 1317 is interesting since
none of the three meetings was called parliament in the records. Councils were called for 9
Feb. at Clarendon, 15 Apr. at Westminster, and 18 July at Nottingham (*CCR 1313–18*,
pp. 451, 456, 459, 482; *CPR 1313–17*, p. 634; *HBC*, p. 554). Lancaster attended none
(Maddicott, *Lancaster*, pp. 191–2). This passage almost certainly refers to the April
meeting; see below, n. 270.

1317 De inimicitiis eorum iam constat euidenter; iam uxorem comitis in
dedecus et obprobium eius rapuerunt,[269] unde affectum quem erga
eum gerunt iam liquido protulerunt. Petit ergo comes quatinus
malefactores illos a familiaritate uestra uelitis expellere, et tunc
ueniet ad uos ubicunque uolueritis assignare. Petit eciam quod
possit sine offencione uestra de iniuria sibi illata uindictam sumere
et satisfaccionem qualem poterit impetrare.'[270]

Respondit rex: 'Ego contemptum comitis iudicabo cum potero;
familiares meos expellere nolo; de raptu uxoris sue remedium iure
querat tantummodo.' Conuocatis itaque familiaribus suis et ceteris
amicis, ait rex coram omnibus: 'Ecce uidetis quomodo comes Lancastrie ad parliamentum non uenit. Videtis quomodo mandatis nostris
parere contempserit. Quid uobis uidetur?' Dicunt quidam: 'Dignum
est ut qui preceptis domini sui parere contempnit contumaciam luat, et
feodum si quod tenet, tamquam periurus consequenter amittat.
Persequatur ergo rex contemptorem suum et comprehendat, et
comprehensum sub carcere cludat uel regno proscribat.' Alii uero
dixerunt: 'Non est leue capere comitem Lancastrie. Scoti succurrent ei
et magna pars Wallie; set melius est aliam uiam assumere, et prius
tractare de forma concordie. Satis enim liquet ex Britonum historia
quam sit plena periculis ciuilis discordia. Nam quod Iulius Cesar
regnum Britannie sibi subiugauit, et quod gens Saxonum fugatis
Britonibus regnum occupauit, quod Normanni regimen Anglie consequenter,[a] ex simili discordia cuncta peruenisse noscuntur.'

Interuenientibus ergo magnatibus, concessum est ut dominus rex
et comes conuenirent[b] ad quendam locum sicut fieri decet ad diem
amoris[271] sine strepitu armorum. Sperabatur enim quod, si inter se
raciones suas et uerba conferent,[c] cicius efficerentur unanimes, quam
per mediatores mandata parcium sepe peruertentes. Set quia secreta
diuitum occultari non possunt, statim nunciatum est comiti regem
iurasse quod, si comes uix modo[d] conuentum accederet, aut capite
priuaret eum aut carceri manciparet.

---

 [a] sic R; poss. for consequentur MW; prob. a verb is missing, ed.   [b] conuenerunt MS;
conuenirent He, St, Den-Y   [c] sic MS; conferrent He, St, Den-Y   [d] modum MS;
uix modo He, Den-Y; uixdum St

---

[269] Alice left Thomas on 11 Apr. 1317, possibly with court connivance (Maddicott,
Lancaster, pp. 197–8).
[270] The reference to his wife's abduction strongly suggests that these messengers were
excusing his absence at the April council meeting, held very shortly after the abduction.
Lancaster's letter of excuse for his later absence in July did not refer to his wife (*Murimuth*,
pp. 271–4; *Brid.*, pp. 50–2). However, it remains possible that the messengers mentioned

enmity is already clearly well known; they have already carried off the   1317
earl's wife to his disgrace and shame,[269] whereby they have plainly
displayed the feelings that they bear towards him. The earl therefore
asks you to drive these evildoers from their position in your household, and then he will come to you wherever you wish to choose. He
also asks that he may without offence take revenge and such
satisfaction as he can get for the wrong done to him.'[270]

The king replied: 'I will punish the affront to the earl when I can; I
will not to send away members of my household; for the abduction of
his wife let him seek a remedy only at law.' And so, having summoned
his household and other friends, the king said in the presence of all:
'You see how the earl of Lancaster has not come to parliament. You
see how he scorns to obey our commands. How does it seem to you?'
Some said: 'It is right that he who scorns to obey his lord's commands
shall pay for his obstinate disobedience, and consequently, as a
perjurer, lose his fief if he holds one. Let the king therefore pursue
and seize the man who has scorned him, and when he is seized put
him in prison or exile him from the kingdom.' But others said: 'It is
not a small matter to take the earl of Lancaster. The Scots will
support him and a great part of Wales; but it is better to adopt
another way, and to discuss first a form of agreement. For it is very
clear from the history of the Britons, how civil discord is filled with
dangers. For that Julius Caesar made the kingdom of Britain subject
to him, that the Saxon race seized the kingdom once the Britons had
fled, that the Normans in their turn [took over] the rule of England
are all known to have resulted from a similar discord.'

So, with the great men acting as mediators, it was agreed that the
lord king and the earl should meet at a certain place as it is
appropriate to do for a loveday[271] without the clash of arms. For it
was hoped that if they talked their reasons and arguments over
between themselves, they would come to an agreement more quickly
than through mediators who often twist the meaning of their
instructions from both sides. But because the secrets of the rich
cannot be hidden, it was immediately reported to the earl that the
king had sworn that if only the earl should come to the meeting, he
would either have his head or throw him in prison.

here were those of July, delivering an additional verbal message to supplement the July
letter (Maddicott, *Lancaster*, p. 198).

[271] A loveday was 'a day appointed for a meeting with a view to an amicable settlement
of a dispute' (*OED*). It was a term used for meetings to manage breaches of truce and to
extend truces (Keen, *Laws of War*, p. 215).

1317   Ab illa die in antea cogitauit comes regem non adire sine tutela.
Congregauit sibi comes omnes sibi adherentes apud Pountefreyt*a*
castrum suum, et erat rex eo tempore apud Eboracum, ubi mandauerat exercitum suum conuenire;[272] set qui properabant ad regem
non permittuntur cum armis transire. Obseruabat enim comes
pontes, et diligenter fecit inhiberi dextrarios transduci uel arma
transferri; et hoc asserebat se facere eo quod senescallus sit Anglie,
cuius interest utilitatibus regni prospicere, et, si rex contra aliquem
arma uellet assumere, senescallo precipue deberet innotescere.[273]
Cernens autem rex suum impediri propositum, et consilium eius
pro parte denudatum, quid faceret uel quo se uerteret penitus
ignorauit. Denique procurante comite de Penbrok, interponentibus
se eciam cardinalibus legatis *b*iam qui*b* uenerant in Angliam, sic actum
est, ut in quindena sancti Hillarii[274] apud Lyncolniam conuenirent
uniuersi, et tunc repararentur omnia indirecta, et de malefactoribus
fieret iusticia.

Hiis itaque dispositis dominus rex cum tota comitiua sua uersus
Londonias aggreditur, et, cum uenisset prope castrum de Pountfreit
pertinens ad comitem Lancastrie, iussit omnes suos arma resumere,
quia forsan timuit sibi ubi non erat timendum, aut certe ab
insipientibus processit consilium. Armati uero et per turmas distincti
processerunt quasi uillam expungnaturi; et ecce, comes Penbrok
regem alloquitur: 'Domine,' inquid comes, 'quale consilium accepisti?
quid est quod ita precipitanter arma sumpsisti? Aduersarius non
instat, nec aliquis nos expungnat. Nonne omnia ad certum tempus
sunt suspensa, pacta inita, fide pariter et scriptis confirmata? Turpe
est contra pacta uenire, credentem fallere et fidem infringere.' Et rex
ad comitem; 'Relatum est michi quod comes Lancastrie in insidiis
latitat, et nos omnes inprouisos inuadere studiose procurat.'

---

a Pountesfreyt *R*; Pountefreyt *St, Den-Y*   *b–b* *sic R*; qui iam *St, Den-Y*

---

[272] Lancaster was certainly at Pontefract as early as 24 July 1317 (Maddicott, *Lancaster*,
p. 345) and may have been there throughout Aug. Edward was at York from 4 Sept. (*Itin.*,
p. 159). After preliminary meetings at York, the main army was due to muster at
Newcastle on 15 Sept. (*PW*, ii. 1. 494–9).

[273] This appears to be the earliest reference to Lancaster's exploitation of the stewardship of England in the middle years of the reign. He made a further statement in 1318 and
claimed in 1319 the right to appoint the steward of the household. Lancaster claimed the
stewardship through its links with the earldom of Leicester. The earldom had been granted
to his father, Edmund, in 1265, but the stewardship was granted to Edmund only in 1268
and then only for life. Thomas made no claim to the office while Edward I was alive, but

From that day forward the earl took care not to approach the king 1317 without protection. The earl collected all his supporters at his castle of Pontefract, and the king at that time was at York, where he had ordered his army to muster;[272] but those who were hastening to the king were not allowed to pass by armed. For the earl guarded the bridges, and assiduously prevented war-horses or weapons from being taken across; and he said that he did this because he was steward of England, whose business it was to look to the advantage of the kingdom, and if the king wished to take up arms against anyone he ought first to notify the steward.[273] The king seeing that his purpose was frustrated and his plan partly laid bare, had absolutely no idea what to do or which way to turn. At length at the instance of the earl of Pembroke, and by the intervention of the cardinal legates who had now reached England, it was decided thus: that they should all meet a fortnight after the feast of St Hilary[274] at Lincoln, and then all wrongs would be righted, and justice done to evildoers.

When these things had been settled the lord king marched towards London with all his retinue, and when he had come close to the earl of Lancaster's castle of Pontefract he ordered all his men to take up their arms, perhaps because he was afraid where there was nothing to be feared, or else, in fact, because the advice came from foolish people. In truth, armed and divided up into troops they marched on as if about to besiege the town; and see, the earl of Pembroke addresses the king: 'My Lord,' said the earl, 'What kind of counsel have you taken? Why have you so hastily taken up arms? No enemy presses us, no one is fighting us. Has not everything been postponed until an appointed date, agreements entered into, confirmed equally by a pledge and being set down in writing? It is shameful to go against the agreement, to deceive those trusting in it, and to break faith.' And the king replied to the earl: 'I have been told that the earl of Lancaster is lying in ambush, and is carefully preparing to attack us all by surprise.'

obtained it for himself and his heirs from Edward II in 1308. His claim to supervise the good of the kingdom reflects the first part of the tract on the steward (usually assigned to 1321), but the claim to a military role is not made there. The military claim may have been based on the right to supervise the king's castles granted to Edmund soon after he had been made steward (L. W. Vernon Harcourt, *His Grace the Steward and Trial of Peers* (London, 1907), pp. 148–51, 164–7; Maddicott, *Lancaster*, pp. 76–7, 241–3).

[274] 27 Jan. 1318. The cardinals (Gaucelin d'Euse and Luca dei Fieschi) had been in England since 1 July 1317 (see n. 266 above). They arrived at York c.7 Sept. following the attack on them near Durham (see below, p. 142–3). Negotiations took place until 29 Sept., when Edward left York (*Cont. Trivet*, p. 23; *Itin.*, p. 159). The parliament was later postponed (see n. 283 below).

1317 'Certe,' inquid comes, 'domine, non est ita. Regnum et feodum, et uniuersa que possidet, comes ipse relinqueret priusquam huiusmodi prodicionem inchoaret.' Sic tandem ad suggestionem comitis rex ab inceptis destitit, et uersus Londonias iter arripuit.[275]

Rebus sic se habentibus,[a] reuersi sunt eciam cardinales Londonias. Processerant enim uersus Scociam ut[b] ibidem legacionem suam[c] fungerentur; set per terram Northamhimbrorum iter facientes a quibusdam predonibus[d] male tractabantur. Nam Gilbertum quendam de Middeltone dictum cum suis complicibus obuiam habuerunt,[e] qui sarcinulas eorum scrutantes maximam summam pecunie legatis abstulerunt.[276] Suspendebant ergo legati partes legacionis sue ad tempus, donec in parliamento optinuerunt[f] fieri ulcionem de malefactoribus illis; procedentes nichilominus spiritualiter contra dictos predones, Gilbertum de Middeltone cum suis fautoribus solempniter et publice a communione fidelium separantes. Vt[g] expressa pena inmanitas excessus appareat, tenorem quem ex constitucione Bonefacii octaui pro parte recolui lector aduertat. Bonefacius octauus in titulo *de penis* sic statuit:[277]

Si quis in hoc sacrilegii genus irrepserit quod ecclesie Romane cardinalem hostiliter insecutus fuerit, percusserit aut ceperit, fieri mandauerit uel factum ratum habuerit, consilium facienti dederit uel fauorem, aut scienter receptauerit uel defensauerit eundem, tanquam reus lese magestatis perpetuo sit infamis, bannitus et intestabilis,[h] et ab omni successione repulsus; omnia edificia eius diruantur, et, ut perpetuam notam[i] infamie perpetua ruina testetur, et[j] nullo tempore reparentur. Nullus ei debita cogatur reddere, nullus in iudicio sibi teneatur respondere, set quicquid in bonis ipsius inuenitur, fisco uel rei publice dominio applicetur, nulla parte bonorum ad posteros eius transmissa, ut sic quodammodo cum ipso dampnentur et sua, et si quid ab ecclesia forsan optineant ipso iure beneficium perdant, de quo

---

[a] dehabentibus *MS*; se habentibus *He, St, Den-Y*   [b] et *MS*; ut *He, St, Den-Y*
[c] sic *MS*; suum *St, Den-Y*   [d] predonis *MS*; predonibus *He, St, Den-Y*   [e] habuit
MS; habuerunt *He, St, Den-Y*   [f] sic *R*; *He corrected his first reading of* optinuerunt *to*
optinerent *without comment*; optinerent *St, Den-Y*   [g] et *MS*; ut *He, St, Den-Y*
[h] indetestabilis *MS*; intestabilis *He, St, Den-Y*   [i] uotam *MS*; notam *He, St, Den-Y*
[j] sic *MS*; redundant *MW*

---

[275] This incident took place between 29 Sept. 1317, when Edward left York, and 3 Oct., by which time he had reached Doncaster (*Itin.*, pp. 159–60).

[276] The attack occurred on 1 Sept. 1317 at Ferryhill, between Darlington and Durham. The cardinals were accompanying Louis Beaumont, bishop-elect of Durham, and his brother Henry Beaumont to Durham for Louis's consecration. Although the perpetrator was Gilbert Middleton, a Northumbrian and a royal household knight, Lancaster may have been implicated in the attack. He disliked Henry Beaumont as a symbol of the king's non-

'Indeed, my lord, it is not so', said the earl. 'The earl himself would 1317
leave the kingdom, his fee, and everything that he has, before he
would set such treachery in motion.' So at length at the earl's
prompting the king gave up his intentions, and made his way towards
London.[275]

This was the state of affairs when the cardinals too returned to
London. They had set out for Scotland to carry out their commission
there; but journeying through Northumbria they were badly treated
by certain robbers. For they met a certain Gilbert, called of
Middleton, with his accomplices, who searched their baggage and
took from the legates a very large sum of money.[276] Therefore the
legates postponed part of their mission for a time, until they should
obtain redress in parliament against those wrongdoers; nevertheless
they proceeded spiritually against the said robbers, solemnly and
publicly cutting Gilbert Middleton and his accomplices out of the
communion of the faithful. So that the enormity of the outrage may
appear from the penalty laid down for it, the reader may note the
wording of Boniface VIII's constitution which I have recorded in
part. Boniface VIII under the title 'Of Penalties' decreed thus:[277]

If any one fall into this kind of sacrilege, namely that he has attacked,
struck, or seized a cardinal of the Roman church, or has ordered it to be
done, or approved it when done, or given counsel or aid to the doer, or has
knowingly received or defended the same, as one guilty of treason he shall
be for ever disgraced, banned, and incapable of making a will, and excluded
from every succession; all his buildings shall be destroyed, and, so that their
permanent ruin may bear witness as an everlasting mark of disgrace, they
shall never be repaired. No one shall be forced to pay debts to him, no one
bound to answer to him in judgment, but whatever is found of his goods
shall be made over to the treasury of public funds, no part of his property
shall be transmitted to his descendants, so that in a way they are
condemned with him and his goods, and if by chance they hold anything
from the church, by the same law they shall lose the benefice, which the

enforcement of the Ordinances, and Louis Beaumont because he had been favoured above
Lancaster's candidate for the bishopric of Durham. The Beaumonts were detained in
Mitford Castle until payment of ransom in Oct. The cardinals' presence in the party seems
to have been unexpected: they were immediately released and Lancaster offered his
personal protection for their journey from Durham to York (Maddicott, *Lancaster*,
pp. 204–6; Phillips, *Pembroke*, pp. 126–8). For a full account, see A. E. Middleton, *Sir
Gilbert de Middleton* (Newcastle, 1918); for doubt cast on Lancaster's role, see
M. Prestwich, 'Gilbert de Middleton and the attack on the cardinals, 1317', in
T. Reuter (ed.), *Warriors and Churchmen in the High Middle Ages: Essays Presented to
Karl Leyser* (London, 1992), pp. 179–94, esp. 186–90, 194.
[277] Cf. *Sext.* L. 5 t. 9 c. 5, *Corpus Iuris Canonici*, cols. 1091–2.

1317 superior ecclesie pro sua uoluntate disponat. Insuper filii eius et nepotes per masculinam lineam descendentes, si beneficium aliquod uel eciam pontificalem dignitatem fuerint adepti, sint eis ipso iure priuati; sit talibus omnis preclusa dignitas, sit postulandi negata facultas, officium et quodlibet ministerium*a* publicum utrobique sic sit eis interdictum. Non credatur in iudiciis eorum assercioni; ad testimonium prorsus reddantur indigni.*b* Sit eis ad ordines ascensus inhibitus; sit ad beneficium ecclesiasticum negatus accessus; et, ut magis famosa sit eorum infamia, super omnibus premissis sit eis spes dispensacionis penitus adempta, et tam insecutor quam uiolente manus*c* iniector, ipso facto sentenciam excommunicacionis maioris incurrat, quam non nisi per summum pontificem, nisi duntaxat in mortis articulo constitutus, euadat.

Et hec quidem sentencia in predictum Gilbertum et suos fautores tam terribiliter erat promulgata.

Reuera nimis erat audax uersucia et uersuta nimis audacia que tantis uiris non pepercit. Cui capiti cuiusque persone reuerencia debetur, si patribus conscriptis, si*d* legatis a latere pape transmissis non defertur? Ceterum quantumcunque peccauerit*e* uir in uirum,[278] solet ecclesia Romana humiliter petenti ueniam prestare; set si manus sacrilega curiam ipsam inuaserit, qua fronte, queso, poterit ueniam postulare, cum iure caueatur quod frustra legis auxilium inuocat qui committit in legem?[279] Denique cuius efficacie fuerit sentencia statim apparuit; nam paucis euolutis diebus Gilbertus capitur et coram iusticiariis regis Londoniis condempnatur. Deinde protractus, suspensus et exenteratus, capite truncatur.[280]

Quia in festo sancti Hillarii[281] dominum regem et ceteros magnates ad parliamentum conuenire oportuit, ex condicto conuenerunt hii qui erant de consilio domini regis,[282] dicentes: 'Non est bonum inire parliamentum sub hoc modo. Nam si dominus rex ueniat et comes Lancastrie ueniat, utique et omnes qui sunt de eorum retencione, et*f* certe tanta et tam effrenata*g* multitudo mali pocius quam boni foret occasio. Iccirco melius est per medias personas inter dominum regem et comitem Lancastrie firmam concordiam et plenam securitatem

---

a misterium *R*; ministerium *St, Den-Y*   *b* indignum *MS*; indigni *He, St, Den-Y*
c ma manus *MS*; manus *He, St, Den-Y*   *d* se *MS*; si *He, St, Den-Y*   *e* placuerit *MS*; fecerit, *or else* faciat *to be understood He*; peccauerit *St, Den-Y*   *f* sic *MS*; *redundant MW*   *g* effranata *MS*; effrenata *He, St, Den-Y*

[278] I Kgs. (I Sam.) 2: 25.
[279] *Dig.* iv. 4. 37, *Corpus Iuris Ciuilis*, i. 61.

ecclesiastical superior shall dispose of as he wills. Moreover his sons and 1317 grandsons descending in the male line, if they have acquired any benefice or even the episcopal dignity, are by the same law deprived of them; such persons are precluded from every dignity, denied the opportunity of postulation, office and any kind of public service is alike forbidden to them. No faith is to be placed in their statements in courts of law; they are rendered utterly unworthy of bearing witness. They may not proceed to Holy Orders; they may not receive an ecclesiastical benefice; and that their infamy may be the more notorious, all hope of dispensation for all the aforesaid is utterly taken away, and the persecutor as well as the one who attacks with violence shall automatically incur the sentence of the greater excommunication, from which he shall not escape, except at the hands of the pope alone, unless he is at the point of death.

And this sentence was indeed, terrifyingly, promulgated against the said Gilbert and his supporters.

Indeed too rash was the deceit and too deceitful the rashness that did not spare such men. To whose head, to whose person is reverence due, if it is not given to senators, to legates specially sent by the pope? In other respects, however much one man shall sin against another,[278] the Roman church is accustomed to bestow pardon on the humble petitioner; but if the sacrilegious hand attacks the curia itself, with what assurance, I ask, can pardon be demanded, since we are warned by law that the support of the law is sought in vain by the lawbreaker?[279] At any rate the efficacy of the sentence was at once apparent; for after a few days Gilbert was taken and condemned before the king's justices at London. Then he was drawn, hanged, and disembowelled, and his head cut off.[280]

Because the lord king and the other great men were to meet in parliament on the feast of St Hilary,[281] those who were of the lord king's council met by agreement,[282] saying: 'It is not good to begin a parliament like this. For if the lord king comes and the earl of Lancaster comes, and all on both sides who are retained by them, surely so great and so unruly a crowd would be the occasion of evil rather than good. Therefore it is better to restore true harmony and full confidence between the lord king and the earl of Lancaster by

[280] Middleton held out until Dec. in Mitford Castle; he was executed in London on 26 Jan. 1318 (*Ann. Paul.*, pp. 281–2) or about 2 Feb. (*Brid.*, p. 52; *Flores*, iii. 180).
[281] 13 Jan. 1318; the date is given correctly as the quinzaine of St Hilary (27 Jan.) above, pp. 140–1.
[282] The council met on 30 Dec. 1317 (*CCR 1313–18*, p. 586; *PW*, ii. 2. 174; Phillips, *Pembroke*, p. 154).

1317 prius reformare, ac deinde diem et locum parliamenti sicut decet
1318 assignare.' Et actum est.[283] Nam de consensu conuenerunt apud
Leicestriam archiepiscopi, comites et barones ex parte domini regis,
et consiliarii comitis, tractaturi super istis negociis.[284] Vbi cum multa
ex parte regis peterentur quibus et comes ipse, si placeret ei, prestaret
assensum, ad nichil penitus inclinari potuit sine plenaria obseruacione
ordinacionum.

Videntes igitur archiepiscopi[a] et ceteri comites animum comitis
immobilem, concesserunt pro domino rege et pro se ordinaciones
uniuersas fideliter obseruari, et cartam testimonii sacramento singulorum et sigillorum impressione roborari. Et comes Lancastrie e
contra domino regi et suis debitam fidelitatem et securitatem sub
fide promisit, excepta querela quam contra comitem Warennie de
raptu uxoris dudum instituit.

Hiis igitur sub tali forma excessis,[b] acceperunt diem parliamenti
apud Lyncolniam in crastino Trinitatis.[285] [c]O quantum[c] nocuit ista
dissencio, O quantum exstitit malis occasio! Dum rex delirat cum
baronibus, fiducia[d] rebellandi datur hostibus. Sic[e] iam amittitur tota
Scocia, et terra Northamhimbrorum iacet inculta. Vna uilla regi
remanserat in Scocia. Hec erat Berewyke, fortis et ualida et muro
inexpungnabili decenter ambita. Hanc dum rex committeret burgen-
sium custodie, uillam tradunt hostibus famuli perfidie.[286] Reuera nec
locus tutissimus nec uir potentissimus resistit proditoribus; set Troia
obsessa[f] decennio, que uinci non potuit in prelio, proditorum tandem
subcubuit ingenio. Sic ille magnus Grecorum imperator Allexander,[g]
tocius orbis domitor, cum cunctas naciones armis subicit, per
familiares proditores toxicatus occubuit.[287] Studeat amodo rex

[a] sic R; archiepiscopus St, Den-Y   [b] sic R; concessis Den-Y   [c-c] Equantum MS;
O quantum He, St, Den-Y   [d] fudicia MS; fiducia He, St, Den-Y   [e] sit MS; sic He,
St, Den-Y   [f] obcessa MS; obsessa He, St, Den-Y   [g] sic R; Alexander St, Den-Y

[283] The parliament was postponed on 4 Jan. 1318 to 12 Mar., and on 3 Mar. to 19 June,
in order to accommodate negotiations with Lancaster through the spring. On 8 June the
summons was revoked because of the need to combat the Scottish raids. Parliament finally
met on 20 Oct. 1318 at York and implemented the terms of the treaty of Leake (CCR
1313–18, pp. 590, 601, 619; CCR 1318–23, p. 99; PW, ii. 1. 175–7, 178, 181–2).
[284] They met at Leicester in early Apr. 1318 and final agreement was probably reached
by 12 Apr. 1318. The canon of Bridlington is the best source for this meeting, although he
wrongly called it a parliament (Brid., pp. 54–5). At this stage Lancaster appeared to have
achieved everything he wanted, but over the next four months, under pressure, he made
concessions (Maddicott, Lancaster, pp. 216–29, 237–9). The recipients of royal grants had
every reason to block the agreement, but it is also possible that royal envoys had made the
agreement expecting further negotiations (Phillips, Pembroke, p. 163).
[285] 19 June 1318. The author is mistaken in placing the decision about the new date for

intermediaries, and then appoint a day and place for parliament as is 1317
fitting.' And so it was done.[283] For the archbishops, earls and barons 1318
on the lord king's part, and the earl's counsellors met by agreement at
Leicester to discuss this business.[284] There, when many things were
sought on the king's behalf to which the earl should give assent if it
pleased him, he could not be persuaded to accept anything at all
without full observance of the Ordinances.

Seeing, therefore, that the earl's mind was made up, the archbishops and the other earls granted on behalf of the lord king and
themselves that all the Ordinances should be faithfully observed, and
that a charter in witness of this should be confirmed by the oath of
each and the impression of their seals. And the earl of Lancaster for
his part promised on his oath due fealty and security to the lord king
and his men, saving the complaint that he had long ago lodged against
Earl Warenne for the abduction of his wife.

When these things had been granted in this way, they received a
date for parliament at Lincoln on the morrow of Holy Trinity.[285] Oh!
How harmful was this quarrel! Oh! How great an occasion for evil!
While the king raves against the barons, his enemies are given the
confidence to rebel. In this way the whole of Scotland is now lost and
the land of Northumbria lies waste. One town alone remained to the
king in Scotland. This was Berwick, sturdy and strong and well
surrounded by an impregnable wall. When the king committed this
town to the care of the burgesses, the treacherous servants handed it
over to the enemy.[286] Indeed there is no place safe enough or any man
powerful enough to withstand traitors: Troy, besieged for a decade,
which could not be conquered in battle, at length succumbed to the
trickery of traitors. So too that great emperor of the Greeks,
Alexander, conqueror of the whole world, while he subdued all the
nations in war, was poisoned by traitors in his own household.[287] Let

parliament after the meeting at Leicester in April. The writ postponing parliament had
already been issued on 3 Mar. (*CCR 1313–18*, p. 601; *PW*, ii. 2. 178). Otherwise
the author's information is good and he is the only chronicler to show knowledge of the
postponed parliaments.

[286] The town was lost between 2 and 8 Apr. 1318. Berwick had been taken by Edward I
in 1296 and was of great strategic importance to the English for channelling men
and supplies to the Scottish wars. Its loss was also a great blow to Edward's prestige,
and helped to speed up the negotiations with Lancaster so that a united force could be
organized to retake the town.

[287] Troy was taken by the Greeks' ruse of the wooden horse, but those advising the
acceptance of the gift were suspected of betrayal. Rumours that Alexander the Great was
poisoned arose soon after his death. Most commentators have discounted them but a recent

1318 noster uel Scociam recupare, uel saltem terram propriam ab hostibus defendere. Nam licet Scotis fortuna semel arriserit, manum forsan retrahens ad Anglos conuolabit. Prodicio, periurium et homicidium, que Roberto de Brutz regnandi dederunt inicium, perducent eum tandem ad finem desolatum.[288]

Appropinquante die parliamenti prefixo uenit rex apud Northamtoniam cum electa multitudine armatorum;[289] ubi dum uellet omnimodo expectare magnates, apparuit quidam Oxonie qui diceret se filium regis esse et regnum Anglie iure sanguinis ad se pertinere. Dicebat enim se in cunis fuisse sublatum et regem qui nunc regnat pro ipso suppositum.[290] Accessit autem ad aulam regiam, ubi fratres Carmelitani[a] ceperunt edificare,[291] uolens ibidem seisinam capere. Peruenit itaque uerbum ad regem, et statim iussu regis capitur, et in crastino domino regi presentatur. Verumptamen coram rege constitutus priora dicta sua non negauit, set se uerum regni heredem, regem autem iniuste regnare, constanter affirmauit.

Huius rei celebris erat fama per totam terram, et ultra quam dici potest molestabat reginam. Cepit igitur inter sapientes esse consultum quid in hoc casu foret agendum, ac post magnam disceptacionem consideratum est inter eosdem quod qui fame principis et honori non parcit tanquam proditor[b] capitali pena[c] dampnetur, sicut scriptum est, qui maledixit principi morte moriatur.[292] Itaque fatuus ille ex decreto curie protrahitur, ac post illam proditorum penam laqueo suffocatur.[293] Reuera male uendicauit, et accionem non recte instituit, dum uitam et regnum simul amisit.

---

[a] Carmelini *MS*; Carmelitani *He, St, Den-Y*   [b] proditori *MS*; proditor *He, St, Den-Y*   [c] penam *MS*; pena *He, St, Den-Y*

re-examination of the evidence leaves the question open (see Hamilton, *Plutarch: Alexander*, pp. 213–14; Green, *Alexander*, pp. 476–80). For medieval interest in Alexander and the use of his death in exempla, see Cary, *Medieval Alexander*, pp. 190–4, and above, pp. xxviii–xxx). The author's earlier quotation from Walter of Châtillon's *Alexandreis* suggests he may have acquired his information on Alexander from that work, where death by poison is described in book x (*PL* ccix. 566–7).

[288] This comment indicates that the author wrote before the Anglo-Scottish treaty of 1328 acknowledged Bruce as king of Scotland (Stones, *Anglo-Scottish Relations*, pp. 323–41).

[289] The summons to parliament for 19 June had, in fact, been cancelled on 8 June (see n. 283 above), but the king was expecting a major meeting at Northampton to witness reconciliation with Lancaster, who had been given a safe conduct to come to the king on 29 June (*CPR 1317–21*, p. 162). The king was at Northampton 30 June–3 Aug. 1318 except for a brief visit to Woodstock at about 22–7 July (*Itin.*, pp. 169–71).

[290] The claim was made by John of Powderham, son of an Exeter tanner. It made considerable public impact and was recorded in most chronicles (Childs, '"Welcome"').

our king now take thought either for the recovery of Scotland, or at 1318
least for the defence of his own land against his enemies. For, though
Fortune has once smiled upon the Scots, perhaps she will withdraw
her hand and fly over to the English. Treachery, perjury, and
homicide, which brought Robert Bruce to the throne, will lead him
at last to a desolate end.[288]

As the day fixed for parliament approached, the king came with a
chosen body of men-at-arms to Northampton.[289] While he was
waiting there for the great men, a person appeared at Oxford who
said that he was the king's son and that the kingdom of England
belonged to him by right of blood. He claimed that he had been taken
from the cradle, and that the king who now reigned was put in his
place.[290] So he came to the royal palace, where the Carmelite friars
were beginning to build,[291] wishing to take possession there. Then
word reached the king, and the man was at once arrested by the king's
order, and brought before the lord king the next day. Even brought
face to face with the king he did not deny what he had already said,
but stated firmly that he was the true heir to the kingdom, and that
the king had no right to reign.

The notoriety of this spread throughout the whole country, and
annoyed the queen beyond all words. Therefore the wise began to
take counsel on what should be done in this case, and after much
discussion it was decided amongst them that he who does not spare
the good reputation and honour of the prince, shall be condemned to
the extreme penalty as a traitor, as it is written: 'He that curseth the
ruler shall die the death'.[292] So by the verdict of the court, this fool
was drawn and after that was strangled by a noose, the punishment of
traitors.[293] Indeed he had a bad claim and he did not bring a true
action, for he lost his life and the kingdom together.

Another impostor had been recorded in 1313, when a Gascon claimed to be Edward's
brother, but he was treated very leniently and the incident received no attention in the
chronicles (Chaplais, *Gaveston*, pp. 111–12). A certain Thomas de Tynewelle had also been
accused in 1316 of doubting that Edward II was Edward I's son (H. Johnstone, 'Isabella,
the she-wolf of France', *History*, xxi (1936–7), 212–13).

[291] The King's Hall in Oxford was granted to the Carmelites on 1 Feb. 1318 (*CPR
1317–21*, pp. 75, 103–4, 168–9, 237).

[292] Cf. Exod. 21:17, 22: 28; Matt. 15: 4.

[293] Edward laughed at the claim (*Anon.*, pp. 94–5). Others thought the man mad or
possessed (*Brid.*, p. 55), but some saw the claim as dangerous in the delicate political
situation of summer 1318 and quickly had Powderham arrested. An order for his delivery
from Northampton gaol was made on 20 July (TNA, E 37/4 m. 3), and his execution may
have been then or *c*.23 July (*CPR 1317–21*, p. 273; *Ann. Paul.*, p. 283; *Brid.*, p. 55; *Anon.*,
p. 95).

1318   Igitur sicut predixi dominus rex apud Northamtoniam exspectabat;
magnates autem erant cum eo comes de Warennia, Rogerus Dammori, Hugo Despenser pater et filius, Hugo Daudeleghe, Willelmus
de Mountagu; et hii omnes cum magna sequela, ita ut reputares eos
non ad parliamentum uenisse, set pocius ad bella. Quod cum audisset
comes Lancastrie, licet pluries uocatus noluit accedere.²⁹⁴ Nam hos
omnes prenominatos reputabat comes sibi capitales inimicos. Causas
autem inimicicie breuiter, si placet, licet exponere.

Comes de Warennia comitis Lancastrie rapuit uxorem, uel saltem
rapientibus prestabat assensum, de quo nimirum si unus uindictam
uellet expetere, et alter si posset penam euadere.²⁹⁵ Oderant eciam
comitem reliqui omnes eo quod tueri uolebat ordinaciones. Illi
namque iuxta ordinaciones a curia regis erant amouendi, et terras
quas a domino rege acceperant similiter amissuri. Ideo insidiabantur^a
comiti in quantum potuerunt; set insidie eorum effectum non
habuerunt; statim enim notificatur comiti quicquid contra eum
machinantur inimici.

Videns igitur rex quod proficeret nichil, ⟨nichil⟩^b ageret in
omnibus que contra comitem excogitaret, pensans eciam sibi
periculosam esse huiusmodi dissencionem, eo quod Scotorum
contra se firmaret rebellionem, nec posse eum contra Scotos
proficere sine auxilio comitis Lancastrie; pensans eciam uillam de
Berewyk turpiter amissam et uillam de Northam nouiter amittendam
nisi succurratur obsessis, qui resistere non possunt ultra festum
sancti Michaelis;²⁹⁶ pensans et expensas inmensas quas faciebat
contra comitem, requirere quatinus, omni rancore deposito, ad
locum quem uellet accederet, ubi cum eo super omnibus commissis
ᶜpro seᶜ et suis amicabiliter componeret; set et omnes hii, contra quos
diceret se comes habere querelam, ad arbitrium comitis satisfacerent,

^a insidiebantur *MS*; insidiabantur *He, St, Den-Y*   ^b *om. MS*; *supplied He, St, Den-Y*
ᶜ⁻ᶜ per se *MS*; per suos *He*; pro se *St, Den-Y*

²⁹⁴ Lancaster had a safe conduct to meet the king for 29 June (see above, n. 289). Amory
and Audley and Montague were also identified by the continuator of the *Flores* as the
king's new favourites and worse than Gaveston (*Flores*, iii. 178). The young Despenser,
Audley, and Amory had risen in wealth and standing after the death of Gilbert de Clare in
1314, through their marriages to the three Gloucester heiresses. Despenser had married
Eleanor, the eldest sister, in 1306 (*CP*, iv. 269). Audley, from an Oxfordshire family, began
his career in royal service around 1312–13 and married Margaret, widow of Gaveston, 28
Apr. 1317 (Maddicott, *Lancaster*, pp. 194–5; *CP*, i. 346; ibid. v. 715). Amory, at this time
probably closest of the three to the king, also from an Oxfordshire family and originally a
Gloucester retainer, was a later arrival to royal favour. He began to rise in royal service
only after Bannockburn, and married Elizabeth, the youngest sister, widow of John de

Thus, as I have said, the lord king was waiting at Northampton: the 1318
magnates with him were the Earl Warenne, Roger Amory, Hugh
Despenser, the father and the son, Hugh Audley, William Montague;
and these were all there in great strength, so that you would have
thought they had come not to parliament, but rather to battle. When
the earl of Lancaster heard this, though often summoned, he refused
to come.[294] For the earl reckoned all these mentioned above to be his
deadly enemies. The causes of this enmity may, by your leave, be
briefly set forth.

The Earl Warenne abducted the earl of Lancaster's wife, or at least
gave his consent to those who did, so that it is not surprising if the
one should wish to look for vengeance, and the other to escape
punishment if he could.[295] All the others also hated the earl because
he wanted to uphold the Ordinances. For they, according to the
Ordinances, were to be removed from the king's court and would
likewise lose the lands they had received from the lord king. They
therefore intrigued against the earl as much as they could; but their
conspiracies had no effect, for the earl was at once notified of
whatever his enemies plotted against him.

Thus the king, seeing that he profited nothing, achieved nothing by
all the plans he made against the earl; also considering that such
discord was dangerous to him, because it encouraged the Scottish
rebellion against him, and he could make no headway against the
Scots without the help of the earl of Lancaster; considering, too, that
the town of Berwick had been disgracefully lost and the town of
Norham was on the point of being lost unless help was brought to the
besieged, who could not hold out beyond Michaelmas;[296] and
considering the enormous expenses he incurred against the earl,
asked that, all ill-feeling laid aside, [the earl] should go to a place
of his own choosing, where a friendly agreement might be made with
him and his men about everything done in his name; moreover all
those against whom the earl said that he had any complaint, should
make satisfaction at the earl's discretion, and for this should offer

Burgh, before 3 May 1317 (Maddicott, *Lancaster*, pp. 193–4; *CP*, iv. 42–5). The final
division of the lands was made 15 Nov. 1317 (*RP*, i. 355; *CPR 1313–18*, pp. 660–1, 666;
CFR 1307–19, pp. 350–1). Montague also held Oxfordshire lands, and had been active on
royal military service since 1301. He continued to serve Edward II as soldier, diplomat,
and courtier, and was royal steward by 1317 (*CP*, ix. 80–2; Maddicott, *Lancaster*, pp. 194–
5; *HBC*, p. 76). [295] See above, n. 269.
[296] Norham was on the English side of the border, strategically placed on the River
Tweed about ten miles south-west of Berwick.

1318 et super hoc fideiussores, cautionem aut pignora prestarent; et ita ad
instanciam domine regine, comitis Herfordie, et aliorum nobilium
quos comes Lancastrie reputabat fideles, optentum est.[297]
    Conuenerunt igitur dominus rex et comes,[298] et diu familiariter
alloquentes debitam amiciciam et mutuam graciam renouarunt, atque
in signum federis eadem die cibum simul acceperunt; set et Rogerus
Dammori et ceteri, exceptis Hugone Despenser et comite de Warenna
ad comitis presenciam humiliter accedentes, in graciam eius admissi
sunt. Preterea quia in ordinacionibus cautum erat quod dominus rex
nichil alienaret, nichil grande uel arduum inchoaret nisi per assensum
comitum et baronum et hoc in communi parliamento solempniter
expressum, prouisum est quod eligerentur duodecim uiri de discrecioribus tocius regni, quorum quatuor episcopi, quatuor comites,
et quatuor barones essent, et de hiis tres ad minus dominum regem
semper comitantes,[a] si aliquid arduum in curia regis emergeret,
auctoritas istorum duodecim statim expediret. Nam difficile foret,
pro singulis negociis que solent in curia regis accidere omnes
magnates tocius regni congregare.[299]
    Nabugodonosor ille potentissimus rex Assiriorum ante annum
regni sui duodecimum nichil egisse legitur memorandum, quod
anno uero regni sui duodecimo cepit florere et gentes et regna sibi
subicere. Arphaxat regem Medorum in bello deuicit, et de multis
regnis unam monarchiam potenter effecit.[300] Nec eciam rex noster
Edwardus, qui undecim annis regnauit et amplius, aliquid egit quod
predicari debeat in foro uel in tectis. Vtinam ad exemplum regis
Nabugodonosor hostes suos nunc[b] saltem niteretur inuadere, ut
dampna et obprobria que diu sustinuit posset resarsire.

---

[a] communicantes *MS*; *prob. for* comitantes *He, St, Den-Y*   [b] nec *R*; nunc *St, Den-Y*

[297] Although brief, these three paragraphs show an acute awareness of the tensions of
June and July. The agreement of 12 Apr. was renegotiated at meetings on 23 June (at
Horninglow near Tutbury), 4–16 July, and 20–5 July. A final meeting on 1 Aug. made
arrangements for formal reconciliation. The best modern surveys are in Maddicott,
Lancaster, pp. 217–38, and Phillips, *Pembroke*, pp. 159–76.
[298] The king and Lancaster met on 7 Aug. for the kiss of peace; the final agreement was
sealed at Leake on 9 Aug. 1318 (HMC, 55, *Var. Colls.*, i. [Dean and Chapter of
Canterbury] 269; *CCR, 1318–23*, pp. 112–14).
[299] This is a reasonable résumé of the treaty of Leake. It set up a standing council to
advise the king; it gave unconditional pardons to Lancaster and his followers, while
Lancaster released all claims on his opponents except for Warenne; and it confirmed the
Ordinances. No specific reference was made to the resumption of gifts, although this
would be covered by confirmation of the Ordinances, and in particular no reference was
made to punishment of those receiving grants. Whether Lancaster had intended to be one

sureties, caution money, or pledges. And so at the request of the lady 1318 queen, the earl of Hereford, and other nobles whom the earl of Lancaster accounted faithful to him, this was achieved.[297]

So the lord king and the earl met[298] and, speaking together long and intimately, they renewed due friendship and mutual goodwill, and to mark the pact they ate together on that same day; and Roger Amory and the rest, except Hugh Despenser and the Earl Warenne, humbly presenting themselves before the earl, were received into his grace. Moreover, because it had been carefully laid down in the Ordinances that the lord king should alienate nothing, and should initiate nothing important or difficult without the assent of the earls and barons and that solemnly expressed in a general parliament, it was provided that twelve of the more discreet men of the whole realm should be elected, of whom four should be bishops, four earls, and four barons, and, with at least three of these always accompanying the lord king, if anything difficult should arise in the king's court, the authority of those twelve would at once deal with it. For it would be difficult, in individual cases which occur from time to time in the king's court, to bring together all the great men of the whole realm.[299]

Nebuchadnezzar, that most powerful king of the Assyrians, before the twelfth year of his reign did, we are told, nothing memorable, but in that twelfth year of his reign he began to flourish and to conquer nations and kingdoms. He overcame Arphaxad, king of the Medes, in war, and out of many kingdoms constructed one powerful monarchy.[300] Neither has our King Edward who has reigned eleven years and more, done anything that ought to be preached in the marketplace or from the rooftops. Would that, following the example of King Nebuchadnezzar, he would now at least try to attack his enemies, so that he might repair the damage and disgrace which he has borne so long.

of the named council is unclear, but his position was certainly weakened when he was only represented by a banneret (*PW*, ii. 2. 184–5). The detailed arrangements were further worked out at the York parliament in Oct. (see below, n. 306). Substantial payments of money by Amory, Audley, and Montague in Nov. 1318 were probably part of the arrangements to compensate Lancaster (Maddicott, *Lancaster*, pp. 233–4). The council is reminiscent of that proposed for Henry III in 1258, and its importance or its novelty prompted the author to report it fully; he is, however, mistaken in his numbers. There was to be a group of sixteen of whom four would always be with the king. A further seven names were added to the list at the York parliament (Cole, *Docs. Illus.*, pp. 1–2, 12).

[300] Cf. Judith 1: 1, 5, 11, 13. There it was not until the seventeenth year that Nebuchadnezzar, king of the Assyrians, defeated Arphaxad, king of the Medes.

1318   Spes magna hiis diebus nobis accreuit eo quod Deus in multis prosperis regem et populum exhillarauit. In primis regi et populo Anglorum feliciter contigit quod dominus papa, cuius est dissensiones*a* sedare, Scotis et eorum ducibus treugas biennales indixit, ut interim uiam concordie et formam pacis excogitaret. Set Robertus de Brutz spretis*b* mandatis apostolicis regem Anglie multipliciter infestauit. Visum est itaque domino pape transgressoribus penam infligere, et post monita censuram adicere. Igitur Robertum de Brutz et suos sequaces anathematizauit, et terram Scotorum interdicto supposuit, ita ut nullus nisi ianuis clausis, interdictis et excommunicatis exclusis, diuina celebraret.[301] Cuius efficacie fuerat interdictum dignatus est Deus ostendere ad oculum. Nam dum quadam die Robertus de Brutz peteret sibi missam celebrari, capellanus pretextu interdicti nitebatur excusari; set iussum*c* tiranni preualuit, et capellanus nimio*d* timore coactus, ad altare diuina celebraturus accessit. Cum autem sacerdos missam usque ad eleuacionem Corporis Domini rite peregisset, sacerdos, sicut mos est, hostiam nitebatur erigere, et columba desuper ueniens manifeste cunctis apparuit et hostiam de manu sacerdotis ereptam cunctis uidentibus asportauit. Quid aliud pretendere potest huiuscemodi uisio, nisi quod presentes ibidem indigni erant sacramento? Et hoc quidem acceptabile nobis et gratum, dum scimus hostem nostrum a Deo reprobatum eo quod non seruauit interdictum.

Secundo dedit nobis Deus uictoriam super inimicos nostros in Hibernia. Edwardus de Brutz et sui milites, qui iam per biennium dominium ibidem usurparunt, uenientes uersus Dondalk ut uillam caperent, exercitum nostrum obuiam habuerunt; set inito conflictu cecidit Edwardus *e* et quingenti cum eo ualentes armati ipsa die coram nostris.[302]

⟨Tercio, cessauit⟩*f* sterilitas illa que diu nos afflixit, et habundancia omnium*g* bonorum terram Anglorum multipliciter fecundauit.[303]

---

a descenciones *MS*; dissensiones *He, St, Den-Y*   *b* spectis *MS*; spretis *He, St, Den-Y*   *c* iussu *MS*; iussum *He, St, Den-Y*   *d* non uno *R*; nimio *St, Den-Y*   *e* Edwardum *MS*; Edwardus *He, St, Den-Y*   *f* om. *R*; supplied *St, Den-Y*   *g* omni *R*; omnium *St, Den-Y*

---

[301] Edward asked for support against the Scots in Nov. 1317; the pope declared the truce on 17 Mar. 1318 (*Foed.*, ii. 1. 347–8; *CPL 1305–42*, p. 127). Bruce ignored the truce by capturing Berwick, Wark, Harbottle, and Mitford, and raiding as far south as Ripon, Knaresborough, and Skipton in Yorkshire (*Lanercost*, pp. 234–5; I. Kershaw, 'A note on Scottish raids in the West Riding 1316–18', *Northern History*, xvii (1981), 231–9). The papal bull of excommunication was dated 28 June (*Foed.*, ii. 1. 362–3), but was not

Great hope has latterly grown up in us, because God has gladdened 1318 king and people with many signs of prosperity. In the first place, it turned out happily for the English king and people that the lord pope, whose business it is to settle quarrels, imposed upon the Scots and their leaders a two years' truce, so that in the meanwhile he might devise a way to bring harmony, and a form of peace. But Robert Bruce scorned the apostolic commands and attacked the king of England many times. So it seemed good to the lord pope to penalize the transgressors and, after warnings, to add censure. He therefore anathematized Robert Bruce and his followers, and placed the land of the Scots under an interdict, so that no one could celebrate the holy offices except behind closed doors, with interdicted and excommunicate persons excluded.[301] God deigned to show the efficacy of this interdict. For when one day Robert Bruce asked for Mass to be celebrated for himself, the chaplain sought to be excused by reason of the interdict; but the tyrant's order prevailed, and the chaplain, overwhelmed with fear, approached the altar to celebrate Mass. But when the priest had performed the office as far as the elevation of the Body of our Lord, the priest, as usual, attempted to elevate the Host, and a dove coming down from above clearly appeared to all, and in the sight of everyone carried off the Host, plucked from the priest's hand. What else can such a vision mean, except that those present were unworthy of the sacrament? This indeed was welcome and pleasing to us, for we knew that our enemy had been rebuked by God for not observing the interdict.

Secondly, God gave us victory over our enemies in Ireland. Edward Bruce and his knights, who now for two years had usurped lordship there, approaching Dundalk to take the town, came up against our army; but when battle was joined Edward fell before our men that day, and five hundred stout-hearted men-at-arms with him.[302]

Thirdly, the dearth that had so long plagued us ceased, and England became fruitful with a lavish profusion of all good things.[303] A bushel

published until 3 Sept. 1318 (*Ann. Paul.*, p. 283). Before then, the Scots would have been covered by the general excommunication in 1312 of those disturbing the peace of the kingdom (Wright, *Reynolds*, pp. 350, 351, 352).

[302] The battle of Dundalk took place on 14 Oct. 1318 (Lydon, 'Impact', pp. 293–4).

[303] The famine had begun in 1315; see above pp. 110–11. Although in many places conditions improved after two to three years, in some areas hardship continued longer, and the Bridlington chronicler recorded that in Yorkshire the scarcity lasted as long as six years (*Brid.*, p. 48; Kershaw, 'Agrarian crisis', pp. 13–15).

1318 Modius tritici, qui anno preterito pro quadraginta denariis uendebatur, hodie pro sex denariis emptori libenter offertur. Sic olim tamdiu obsessa Samaria, ut mater filii carnibus uesceretur pro penuria[a] uictualium, recuperauit diuina gracia. Nam capud asini, quod octoginta aureis pridie uendebatur, omnibus inmundum in crastino reputatum erat, et modius simile pro statere uno uenundatus, sicut predixerat uir Dei Heliseus.[304]

Quarto, factus est unanimis rex noster cum baronibus suis. Nam nugis postpositis[b] consilia baronum auscultat,[c] nec est qui regem ad malum instigat amplius, quia priuata familia que baronibus erat contraria hodie recessit ab aula. Hiis igitur omnibus per graciam Dei concurrentibus, non est timendum nobis ab inimicis nostris, sicut scriptum est ad Romanos, si Deus nobiscum, quis contra nos?[305]

Habita concordia inter dominum regem et comitem Lancastrie, bonum uisum est magnatibus concordiam et unitatem in populo facere, iniurias ulcisci et regnum innouare. Tunc assignati sunt et destinati ad quemlibet comitatum uiri discreti et bone opinionis, ad audiendum et terminandum querelas subditorum. Ministrales enim regii auctoritate publice potestatis concuciebant simplices, spoliarunt innocentes, ut[d] nemo negocium suum consummaret, nisi huiusmodi officialium[e] manum impleret. Amoti sunt omnes tales ab officio ut liberius procederet inquisicio.[306] Insuper ordinatum est ut conuicti[f] lesis in duplo satisfacerent, et ad officium nunquam redirent.

Hec ordinacio terruit multos, et ad satisfaciendum induxit nondum conuictos. Reuera de officialibus domini regis ueraciter hoc possumus dicere, quia a minimo usque ad maximum omnes student auaricie; a summo iusticiario usque ad minimum pedaneum iudicem,[307] nullus recusat accipere. Porro, licet aliqui non exigant uel extorqueant offerrendum,[g] nullus tamen eorum respuit oblatum. Verumtamen quod offertur ex gracia licenter recipi[h] potest, set cum mensura; quia a nemine accipere est ualde inhumanum,[i][308] set passim et indifferenter, turpissimum. Oporteret certe dominum regem; a maioribus

    [a] pennuria *MS*; penuria *He, St, Den-Y*   [b] prepositis *MS*; postpositis *He, St, Den-Y*   [c] ascultat *MS*; auscultat *He, St*   [d] et *MS*; ut *He, St, Den-Y*   [e] efficialium *MS*; officialium *He, St, Den-Y*   [f] comiti *R*; conuicti *St, Den-Y*   [g] sic *MS*; offerrendum *He, St, Den-Y*   [h] recepi *MS*; recipi *He, St, Den-Y*   [i] inhumatum *MS*; inhumanum *He, St, Den-Y*

    [304] Cf. 4 Kgs. (2 Kgs.) 6: 25–9, 7: 1, 16.   [305] Rom. 8: 31.
    [306] At the York parliament in Oct. 1318 the practical details following from the treaty of Leake were worked out. The king also agreed to a reform of his household, a review of offices, and an inquiry into county administration at all levels (Cole, *Docs. Illus.*, pp. 1–4,

of wheat, which the year before was sold for 40 pence, today is freely 1318
offered to the buyer for sixpence. So once Samaria, which had been
besieged for so long that for lack of food a mother fed upon the flesh of
her son, recovered through divine grace. For an ass's head, which the
day before had sold for 80 pieces of gold, was on the next day held
unclean by all, and a bushel of fine flour was sold for a stater, as Elisha,
the man of God, had foretold.[304]

Fourthly, our king became reconciled with his barons. For putting
aside trifles, he listens to the barons' advice, and there is no longer
anyone to incite the king to do wrong, because his close supporters
who were hostile to the barons have now left the court. Therefore,
with all these things coinciding by the grace of God, we need not fear
our enemies, as it is written in the Epistle to the Romans, 'If God be
for us, who is against us?'[305]

When peace had been made between the lord king and the earl of
Lancaster, it seemed good to the great men to promote peace and
unity among the people, to punish wrongs and overhaul the kingdom.
Discreet men of good reputation were assigned and appointed to each
county, to hear and determine the complaints of the people. For the
king's officials with the authority of public power terrorized the
simple, robbed the innocent, and no one could finish his business
without greasing the official palm. All such men were removed from
office so that the investigation might proceed more freely.[306] Furthermore, it was decreed that those found guilty should pay the injured
party double, and never return to office.

This decree terrified many and persuaded those not yet convicted
to make satisfaction. Indeed, we can truly say this of the lord king's
officials, that from the lowest to the highest they all eagerly apply
themselves to avarice; from the lord chief justice to the least petty
judge[307] no one rejects a bribe. Furthermore, although some may not
demand or extort money, nevertheless none of them has refused what
is offered. Of course, what is offered freely may properly be received,
but in moderation; for to take from no one is scarcely human,[308] but to
do so promiscuously and indiscriminately is most scandalous.
Certainly it should be essential for the lord king; for men take an

6–13). As part of this review, twenty sheriffs were replaced on 29 Nov. and one more on 1
Dec. 1318 (*CFR 1307–19*, pp. 381–3).

[307] *Pedaneus* ('foot-high') in juridical Latin signified a minor judge, who sat on a low
seat, had no tribunal, and tried minor cases (*Dig.* iii. 1. 1 (6), xlviii. 19. 38 (10), *Corpus Iuris
Civilis*, i. 35, 817).

[308] *Dig.* i. 16. 6 (3), *Corpus Iuris Civilis*, i. 15.

1318 sumitur enim exemplum, et a capite diriuatur omnis malicia. Sic ille regum prudentissimus rex noster Edwardus proximus Thomam de Weilonde capitalem iusticiarium, propter quasdam transgressiones et oppressiones subditorum, omni honore, beneficio et dignitate priuauit, et capitali pene uel carceri perpetuo addictus fuisset, nisi ad ordinem minorum cicius conuolasset.*a* Set nec corda minorum eidem prestabat*b* confugium, quin idem Thomas nudatus pedes et caput subiret exilium.³⁰⁹ Eodem tempore multi et magni uiri inter potestates domini regis precipui, de turpibus sceleribus conuicti, cum magna iactura et ignominia ab officio et dignitate repulsi sunt. Inter quos quidam clericus, inter officiales regis non minimus, de tirannide quam exercuit ab ipsis specialibus domini regis accusatus et con- uictus, omni feodo laicali quod in regno possidebat est priuatus.³¹⁰ Insuper in auro et argento et uaria suppellectili ad ualorem triginta milium marcarum perdidit, que manus regia, utpote de bonis regis collecta, sibi confiscauit. O quanta cura in hiis adunandis prius impendidit, et uno die uel uno momento ualefecit! O fallax rerum copia que, cum possessorem suum felicem facere deberet, infelicissi- mum reddit, que nec eum dormire nec saltem unam horam in gaudio consummare permittit. Nam solicitudines et uigilie inimici sunt nature. Hoc est quod Ecclesiastes deplorando conqueritur: Vide,*c* inquid, quod est sub sole et quidem*d* frequens apud homines; uir cui dedit ⟨Deus⟩*e* diuicias, substanciam et honorem, et nichil deest anime eius ex omnibus que desiderat; nec tribuit ei Deus potestatem ⟨ut⟩*f* ex eo commedat, set homo extraneus deuorabat illud. Deinde addit Ecclesiastes et diffinit de talibus, dicens quod melior illo est abortiuus. Frustra enim uenit, et pergit ad tenebras, et obliuioni dabitur nomen eius.³¹¹

Inter comitem Lancastrie et comitem de Warenna facta est concordia per excambium quarundam terrarum, quas autem comes imperpetuum possidebit hereditate. Iacturam fecit ut euitaret maius*g* periculum, quia de duobus malis minus malum est

---

a conualescet *MS*; conuolasset *He, St, Den-Y*   *b* sic *MS*; prestabant *He*   *c* sic *MS*; uidi *He*   *d* qui deus *MS*; quidem *He, St, Den-Y*   *e* om. *MS*; supplied *He, St, Den-Y*   *f* om. *MS*; supplied *He, St, Den-Y*   *g* manus *MS*; maius *He, St, Den-Y*

---

³⁰⁹ Thomas Weyland, chief justice of common pleas, was removed in Sept. 1289 for protecting two of his followers who had committed murder. He took refuge with the Franciscans at Bury St Edmunds, but was starved out and exiled at the following parliament, which met between Dec. 1289 and Jan. 1290 (Prestwich, *Ed. I*, p. 339).

³¹⁰ Adam Stratton, chamberlain of the Exchequer, was removed in 1290. He had already

example from those greater than themselves and from the head is ᵢ₃ᵢ₈
derived all evil. Thus, that wisest of kings, our previous king Edward,
for certain crimes and oppressions done to the people deprived
Thomas Weyland, the chief justice, of every honour, benefice, and
dignity, and he would have been condemned to death or life
imprisonment, if he had not taken refuge quickly with the Franciscans. But even the cord of the Franciscans did not protect the same
Thomas from going into exile with bared head and feet.[309] At the
same time many great men amongst the lord king's principal officials,
found guilty of disgraceful crimes, were driven from office and
honour to their great loss and disgrace. Amongst them was a certain
clerk, not the least of the king's officials, who, accused and found
guilty of tyrannous behaviour by very special justices of the lord king,
was deprived of all the lay fees that he possessed in the kingdom.[310]
Moreover he lost gold and silver and other moveables to the value of
30,000 marks, which the crown confiscated for itself as these had been
amassed from the king's goods. Think of the trouble he had taken to
gather all this wealth together, only to lose it all in a day, in a moment!
Oh! How deceptive is material wealth, which, when it ought to make
its possessor happy, renders him most unhappy, which allows him
neither to sleep nor to pass even one joyful hour. For anxiety and
sleeplessness are nature's enemies. It is this that the Preacher deplores
in his lament: 'See', he says, 'what I have seen under the sun, and that
frequent among men; a man to whom God hath given riches, and
substance, and honour, and his soul wanteth nothing of all that he
desireth: yet God doth not give him power to eat thereof, but a
stranger shall eat it up.' Then the Preacher adds and explains such
things, saying that 'the untimely born is better than he. For he came
in vain, and goeth to darkness, and his name shall be wholly
forgotten.'[311]

An agreement was made between the earl of Lancaster and Earl
Warenne for the exchange of certain estates, which the earl will
possess forever by hereditary right. He [Earl Warenne] cut his losses
to escape a greater danger, for of two evils the lesser evil is to be

---

faced complaints in 1279. He was a major pluralist, holding twenty-three benefices in 1280,
and a moneylender. At his arrest in 1290 he had the spectacular sum of £11,333 in new
money and £1,317 in old coin as well as many debts owed to him (N. Denholm-Young,
Seignorial Administration in England (Oxford, 1937), pp. 77–85; Prestwich, *Ed. I*, p. 341;
R. H. Bowers, 'From rolls to riches: King's clerks and money-lending in thirteenth-
century England', *Speculum*, lviii (1983), 60–71, at p. 69).
   [311] Eccles. 6: 1–4.

1318 eligendum.[312] Sic comes Lancastrie aduersarios suos ad satisfaccionem reduxit caute; set Hugonem Despenser adhuc pro libito superare non potuit. Hugo semper et caute querit subterfugia ut redimat tempus et euitet pericula. Nam secundum relatum aliquorum iam adiuit sanctum Iacobum,[313] quia timuit uenire ad parliamentum.

1319 Post Pascha conuenerunt omnes magnates terre cum domino rege apud Eboracum,[314] et consilio facto consenserunt unanimiter in festo sancte Marie Magdalene omnes apud Nouum Castrum cum armis conuenire,[315] et extunc quod ad expedicionem belli pertinet, Deo dante, feliciter incohare.[a] Concesserunt eciam proceres domino regi in subsidium guerre sue duodeuicensimum denarium tocius Anglie.[316]

Hiis ita dispositis[b] misit dominus rex nuncios in Scociam qui regnum peterent, pacem offerrent, et Roberto de Brutz uitam et membra sic salua permitterent.[317] Sic enim decet regem facere, et pace repulsa hostes impetere. Sic eciam habuerunt filii Israelis in preceptis, ut, cum ciuitatem aliquam expungnarent, pacem prius offerrent, qua non admissa ad pungnacionem citanter[c] rite procederent.[318] Sic Greci post raptum Helene leguntur Troianis pacem optulisse. Sic potens ille Nabugodonosor rex Assiriorum, antequam expungnaret exteras naciones, petiit sub pace tributum.[319] Respondit Robertus de Brutz se de pace regis Anglie non multum curare; regnum Scocie suum esse et iure hereditario et iure belli ad se pertinere. Hiis titulis dicebat se munitum esse, protestans se nec debere nec uelle aliquem superiorem uel dominum terrenum agnoscere.

---

[a] sic R; inchoare St, Den-Y   [b] depositis MS; dispositis He, St, Den-Y   [c] sic R; cito or citatim also possible readings, He; MS was evidently unclear ed.

---

[312] Warenne released all his lands in Yorkshire and North Wales and the reversion of his lands in Norfolk to Lancaster on 29–30 Nov. 1318. He also pledged to pay Lancaster £50,000 by 25 Dec. In return he received a few estates in the west country. The money was not paid, but the land exchange was complete by Mar. 1319. The exchange was to Warenne's immense disadvantage, and he claimed in 1322 that the agreements were made under duress while he was at Pontefract (Maddicott, *Lancaster*, pp. 234–7).

[313] The elder Despenser had letters of safe conduct and protection dated 1 Jan. 1319 to last to 29 Sept. for a journey to Spain on the king's business. The king also addressed letters on 5 Feb. 1319 to the Castilian princes on his behalf, asking for a safe conduct and permission to export war horses (*CPR 1317–21*, p. 262; *CCR 1319–23*, p. 123). Despenser may have made a pilgrimage to Santiago de Compostela in Galicia during this visit.

[314] Parliament (with commons) was summoned to York for 6 May 1319 and dismissed on 25 May (*HBC*, p. 554).

preferred.[312] Thus the earl of Lancaster shrewdly brought his 1318
enemies to make amends; but as yet he could not overcome Hugh
Despenser as he wished. Always Hugh cautiously took evasive actions
to gain time and keep out of danger. In fact, according to the reports
of some people, he now went to Santiago,[313] because he was afraid to
come to parliament.

After Easter all the great men of the land met the lord king at 1319
York,[314] and, having held council, they unanimously agreed that all
should muster in arms at Newcastle on St Mary Magdalene's day,[315]
and then, God willing, happily make a start on the preparations for a
campaign. The nobles also granted to the lord king the eighteenth
penny from all England as a war subsidy.[316]

When these things had been thus arranged, the lord king sent
envoys to Scotland to claim the kingdom, offer peace, and allow safety
in life and limb to Robert Bruce.[317] For it is fitting for a king to act
thus, and to attack his enemies when peace is refused. This
commandment, too, was laid upon the children of Israel, that when
they were to besiege a city, they should first offer peace, and if this
was not accepted, they might justly move on quickly to the battle.[318]
Thus the Greeks after the abduction of Helen are said to have offered
peace to the Trojans. Thus that mighty Nebuchadnezzar king of the
Assyrians, before he attacked other nations, sought peaceful tribute.[319] Robert Bruce replied that he did not much care for the
king of England's peace; the kingdom of Scotland was his and
belonged to him both by hereditary right and by right of battle. He
said that he was justified by these titles, and protested that he neither
ought to nor would acknowledge any superior or earthly lord.

---

[315] 22 July. The parliament of York in Oct. 1318 had agreed to a muster for 10 June
1319 (Cole, *Docs. Illus.*, p. 4), but at this parliament writs dated 22 May postponed the
muster until 22 July (*CCR 1318–23*, p. 141).

[316] This is the second of Edward's parliamentary taxes to be mentioned by this writer
(see above, pp. 76–7). Again he ignores the commons' role and the tax on towns: the
countryside was to give one-eighteenth and the towns one-twelfth; the tax raised £36,396.
1s. 1d. (*Lay Taxes*, pp. 34–5; Willard, *Parliamentary Taxes*, p. 344).

[317] It is unclear when these envoys were sent to Scotland. As early as 8 Mar. 1319 the
king requested permission from the pope to treat with the excommunicated Scots (*Foed.*,
ii. 1. 381).

[318] Cf. Deut. 20: 10–12. The same sentiment is expressed above, pp. 58–9.

[319] The examples chosen are of extremes of bitter hostility, to emphasize the contrast of
offering peace. The Trojan war was marked by its savagery, and Nebuchadnezzar was the
epitome of the merciless attacker, a punishment from God. There is little biblical evidence
to show that he ever offered quarter; see 4 Kgs. 24: 1, 8–19, 25: 1–22; 2 Chr. 36: 6–13, 17–
20; Jer. 38: 17–27, 40: 1–8.

1319   Termino prefixo conuenerunt rex, apud Nouum Castrum, comites et barones.[320] Aderat Thomas comes Lancastrie, comes de Penbrok, comes de Arundel et comes de Herford, comes de Warenna et frater domini regis comes Marescallie. Affuit eciam Hugo Despenser, Rogerus Dammori et Hugo Daudeleye, et hii tres *uice comitis*[a] Gloucestrie; hii tres enim tres sorores duxerant que, familie[b] iudicio, comitatum[c] Gloucestrie inter se diuiserant.[321] Aderant eciam reliqui barones Anglie, qui, domino regi certum patrocinium tenentur conferre; et multa milia peditum similiter confluxerant; et omnes uoluntarie, eo quod dominus rex concesserat unicuique usque[d] ad summam centum librarum sine restitucione, quantum posset in bonis hostium occupare. Item concessit dominus rex nautis omnibus, ut scilicet a parte maris hostes uiriliter impeterent, ut[e] de spoliis hostium quantum possent [f]sua dominia amplificarent.[f] Hec utique concessio in depredacionem Scotorum uoluntarios multos armauit, quia restitucio, que post concordiam frequenter fiebat, timenda non fuit.[322]

Profectus inde dominus rex in Scociam apud Berewyk cum toto exercitu primo peruenit, et hanc primam expungnacionem de consilio fore decreuit, eo quod ultro[g] recesserat ab imperio suo, et ne se ipsos exponerent periculo dum hostes inuictos dimitterent a tergo.[323] Diffusus est igitur exercitus uille[h] in circuitu a parte terrestri et ceperunt contra eam municiones et expungnacula[i] properari. A parte uero maris naute qui[j] presunt quinque portubus ita obseruabant introitus et exitus[k] ut nulli omnino pateret egressus.

Dum hec aguntur in Scocia, nec uideretur esse timendum ab hostibus in Anglia, Iacobus Douglas cum suis complicibus, qui semper machinacionibus fuit intentus, nisi Deus et Dominus omnium nobis precauisset, magnam iacturam et dampnum inestimabile[l] nobis intulisset. Nam iuxta consilium Achitofel decem milia uirorum sibi elegerat,[m][324] et reginam Anglie, que iuxta Eboracum morabatur, rapuisse decreuerat. Certe si capta fuisset tunc regina,

---

[a–a] uices comites *MS*; uicecomites *He, St*; uice comitis *Den-Y*   [b] famulie *MS*; familie *He, St, Den-Y*   [c] comitum *MS*; comitatum *He, St, Den-Y*   [d] sic *R*; om. *St, Den-Y*   [e] et *R; for* ut *ed.*   [f–f] suo dominio amplicarent *MS*; sua dominia amplificarent *He, St*; suo dominio amplicarent *Den-Y*   [g] ulcio *R*; ultro *St, Den-Y*   [h] uillam *MS*; circa uillam *He*; uille *MW*   [i] sic *R; or* propugnacula *He (leaving in doubt which was in West's MS, ed.)*; propungnacula *Den-Y*   [j] que *MS*; qui *He, St, Den-Y*   [k] exercitus *MS*; exitus *He, St, Den-Y*   [l] inestimabilem *MS*; inestimabile *He, St, Den-Y*   [m] eligerat *MS*; elegerat *St*

---

[320] Edward was in or near Newcastle on 2 Aug.–21 Sept.; by 29 Sept. he was back at Durham (*Itin.*, pp. 185–8).

At the date arranged the king, earls, and barons assembled at   1319
Newcastle.[320] There were present Thomas, earl of Lancaster, the earl
of Pembroke, the earl of Arundel, and the earl of Hereford, Earl
Warenne, and the lord king's brother, the earl marshal. Present, too,
were Hugh Despenser, Roger Amory, and Hugh Audley, and these
three in place of the earl of Gloucester; for these three had married
three sisters who by a family arrangement had divided the earldom of
Gloucester between themselves.[321] The other English barons, who are
bound to render a fixed service to the lord king, were there too; and
many thousands of infantry likewise had assembled; and all these
came voluntarily, because the lord king had granted to each man as
much of the enemies' goods as he could seize up to the value of a
hundred pounds without restitution. Also the lord king granted to all
the sailors, so that they should eagerly attack the enemy by sea, that
they might increase their own possessions with as much booty from
the enemy as they could take. This right to plunder the Scots
certainly roused many volunteers to arms, because they need not
fear the restitution which was frequently made after a truce.[322]

Then the lord king set out for Scotland and came first to Berwick
with his whole army, and decided on advice that this should be the
first place to be besieged, both because it had withdrawn from his
authority, and so that they should not expose themselves to danger by
leaving an unconquered enemy in their rear.[323] The army was
therefore disposed about the town on the landward side, and they
began to prepare fortifications and siege-works against it. By sea the
sailors in charge of the Cinque Ports' fleet kept so close a watch on the
entrances and exits, that no one at all could come out.

While this was happening in Scotland, and it seemed as if there was
nothing to fear from enemies in England, James Douglas and his
supporters, always ready for intrigue, would have inflicted great loss
and immeasurable damage upon us, had not God, the Lord of all,
provided for us. For according to the advice of Ahitophel he had
chosen ten thousand men,[324] and had resolved to carry off the queen
of England, who was staying near York. Indeed if the queen had at

---

[321] For the marriages see above, n. 294. The final division of the Gloucester lands took
place in Nov. 1317 (*CFR 1307–19*, p. 350).
[322] This was the only campaign in which Edward had the support of all the earls and
barons. The army was not as large as the one at Bannockburn, but was of good size with about
400–500 horse and probably about 10,000 infantry (Maddicott, *Lancaster*, pp. 244–5).
[323] The siege began on 7 Sept. 1319 (*CDS*, iii. no. 663).
[324] Cf. 2 Kgs. (2 Sam.) 17: 1.

1319 credo quod pacem emisset sibi Scocia. Set dissipatum est consilium
proditoris Achitofel, nec passus est tantum discrimen nobis inferri
Deus Israel.³²⁵ Nam quadam die captus est quidam explorator apud
Eboracum; et, cum uidisset se questionibus addictum, promisit se,ᵃ si
daretur ei penam euadere, totam machinacionem Scotorum reuelare;
et placuit pactum maioribus ciuitatis; erant enim ibidem archiepiscopus Eboracensis et regis cancellarius episcopus tunc Eliensis.³²⁶
Explorator ille indicauit quod inimicus noster Iacobus Douglas
clam uenturus esset cum electa manu ad partes illas, ut uidelicet
reginam adduceret et quos reperiret inprouisos simul occideret.ᵇ
'Tali,' inquid, 'die et tali loco latitabunt,ᶜ et, cum tempus acceperint
ydoneum, propositum consummabunt.' Vix erat qui dictis adhiberet
credentiam, eo quod dominus rex Anglie terras Scotorum uastareᵈ
iam inciperet, et magis uidebatur necessarium talem exercitum
proprios fines defendere quam extra propria loca per centum miliaria
pungnam appetere. Addidit autem explorator ille quodᵉ nisi euentus
rei dictis suis fidem afferret, capitalem penam libenter acciperet.³²⁷

   Tunc exierunt de ciuitate illa archiepiscopus et cancellarius, cum
communi sequela sua, uicecomes et burgenses et eorum familiares,
monachi et canonici et ceteri regulares, necnon et omnes alii qui ad
arma ferenda inuenti sunt habiles, reduxerunt reginam ad ciuitatem;
deinde per aquam reducta est apud Notyngham.³²⁸ Ibi fuit tutior
locus regine, nec Iacobus timendus nec eius insidie.

   Altera autem die qua iuxta uerbum exploratoris reperiendi erant
Scoti in suis latibulis, exierunt iterum de ciuitate Eboracensi laici,
clerici et religiosi. Ibant igitur clam et sine tumultu, ut hostes
inprouisos inuaderent, ne et ipsi premuniti fugam forsan arriperent.
Verumptamen satis erant premuniti, nec tamen in fugam conuersi.
Nam cum homines nostros inordinate uenientes asspicerent, 'Hii',
inquiunt, 'non bellatores set uenatores; non multum proficient.'
Incenderunt autem Scoti fenum multum quod erat in loco illo

ᵃ sic R; om. St, Den-Y   ᵇ occidirent MS; occiderent or occideret He; occiderent St,
Den-Y   ᶜ latitabant MS; latitabunt He   ᵈ uastaret MS; uastare He, St, Den-Y
ᵉ qui MS; quod He, St, Den-Y

³²⁵ Cf. 2 Kgs. (2 Sam.) 17: 14.
³²⁶ William Melton, archbishop of York from 1316 to 1340, and John Hotham, bishop
of Ely from 1316 to 1337 and chancellor from June 1318 to Jan. 1320 (HBC, pp. 86, 244,
282).
³²⁷ Two chronicles name Edmund Darel as the English knight who was suspected of
conspiring with the Scots to betray the queen, and who was captured and taken to London
(Flores, iii. 188–9; Ann. Paul., p. 288). Although there seems to be little proof of Darel's

that time been captured, I believe that Scotland would have bought 1319 peace for herself. But the counsel of the traitor Ahitophel came to nought, and the God of Israel did not suffer so great a peril to fall upon us.[325] For one day a certain spy was captured at York; and when he saw that he would be interrogated, he promised, if he should be allowed to escape punishment, to disclose the whole conspiracy of the Scots; this bargain pleased the greater men of the city; the archbishop of York and the king's chancellor, at that time the bishop of Ely, were there too.[326] That spy explained that our enemy James Douglas was to come there secretly with his chosen band, to abduct the queen and also kill all those whom he should take unawares. 'They will hide,' he said, 'on such a day and in such a place, and when they see the appropriate moment, they will carry out their plan.' There was hardly anyone who believed this story, because the lord king of England was already beginning to lay waste the lands of the Scots, and it seemed more necessary for such an army to defend its own frontiers than to seek battle a hundred miles outside its own territory. However, the spy added that if what happened did not bear out his words, he would willingly submit to capital punishment.[327]

Then the archbishop and the chancellor went forth from the city, with their combined retinue, the sheriff and the burgesses and their followers, the monks and canons and other regulars, as well as all the others who were found able to handle a weapon, and they brought the queen back into the city; then she was taken by water to Nottingham.[328] That was a safer place for the queen where neither James nor his traps were to be feared.

The next day, on which, according to the spy, the Scots would be found in their hiding places, the laymen, clerks, and men of religion went out again from the city of York. They went stealthily and without noise to take the enemy by surprise, lest, if they were forewarned, they should perhaps take flight. Even so, they were well enough warned, but they did not flee. For when they saw our men advancing without military order, they said: 'These are not soldiers but huntsmen; they will not achieve much.' So the Scots set

complicity in this attack (Doherty, *Isabella*, pp. 63–4), he was troublesome. He had links with the opposition to Edward in 1312–13 and in 1322, and was a violent neighbour in Yorkshire in 1318 (Phillips, *Pembroke*, pp. 54–5; Fryde, *Tyranny*, p. 62; *CPR 1317–21*, pp. 181, 183).

[328] The main sources for the battle do not record the queen's proximity (*Brid.*, pp. 57–8; *Brut*, pp. 211–12; *Lanercost*, p. 239), but it is reported in *Flores*, iii. 189 and *Ann. Paul.*, p. 287.

1319 congestum, et ascendit fumus late dispersus in celum. Fumus[a]
impediebat uisum nostrorum, unde et quos credebant in fugam
conuersos inuenerunt paratos ad bellum. Erant quippe uiri ex omni
Scocia electi ad preliandum apti, ad omnem laborem apti. Nostri uero
plures in re militari minus instructi, ad fugandum quam ad preliandum magis intenti. Inito igitur conflictu plures ex nostris
perimuntur et multi super[b] capiuntur; set et Scoti in Scociam cum
suis captiuis indempnes reuertuntur, etc.[329]

Peruenit uerbum ad regem Anglie et ad exercitum nostrum qui
morabatur in obsidione, et statim nescio quorum consilio derelicta est
penitus obsidio.[330] Rex enim nitebatur obuiare Scotis fugientibus per
unam semitam, et comes Lancastrie per alteram. Scoti uero felici usi[c]
duplomate per alteram uiam reuersi sunt in regionem suam.[331] Set
quare derelicta est obsidio tanto opere inchoata? Dicunt quidam quod
Robertus de Brutz habuit amicos. Certe Dauid non euasisset manus
Saul regis, si non habuisset in familiaribus amicos eius.[332] Inputatur
comiti Lancastrie quod rex recessit de obsidione; inputatur eciam
eidem quod Scoti uenerunt rapere reginam, et quod inimici regis illesi
in patriam suam sunt reuersi. Argumenta quedam prodicionis publice
proclamantur,[d] unde comes et sui sequaces enormiter diffamantur.[333]
Vulgariter enim dicitur quod comes ille recepit a Roberto de Brutz
quadraginta milia librarum, ut sibi et suis occulte ferret auxilium; et
quod in obsedione, dum omnes expungnarent murum, nullus[e] ex
priuatis comitis fecit insultum, et uilla de Berewyk dedita fuisset si
cautela comitis nusquam repungnasset; et Iacobus Douglas reuertens
in Scociam per exercitum comitis transibat, comes autem inhermis
per medium Scotorum ibat.

[a] fug' MS; poss. for foc', focus ed.; fumus He, St, Den-Y   [b] sic MS; insuper He
[c] uisu MS; usi He, St, Den-Y   [d] proclamatur MS; proclamantur He, St, Den-Y
[e] nullis MS; nullus He, St, Den-Y

[329] The battle of Myton-on-Swale made a great public impact because of the number of
English who were slaughtered and the number of religious who fought, from which it
received the name the 'white battle' (Brut, p. 212) or the 'Chapter of Myton' (The Bruce,
xvii. 587: pp. 646–7). The beginning of this passage, 'on the second day', and the
conclusion, 'etc.', suggests the use of a newsletter, and it was probably through this means
that details reached so many chroniclers. The battle probably took place on 12 Sept. 1319
(Brid., p. 58), which would allow time for the news to reach Berwick by 17 Sept. when the
siege ended. Other clerics who fought were the abbots of York and Selby, the dean of
York, and William Airmyn, then chief clerk of the chancery (Brid., p. 57–8; Flores, iii.
189). The Brut confirms the story of the Scottish smokescreen, and both it and the
Lanercost chronicle describe the Scottish use of the wedge formation which devastated the
untrained English forces (Brut, pp. 211–12; Lanercost, p. 239).
[330] The siege was raised on 17 Sept. (Maddicott, Lancaster, p. 247 n. 3). In a letter of 21

fire to a large amount of hay that had been gathered there, and the 1319
smoke rose, spreading widely in the air. The smoke made it difficult
for our men to see, so that those whom they thought had fled they
found ready for battle. They were indeed men picked from the whole
of Scotland, fit for fighting, fit for every task. Many of our men on the
other hand were untrained in the art of war, and were readier to flee
than to fight. Therefore, when battle was joined many of our men
were killed and many more taken prisoner; but the Scots returned
unharmed to Scotland with their captives, etc.[329]

Word of this came to the king of England and to our army
remaining at the siege, and at once by someone's advice the siege
was completely raised.[330] Indeed, the king tried to cut off the
retreating Scots by one road and the earl of Lancaster by the other.
In truth, the Scots, in possession of a fortunate permit to pass,
returned by the other road to their territory.[331] But why was a siege
given up that had cost so much labour to begin? Some say that Robert
Bruce had friends. Certainly David would not have escaped the hand
of King Saul had he not had his friends amongst the household.[332]
That the king raised the siege was blamed on the earl of Lancaster; he
was also blamed for the Scots coming to seize the queen, and the
king's enemies returning unscathed to their own country. Some
evidence of treachery was openly spoken of, from which the
reputation of the earl and his followers was seriously damaged.[333]
For it was commonly said that the earl received 40,000 pounds from
Robert Bruce to help him and his men secretly, and that at the siege,
while everyone was attacking the wall, none of the earl's retinue
assaulted it, and that the town of Berwick would have surrendered if
the earl's scheming had not hindered this, and that James Douglas on
his way back to Scotland passed through the earl's lines, and that the
earl went unarmed through the midst of the Scots.

Sept. to his sheriff in Glamorgan Hugh Despenser blamed Lancaster, although not overtly
accusing him of collusion with the Scots (*CDS*, v. no. 654). Barbour also repeated the story
of Lancaster's speed in leaving the siege (*The Bruce*, xvii. 853–85: pp. 658–61).

[331] Matt. 2: 12. This sentence seems to be a reference to Lancaster's deliberate help to
the Scots. The author writes of two routes only, and that it was 'the other', i.e. the one
guarded by Lancaster, that the Scots took; *usi duplomate* may therefore have its original
meaning of 'permission to travel'. The Scots' safe return through Lancaster's lines is made
explicit in the last sentence of this paragraph.

[332] Cf. 1 Kgs. (1 Sam.) 19: 1–2, 11–12.

[333] In the following pages the author makes his longest lament on Lancaster's behaviour
and despite Lancaster's purging himself of the accusation, the author clearly does not
believe his innocence; see below, pp. 174–5. For the author's interest in treason, see above,
pp. lii–lv.

1319   O comes Lancastrie, cuius sunt tante diuicie, cur pro tanta summa
pecunie perdidisti famam et nomen constancie? Vtinam non fuisset
illa pecunia pro qua fama tua periit et creuit infamia!ᵃ Magna est
iactura in fame periculo, in cuius dispendio nulla est estimacio, quia
cumᵇ semel lesionem patitur uix uel nunquam recuperatur. Certe, si
totum thesaurum tuum in munera disperges,ᶜ famam tuam pristinam
nunquam reuocares. O ᵈquante laudisᵈ habebas precones dum iugiter
defenderes ordinaciones! Fauor populi in odium conuertitur, et fama
tua in infamiam commutatur. Sic licet Ioab multa fortiter gessit,
prodicio in Abner et Amasam omnem laudem eius denigrauit.³³⁴

O generose comes, cur non ad mentem reuocas genus electum,³³⁵
regalem prosapiam tuam quam infamas? Cur non aduertis, comes
egregie, quantum sit crimen scelus perfidie? Nam si facta reorumᵉ
diuersimodeᶠ puniuntur, proditores tamen iusteᵍ maxima pena plec-
tuntur. Proprium enim proditorum est pessimum finem capere, et quis
unquam talem transiuit impune? Filotas quondam pungnator strenuus
sub magno Alexandro, miles egregius, quia delacionem proditoris
triduo suppressit, ex decreto curie sentenciam proditoris accepit.³³⁶
Eneas et ceteri Troiani, qui urbem suam inclitam prodiderunt, post
mortem Priami exules defecti Troiamʰ reliquerunt.³³⁷ Veniamus ad
exempla domestica. Thomas Torboruile, qui regem Anglie prodidit in
Francia, nouam penam suam pertulit postmodum in Anglia.³³⁸ Comes
de Arselles, Symon Frysel, Willelmus Waleys, non quia Scoti fuerunt
set quia proditores, sentenciam proditorum acceperunt.³³⁹ Quid itaque

---

ᵃ infamiam *MS*; infamia *He, St, Den-Y*   ᵇ tunc *MS*; cum *He, St, Den-Y*   ᶜ sic
MS; *poss. for* dispergeres *MW*   ᵈ⁻ᵈ quante laudes *MS*; quantos laudis *He*; quante laudis
St, Den-Y   ᵉ eorum *MS*; malorum *He*; reorum *Den-Y*   ᶠ sic *MS*; *for* diuerso modo
ML   ᵍ iniuste *MS*; iuste *He, St, Den-Y*   ʰ Troiani *MS*; Troiam *He, St, Den-Y*

---

³³⁴ Cf. 2 Kgs. (2 Sam.) 3: 27, 20: 10.   ³³⁵ 1 Pet. 2: 9.

³³⁶ Philotas was a successful but arrogant cavalry leader, and son of Parmenio,
Alexander's leading military commander. He was informed of a plot against Alexander,
but failed to pass the information on, saying in his defence that he did not take it seriously. It
is not clear if Alexander believed in Philotas's complicity, or simply took the opportunity to
remove a group of Macedonians who opposed further Persian adventures. For modern
narratives and commentaries, see J. A. Hamilton, *Alexander the Great* (London, 1973),
pp. 94–5; Green, *Alexander*, pp. 339–45; Hamilton, *Plutarch: Alexander*, pp. 132–7. The
author may have used Walter of Châtillon's *Alexandreis* as his source, where the story of
Philotas appears in book viii, and the reference to three days at lines 80–91 (*PL* ccix. 542).
For the medieval interest in Alexander and the author's use of Châtillon, see above, p. xxix.
Concealing conspiracy was one of the formal acts of treason: Bracton declared *lesa maiestas* to
be manifest if plots were not disclosed immediately (Bracton, *De Legibus*, ii. 335).

³³⁷ Aeneas could be viewed both as the noble founder of Rome and as one who fled
from, and thus betrayed, Troy. The view of Aeneas as traitor reappeared at this time and is

Oh! earl of Lancaster, whose riches are so great, why for such a 1319 sum of money have you lost your reputation and your name for constancy? Would that that money had never been, for which your reputation died and dishonour was born! There is great damage when reputation is in danger, the cost of which is immeasurable, because once injured it can scarcely ever be regained. Indeed if you scattered all your riches in gifts, you would never recover your former reputation. Oh! What paeans of praise you had while you were constantly upholding the Ordinances! The goodwill of the people is turned to hatred, and your fame is changed to infamy. Thus although Joab performed many brave deeds, his treachery towards Abner and Amasab thoroughly tarnished all his renown.[334]

Oh! noble earl, why do you not recall to mind the 'chosen generation',[335] your royal family which you disgrace! Why do you not take thought, distinguished earl, how great a charge is the crime of broken faith! For, although the deeds of guilty men are punished in a variety of ways, nevertheless traitors justly suffer the extreme penalty. For it is proper that traitors should undergo the worst fate, and who has ever committed such a deed with impunity? Long ago Philotas, a valiant warrior under Alexander the Great, a distinguished soldier, because he held back his denunciation of a traitor for three days, by decree of the court received a traitor's sentence.[336] Aeneas and the other Trojans, who betrayed their famous city, on Priam's death left Troy as homeless exiles.[337] Let us come to examples nearer home. Thomas Turberville, who betrayed the king of England in France, afterwards received his new sentence in England.[338] The earl of Atholl, Simon Fraser, William Wallace, were sentenced as traitors, not because they were Scots, but because they were traitors.[339] What then are you doing, earl of Lancaster? If

found also in Trevet's and Higden's writings (F. Ingledew, 'The Book of Troy and the genealogical construction of history: The case of Geoffrey of Monmouth's *Historia regum Britanniae*', *Speculum*, lxix (1994), 665–704, at p. 700).

[338] Turberville, a household knight, had been captured by the French and released on condition that he spied against Edward I for France. This he did, was discovered and executed in 1295 (J. G. Edwards, 'The treason of Thomas Turberville, 1295', in R. W. Hunt, W. A. Pantin, R. W. Southern (eds.), *Studies in Medieval History Presented to F. M. Powicke* (Oxford, 1948), pp. 296–309).

[339] John Strathbogie, earl of Atholl, joined Bruce's rising of 1306, was captured in Sept. and executed 7 Nov. 1306 in London. Fraser supported Wallace, then Bruce, was captured in Aug. 1306 and executed in London. Wallace rebelled in 1297, was finally captured in Aug. 1305 and executed. All three were considered by Edward I as traitors for fighting against him as their overlord; Fraser's crime was greatest because he had been closest to Edward as one of his household knights (Prestwich, *Ed. I*, pp. 501, 503, 507–8; *CP*, i. 306).

1319 facies, comes Lancastrie? Si uiam nephariam proponas incedere, totus
mundus insurget contra te, nec penam debitam poteris euadere. Igitur
uel[a] labia dolosa[340] de falso conuincas, uel mala opera tua in meliora cito
conuertas.

Inter cetera uicia duo sunt diuitibus ualde inconueniencia, cupiditas et fallacia cupiditatis socia. Vt quid enim cupit qui satis habundat,
ut quid fallit qui alieno non eget? Reuera pauperes et tenues, ⟨qui⟩[b]
que necessaria sunt non habent, huiusmodi uicio laborare solent.
Nam et in iudiciis testimonium eorum solet reprobari, eo quod
presumitur tales facilius posse corrumpi. Set nunc cupiditas assen-
ciones suas ita disposuit, ut pre ceteris uiciis ueraciter dicere possit,
'Ego in sublimibus habito, et tronus meus in diuitum consorcio'.[341]

Sic igitur concurrunt et stant pariter simul in unum diues et
pauper, nisi quod de paupere frequenter fit iudicium, set contra
iniuriam diuitis non est remedium. Heu multa mala inducit cupiditas,
periurium, homicidium, et machinaciones innumeras. Hec animam
hominis uenalem facit et de periculo anime nichil curat, dum tamen
id quod concupiscit adquirit.

Maledicta cupiditas, et eius commercium, per quam caritas abiit et
fides in exilium. Ecce comites et ceteri magnates terre, qui de
patrimonio suo satis possent decenter uiuere, iam totum tempus
suum computant pro nichilo, nisi patrimonium augeant in duplo uel
in triplo; unde uicinos pauperes ad uendicionem paternarum rerum
studiose solicitant, et quos sic inducere non possunt multipliciter
infestant, donec angustiati pro modico forsan offerant, quod pro
magno prius uendidisse potuerant. Et, quia res concordat materie,
factum [c]quoddam libet[c] apponere.

Erat quidam miles uir simplex et multe innocencie sicut ex quodam
eius actu consueto potest apparere. Nam cum seruos eius[d] ex decreto
balliui contingeret quandoque pro transgressione facta puniri, solebat
miles ille apud balliuum pro seruis intercedere, et penam inflictam
frequenter remittere. Dicebat se ex rapinis et spoliis nolle uiuere;
magnum erat opus hoc misericordie. Reliquit post se filios bene
ualentes quorum conuersacio placens erat apud Dominum et
homines. Venit autem magnus quidam et potens filius diaboli,
minister Sathane, et pueros expulit a paterna hereditate. Illi uero

---

[a] ut MS; uel He, St, Den-Y   [b] om. MS; supplied He, St, Den-Y   [c-c] quod
ubilibet MS; quoddam libet He, St, Den-Y   [d] sic R; suos St, Den-Y

[340] Ps. 11 (12): 3; see also Ps. 30 (31): 19.   [341] Cf. Ecclus. 24: 7.

you intend to take the path of wickedness, the whole world will rise 1319 against you, and you will not be able to escape the due punishment. Therefore you should either convict the deceitful lips[340] of falsehood, or quickly turn your evil deeds into better actions.

Two vices amongst others are most unbecoming to the rich, avarice and deceit, the companion of avarice. For what sort of man covets when he has abundance enough, what sort of man cheats when he does not need another's goods? It is true that the poor and needy, who have not the necessaries of life, commonly indulge in this vice. And their testimony is commonly rejected in judicial decisions, because it is presumed that such people can be more easily corrupted. But now avarice has so organized its rise that, beyond other vices, it can truly say: 'I dwell in high places, and my throne is set in the company of the rich.'[341]

Thus rich and poor come together and stand equally side by side, save only that judgment is frequently obtained against the poor, but there is no remedy against the evildoing of the rich. Alas! avarice leads to many evils—perjury, homicide, and innumerable conspiracies. It corrupts man's soul and he cares nothing for the danger to his soul, so long as he gets what he covets.

Cursed be avarice, and its dealings, through which charity has departed and faith is exiled. See how the earls and other great men of the land, who could live fittingly enough on their inheritance, now regard all their time as wasted, unless they double or treble their patrimony; wherefore they assiduously pester their poorer neighbours to sell what they have inherited, and those whom they cannot persuade they plague in many ways, until, in distress, they may perhaps offer for a song what they could earlier have sold for a good price. And since it is relevant to my theme, I am disposed to add an example.

There was a certain knight, a simple man of great innocence, as can appear from a certain habit of his. For when it happened that by order of his bailiff his servants were at some time or other punished for a misdeed, the knight used to intervene with the bailiff on behalf of his servants, and often remitted the penalty imposed. He used to say that he did not wish to live on plunder and robbery; this was a work of great mercy. He left behind him strong sons whose way of life was pleasing to God and man. But there came a certain great and powerful son of the devil, a minister of Satan, and expelled the children from their paternal inheritance. They, in truth not daring

1319 non audentes querelam instituere, coacti sunt pro iure suo modicum accipere.

Set cum prouidencia Dei regatur mundus, ut credimus, cur subcumbit innocens et floret impius, cur non est sumpta uindicta de nocentibus? Sane hec uetus querela magnos et sanctos*a* afflixit, set et regis David animum quandoque concussit. Cum enim rex ille propheta pressuras iustorum cerneret, et iniquos ad omnes uite huius illecebras licencius euagari conspiceret, querebat si utique esset fructus iustorum, et esset Deus iudicans iniquos in terra. 'Mei,' inquid, 'pene moti sunt pedes, pene effusi sunt gressus mei, quia zelaui super iniquos, pacem peccatorum uidens. In labore hominum non sunt, et cum hominibus non flagellantur. Ideo tenuit eos superbia; ecce ipsi peccatores habundantes in seculo optinuerunt diuicias. Et dixi, ergo sine causa iustificaui cor meum et laui inter innocentes manus meas, et fui flagellatus tota die.'[342] Tandem ad occulta Dei iudicia descendens nodum*b* questionis enucleat dicens; 'uerumtamen propter dolos posuisti eis, deiecisti eos dum alleuarentur. Quomodo facti sunt in desolacionem, subito defecerunt, perierunt propter iniquitatem suam.'[343] Manifeste igitur insinuat, qualiter diuicie fallaces et proditorie amatores suos decipiunt, et quos dolose erigunt cum dolore prosternunt. Beatus igitur Iob in dolore et affliccione positus eandem querelam mouet, et postea diuine dispensacionis iusticiam assignat: 'Quare impii uiuunt, sublevati sunt et confortati diuiciis? Semen eorum permanet coram eis, domus eorum secure sunt et parate,*c* et non est uirga Dei super eos';[344] et cetera prosequitur in hunc modum. Nunc diuine dispensacionis iudicium: 'Ducunt in bonis dies suos, et in puncto ad inferna descendunt.'[345] Ecce quomodo exaltati sunt sicut cedrus Libani, et deiecit eos consilium Altissimi.[346] Diuicie date sunt eis in laqueum, delicie et uoluptates in capturam. Super hac re similiter disputat Ieremias; 'Quare,' inquid, 'uia impiorum prosperatur, bene est omnibus qui male agunt et preuaricantur? Plantasti eos, radices miserunt, proficiunt et faciunt fructum.'[347] Et tandem suam mittit sentenciam: 'Congregabuntur,' inquit, 'in die occisionis quasi greges ad uicti-

---

a querelam *inserted after* sanctos *in MS*; *om. He, St, Den-Y*   *b* nondum *MS*; nodum *He, St, Den-Y*   *c* *sic MS*; pacate *He, St, Den-Y*; pacate *conforms with Vulgate reading,* ed.

[342] Ps. 72 (73): 2–3, 5–6, 12–14.   [343] Ps. 72 (73): 18–19.
[344] Job 21: 7–9.   [345] Job 21: 13.
[346] Cf. Isa. 2: 12–13.   [347] Jer. 12: 1–2.

to lodge a complaint, were forced to accept a pittance for what was 1319 theirs by law.

But since the world is ruled by the providence of God, as we believe, why is the innocent overcome and why does the wicked flourish, why is not vengeance taken on evildoers? Truly, this old complaint has tormented great men and saints, and even at times troubled the mind of King David. For when that prophet-king perceived the oppression of the righteous, and observed the wicked turning aside without restraint in pursuit of all the attractions of this life, he asked if this was the reward of the just, and if God judged the wicked upon earth. 'My feet', he said, 'were almost moved, my steps had well nigh slipped; because I was jealous of the wicked, seeing the prosperity of sinners. They are not in trouble as other men, neither are they scourged like other men. Therefore pride hath held them fast; behold these are sinners, and yet prospering in the world, they have obtained riches. And I said, Then have I in vain justified my heart, and washed my hands among the innocent, and I have been scourged all the day.'[342] Coming at last to the secret judgements of God, he sets out the nub of the question, saying: 'But indeed for deceits thou hast put it to them, when they were lifted up, thou hast cast them down. How are they brought to desolation, they have suddenly ceased to be, they have perished by reason of their iniquity.'[343] Therefore he clearly implies how false and treacherous riches deceive those who pursue them, and those whom they raise up by deceit they cast down in sorrow. The blessed Job, placed in grief and affliction, raises the same complaint, and later admits the justice of divine dispensation: 'Why then do the wicked live, are they advanced and strengthened with riches? Their seed continueth before them, their houses are secure and provisioned, and the rod of God is not upon them',[344] and thus he elaborates his theme. Now this is the judgement of the divine dispensation: 'They spend their days in wealth and in a moment they go down to hell.'[345] Behold how they were raised like the cedar of Lebanon, and the counsel of the Most High has cast them down.[346] Their riches are given to them for a snare, delights and pleasure for their capture. On this matter Jeremiah argues in like manner: 'Why', he says, ' doth the way of the wicked prosper, why is it well with all them that transgress, and do wickedly? Thou hast planted them, and they have taken root; they prosper and bring forth fruit.'[347] And at length he gives his opinion: 'They shall be gathered together on the day of slaughter like sheep for

1319 mam.'[348] Quidam eciam poeta, dum de prosperitate impiorum[a] conqueritur simile iudicium prosequitur. Ait enim, 'Tolluntur in altum, ut lapsu grauiore ruant.'[349] Ecce Dauid et Iob, Ieremias et poeta, eandem[b] instituunt querelam, quorum similia sunt iudicia et in unum consona dicta. Certe 'quia non profertur cito contra malos sentencia, absque ullo timore filii hominum impetrant[c] mala'.[350] Nunc autem due semite nobis exponuntur, una uite, altera interitus, et utriusque noticiam habemus. Qui ergo salutis sue tam prodigus extiterit ut relicta semita uite uiam interitus maluerit incedere, sibi imputare debet qui potuit eligere.

Audiens autem comes Lancastrie sic nomen suum diffamatum in populo, et quod publica uox et fama testimonium perhiberet de malo, accessit ad regem et dixit, 'Scitis, domine, quod fueram cum omni retencione mea uobiscum in Scocia, et quod non modicos sumptus ibidem fecerim pro uilla de Berewyk recuperanda.[351] Set nunc imputatur per totum regnum quod res non successit nobis ad uotum. Ego autem ora hominum obturare non possum, uerumptamen ad arbitrium boni uiri, et, si necesse fuerit, [g]in ferro candenti[d] offerro me purgaturum, uel, si appareat[e] accusator et uelit se inscribere, offerro me legitime innocenciam meam ostendere.' Et uidebatur oblacio comitis iusta, eo quod sola fama laborabat, nec erat transgressio manifesta. Admissa est igitur purgacio comitis cum quadam[f] manu parium. Sic spina in lilium, rubigo in ferrum, et scoria redit[g] in aurum, et cetera.

Post hec exegit nouus rex Francie a rege Anglie homagium pro terra Vasconie; et, quia huiusmodi seruicium non nisi personaliter prestari potuit,[352] rex de consilio suo treugas biennales cum Scotis iniit,[353] et sic in breui transfretare disposuit. Displicuerunt treuge quibuscumque[h] proceribus, eo quod status domini regis uideretur in

---

[a] imperiorum *MS*; impiorum *He, St, Den-Y*   [b] eadem *MS*; eandem *He, St, Den-Y*
[c] sic *MS*; perpetrant *He, St, Den-Y*; perpetrant *conforms with Vulgate reading, ed.*
[d-d] insero cadenti *MS*; in ferro candenti *He, St, Den-Y*   [e] apperiat *MS*; appareat *He, St, Den-Y*   [f] qua *MS*; quadam *He, St, Den-Y*; qua *poss. for* quarta *or* quinta *St; meaning 'with four or five oath helpers', Den-Y*   [g] reddit *MS*; redit *He, St, Den-Y*
[h] sic *R*; quibuscunque *St*

---

[348] Cf. Jer. 12: 3.   [349] Claudian, *In Ruf.* i. 22.   [350] Eccles. 8: 11.
[351] There are indeed no records of payment to Lancaster for his service at Berwick. Greater magnates had sometimes served at their own expense under Edward I and continued to do so under Edward II (M. Prestwich, 'Cavalry service in early fourteenth-century England', in J. Gillingham and J. C. Holt (eds.), *War and Government in the Middle Ages: Essays in Honour of J. O. Prestwich* (Woodbridge, 1984), pp. 147–58, at pp. 152–3).

the sacrifice.'[348] Also a certain poet, complaining of the prosperity of 1319
the wicked, passes a similar judgement. For he says, 'They are raised
up on high that they may fall headlong into more grievous ruin'.[349]
See how David and Job, Jeremiah and the poet make the same
complaint, their judgements are alike and their words are in harmony.
Indeed 'because sentence is not speedily pronounced against the evil,
the children of men commit evils without any fear'.[350] And now two
paths are open to us, the one of life, the other of destruction, and we
are informed of each. He therefore who remains so careless of his
safety that abandoning the path of life he prefers rather to follow the
way of destruction, must blame himself, for he has had his choice.

The earl of Lancaster hearing that his name was thus maligned
amongst the people, and that public opinion and rumour bore witness
as to his wrongdoing, approached the king and said, 'You know, my
lord, that I was with you in Scotland with my whole retinue, and that
there I was put to no little expense in recovering the town of
Berwick.[351] But now I am blamed by the whole kingdom that we
did not get the success we wanted. I cannot stop men talking, but I
offer to clear myself by the arbitration of a good man, and, if it should
be necessary, by the white-hot iron, or even if an accuser shall appear
and wish to put himself on record, I offer to show my innocence by
legal process.' And the earl's offer seemed a fair one, because only
rumour had been brought against him; the offence was not proved by
evidence. The earl was therefore allowed to purge himself with the
help of his peers. Thus the thorn turns into a lily, rust into iron, and
dross into gold, etc.

After this the new king of France demanded homage from the king
of England for the land of Gascony; and because this kind of service
could only be performed in person,[352] the king on advice entered
upon a two years' truce with the Scots,[353] and so arranged to cross the
channel in the near future. The truce annoyed certain nobles because

Lancaster possibly refused payment in order to maintain his independence in the face of
the court (Maddicott, *Lancaster*, pp. 245–6).

[352] Philip V had succeeded his brother Louis X on 5 June 1316. Homage by proxy had
been permitted in the past, but Philip now insisted on personal homage, although Edward
was not pushed to give a personal oath of fealty (Chaplais, 'Duché-Pairie', pp. 150–4).

[353] Safe conducts were issued for twelve Scottish negotiators on 24 Oct., powers were
granted to English negotiators 1 Dec., and a two-year truce was arranged to run from 21
Dec. 1319. Further negotiations for a peace treaty or an extension of the truce took place a
year later in Jan.–Apr. 1321 (with French and papal representatives present), but they soon
foundered and the truce was not extended (*Foed.*, ii. 1. 404, 410, 416, 441, 450; Stones,
Anglo-Scottish Relations, pp. 292–307; Barrow, *Bruce*, pp. 240–2).

1319 hoc ualde minoratus. Sane probabiliter sentirent si onus quod regi incumbit caute declinarent. Set nec lex nec racio turpiter fieri presumit quod necessitas ineuitabilis introducit. Legitur quod in *obsidione Troiana* omnes fere mundi principes conuenerant, isti quidem exterioribus, illi uero ad auxilium prestandum obsessis. Set nec hii nec isti erubescebant inducias petere cum oporteret morticina comburere. Porro non iniit rex treugas tantum quia transfretaturus erat, set ut eo pacto ab infestacione suorum gens Scotorum desisteret, quos tempore hiemali precipue uastare consueuerat. Solebat enim rex annis preteritis per totam hiemem munire Marchiam custodibus, set magis nocebat populo oppressio *custodum quam* persecucio inimicorum. Scoti namque pro modico tributo Northamhimbrorum incolis ad tempus parcebant, set hii qui ad tutelam prepositi uidebantur cotidiane exaccioni[c] iugiter uacabant.[354] Preterea non potuit rex simul transfretare et exercitum ad bellum conducere: erat enim transfretaturus[d] post Pascha, quando solent reges preparare conductum ad bella.[355]

1320 Vocauit igitur dominus rex barones suos apud Eboracum ut de statu regni disponerent ante recessum suum.[356] Comes autem Lancastrie, sicut pluries, uocatus non uenit. Non enim decebat habere parliamentum in cameris, ut dixit.[357] Habebat namque regem et collaterales suos sibi suspectos, et ipsos non iam clam set manifeste protestabatur inimicos suos. Set nonne iam dudum erat omnis controuersia et discordia sedata? Reuera sic uidebatur pluribus fuisse res gesta. Verum suspecta est pax inter magnates, ad quam, non amore set ui sublimes ueniunt potestates. Dominus rex apud Berewyke cum firmata fuisset obsidio, et uidebatur res expedienda pro nichilo, huiusmodi uerba protulisse fertur: 'Cum iniquus[e] transierit iste tumultus, ad alia negocia manus conuertemus. Nondum enim nobis excedit *a memoria* fratri meo Petro illata

a–a obsidionem Troianam *MS*; obsidione Troiana *He*   *b–b* custodium quamque *MS*; custodum quam *He, St, Den-Y*   *c* exaccione *MS*; exaccioni *He, St, Den-Y*   *d* transfetaturus *MS*; transfretaturus *He, St, Den-Y*   *e* iniqua *MS*; iniquus *He, St, Den-Y*   *f–f* ad memoriam *R*; a memoria *St, Den-Y*

[354] The office of warden of the Marches first appeared as a permanent post in 1309 as a result of the Edwardian wars (R. R. Reid, 'The office of warden of the Marches; its origin and early history', *EHR*, xxii (1917), 479–96, at p. 479). For examples of exactions by English officials, including the constable of Bamburgh Castle, see Maddicott, *Lancaster*, p. 161, and J. Scammell, 'Robert I and the North of England', *EHR*, lxxiii (1958), 385–403, at p. 389; see also A. King, 'Jack le Irish and the abduction of Lady Clifford, November 1315: the Heiress and the Irishman', *Northern History*, xxxviii: 2 (2001), 187–95.

the lord king's estate seemed to be much diminished by it. Their 1319
judgement would have been quite right if they could have avoided
with safety the obligation that lies upon the king. But neither law nor
reason judges it to be disgraceful to do what unavoidable necessity
brings about. We read that at the siege of Troy almost all the princes
of the world had assembled, some to help the besiegers, others the
besieged. But neither the latter nor the former were ashamed to ask
for a truce when it was necessary to burn their dead. Further, the king
did not make the truce so much because he was about to go overseas,
but so that, when it was made, the Scottish people would stop
attacking his people, whom they used to plunder especially in
wintertime. For in past years the king had been in the habit of
strengthening the March with wardens throughout the winter, but
the oppression of the wardens harmed the people more than the
persecution of their enemies. For the Scots used to spare the
inhabitants of Northumbria for a time in return for a moderate
tribute, but these who were supposed to be set over them for their
protection were free all the time to make exactions every day.[354]
Moreover the king could not cross the channel and at the same time
muster an army for war: for he was to go overseas after Easter when
kings customarily make preparations for war.[355]

The lord king therefore summoned his barons to York to make 1320
arrangements about the state of the realm before his departure.[356] The
earl of Lancaster, however, as frequently happened, when summoned, did not come. He stated that it was improper to hold
parliament in secret.[357] For he regarded the king and his supporters
as suspect, and he declared, no longer privately but publicly, that they
were his enemies. But had not all controversy and discord been
settled a while ago? Indeed many thought that this had been done.
But in truth peace between great men is to be regarded with suspicion
when eminent and powerful men have arrived at it not through love
but by force. When siege had been laid to Berwick and it seemed that
the matter was being pursued to no purpose, the lord king is said to
have uttered some such words as these: 'When this wretched business
is over, we will turn our hands to other matters. For I have not yet

[355] Cf. 2 Kgs. (2 Sam.) 11: 1.
[356] Parliament (without commons) was summoned to York for 20 Jan. 1320 (HBC, p. 555).
[357] Although York could hardly be called 'secret', this may echo cap. 29 of the Ordinances, which says that parliament must be summoned to a convenient place (SR, i. 165b, trans. in 'The New Ordinances, 1311', EHD, iii. 536).

1320 quondam iniuria.' Et hoc quidem uerbum comitem non latuit; unde
nimirum de re apud Berewyk segnius intromisit, uel, si dicere fas sit,
ipsam expedicionem forsan impediuit. Sic^a Achilles iratus commili-
tonibus Grecorum fertur nocuisse, et ab armis suis diu propter uotum
abstinuisse.³⁵⁸ Non uitupero^b comitem si sibi precaueat, nec tamen
laudo si fidem infringat.³⁵⁹

   Igitur quinto sextoue die ante natiuitatem sancti Iohannis baptiste
transfretauit dominus rex in Franciam,³⁶⁰ quem Deus pro sua pietate
salvo custodiat et salvo reducat in Angliam. Precesserant autem regem
frater eius Edmundus, Bartholomeus Badesmere, et quidam alii pro
quibusdam negociis domini regis ad curiam Romanam profecturi.³⁶¹
Eo tempore uacabat in Anglia sedes episcopalis Lyncolniensis, set
canonici ante recessum regis optenta licencia unanimiter consenciebant de eleccione pastoris, qui quidem, magister Antonius de Bek
nominatus, sicut^c generosus et morigeratus et magister erat theolo-
gus^d ecclesie Lyncolniensi satis ydoneus, illius egregii Antonii de Bek
quondam Dunelmensis episcopi et patriarche Ierosolimitane^e con-
sanguineus.³⁶² Habebat dictus Bartholomeus nepotem qui pro etate
industris erat; nondum enim quinque et uiginti annos attigerat.
Procurante itaque Bartholomeo inductus est rex Anglie supplicare
domino pape pro iuuene, ut ad dictam sedem episcopalem dignaretur
eum assumere. Rogabat et rex Francie, et Edmundus frater regis^f
Anglie, et laudabant iuuenem omnes, personam ipsius apud dominum
papam, multipliciter recommendantes. Sic igitur dominus papa, tot et
tantorum precibus solicitatus priorem eleccionem cassauit, et iuuenem illum ecclesie Lyncolniensi prefecit.^g

   Mirabile quidem factum, quia contra legem et racionem^h
actum, nec uisum nec prius auditum ut tam iuuenis preficeretur in

---

   ^a si *MS*; sic *He, St, Den-Y*   ^b uituperio *MS*; uitupero *He, St, Den-Y*   ^c sic *R*;
fuit *St, Den-Y*   ^d sic *MS*; theologie *He, St, Den-Y*; *the copyist uses the same form above*
(p. 78) ed.   ^e sic *MS*; Ierosolimitani *He, St, Den-Y*   ^f eius *R*; regis *St, Den-Y*
^g prefacit *R*; prefecit *St, Den-Y*   ^h armacionem *MS*; *He considered* arramicionem *but*
preferred racionem; racionem *St, Den-Y*

---

   ³⁵⁸ Achilles quarrelled with Agamemnon and refused to fight the Trojans. While he sulked
the Greeks sustained heavy losses including that of his greatest friend Patroclus. See above,
pp. xxix, 28–9. For the quarrel and its outcome see Homer, *Iliad*, esp. bks i, xvi.

   ³⁵⁹ The author's view of Lancaster's guilt seems to have hardened since the previous
entry, where rumour has more emphasis (above, pp. 167–71); the author still, however,
admits mitigating circumstances.

   ³⁶⁰ The date given, that is 18 or 19 June, is accurate. Edward was absent from England
between 19 June and 22 July 1320, and the ceremony took place on 30 June (*HBC*, p. 39;
Chaplais, 'Duché-Pairie', p. 153).

forgotten the wrong that was once done to my brother Piers.' And   1320
this remark did not escape the earl; for this reason without doubt he
took a less active part at Berwick, or, if the truth be told, perhaps he
hindered that expedition. In the same way Achilles in anger is said to
have brought injury upon the Greek co-fighters, and to have
abstained for a long time from the use of arms for a vow.[358] I do
not blame the earl if he is looking after his own interests, nor,
however, do I praise him if he breaks faith.[359]

On the fifth or sixth day before the nativity of St John the Baptist[360]
the lord king accordingly crossed to France, and may God in His
mercy keep him in safety and bring him safely back to England. His
brother Edmund, Bartholomew Badlesmere, and some others who
were going on the lord king's business to the court of Rome had
preceded the king.[361] At that time the episcopal see of Lincoln was
vacant in England, but before the king's departure the canons had
obtained their licence and unanimously agreed on the election of a
pastor, named Master Anthony Bek, who, as a worthy and well-born
man and a master of theology, the kinsman of the famous Anthony
Bek, formerly bishop of Durham and patriarch of Jerusalem, was well
fitted for the church of Lincoln.[362] Now the said Bartholomew had a
nephew who was hard-working for his age; he had not yet reached the
age of 25. So at Bartholomew's instigation the king of England was
persuaded on the young man's behalf to humbly entreat the lord pope
to see fit to promote him to the said episcopal see. Both the king of
France and Edmund, the king of England's brother, requested it, and
everyone praised the youth, repeatedly recommending his person to
the lord pope. So therefore the lord pope, urged on by so many
prayers of so many great men, quashed the former election and
appointed the young man to the church of Lincoln.

This was an extraordinary action, because it was an illegal and
unreasonable act, never before seen or heard of, that so young a man

---

[361] The embassy to Avignon left England on 19 Mar. It was headed by Edmund, earl of
Kent, and included the elder Despenser and Badlesmere (*Foed.*, ii. 1. 418). Its members
joined the king in France at Amiens in late June or early July (Maddicott, *Lancaster*,
p. 255 n.).

[362] John Dalderby, bishop of Lincoln, died on 12 Jan. 1320; Bek was elected on 3 Feb.
(*HBC*, p. 255). The elder Bek, bishop of Durham 1283–1311, had been a royal clerk and,
although not as outspoken as Winchelsey, he had given support to Winchelsey and to the
earls of Norwich and Hereford in 1297. He was known to contemporaries as a mediator
between Edward I and the earls, and in a long eulogy the Bridlington chronicler goes so far
as to say that, if he had lived, the dissension between Edward II and his earls would have
had a happier outcome (*Brid.*, p. 38).

1320 episcopum: contra legem, cum nemo citra triginta annos de iure
cathedram pastoralem possit ascendere, contra racionem quia nemo
iuuenes eligit duces, eo quod non constat eos esse prudentes.³⁶³ Nam
et Salomon incertissimum reputat inter omnia incerta uiam adoles-
centis in iuuentute sua.³⁶⁴ Siquidem admiranda seculo et ridiculosaᵃ
presumpcio, dum iuuenis pastorali locatur in solio. Iuuenem contingit
ad regnum sublimari, set bene non congruit iuuenes episcopari, quia
sanguis et natura attenditur in principe, set uirtus et sciencia
requiritur in episcopo.ᵇ In gregibus et armentis aper, aries et
taurus, corpore et animositate prestancior, ceterorum erit minator
et ductor, set inter racionales hic ordo non seruatur. Hodie enim
quanto quis minus sapit, tanto audacius melioribus ᶜanteuenisseᶜ
presumit. Qui nichil didicit aliorum doctor efficitur, et quasi aes
sonans aut cimbalumᵈ ³⁶⁵ usurpat predicacionis officium, cum sit
cuneus inutilis et ydolum mutum. Nam episcopus illiteratus preco
est mutus. Apud ueteres erat condicio sapientum inestimabiliter
uenerabilis. Hodie uero prudencia tanquam uilis et abiecta calcatur;
et quadam abhominabili mutacione stulticia in sublimi preponitur.
Hoc est quod Ecclesiastes deplorando conqueritur. 'Vidi,' inquit,
'malum quod est sub sole, stultum in sublimi dignitate positum, et
sapientes sedere deorsum.'³⁶⁶ Sacre scripture ᵉprorsus experteseᵉ onus
importabile ᵉdignitatis usurpant,ᶠ de aliena pocius quam de sua
sciencia presumentes.ᵍ Erubescat doleatque prelatus preesse populo
nec prodesse, docentis officium assumpsisse et in doctrina populi
mutum esse. Talem siquidem non prefert honestas set cupiditas, non
moralitas set uenalitas, non sciencia set pecunia, non meritum set
precium, non eleccio set ambicio, et, cum ad regimen plebis et
ducatum populi preficiatur, timendum est ne relicta terra promissio-
nis, in seruitutem incidat et in Egiptum reuertatur. Dignitatis
equidem appetitus nacione celestis est, in celo conceptus, a celo
deiectus, quando affectabat Lucifer ille a parte aquilonis cathedram
erigere, collocari in excelso et fieri similis Altissimo.³⁶⁷ Timendum est

---

ᵃ rediculosa *MS*; ridiculosa *He*, *St*, *Den-Y*   ᵇ principe *R*; episcopo *St*, *Den-Y*
ᶜ⁻ᶜ ante eum esse *MS*; anteeundum *or* anteferendum esse *He*; antecedere (antecedendum)
St; anteuenisse *Den-Y*   ᵈ simbalum *MS*; cimbalum *He*, *St*, *Den-Y*   ᵉ⁻ᵉ prossus ex
perte *MS*; prorsus ex parte *He*, *St*; prorsus expertes *Den-Y*   ᶠ⁻ᶠ dignitate usurpauit *R*;
dignitate usurpant *St* (*who notes the whole sentence as corrupted*); dignitatis usurpant *Den-Y*
ᵍ sic *MS*; presumens *He*

---

³⁶³ Henry Burghersh was provided to the see on 27 May 1320 and held it until his death
in 1340. Most chroniclers disapproved of the appointment, but he was university educated

should be made a bishop. It was illegal, since no one under 30 years of 1320
age can rightfully occupy the pastoral chair, it was unreasonable
because no one chooses young men as leaders, for the reason that their
wisdom is an unknown quantity.[363] Solomon, too, held that the most
uncertain of all uncertainties was 'the way of a man in youth'.[364]
Indeed it astonishes the world and is a laughable presumption for a
young man to be set upon the pastoral throne. It may happen that a
young man is raised to royal authority, but it is not at all fitting for
young men to be made bishops, because blood and birth are looked
for in a prince, but virtue and knowledge are required in a bishop. In
flocks and herds the boar, the ram, and the bull, outstanding in
physique and courage, will dominate and lead the others, but amongst
rational beings this rule is not kept. For today the less a man knows,
the more boldly he dares to push in front of his betters. He who has
learnt nothing is made the teacher of others, and as sounding brass or
cymbal[365] usurps the office of preacher, although he is a useless block
and a dumb idol. For an illiterate bishop is a dumb herald. With the
ancients the position of wise men was one of immeasurable venera-
tion. But today sound judgement is trampled underfoot as vile and
despicable; and by some disgusting change foolishness is raised on
high. This is what the Preacher bitterly laments: 'I have seen', he
said, 'an evil which is under the sun, a fool set in high dignity, and the
wise sitting beneath.'[366] Men completely ignorant of Holy Scripture
usurp the burden of an office they cannot uphold, drawing on other
people's knowledge rather than their own. May a prelate blush and
grieve to find himself in command of the people without being of use,
to have taken upon himself the duty of teaching, and to be dumb in
instructing the people. It is indeed not honour but greed which
promotes such a man, not morality but venality, not knowledge but
money, not merit but a bribe, not free choice but soliciting votes, and
when he is set up to direct the masses and lead the people, it is to be
feared that, having left the promised land, he will fall into slavery and
return to Egypt. Indeed the lust for authority is of heavenly birth,
conceived in heaven, but from heaven cast down, when the famous
Lucifer attempted to raise aloft his throne from the northern parts, to
be set on high and to be regarded like the All Highest.[367] Therefore

---

and in at least his twenty-ninth year and therefore near canonical age (*HBC*, p. 255;
BRUO, iii. 2157–8; Smith, *Appointments*, pp. 35–6).   [364] Prov. 30: 18–19.
[365] 1 Cor. 13: 1.   [366] Eccles. 10: 5–6; wherein *diuites* for the author's *sapientes*.
[367] Cf. Isa. 14: 13–14.

1320 itaque miseris prelatis ne, dum cathedram erigunt ad aquilonem, id est dum indigne cathedram ascendunt pastoralem, cum Lucifero precipitentur in gehennam.

Qua fronte, queso, preesse presumit qui prodesse non nouit? Nonne uideretur insanus qui omnino nauigacionis ignarus in discrimine[a] tempestatis peritissimos nautas contempneret, ipse autem in suam et aliorum perniciem propter temeritatem magisterium nauis usurparet? Set nullus hodie ab onere pontificali se excusat; nullus inuitus trahitur aut reclamans.[b] Vbi hodie similis Amonio reperitur, qui cum ab omni populo ad pontificatus apicem peteretur, 'Oculos meos,' inquid, 'effodiam, linguam[c] per quam uobis me placeo nisi me dimittatis abscidam.'[368] Certe cum ad erudicionem populi mitteret Dominus Ieremiam, quem[d] sanctificauerat ex utero, suam inperfeccionem propheta formidans, 'A! A! A! ' inquid, 'Domine, ecce loqui nescio.'[369] Moises eciam, dum a Domino ad liberacionem[e] populi in Egiptum destinatur, inpedicionem lingue pretendens alium mittendum humiliter inprecatur.[370] Iccirco propter insufficienciam et cupiditatem pontificum translata est hodie archa Dei de Israel in Azotum, id est, a sanctitate in ignem concupiscentie, et de Azoto[f] transfertur in templum Dagon,[371] id est, desolacionis et tristicie. Nam in Matheo scriptum est, cum uideritis abhominacionem desolacionis sedentem in templo, tunc ue pregnantibus et nutrientibus,[372] ac si diceret, cum uideritis [g]ambiciosum, illiteratum[g] et fatuum in ecclesia Dei preminere, ue illis qui talibus prelatis coguntur subiacere. Illi uero qui spem salutis conceperant, exemplo[h] talium suffocantur, qui[i] uero uite celestis alimenta[j] petebant nullo[k] uerbi Domini pabulo sustentantur. 'Paruuli,' inquid propheta, 'petierunt panem et non erat qui frangeret eis.'[373]

Post reuersionem domini regis orta est magna discordia inter quosdam maiores baronum et Hugonem Despenser filium, domini regis camerarium.[374] Hugo namque, qui primogenitam heredum

---

[a] discrimen *MS*; discrimine *He, St, Den-Y*   [b] reclamas *MS*; reclamans *He, St, Den-Y*   [c] liguam *MS*; linguam *He, St, Den-Y*   [d] q' *MS*; qui *He*; quem *St, Den-Y*   [e] obliberacionem *MS*; liberacionem *He, St, Den-Y*   [f] Azota *MS*; Azoto *He, St, Den-Y*   [g-g] ambicom, illaratum *MS*; ambitiosum, illiteratum *He, St, Den-Y*   [h] exemplum *MS*; exemplo *He, St, Den-Y*   [i] quo *MS*; qui *He, St, Den-Y*   [j] alimentam *MS*; alimenta *He, St, Den-Y*   [k] nulle *MS*; nullo *He, St, Den-Y*

---

[368] Palladius, *Historia Lausiaca*, xii (*PL* lxxiii. 1104).   [369] Jer. 1: 6.
[370] Cf. Exod. 4: 10, 13.   [371] 1 Kgs. (1 Sam.) 5: 2.
[372] Matt. 24: 15, 19 (wherein *stantem in loco sancto* for the author's *sedentem in templo*).
[373] Lam. 4: 4.
[374] The king returned from France on 22 July 1320 (*HBC*, p. 39). Despenser's

these wretched prelates should be alarmed lest, when they raise their 1320
throne in the North, that is when they unworthily ascend the pastoral
throne, they be cast down with Lucifer into the pit.

With what effrontery, I ask, does he presume to command, who
does not know how to be of use? Does it not seem altogether mad
that he who is wholly ignorant of navigation should scorn the most
expert sailors at the height of the storm, while out of rashness he
seizes command of the ship to the destruction of himself and others?
But no one today excuses himself from the burden of the pontificate;
no one is dragged forth unwillingly, or protesting. Where today is
one found like Amonius, who, when he was begged by all the people
to become their bishop, said 'I will pluck out my eyes and cut off the
tongue through which I please you, unless you suffer me to
depart'?[368] Indeed when the Lord sent Jeremiah, whom He had
sanctified from birth, to instruct the people, the prophet, fearing his
inadequacy, cried 'Ah! Ah! Ah! Lord, behold I cannot speak.'[369]
Moses, too, when he was sent by the Lord into Egypt to deliver his
people, protesting his imperfection of speech, humbly begged that
another might be sent.[370] Therefore through the incompetence and
greed of the bishops the ark of God is today removed from Israel to
Azotus, that is from holiness to the fire of lust, and from Azotus it is
taken to the temple of Dagon,[371] that is of desolation and grief. For
in Matthew it is written, 'When you shall see the abomination of
desolation sitting in the temple, then woe to them that are with
child, and that give suck',[372] as if he were to say: when you shall see
the ambitious, the illiterate, and the fool pre-eminent in the church
of God, woe to those who are placed under such prelates. Indeed
those who had taken hope of safety are choked by the example of
such men, those who sought the food of celestial life are not
sustained by the nourishment of the Lord's word. 'The little
ones', says the prophet, 'have asked for bread, and there was none
to break it unto them.'[373]

After the lord king's return a great quarrel arose between some of
the greater barons and Hugh Despenser the son, the lord king's
chamberlain.[374] For Hugh, who had married the eldest of the

appointment as chamberlain took place sometime between 19 Apr. 1318, when John
Charlton was still chamberlain, and 20 Oct. 1318, when Despenser's appointment was
confirmed in the York parliament (Tout, *Ed. II*, p. 315; Cole, *Docs. Illus.*, p. 4). The
French prose Brut's suggestion that opponents tried to oust Despenser from the office of
chamberlain at Northampton, if correct, would indicate he was in office by July 1318
(*Anon.*, pp. 39–40, 93).

1320 Gloucestrie duxerat uxorem, et cui fere totum Glamorgan cesserat in partem, omni studio et tota mente terras uicinas^a dominio suo nitebatur amplificare;^{b} et primo castrum de Neuport, quod Hugo de Augeleghe^c in partem accepit, fraudulenter^d intrauit et tenuit;^{375} et castra quedam, ex regia munificencia Rogero de Mortemer dudum collata, uehementer affectauit, et dominum regem ad repeticionem dictorum castrorum consequenter induxit.^{376}

Preterea terram de Gower, ex quibusdam causis in legibus Marchie preiudicium exquisitis, fisco applicari censebat, pro eo quod Iohannes Moubray in ipsam, cum de rege teneretur in capite, sine licencia regis ingressum fecerat; set et dominus rex, qui uotis Hugonis pro posse fauebat, processum quendam in predictum Iohannem, et legi Marchie preiudicialem, fieri discernebat.$^{e\ 377}$ ^{f}Obstabat Iohannes, obstabat^f et comes Herfordie, commune preiudicium aduertentes, domino regi ne nouam legem, quam^g consuetudines^h ab antiquo usitatas et approbatas, induceret humiliter supplicantes. Instabat Hugo Despenser pertinaciter dicens dominum regem tam in Wallia quam in Anglia hac semper prerogatiua gaudere, ut nullus sine licencia regis ingressum^i haberet in feodum quod de rege teneretur in capite; et si contrarium a quocunque foret attemptatum feodum sic occupatum redigeretur in fiscum. Allegabant alii legem marchie et consuetudines quas non licebat infringere.^{378} Spreuit Hugo et consuetudines et legem Marchie, set et barones talia allegantes lese maiestatis uidebatur arguere.

Tanta contumelia barones affecti indignanter recesserunt, et conuenientes in Wallia Hugonem Despenser prosequendum, deponendum et penitus destruendum, unanimiter decreuerunt. Huic autem decreto principaliter consencientes et iuramento astricti fuerunt

---

^{a} uicinias *MS*; uicinas *He, St, Den-Y* ^{b} amplicare *MS*; amplificare *He, St*
^{c} Augelegh' *R*; Angeleghe *He*; Audeleghe *St, Den-Y* ^{d} fraudelenter *MS*; fraudulenter
He, St, Den-Y ^{e} *sic MS; poss.* decernebat *He* $^{f-f}$ ostabat *MS in both places; for*
obstabat *St, Den-Y*; instabat *He* ^{g} *sic R;* contra *St, Den-Y* ^{h} consuetudinis *MS*;
consuetudines *He, St, Den-Y* ^{o} in *before* ingressum *MS; om. He, St, Den-Y*

---

^{375} By Dec. 1318, and clearly under pressure, the Audleys granted Newport to Despenser. They confirmed the grant in 1320 (*CPR 1317–21*, pp. 257, 415, 456).

^{376} This is probably a reference to the castles of Blaenllyfni and Dinas in the lordship of Blaenllyfni, both of which Roger Mortimer of Chirk held as keeper from 1310 and which were granted to him in 1316. Despenser did not acquire them until after Mortimer's rebellion. He became keeper of Blaenllyfni in 1322, and was granted both castles in 1324 (*CFR 1307–1319*, p. 58; ibid., *1319–27*, pp. 143, 179; *CChR 1300–1326*, pp. 306, 469). I am indebted to Barbara Wright for detailed discussion of Mortimer's association with the castles. For Mortimer, see above, n. 226.

Gloucester heiresses, and to whose share almost all Glamorgan had 1320
fallen, now devoted all his energy and thoughts to extending his
lordship over the neighbouring lands; and first he deceitfully seized
and held Newport castle, which had fallen to Hugh Audley's share;[375]
and he passionately coveted certain castles bestowed on Roger
Mortimer a little while ago of the king's gift, and so persuaded the
lord king to reclaim the said castles.[376]

Further, he proposed that the land of Gower, for certain reasons
carefully chosen to be prejudicial to the laws of the March, should be
put under the royal treasury, because John Mowbray had entered it
without the king's licence, although it was held from the king in chief;
and the lord king, who furthered Hugh's designs as far as he could,
decided that an action should lie against the said John, prejudicial to
Marcher law.[377] John opposed this, the earl of Hereford also opposed
it, pointing out the general disadvantage, humbly begging the lord
king not to introduce a new law, rather than [keep] customs used and
approved from time out of mind. Hugh Despenser stubbornly
insisted, saying that the lord king had always enjoyed this prerogative
in Wales as in England, that no one without the king's licence should
have entry upon any fee held of the king in chief; and if, on the other
hand, this should be attempted by anyone, the fee so seized should be
assigned to the royal treasury. Others cited the law and customs of the
March which could not be infringed.[378] Hugh took no notice of the
customs and law of the March, and appeared to accuse the barons
who cited such things of treason.

Deeply upset by such an affront the barons departed full of
indignation, and, meeting in Wales, they unanimously decided that
Hugh Despenser must be pursued, laid low, and utterly destroyed.

---

[377] John Mowbray of Axholme (Lincs.) was knighted alongside Mortimer and Prince
Edward 1306, and served regularly in the Scottish wars. He was William Braose's son-in-
law and expected to obtain Gower through right of his wife and a contract made with
Braose (CP, ix. 377–9; Maddicott, Lancaster, p. 260 n. 7). In need of money, Braose also
made bargains with Hereford, Mortimer of Wigmore, and Despenser. Mowbray entered
Gower without the king's licence to forestall other claimants including Despenser, and the
king confiscated the lordship on 26 Oct. 1320 (CCR 1318–23, p. 268; J. Conway Davies,
'The Despenser war in Glamorgan', TRHS, 3rd ser., ix (1915), pp. 34–41). The king's
men met resistance to the confiscation of Gower in Nov. 1320, and finally took possession
14 Dec. (CFR 1319–27, pp. 40–2; Maddicott, Lancaster, p. 260).

[378] Over a long period, as defenders of English borders against the Welsh princes,
Marcher lords had acquired considerable independent jurisdictions, where the writ of the
king did not run. When Edward I conquered Wales, English administration and law were
applied to the conquered lands, but not to the entrenched Marcher jurisdictions. For the
peculiar status of the Marcher lordships see Davies, Wales 1063–1415, pp. 391–2, 404–5.

1320 subscripti: Iohannes de Mounbray, comes de Herford, Hugo Daudeleye, et Rogerus de Clifford, Rogerus Dammory, et inter alios
Rogerus de Mortymer auunculus et nepos. Isti uenerunt cum multis
1321 aliis; et manus comitis Lancastrie erat cum illis.[379] Quilibet[a] istorum
Hugonem[b] diffiderat,[c] quia contra singulos Hugo deliquerat: Iohannes
de Moubray pro terra de Gower, quem supplantare nititur Hugo
Despenser; Hugo[d] Daudeleye pro castro detento; comes de Herford
pro leso filio;[380] Rogerus de Clifford pro exheredacione matris, quam
Hugo procurauerat in preiudicium ipsius;[381] Rogerus Dammori,
coheres comitis Gloucestrie, inuidum suum non potest diligere.
Rogerus de Mortimer et Rogerus de Mortimer inimici facti sunt
Hugoni Despenser quia unum spoliare disposuit et in utrumque
mortem aui sui uindicare promisit.[382] Comes Lancastrie notam
infamie, quam apud Berewyk pertulit, imputat Hugoni,[383] quam
uult uindicari cum tempus acceperit.

Igitur antequam rem in actum proferrent, mandarunt domino regi
quatinus Hugonem Despenser a se dimitteret, aut electe custodie
ipsum committeret, ut[e] certo die iudicio sisti posset, quo ad sibi
obicienda responderet; alioquin regem pro rege deinceps non haberent, set homagium et fidelitatem et iusiurandum quodlibet regi
prestitum penitus declinarent, et tanquam homines sine rege, sine
rectore et sine iudice, pro defectu iusticie in ulcionem Hugonis
propria auctoritate procederent, et uindictam qualem possent de
malefactis tantorum malefactorum expeterent.[384]

---

[a] He read quibus *and suggested* omnibus; quilibet *St, Den-Y*   [b] Hugo *R*; Hugonem
St, Den-Y   [c] diffidat *MS*; diffiderat *Den-Y*   [d] Hugonem *MS*; Hugo *He, St, Den-Y*
[e] et *MS*; ut *He, St, Den-Y*

[379] This meeting probably took place in Feb. 1321. On 30 Jan. 1321 the king had
forbidden the Despensers' opponents to assemble together, but a letter of 27 Feb. reported
that the Marchers and Lancaster had met. It appears to be the only source for such a
meeting at this time (*CCR 1318–23*, p. 355; *Foed.*, ii. 1. 442; Davies, 'Despenser war', p. 47,
citing TNA Anc. Corr. 35/8). Lancaster took no part in the subsequent violence, although
most chronicles record his support for the Despensers' opponents (Maddicott, *Lancaster*,
p. 267).
[380] Hereford's son was to have the reversion of Gower (see above, n. 377).
[381] Roger Clifford, born 1300 and one of the youngest contrariants, was the son of
Robert Clifford who died at Bannockburn (see above, n. 167). His mother was heiress to
the lands of her nephew Thomas Clare, son of Richard Clare of Connaught. Thomas was
dead by spring 1321, but this seems rather late to have caused trouble over inheritance in
1320, unless there were previous problems over wardship (*CP*, iii. 247, 291; Davies
'Despenser war', p. 43 n.).
[382] For the Mortimers, see above, n. 226. This is a reference to Despenser's attempt to
rob Wigmore of Gower, but the author has also mentioned Despenser's designs on Chirk's

The leaders of those agreeing with this decision and bound by oath 1320
were as written below: John Mowbray, the earl of Hereford, Hugh
Audley, and Roger Clifford, Roger Amory, and amongst others Roger
Mortimer, the uncle and the nephew. These came with many others;
and they had the support of the earl of Lancaster.[379] Each of these had 1321
renounced allegiance to Hugh, because Hugh had wronged each of
them: John Mowbray for the land of Gower, in which Hugh
Despenser is trying to overthrow him; Hugh Audley for the castle
withheld; the earl of Hereford for the wrong done to his son;[380] Roger
Clifford for the disinheritance of his mother, which Hugh had
brought about to his damage;[381] Roger Amory, co-heir of the earl
of Gloucester, could not love his jealous rival. The two Roger
Mortimers were hostile to Hugh Despenser because he proposed to
rob the one, and promised to avenge the death of his grandfather
upon each of them.[382] The earl of Lancaster blames Hugh for the
mark of dishonour which he suffered at Berwick,[383] which he wishes
to avenge when the opportunity arises.

Thereupon, before they put plans into action, they told the lord
king to dismiss Hugh Despenser from his presence, or to commit him
to a picked guard, in order that he could be put on trial on a certain
day, when he might answer the charges against him; otherwise they
would no longer have the king for king, but would utterly renounce
their homage and fealty and whatever oath they had sworn to the
king, and as men without a king, without a ruler, and without a judge,
they would proceed to take vengeance upon Hugh on their own
authority for lack of justice, and they would take what revenge they
could from the perpetrators of such enormities.[384]

castles; see above, n. 376. The reference to revenge is because the Mortimers and
Despensers had fought on opposite sides at the battle of Evesham in 1265, and Wigmore's
grandfather (Chirk's father) had been instrumental in blocking the bridge which trapped
Montfort's army and ultimately led to Despenser's grandfather's death in battle. Mortimer
seems to have been particularly brutal there (Prestwich, *Ed. I*, p. 51; J. R. Maddicott,
Simon de Montfort (Cambridge, 1996), pp. 340–2).

[383] The *Vita* devotes more space than other chronicles to discussing Lancaster's blame
for the failure to retake Berwick (see above pp. 166–71, 174–5). Despenser certainly helped
to circulate the rumours in a letter to John Inge, his sheriff in Glamorgan (Maddicott,
Lancaster, p. 249).

[384] The first part of this passage reflects closely the letter sent by Hereford to excuse
himself from meeting the king at Gloucester in Apr. The passage threatening renunciation
of fealty does not, however, appear in that letter (*CCR 1318–23*, pp. 367–8; *PW*, ii. 1. 231–
2; Davies, 'Despenser war', pp. 50–2). For threats against Edward see above, pp. 18–21,
60–3, and below pp. 192–3.

1321 Indignatus*a* rex uehementer super mandato baronum, uersus
Gloucestriam iter arripuit,[385] et ultra progressus Rogero Dammory,
qui partem aduersam sustinuit, castrum de Sancto Briauello cum
libertate et pertinenciis statim abstulit,[386] et terras Hugonis Daudeleye confiscari iussit, quia, ut rex asserit,*b* contra iuramentum quod
regi prestiterant baronibus adhesit.[387] Deinde cum propositum baronum sine forma predicta suspendere non posset, cum suo Hugone
semper a latere Londonias reuertitur.

Set propositum baronum ulterius non differtur, nam castrum de
Neuport primitus obsidentes leuiter capiunt,[388] et Hugonem Daudeleye, prout ius dictabat, in possessionem mittunt. Cetera castella, que
Hugo Despenser tenebat in Wallia, modico labore barones occupant.
Nec custodes defendere nec Walenses, dominacionem Hugonis
execrantes, tuicionem inferre procurant; erat enim cum baronibus
fortitudo copiosa armatorum octingenti et peditum multa milia; nec
Hugo Despenser uenerat defendere nec custodes indefensi poterant
resistere. Quicquam*c* autem preciosam in castris reperiunt, econtra
lege*d* iuris belli inter ipsos diuidunt.[389] Oues, boues et equos non
dimittunt, set quid quis tolleret sine lite statuunt. Dignum namque
iudicant ut publicentur ⟨bona⟩*e* eius, per quem regnum et optimates
regni grauiter perturbantur.

Conuenerunt autem incole illius terre ad barones quasi triginta
milia hominum, dicentes: 'Cesset indignacio uestra circa nos; dominacionem Hugonis Despenser nunquam gratam habuimus; parati
sumus unanimiter obedire mandatis uestris.' Admissi sunt sub tali
pacto, ut ab homagio Hugonis Despenser penitus discederent, ut eum
pro domino nunquam agnoscerent, set domino regi per omnia fideles
existerent, et uero heredi pro loco et tempore debita seruicia illesa
seruarent; et hec omnia tactis sacrosanctis euangeliis*f* et oretenus
appositis specialiter confirmarunt.

Post rem sic consummatam in Wallia, idem iudicium decreuerunt
barones exercendum in Anglia. Nam omnia bona Hugonis tam patris

---

a indignatur *MS*; indignatus *He, St, Den-Y*   *b* sic *MS*; poss. asseruit *He*   *c* sic
MS; quicquid *He, St, Den-Y*   *d* sic *MS*; poss. legem or leges *He*   *e* om. *MS*; supplied
Den-Y   *f* euuangeliis *R*; euangeliis *St, Den-Y*

[385] The king was at Gloucester by 26 Mar. 1321 (*Itin.*, p. 208). The rebels were
summoned to appear before him there on 5 Apr. (*CCR 1318–1323*, p. 364).
[386] The king was at St Briavels 2–6 Apr. 1321 (*Itin.*, p. 209).
[387] The king ordered the confiscation of Audley's lands on 9 Apr. (*CFR 1319–27*,
pp. 51–2; *PW*, ii. 2. App. 158).

Highly displeased at the baronial demand the king set out towards 1321
Gloucester,[385] and going beyond it immediately took the castle of St
Briavel's, with its liberty and appurtenances, from Roger Amory who
supported the other side,[386] and ordered Hugh Audley's estates to be
confiscated, because, as the king asserted, he supported the barons
contrary to the oath which they had sworn to the king.[387] Then, since
he could not put a stop to the baronial plan unless he agreed to their
terms, he returned to London with his own Hugh always at his side.

But the baronial plan was put off no longer, for, first besieging
Newport Castle, they easily took it,[388] and put Hugh Audley in
possession, as right dictated. The barons seized the other castles
which Hugh Despenser held in Wales without much difficulty. The
keepers did not defend them, nor did the Welsh, hating Hugh's
lordship, give them any protection; for with the barons there was an
ample contingent of eight hundred men-at-arms and many thousand
foot soldiers; and Hugh Despenser had not come to defend the
castles, nor had the keepers been able to offer resistance without
help. Whatever they found of value in the castles they divided
between themselves, contrary to the law of war.[389] They did not
forgo sheep, oxen, and horses, but agreed without dispute what each
might take. For they judged it right to confiscate the goods of the
one through whom the kingdom and its great men were severely
troubled.

However, the inhabitants of that region, some 30,000 men, came
to the barons saying: 'give up your displeasure towards us; we have
never liked Hugh Despenser's lordship; we are all prepared to obey
your orders'. They were accepted on these terms, that they would
wholly renounce their homage to Hugh Despenser, that they would
never acknowledge him as lord, but would remain faithful to the
lord king in all things, and would maintain unimpaired the due
services for the true heir at the proper time and place; and having
touched and kissed the Holy Gospels, they solemnly confirmed all
these things.

When this business had been settled in Wales, the barons resolved
that the same judgment was to be carried out in England. They

---

[388] The Marchers turned from threats to violence at the beginning of May, and attacked
Newport on 6 May (*CCR 1318–23*, p. 541). The Tintern version of the *Flores*, however,
records the attack as on 4 May and Newport's fall as on 8 May (*Flores*, iii. 344).
[389] By the commonly accepted laws of war towns which surrendered without fighting
should not be pillaged; only those which resisted and were taken unconditionally were
open to the full rigours of plunder (Keen, *Laws of War*, pp. 119–23).

1321 quam filii ubicumque reperta occuparunt, disperserunt, et publicarunt. Voluntas enim comitis Lancastrie fuit ut non solum insurgerent in filium, set ut patrem cum filio mitterent in exterminium, quia antiquum odium erga patrem conceptum tempus uindicte non uiderat acceptum. Et sic interim coniurati sunt barones Marchie cum comite Lancastrie in exilium Hugonis Despenser tam patris quam filii, in persecucionem eorum, in dampnacionem, in perpetuam exheredacionem.[390] Igitur, sicut dixi, occupantur bona eorum, maneria spoliantur, franguntur claustra ferarum, et, forsan quia Hugo pater olim a multis pro feris regiis iniustam extorsit redempcionem,[391] nunc in feris propriis, quas multum dilexit, patitur ulcionem. Sic Pharao submergitur quia infantes submersit;[392] et sic frequenter[a] iuste contingit ut quis puniatur in quo deliquit.

    Cum audisset rex tantam feritatem baronum, conuocatis consiliariis suis proposuit[b] concilium.[393] Erant quidam qui iustum reputabant esse iudicium inuadere et occupare castra baronum, ut exemplum quod ipsi prestiterant retorqueretur in caput eorum. Et huic quidem consilio dominus rex libenter acquieuisset si consentaneos[c] sufficientes habuisset. Alii uero sanioris consilii dissuadebant sic fieri. Dicebant enim ex huiusmodi processu nichil aliud euenire quam communem guerram suscitare, terram destruere, et ad perdicionem regni properare. Consulebant autem ut rex barones ad parliamentum conuocaret, et ibidem sicut decet querelas singulorum audiret, et eas secundum leges terminaret. Vocauit igitur barones ad parliamentum, ut interim cessaret impetus eorum.[394] Venerunt itaque ad parliamentum, set cum maxima multitudine armatorum.[395]

    Videns autem rex propositum baronum, animaduertens peticiones

---

[a] sic frequenter et sic frequenter *MS*   [b] posuit *R*; proposuit *St, Den-Y*
[c] concentaneos *MS*; consentaneos *He, St, Den-Y*

---

[390] Although this conspiracy is placed in the text before the council meeting in May, it must allude to the meeting at Sherburn on 28 June 1321. The author explicitly places it after the Welsh seizures in May, so it cannot refer to the meeting between the Marchers and Lancaster in Feb. (see above, n. 379), but Marchers were not present at Lancaster's meeting with northern barons at Pontefract on 24 May (*Brid.*, pp. 61–2). Hereford and other unnamed southern barons were, however, at the meeting Lancaster called at Sherburn on 28 June, at which the indictment against the Despensers was first drawn up (*Brid.*, pp. 62–5). Maddicott has convincingly shown that there was only one meeting at Sherburn that summer (Maddicott, *Lancaster*, pp. 270–9).

[391] Except for two short periods in 1307–8 and 1311–12, the elder Despenser had been justiciar of the forest south of Trent for nearly eighteen years between 1297 and 1315. He would be appointed again, for life, in June 1324 (Tout, *Ed. II*, pp. 320–1). For this author's further comment see below, pp. 238–9.   [392] Cf. Exod. 1: 22, 14: 28.

seized, divided up, and confiscated all the goods of Hugh (the father
as well as the son) wherever they were found. For it was the wish of
the earl of Lancaster that they should not only rise against the son,
but destroy the father along with the son, because he had seen no
opportunity for satisfying his old hatred against the father. And so for
a time the barons of the March made a sworn conspiracy with the earl
of Lancaster to banish, prosecute, condemn, and perpetually disin-
herit the Despensers, father and son.[390] Thus, as I have said, their
goods are seized, their manors plundered, their game preserves
broken open, and, perhaps because Hugh the father once squeezed
unjust fines from many for offences against the royal beasts of the
chase,[391] he now suffers vengeance against his own beasts, in which he
has taken much pleasure. Thus Pharaoh is drowned because he
drowned the children;[392] and thus it often justly happens that the
punishment fits the crime.

When the king heard that the barons were behaving so savagely, he
called together his advisers and held a council.[393] Some thought it
would be right to attack and seize the baronial castles, so that the
precedent which they had established should recoil upon their heads.
This advice the lord king would willingly have followed, if it had had
sufficient support. Others, however, of wiser counsel argued against
doing this. For they said that nothing would emerge from such a
course except that it would stir up a general war, destroy the country,
and hasten the ruin of the kingdom. They advised the king to
summon the barons to parliament, and there, as was fitting, hear
the complaints of each, and settle them according to the law. He
therefore called the barons to parliament, so that their attacks might
cease for a time.[394] So they came to parliament, but with a very great
crowd of men-at-arms.[395]

When the king saw the barons' intention, and heard their petitions,

---

[393] The council was called at London for 13 May 1321, then postponed to 17 May
(*PW*, ii. 2. 159).
[394] Parliament (with commons) was summoned on 15 May 1321 to meet on 15 July at
Westminster. It was dismissed on 22 Aug. (*HBC*, p. 555).
[395] Detailed descriptions of this parliament are also to be found in *Ann. Paul.*, pp. 294–7
and *Hist. Roff.*, pp. 166–7. The *Annales Paulini* add the queen as mediator, and the
Historia Roffensis records Badlesmere's plot to saddle the Despensers with the declaration
on homage which had been used against Gaveston in 1308. Both the *Historia Roffensis* and
the *Brut* (p. 213) show the cohesion of the rebel forces in their use of a common green and
yellow livery. For a discussion of the charges against the Despensers and their evolution,
see Maddicott, *Lancaster*, pp. 280–6, and M. Prestwich, 'The charges against the
Despensers, 1321', *BIHR*, lviii (1985), 95–100.

1321 eorum, et quod ad hoc tendebant omnimodo, ut exterminarent priuatum*a* suum, nitebatur differre negocium. Nolebant dilacionem ferre magnates. Noluit rex audire barones, et ita per aliquot dies suspendebat rex peticiones eorum, donec unanimiter omnes unum conformauerunt decretum, mandantes domino regi quatinus querelas eorum audiret et peticionibus eorum secundum iusticiam satisfaceret, aut ab homagio suo penitus discederent et alium rectorem sibi preficerent qui iusticiam omnibus faceret et collum nocentium et superborum humiliaret;³⁹⁶ et hoc quidem mandatum comes de Penbrok et alii magnates qui uidebantur mediatores regi differrebant,*b* qui tamen cum baronibus de*c* querelis eorum defendendis usque ad mortem iuramentum prestiterant.

Tunc comes Adomarus coram rege huiusmodi uerba fertur protulisse. 'Considera,' inquid, 'domine rex, potenciam baronum; imminens*d* aduerte periculum; nec frater nec soror te tibi debet esse carior. Noli ergo pro aliquo uiuente perdere regnum tuum. Alpibus ille perit qui plus se diligit ullum. Nec dicat dominus rex in contumeliam suam hec a baronibus incohata;*e* set, quia publice utile est ut malis hominibus euacuetur patria, et ad hoc, domine rex, prestitisti iuramentum in coronacione tua, ergo si barones audieris, potenter et gloriose regnare poteris; sin autem, et a peticionibus eorum ⟨et⟩*f* a nostris*g* auertis,*h* regnum forsan et nos omnes consequenter amittes.*i* Coniurati enim sumus, quia paribus nostris contradicere non possumus.'

Videns ergo rex quod uehementer irruerunt in eum, annuebat licet inuitus peticionibus eorum. Tunc missus est ex parte regis archiepiscopus Cantuariensis, qui barones ad Westmonasterium conuocaret, ubi coram rege conuenirent, et quod racio dictaret sine dilacione reportarent. Nec mora, congregatis omnibus apud Westmonasterium, perlecte sunt coram rege querele eorum baronum et protinus adiecte peticiones eorum, et quia nemo contradicere posset sequebatur conforme iudicium. Summam autem querele paucis uerbis libet exprimere.

Arguebatur Hugo nimium cupidus et per hoc regi minus ydoneus; arguebatur malus consiliarius; arguebatur conspirator et falsus; arguebatur destructor*j* populi, exheredator corone, inimicus regis et

---

a sic MS; poss. primatum He   *b* sic MS; defferebant He; deferebant St, Den-Y   *c* et MS; pro or de He; de Den-Y   *d* iminens MS; imminens He, St, Den-Y   *e* sic MS; inchoata St;   *f* om. MS; supplied He   *g* sic R; aures St, Den-Y   *h* aduertis MS; auertis He, St, Den-Y   *i* amittis MS; amittes He, St, Den-Y   *j* distructor R; destructor St

and that they were utterly determined upon the expulsion of his 1321
favourite, he strove to delay the matter. The magnates would not
tolerate this delay. The king would not listen to the barons, and so for
some days the king held up their petitions, until at length they all
unanimously drew up a single resolution, requesting the lord king to
hear their complaints and satisfy their petitions according to justice,
or they would utterly renounce their homage and set up another ruler
to do justice to all and make the guilty and the arrogant bow their
necks;[396] the earl of Pembroke and other great men brought this
message to the king, appearing to be mediators, although they had
taken an oath with the barons to defend their grievances to the death.

At this time Earl Aymer is said to have uttered these words in the
presence of the king: 'Consider, lord king', he said, 'the power of the
barons; pay heed to the looming danger; neither brother nor sister
should be dearer to you than yourself. Do not therefore for any living
soul lose your kingdom. He perishes on the rocks who loves another
more than himself. Let not the lord king say, to his own dishonour,
that this business was begun by the barons; but, since it is for the
good of the people that the country be rid of wicked men, and to this
[public good], lord king, you swore an oath at your coronation, if
therefore you will listen to the barons you will be able to reign in
power and glory; but if not, and you turn away from their petitions
[and] from ours, you may perhaps because of that lose the kingdom
and all of us. For we are sworn allies, and we cannot oppose our
peers.'

So the king, seeing how violently they attacked him, unwillingly
granted their requests. Then the archbishop of Canterbury was sent
on the king's behalf to summon the barons to Westminster, where
they should meet in the king's presence, and they would immediately
obtain what reason demanded. Nor was there any delay; when they
had all gathered at Westminster the barons' complaints were read out
before the king and their petitions added forthwith, and, as no one
could contradict them, an appropriate judgment followed. The sum
of their complaints can be expressed in a few words.

Hugh was accused of being too greedy and thus unsuitable to be
with the king; he was accused of being an evil counsellor; he was
accused of being a conspirator and a liar; he was accused of being a

[396] This the most extreme threat to Edward recorded by the author, but even so it is not
yet a threat to choose another king, but a 'rector', perhaps a governor or keeper of the
realm. For similar threats see above, pp. 18–21, 60–3, 186–7.

1321 regni. Hec omnia contra Hugonem barones allegabant, et super hiis tam patrem quam filium constanter accusabant. Non erat qui patrem uel filium defenderet, non erat qui pro ipsis contra barones disputaret.

Tunc in conspectu domini regis, prelatorum, comitum et baronum, prolatum est iudicium in Hugonem Despenser patrem et filium. Nam uterque tanquam malus et falsus domini regis consiliarius, tanquam seductor et conspirator uel exheredator corone et destructor populi, et inimicus regis et regni, condempnatur, proscribitur et exheredatur; et super hoc editum est statutum, ut iudicium, tanta auctoritate firmatum, nullum reuocetur in euum.[397]

Ecce duo uiri inter magnates terre, et ipsius regis speciales nuper precipui, natale solum et solium deseruerunt licet inuiti. Res miranda quia tam subita, subitas enim mutaciones odit et miratur natura. Reuera iudicio multorum iuste accidit eis hoc infortunium. Pater namque ferus et cupidus olim multis nocuit, et excommunicaciones multorum promeruit. Cum enim esset iusticiarius de foresta, multos accusauit de uenacione regia, multos nequiter exheredauit, quosdam in exilium compulit, iniquas redempciones a pluribus extorsit, mille libratas terre per concussionem adunauit, et ecce manum Dei uel corrigentem uel prouenientem iam sensit. Communi uero iudicio iuste perdidit quod per iacturam aliorum prius congregauit. Set nonne legitur in sacris scripturis: 'Filius non portabit iniquitatem patris'?[398]

Ad hoc uidentur respondere, uidelicet quod commoditas iniquitatis paterne ad filium debuit deuenire, iustum fuit ut paternum uicium communiter redundaret in filium. Set et secundum quosdam malicia filii preponderebat[a] paterne seueritati. Nam de regio fauore confisus omnia pro imperio agebat, omnis captabat, nulli nec alicui quantumcunque auctoritatis deferebat, coheredibus suis moliebatur insidias; sic, si fieri posset, per occasiones fictas uterque partem suam amitteret, et ipse solus solidum comitatum optineret. Ipsi uero, auxilio freti baronum, malicie eius occurrerunt. Nam et patrem et filium simul in exilium agitarunt. Verumptamen iudicio fide-

---

[a] *sic MS*; preponderabat *He, St, Den-Y*

[397] The official indictment was read in Westminster Hall and finally accepted by the king on 14 Aug. 1321 (*Ann. Paul.*, p. 297; *Anon.*, pp. 100–1). The author of the *Vita* closely reflects the general wording of the accusations but is mistaken on the matter of statute. A statute was indeed requested, but on the king's refusal the judgement was finally made by an award; the indictment was therefore entered on the close roll not among the

destroyer of the people, a disinheritor of the crown, an enemy of king 1321 and kingdom. All these things the barons alleged against Hugh, and persistently accused both father and son of these offences. There was no one to defend either the father or the son, no one to speak for them against the barons.

Then in the presence of the lord king, the prelates, earls, and barons, judgment was given against Hugh Despenser, the father and the son. Each was found guilty, proscribed, and disinherited, as an evil and false counsellor of the lord king, as a deceiver and conspirator, and even a disinheritor of the crown and a destroyer of the people, and an enemy of the king and kingdom; and a statute was published on this so that the judgment, confirmed by such authority, should never be revoked.[397]

See now how two men, counted amongst the great men of the land, and until recently the particular intimates of the king himself, reluctantly left their native soil and splendour. An astonishing thing because so sudden, for nature abhors and marvels at sudden changes. But in truth in the opinion of many this misfortune fell upon them justly. For the cruel and greedy father had in the past wronged many, and obtained the excommunication of many. For when he was justice of the forest he accused many of illegal hunting, he wretchedly disinherited many, forced some into exile, extorted unjust ransoms from many, collected a thousand pounds' worth of land by means of threats, and behold now he feels the hand of God coming to correct him. The general judgement was that he justly lost what he had formerly accumulated from the loss of others. But is it not written in the Holy Scriptures: 'The son shall not bear the iniquity of the father'?[398]

In reply it may be said that, as the profit from the father's evildoing had to pass by inheritance to the son, it was right that the father's crime should also accrue to the son. But according to some the son's wickedness outweighed the father's harshness. For, confident of the royal favour, he did everything on his own authority, grabbed everything, had no regard for the authority of anyone whomsoever, set traps for his co-heirs; thus, if he could manage it, each would lose his share through trumped up accusations and he alone would obtain the whole earldom. But they, relying on the help of the barons, were a match for his wickedness. For they drove both father and son into

statutes (Prestwich, 'The charges against the Despensers', pp. 95, 97; *RP*, iii. 363; *CCR 1318–23*, pp. 492–4).

[398] Ezek. 18: 20. For Despenser as forester, see above, pp. 74–7, 194–5, and n. 197.

1321 dignorum barones in persecucione sua excesserunt modum. Nam, si causas exilii iustas inuenerunt, bona tamen eorum non iuste occuparunt. Quare maneria eorum destruxerunt, quamobrem a familiaribus*[a] redempciones extorserunt? Si iustam causam prius habuerunt, ius et iniuriam*[b] modo conuerterunt. Sic Saul rex dum percussit Amalec Deo placuit, set, postquam ad predam uersus armentis pepercit et gregibus, Deo displicuit, quia quod non debuit perpetrauit.[399] Cartas autem remissionis quas a rege barones impetrauerunt*[c] non sicut decuit exegerunt, et iccirco comodo*[d] eorum*[e] postmodum caruerunt.[400] Sic Babilonii induxerunt regem inuitum, ut Danielem mitteret in lacum leonum,[401] et, quia hoc iniuste fecerunt, penam condignam postmodum pertulerunt.

Hiis itaque gestis Hugo pater transmarinas*[f] partes se transtulit; Hugo uero filius in mari remansit, quem dominus rex tutele nautarum de portubus obnixe commendarat. Et factus est Hugo belua marina insidians mercatoribus qui transibant. Maria occupauit, merces eorum et cetera bona, et nulla nauis transibat intacta; set in grandem nauem Ianuensem quam uulgo appellant*[g] dromonem inuasit, et nautis peremptis infinita bona que naui inerant*[h] ad suos usus sequestrauit.[402]

Interim dominus rex magnatos illos, qui Hugonem in exilium compulerant, expugnare decreuit, pro eo quod castella exulantium occupauerant, et maneria exulantium tam patris quam filii turpiter destruxerant; et quia bona exulum, que fisco magis applicari debuerant,[403] in suos usus sumpserant et consumpserant; et licet dominus rex huiusmodi transgressiones diceretur remisisse, et unicuique cartam concessisse, dicebat tamen et protestabatur se inuitum hoc fecisse et uoluntatem coactam nullam esse.

Igitur dominus rex Bartholomeum de Badelesmere primitus expugnauit, et castrum ipsius apud Ledes personaliter obsedit.[404]

---

*[a] familiaribus *MS*; familiaribus *He, St, Den-Y*   *[b] et in iniuriam *R*; in *om. St, Den-Y*
*[c] impetrauit *MS*; impetrarunt *He, St, Den-Y*; impetrauerunt *ed.*   *[d] sic *MS*; commodo *He, St, Den-Y*   *[e] eorum *MS*; earum *He, St, Den-Y*   *[f] sic *MS*; in *or* ad *to be supplied He*   *[g] appellat *MS*; appellant *He, St, Den-Y*   *[h] inierant *MS*; inerant *He, St, Den-Y*

[399] Cf. 1 Kgs. (1 Sam.) 15: 3, 9–11, 15–23.
[400] Pardons were granted on 20 Aug. 1321 (*CPR 1321–24*, pp. 15–20). Promises extorted under duress were invalid, as the author notes below.   [401] Dan. 6: 16.
[402] The Despensers were to leave England by 29 Aug. (*CCR 1318–23*, p. 494). Hugh the elder went to Poitou (*Flores*, iii. 198). Hugh the younger's seizure of two Genoese dromonds with cargoes said to be worth £60,000 appears in the accusations against him in 1326. The Genoese claimed 14,000 marks compensation (£9,333. 6s. 8d.), and Edward III eventually paid them 8,000 marks (£5,333. 6s. 8d.), while pointing out that he had no

exile at the same time. Yet in the judgement of some worthy men the 1321
barons went too far in their persecution. For even if they found just
reason for the banishment, nevertheless they did not seize their goods
justly. Why did they destroy their manors, for what reason did they
extort ransoms from their followers? Although they had a just cause
before, they now turned right into wrong. Thus King Saul pleased
God when he smote Amalek, but afterwards, when he spared their
herds and flocks for plunder, he angered God, because he had done
what he ought not to have done.[399] The barons did not claim the
charters of pardon, which they sought from the king, in the proper
way, and so later they failed to get any benefit from them.[400] Thus the
Babylonians persuaded the unwilling king to cast Daniel into the
lions' den,[401] and because they did this unjustly they afterwards
suffered the punishment they deserved.

When these things had been done, the elder Hugh took himself
abroad; but Hugh the son remained at sea, as the lord king had firmly
commended him to the protection of the sailors of the Cinque Ports.
And he became a sea monster, lying in wait for merchants who
crossed the sea. He was master of the seas, their merchandise, and
other goods, and no ship got through unharmed; he even attacked a
great Genoese ship, commonly called a dromond, and having killed
the crew, he appropriated to himself the vast amount of goods that
were in the ship.[402]

Meanwhile the lord king determined to attack those great men who
had forced Hugh into exile, because they had seized the fortresses of
the banished men, and had disgracefully destroyed the manors of
both the exiles, father and son; and further because they had taken for
their own use and wasted the goods of the exiles, which ought rather
to have gone to the treasury;[403] and, although the lord king might be
said to have pardoned these trespasses and to have granted a charter
to each man, he nevertheless said and declared that he had done this
unwillingly and that any grant under duress is void.

So to begin with the lord king attacked Bartholomew Badlesmere,
and personally besieged his castle at Leeds.[404] Then the greater

obligation to do so (G. A. Holmes, 'The judgement on the Younger Despenser, 1326',
EHR, lxx (1955), 261–7, at p. 264; *Foed.*, ii. 2. 941).
[403] For the author's use of *erarium* and *fiscus*, see above, n. 40.
[404] Badlesmere held Leeds Castle (Kent) from the king. On 13 Oct. Badlesmere's wife
refused to admit Queen Isabella to the castle. The refusal, possibly deliberately provoked
by the king, was treason and brought a fast response. Edward's hatred of Badlesmere
probably had two main roots: Badlesmere had been close to the king as royal steward at the

1321 Tunc congregati sunt maiores de Marchia ⟨ut⟩ᵃ succursum obsessis
prestarent, set prohibicio comitis Lancastrie fecit quominus auxilium
promissum inferrent.⁴⁰⁵ Comes enim dictum Bartholomeum odio
habuit, et plures transgressiones sibi imposuit, ob quas uel carcere
perpetuo uel saltem exilio dignum fore decreuit; et sic obsessi in
castro succursu caruerunt, unde et nonᵇ ualentes resistere castrum
reddiderunt. Reperit autem rex infra castrum predones, homicidas et
proditores; et hos quidem protrahi iussit, illos suspendit et reliquos
carceri mancipauit.⁴⁰⁶ Voluit enim rex exemplum aliis prebere, ut
nullus de cetero audeat contra eum municiones tenere. Sicut enim
nullus potest in terra castra sine regis licencia construere, ita nec fas
est contra regem in regno castra defendere.

Deinde misit rex manus et occupauit cetera castra Bartholomei, et
comitis Herfordie, Rogeri Dammory et Hugonis de Audeleye; nec
inuenti sunt aliqui resistentes, quia ulcio sumpta de hiis apud Ledes
uehementer terruit omnes. Extendit eciam rex manus ad maneria
baronum qui Hugonis procurauerant exilium, et bona eorum occupauit; set et omnes adherentes eis et eorum fautores uniuersos
depredauit.

Cum igitur occupasset rex municiones baronum a parte orientali,
idem disposuit faciendum in parte occidentali. Tunc congregauit
exercitum copiosum iturus in Marchiam, ut magnates expungnaret
qui occupabant partem illam.⁴⁰⁷ Ibi enim fuit tutissimum refugium
baronum, et regi sine manu ualida difficile penetrandum.

Conuenerunt autem in auxilium domini regis duo fratres sui,
uidelicet Thomas comes Marescallus et Edmundus comes Cancie,
pro etate strenui.⁴⁰⁸ Set et comes de Penbrok diuertebat se ad partem
regis eo quod comes Lancastrie imposuerat se prodicionis. Expertus
erat comes Lancastrie, ut dixit, hominem illum infidum et uarium, et
baronibus indixerat auxilium eius repudiandum.⁴⁰⁹ Eratque cum rege

---

ᵃ om. MS; supplied He, St, Den-Y   ᵇ nunc R; non St, Den-Y

time of his defection to the rebels at Sherburn in June, and he then played a leading part in
drawing up the final indictment against Despenser (*Hist. Roff.*, pp. 162–3). The siege
lasted 17–31 Oct. 1321. Edward was at Leeds 26 Oct.–3 Nov. (*Itin.*, pp. 217–18;
Maddicott, *Lancaster*, pp. 293–4).

⁴⁰⁵ The relieving force stopped short at Kingston-on-Thames on 27 Oct. Lancaster's
interference is confirmed by the *Anonimalle Chronicle*, and he is said to have written to ask
the king not to persecute his people (*Ann. Paul.*, p. 299; *Murimuth*, p. 34; *Anon.*,
pp. 102–3). Lancaster's reason for hating Badlesmere is less clear than the king's; possibly
he resented Badlesmere's appointment as steward of the household, which he felt was in
his gift as hereditary steward of England.

Marchers assembled to bring help to the besieged, but the earl of 1321
Lancaster's prohibition made it impossible to send the promised
help.[405] For the earl hated the said Bartholomew, and blamed him for
many offences, for which he considered him worthy of life imprisonment or at least exile; and so those besieged in the castle lacked help,
and not being strong enough to resist they surrendered the castle.
Within the castle the king found robbers, murderers, and traitors;
some he ordered to be drawn, others he hanged, and the rest he
imprisoned.[406] For the king wished to give an example to others, so
that no one in future would dare to hold fortresses against him. For
just as no one can build castles in the land without the king's licence,
so it is wrong to hold castles in the kingdom against the king.

Then the king sent a force to seize the other castles of Bartholomew, and of the earl of Hereford, of Roger Amory, and of Hugh
Audley; nor were any found to resist, because the vengeance exacted
from those at Leeds terrified everyone immensely. The king also laid
hands on the manors of the barons who had brought about Hugh's
exile, and seized their goods; he also plundered all their followers and
every one of their supporters.

Then, when the king had seized the baronial strongholds in the
east, he made ready to do the same in the west. He gathered a large
army to go to the March and attack the great men who held that
area.[407] For it was there that the barons had their safest refuge, and it
was difficult for the king to penetrate it without a strong force.

His two brothers came to the lord king's help, namely Thomas,
Earl Marshal, and Edmund, earl of Kent, active soldiers considering
their age.[408] The earl of Pembroke went over to the king's side
because the earl of Lancaster had accused him of treachery. The earl
of Lancaster knew by experience, as he said, that the man was
faithless and fickle and had pointed out to the barons that his help

[406] The commander of the garrison, Walter Culpeper, and twelve others were executed
on 1 Nov. Lady Badlesmere, Bartholomew Burghersh, and others were sent to the Tower
(*Ann. Paul.*, p. 299; *Anon.*, pp. 102–3).
[407] The royal household left Westminster 7 Dec. and reached Cirencester on 20 Dec.
1321 (*Itin.*, p. 219). Troops had already been ordered to muster at Cirencester on 13 Dec.
(*PW*, ii. 2. 540–2).
[408] These were the sons of Edward I's second marriage to Margaret of France. Thomas
of Brotherton was 21 (b. 1 June 1300) and Edmund of Woodstock was 20 (b. 5 Aug. 1301).
Thomas had been made earl of Norfolk and Earl Marshal (previously held by the Bigod
family) in Dec. 1312 at the age of 12; Edmund had to wait longer for a title and available
lands, and was made earl of Kent only in July 1321 (*HBC*, pp. 38–9, 467, 473).

1321 comes de Arundel propter affinitatem Hugonis Despenser;[410] comes
de Warenna et comes de Rychmund adheserunt domino regi, et alii
barones potentes et multi.[411] Isti promiserunt domino regi auxilium
prestare et iniuriam sibi illatam pro posse uindicare.

Robertus le Ewer, qui alio modo dicitur Aquarius, erat dux
peditum, et Fulco filius Warini milicie conduxit exercitum. Robertus
le Ewer nomen sumpsit a re, quia in aula regis aquam solebat
ministrare.[412] Fulco filius Warini, qui nunc militat, nomen et cogno-
men antecessorum suorum portat.[413] Nam Fulco filius Warini primus
in diebus regis Iohannis miles fuit famosus, cui successit Fulco
secundus, homo remissus et tepidus. Successit isti*a* Fulco tercius,
miles fortis et strenuus et in Hispannia contra paganos pluries
expertus. Sic frequenter euenit quod post probum improbus et e
contra succedit; et talis genealogia*b* racione forte non caret. Nam
probitas uiri per comparacionem lucidius apparet. Sic figulus iuxta
artem suam quedam uasa ad honorem, quedam componit ad contumeliam,[414] ut hec que facit ad honorem comparacione deteriorum
maiorem habeant decorem.

1322   Igitur dominus rex cum exercitu suo uersus Cyrencestriam iter
arripuit, et ibidem propter natale Domini per aliquot dies perhendinauit.[415] Barones autem preoccupauerant Gloucestriam; quamobrem
rex diuertebat Wygorniam,[416] nec ibidem transiuit Sabrinam, quia
barones ex parte aduersa custodiebant ripam. Premisit quoque rex
apud Bruggenorthe uiros armatos et pedites qui preparent transitum

---

a iste *MS*; isti *He, St, Den-Y*   *b* genologia *MS*; genealogia *He, St*

409 Lancaster considered Pembroke had deserted him in 1312 over Gaveston; they also
had substantial disputes over Thorpe Waterville and Mitford Castle (Phillips, *Pembroke*,
pp. 77–82, 127–8).
410 Edmund FitzAlan, earl of Arundel, was one of the young men knighted with Prince
Edward in 1306. At first he was a strong opponent of Gaveston, associated himself with
Warwick and Lancaster in Gaveston's death, and invoked the Ordinances when he refused
to go to Bannockburn in 1314. Thereafter he positioned himself closer to Pembroke and
was a mediator alongside Pembroke in Aug. 1321. Finally, however, he betrothed his son
Richard to the younger Despenser's daughter Isabel in Feb. 1321, and on Despenser's
return he became a firm supporter of the court party. He was executed by Queen Isabella's
forces in Nov. 1326 (*CP*, i. 241–2; Maddicott, *Lancaster*, pp. 127, 280).
411 Like Pembroke, Warenne had split from Lancaster at Gaveston's death; and he also
had substantial land disputes with Lancaster in Yorkshire (Maddicott, *Lancaster*, pp. 207–
8, 232–7). John of Brittany, earl of Richmond 1306–34, was a royal supporter throughout.
Brother of the Duke of Brittany and without marriage connections to the other earls, he
was something of an 'outsider' (*HBC*, p. 479).
412 Ewer was a king's yeoman by 1318 and held lands in Hants. As *aquarius* his official
duties were to dry the king's clothes and prepare his bath (*Vita*, 1st edn., p. 117 n. 4). He

should be rejected.[409] There was also with the king the earl of 1321
Arundel on account of his kinship with Hugh Despenser;[410] Earl
Warenne and the earl of Richmond and many other powerful barons
stood by the lord king.[411] These promised to lend aid to the lord king
and to avenge the wrong done to him in so far as they could.

Robert Ewer, otherwise called the waterbearer, was in command of
the infantry, and Fulk FitzWarin led the cavalry. Robert Ewer
derived his name from the fact that he was accustomed to serve the
water in the king's hall.[412] The Fulk FitzWarin who is now on active
service bears the name and surname of his ancestors.[413] For, in the
days of King John, the first Fulk FitzWarin was a famous knight, who
was succeeded by Fulk II, a mild and faint-hearted man. To him
succeeded Fulk III, a brave and active knight who often proved
himself against the pagans in Spain. So it frequently happens that a
valiant man is succeeded by one less worthy and vice versa; and such a
pedigree is not perhaps without design. For a man's worth appears
more clearly by comparison. Thus the potter of his art makes 'one
vessel unto honour, and another unto dishonour',[414] so that those
which he makes unto honour have the greater glory by comparison
with those of less worth.

So the lord king set out towards Cirencester with his army, and
stayed there for some days over Christmas.[415] The barons had already
occupied Gloucester; so the king turned aside to Worcester,[416] but
did not cross the Severn there because the barons held the opposite
bank. The king also sent ahead men-at-arms and foot soldiers to

was an active but rebellious soldier. In 1311, 'Roberd le Ewer, archers, et tieu manere de
ribaudaille' were dismissed from court (*Ann. Lond.*, p. 199); in 1321 he rebelled and was
temporarily removed from the office of constable of Odiham castle. This had nothing to do
with the Marcher rebellion, and he was a keen royalist in the civil war. Afterwards his
violence continued and included the plundering of contrariant estates and the attack on
Despenser's lands, which led to his arrest and death (*CPR 1317–21*, pp. 136, 505, 586, 595;
CIPM, vi. 543; *CCR 1318–23*, pp. 179, 260, 326; *CPR 1321–24*, pp. 199, 206; Fryde,
Tyranny, pp. 76, 153–5). For his death, see below, pp. 216–19.
  [413] Fulk was a substantial baron with lands in Shropshire and Gloucestershire, who was
a Lancastrian retainer in 1317–19, but his loyalty to the king in 1321 was clear enough for
the king to put him in charge of forces against the rebels. He was suspected in 1330 of
complicity with the earl of Kent in his attempt to release Edward II from prison
(Maddicott, *Lancaster*, pp. 46, 54–6; *CP*, v. 497–9). Fulk's rebellious ancestor in the
reign of King John was the hero of a romance popular in the late 13th and early 14th cc.
(*Gesta Fulconis filii Warini*, in *Radulphi de Coggeshall Chronicon Anglicanum*, ed.
J. Stevenson, RS, lxvi (1875), pp. xxiii, 277–415).
  [414] Rom. 9: 21.
  [415] The king was at Cirencester 20–6 Dec. 1321 (*Itin.*, p. 219).
  [416] Edward was at Worcester 31 Dec. 1321–7 Jan. 1322 (*Itin.*, pp. 219–20).

1322 suum. Restiterunt domini de Mortimer necnon et grauem eis*
fecerunt insultum. Nam magnam partem uille incenderunt, et de
seruis regis plurimos occiderunt. Reliquit autem rex uillam ad
sinistram, et sic adiuit ad Salopiam,[417] ut ibidem transiret in
Marchiam. Poterant ad hec barones si uoluissent cursum regis
impedisse; set domini Mortymer noluerunt ulterius consentire, eo
quod iuxta placitos dies non uenit comes Lancastrie; timebant enim
aliquid magnum aggredi sine comite. Iccirco sine comite noluerunt
domino regi amplius resistere. Vnde uidentes quod comes non
succurreret in articulo necessitatis, relictis sociis, reddiderunt se
uoluntati domini regis.[418] Reliqui *b* uero comites*c* uehementer attoniti
comitem Lancastrie adierunt, et ea que sic gesta erant in lacrimis
narrauerunt. Comes autem in proteccionem suam omnes recepit, et
pro communi querela defendenda sub iureiurando auxilium promisit.

Rex igitur, relicta Salopia,[419] in Marchiam transiuit, et quia nemo
restitit omnia castella faciliter occupauit. Veniensque rex apud
Herfordiam episcopum loci acriter increpauit, eo quod contra natur-
alem dominum suum barones sustinuit, unde et plurima bona ipsius
in ulcionem confiscauit.[420]

Deinde rediit rex apud Gloucestriam, et Mauricium de Berkelee
recepit in graciam suam. Iussit eum nichilominus in custodiam mitti
et castrum de Berkelee cum omnibus bonis suis pariter confiscari.[421]
Exinde misit rex illos de Mortymer ad Turrim Londoniarum ut
ibidem remanerent, ne forte prioris facti penitentes ad socios suos
barones resilirent.

Dum autem rex moram faceret in uilla Gloucestrie, oblatus est
quidam miles de partibus Herfordie, et notificatum est regi quod
miles ille officium uicecomitis gesserat, et nichilominus cum barones
equitauerat, et quod, in illa secta quam barones dabant militibus pro

---

a eius *R*; ei *St, Den-Y*; eis *ed.*   *b* relequi *MS*; reliqui *He, St, Den-Y*   *c* comitis
MS; comites *He, St, Den-Y*

[417] Edward reached Shrewsbury 14 Jan. 1322 (*Itin.*, p. 220). Once the king could cross
the Severn the lands of the Marcher lords were wide open to his forces.
[418] The Mortimers surrendered on 22 Jan. 1322. The first safe-conduct for them was
issued on Sunday 17 Jan. to last until Wednesday 20 Jan. and through the following night.
It was then extended for all Thursday and the following night, then for all Friday and the
following night (*PW*, ii. 2. App. 176). On Friday 22 Jan. Edward wrote to inform London
that the Mortimers had surrendered (*Let. Bk. E.*, p. 150).
[419] Edward left Shrewsbury on 24 Jan. 1322 (*Itin.*, p. 220).
[420] Edward was at Hereford 29 Jan.–4 Feb. (*Itin.*, pp. 220–1). The bishop was Adam
Orleton, formerly a king's clerk and an experienced diplomat in Edward's service.

prepare his crossing at Bridgnorth. And the lords Mortimer likewise offered resistance and made a serious attack upon them. For they burned a great part of the town and killed very many of the king's servants. However, the king left the town on the left, and thus came to Shrewsbury,[417] so that he might cross into the March there. The barons could have hindered the king's march here if they had wished; but the lords Mortimer would not take part any longer, because the earl of Lancaster had not come at the appointed days; for they were afraid to attempt any large-scale operation without the earl. They therefore would not oppose the lord king any further without the earl. Then, seeing that the earl did not help them in their time of need, they deserted their allies, and threw themselves on the lord king's mercy.[418] The other earls were absolutely stunned and approached the earl of Lancaster, and in tears told him what had happened. The earl received them all into his protection, and under oath promised help for the prosecution of their common grievance.

The king, therefore, leaving Shrewsbury,[419] crossed into the March and as no one opposed him he easily took all the castles. Coming to Hereford, the king sharply rebuked the bishop of the place for supporting the barons against their natural lord, and he confiscated many of his goods in revenge.[420]

The king then returned to Gloucester and received Maurice Berkeley into his grace. Nevertheless he ordered him to be arrested, and his castle of Berkeley to be confiscated with all his goods as well.[421] From there the king sent the lords Mortimer to the Tower of London, where they were to remain, in case, perhaps repenting what they had done, they should return to their baronial allies.

While the king was staying in the town of Gloucester, however, a certain Herefordshire knight was brought before him, and the king was informed that this knight had exercised the office of sheriff, and nevertheless had ridden with the barons, and that, wearing the livery that the barons gave to their knights as a distinguishing mark, he

Although he was suspected of sympathy for the Mortimers, formal charges were not made against him until 1323 and his goods were not seized until early 1324. Edward's persecution turned him into a firm supporter of Isabella's invasion and a prime player in the deposition. He moved up the episcopal scale thereafter, to Worcester in 1327 and to Winchester in 1333, where he stayed until his death in 1345 (Haines, *Orleton*, pp. 134–53, 164–77).

[421] Edward was at Gloucester 6–17 Feb. 1322 (*Itin.*, p. 221). During this period Berkeley surrendered. An order to seize all Berkeley's lands, castles, and goods had gone out on 1 Dec. 1321, but a further order to seize the castle was issued on 7 Feb. 1322 (*CFR 1319–27*, pp. 84, 91).

1322 noticia, in contumelia regis placita comitatus tenuerat. Vnde decretum est militem illum tanquam proditorem fore puniendum; set rex
ex gracia penam proditorum remisit, set suspendendum fore decreuit,
et suspensus est miles ille in secta predicta, ut*a* sicut patebat pena,
pateret et causa.[422]

Eodem tempore uenit Andreas de Herkelee miles de partibus
borialibus ad regem dicens; 'Ecce, domine, treuge Scotorum iam
finite; Robertus de Brutz fines Anglorum inuasu incendit, depredatur
et cedit. Non est qui populum defendit, non est qui pro populo se
murum opponit.[423] Iccirco, domine mi rex, bonum esset, aliis negociis
postpositis,*b* populo oppresso primitus succurrere, qui sine auxilio
regis sui seuitie*c* Scotorum non possunt resistere.'[424] Respondit rex:
'Scias,' inquid, 'Andrea, pro certo, quod si michi Robertus de Brutz
immineret*d* a tergo, et homines meos, qui tot et tanta enormia michi
intulerunt, a fronte conspicerem, proditores illos inuaderem, et
Robertum de Brutz inpersecutum dimitterem. Nimirum si Scoti,
qui nullo uinculo michi tenentur obnoxii,*e* regnum meum inuadunt,
cum hii, qui fidelitate et homagio michi tenentur astricti, contra me
insurgunt, homines meos spoliant et uillas incendunt; si dominum
expungnant serui, quanto magis extraneus?' Sic ait Dauid rex cum
persequeretur eum Absolon et malediceret ei Semei: 'Ecce,' inquid,
'filius meus querit animam meam; quanto magis hic filius Gemini*f*
maledicit*g* michi?'[425] et non permisit aliquem nocere ei.

Dixit autem rex ad militem: 'Reuertere ad partes tuas et serua
municiones tibi commissas; ego uero persequar proditores meos
ubicunque se conuertant, et non reuertar donec deficiant.' Iussit
itaque dominus rex uiros fortes et armatos et pedites ex singulis

---

a et *MS*; ut *He, St, Den-Y*   *b* prepositis *MS*; postpositis *He, St, Den-Y*   *c* seuite
MS; seuitie *He, St, Den-Y*   *d* immineret *MS*; immineret *He, St, Den-Y*   *e* obnoxi
MS; obnoxii *He, St, Den-Y*   *f* *He* read Genui, *poss for* Gemi'i *in MS*; Iemini *He, St,*
Den-Y; Gemini *ed.*   *g* sic *MS*; *or* maledicet *He*

[422] The *Flores* records that three knights were hanged at Gloucester while the king was
there, and names them as Roger de Elmerugge, Nicholas de Lauin, and Nicholas de
Torville (*Flores*, iii. 203). Of these Roger Elmerugge was sheriff of Herefordshire from
Nov. 1318 to 5 Jan. 1322 (*List of Sheriffs*, p. 59). However, he is also listed in the *Flores* and
other chronicles among those executed *after* Boroughbridge (*Flores*, iii. 207; *Brid.*, p. 78;
Anon., pp. 110–11; G. L. Haskins, 'A chronicle of the civil wars of Edward II', *Speculum*,
xiv (1939), 78; *Le Baker*, p. 171; see also *Brut*, p. 224, which gives William of Elmebruge).
The livery was, perhaps, the green cloth with one quarter yellow with white bends, as
worn by the rebel forces in London at the parliament of 1321 (see above, n. 395).
[423] Cf. Ezek. 13: 5.
[424] The meeting is not otherwise known, but possibly took place. Scottish raids began

had held the pleas of the county, showing insolence to the king. For 1322 this it was decreed that this knight should be punished as a traitor; but the king graciously remitted the penalty of traitors, and decided that he should be hanged, and the knight was hanged in the said livery, so that just as the penalty was manifest, so too should be the cause.[422]

At the same time Andrew Harclay, a north country knight, came to the king saying: 'Look my lord, the Scottish truce is already at an end; Robert Bruce in an attack on the English frontier, is burning, plundering, and killing. There is no one to defend the people, no one who sets himself up as a wall for the people.[423] Therefore, my lord king, it would be good if, putting aside other business, you came at once to the help of your hard-pressed people, who without their king's help cannot resist the ferocity of the Scots.'[424] The king replied: 'You may be sure, Andrew,' he said, 'that if Robert Bruce threatens me from behind, and I see before me my own men, who have committed so many and such enormities against me, I would attack those traitors and leave Robert Bruce alone. Small wonder if the Scots, who are in no way bound to me, invade my kingdom, when those who are bound to me by fealty and homage rise against me, plunder my men, and set fire to my towns; if the servants attack their lord, how much more will a foreigner?' Thus said King David when Absalom pursued him and Semei cursed him: 'Behold', he said, 'my son seeketh my life; how much more may this Benjamite curse me?',[425] and he did not permit anyone to harm him.

So the king said to the knight: 'Return to your own country and keep the strongholds committed to you; I shall pursue my traitors wherever they go, and I shall not turn back until they give up.' So the lord king ordered a force of men-at-arms and foot soldiers to be assembled from each county, and a large army to be mustered hastily

immediately the truce ended in Jan. 1322. Harclay was given authority to negotiate with Bruce for a truce or peace on 9 Feb. while the king was at Gloucester (*CPR 1321–4*, p. 71), and the king's order may have been prompted by a personal visit from Harclay. Harclay, son of a Cumberland knight, was a professional soldier, whose whole career was spent in the defence of the north-west. He served as sheriff of Cumberland 1312–16 and 1319–23, and was deputy in Westmorland for Roger Clifford, the hereditary sheriff; he defended Carlisle in 1315 (at the fall of which he briefly became a Scottish prisoner), and was keeper of Cumberland and Westmorland in 1319 during the Berwick campaign (*List of Sheriffs*, p. 26; *CP*, iii. 31; J. Mason, 'Sir Andrew Harclay, earl of Carlisle', *Transactions of the Cumberland and Westmorland Antiquarian and Archaeological Society*, xxix, new series (1929), pp. 98–137). For his role at Boroughbridge see below, pp. 210–13.
[425] 2 Kgs. (2 Sam.) 16: 11.

1322 comitatibus congregari, et copiosum exercitum ad inimicos debellandum festinanter adunari. Inimicos suos omnes appellat quos pars baronum secum sustentat, sicut scriptum est qui non est mecum contra me est.[426] Iccirco bis uel ter proclamari fecit solempniter quod omnes hii qui ad partem baronum diuerterant[a] infra certum diem ad pacem regis redirent; alioquin[b] uelut hostes publici regi puniendi sine spe redeundi extunc remanerent.[427]

Circa idem tempus Hugo Despenser pater et filius reuersi sunt ab exilio, eo quod reconciliacio eorum et pax nutu regio proclamata foret in regno.[428] Redierunt, inquam, in Angliam quia rex nouit eos exulasse per inuidiam. Poterant adhuc barones ad pacem uenisse, ueniam et misericordiam regis forsan impetrasse, set modo quicquid agunt aut machinantur in confusionem et dampnacionem totaliter operantur. Nam, de proteccione comitis Lancastrie nimis elati, resistentes cedunt, pacientes spoliant, nec parcunt alicui, et ad maiorem dampnacionem suam castrum ipsius regis apud Tykhulle inuadunt, et ad capcionem castri toto nisu licet incassum laborant.[429]

Dominus rex nimirum super hiis uehementer commotus apud Couentriam iter arripuit, et ibidem exercitum uenturum per aliquot dies exspectauit.[430] Exinde conduxit exercitum usque ad magnum flumen[c] qui dicitur Trente.[431] Est autem ibidem pons magnus qui uiam prebet transeuntibus. Premisit quoque rex ad pontem cuneum fortem armatorum et peditum, scire uolens an[d] aliquis impediret transitum suum. Venerat autem comes Lancastrie cum omni sequela sua in uillam de Burghtone ex parte alia.

Cumque iam fuisset compertum quod rex disposuit transire fluuium, misit comes uiros fortes armatos et pedites qui pontem defenderent. Verum cum per tres pluresue dies inter se partes

---

[a] diuertant MS; diuerterant He, St, Den-Y   [b] aliquin MS; alioquin He, St, Den-Y
[c] sic R; fluuium St, Den-Y   [d] aut R; utrum He; an St, Den-Y

---

[426] Matt. 12: 30.

[427] For the author's interest in treason, see above, pp. liii–lv.

[428] The younger Despenser's appeal against exile, delivered to the king on 30 Nov., may have been placed before an ecclesiastical council on 1 Dec. 1321. The five southern prelates who attended the meeting declared the exile unlawful. Their judgment was confirmed by four earls (Kent, Pembroke, Richmond, Arundel), and then by the royal justices and members of the king's council. The annulment of the sentence was published on 1 Jan. 1322 (CCR 1318–23, pp. 543–6; Ann. Paul., p. 301). Edward gave the younger and elder Despensers safe conducts to return on 8 and 25 Dec. respectively; he also provided a safe conduct for their troops to fight against Scotland in Feb. The Despensers finally joined him on 3 Mar. at Lichfield (CCR 1318–23, pp. 510–11; CPR 1321–4, pp. 45, 47, 64; Phillips, Pembroke, pp. 219–20, 223).

to subdue his enemies. He called all those who supported the baronial 1322
party his enemies, as it is written: 'He that is not with me is against
me.'[426] Therefore two or three times he had it solemnly proclaimed
that all those who had gone over to the baronial party should return to
the king's peace by a certain day; otherwise from henceforth they
were to remain as public enemies of the king to be punished without
hope of returning to the king's grace.[427]

About the same time the Despensers, father and son, returned
from exile, because their reconciliation and release from outlawry was
about to be published in England on the king's command.[428] They
returned to England, I say, because the king knew that they had been
banished out of jealousy. The barons could still have made peace,
could perhaps have sought the king's pardon and mercy, but now
whatever they do or contrive works entirely to their confusion and
loss. For, made arrogant by the earl of Lancaster's protection, they
kill those who oppose them, plunder those who offer no resistance,
spare no one, and to their greater guilt attack the king's own castle at
Tickhill, and put their best efforts into taking the castle, though in
vain.[429]

The lord king, extremely provoked, of course, by these actions, set
out for Coventry, where he awaited the arrival of his army for some
days.[430] Thence he led the army to the great river called the Trent.[431]
There is there a great bridge which offers a passage to those who wish
to cross. The king sent a strong troop of men-at-arms and infantry
ahead to the bridge, wishing to know if anyone would oppose his
crossing. However, the earl of Lancaster had arrived with all his
retinue at the town of Burton on the other side.

Now, when it was known that the king proposed to cross the river,
the earl sent staunch men, men-at-arms and foot soldiers, to defend
the bridge. But when the two sides had fought together for three or
more days and had returned to the same fight the next day, the king

[429] Until now Lancaster had refrained from open violence and the king's attention had
focused on the Marchers. Lancaster's attack on Tickhill was under way by 10 Jan. 1322. It
was possibly aimed at Tickhill's constable, William de Aune, an active informer against
Lancaster, rather than at the king, but an attack on a royal castle was treason. By both
contemporaries and recent historians the attack has been considered a turning point in the
war, with Edward moving to a determined effort to crush Lancaster and his supporters
once and for all (*Lanercost*, p. 242; Maddicott, *Lancaster*, pp. 306–7).

[430] Musters were ordered at Coventry for various dates between 21 Feb. and 7 Mar.
The king arrived on 27 Feb. (*PW*, ii. 2. 547–54; *Itin.*, p. 221).

[431] The king reached Cauldwell, just south of Burton-on-Trent, on 7 Mar. 1322 (*Itin.*,
p. 222).

1322 dimicassent, ac ad eundem conflictum in crastinum rediissent, reperit rex uadum superius, ubi transiit ipse et reliqua pars exercitus.[432] Audientes itaque barones et iam uidentes quod rex flumen transisset, pontem reliquerunt, equos ascenderunt et fugam inierunt. Set quare fugit comes Lancastrie qui tociens solebat regi resistere, precipue cum haberet secum comitem Herfordie et clariorem miliciam tocius Anglie? Reuera magna erat nunc manus regis et ualida. Habebat enim circiter omnibus numeratis trecenta milia numero.[433]

Mandauerat comes Roberto de Hoylond, quem preposuerat[a] gazis[b] suis, quatinus exercitum conduceret de uiris fortissimis, et certum diem ueniendi statuit; set prefixo die Robertus non uenit, immo preuaricator in causa domini sui reddidit se domino regi.[434] Vnde comitis sequaces auxilium parum adesse[c] uidentes pontem reliquerunt, equos ascenderunt, et fugerunt.[d]

Persequebatur rex fugientes usque ad castrum de Totbury,[435] quod erat comitis Lancastrie, inuenitque rex ianuas apertas, eo quod post fugam comitis nullus audebat resistere.[e] Set et custos castri de Kneleworthe,[f] audita fuga comitis, reddidit statim castrum in manus uicecomitis. Repperit autem rex apud Tottebury Rogerum Dammori in extremis laborantem; erat enim infirmitas ad mortem, quia non uixit ultra tercium diem; et bene quidem et honeste sibi contigit quod ad finem desolatum cum sociis non durauit. Iste Rogerus olim pauper miles et tenuis ob industriam et probitatem suam factus est regis specialis, quamobrem dedit ei rex neptem suam in uxorem, et de comitatu Gloucestrie que contingebat eam[g] terciam partem; set quia cum baronibus contra regem tenuit, notam ingratitudinis a multis reportauit.[436]

Comes igitur Lancastrie et comes Herfordie, cum omnibus sibi adherentibus, in fugam conuersi, ad Pountfreit peruenerunt. Ibidem aliquantam moram facientes, tandem diffinito consilio uersus Scociam

---

[a] proposuerat *MS*; preposuerat *He*, *St*, *Den-Y*   [b] garis *R*; gazis *St*, *Den-Y*
[c] abesse *R*; adesse *Den-Y*   [d] only . . . ge . . . *legible in MS*; diligenter *He*; et fugerunt
St, *Den-Y*   [e] recistere *MS*; resistere *He*, *St*, *Den-Y*   [f] *sic MS*; Keneleworthe *He*,
St, *Den-Y*   [g] *sic MS*; *poss.* ei *He*

[432] Skirmishing took place between 7 and 10 Mar., by which day the king's household reached Burton. By 11 Mar. the household was at Tutbury (*Itin.*, p. 222).

[433] This is an obvious exaggeration. It might be a scribal error, but Hearne made no comment on the figures he transcribed.

[434] Holand, of Holland in Lancashire, had served Lancaster since 1298 and seems to have exercised authority equivalent to that of a steward. He also held livery from Audley and Badlesmere and served the king. He was royal justice of Chester for the third time

found a ford higher up, where he himself crossed with the remainder 1322 of his army.[432] When the barons heard, and now saw for themselves, that the king had crossed the river, they left the bridge, mounted their horses, and fled. But why did the earl of Lancaster, who so often used to resist the king, now flee, particularly as he had with him the earl of Hereford and the more celebrated soldiers of all England? In reality the king's force was now great and powerful. For he had about 300,000 men all told.[433]

The earl had ordered Robert Holand, whom he had put in charge of his treasure, to bring an army of his best men, and had arranged a day for his arrival; but on the appointed day Robert did not come; on the contrary, as a renegade in his lord's cause, he surrendered to the lord king.[434] Because of this the earl's followers, seeing that there was not enough support, left the bridge, took horse, and fled.

The king pursued the fugitives to Tutbury Castle,[435] which belonged to the earl of Lancaster, and he found the gates open, because after the earl's flight no one dared to offer resistance. The keeper of Kenilworth Castle, too, on hearing of the earl's flight, at once surrendered the castle to the sheriff. At Tutbury the king found Roger Amory at the point of death; he was indeed mortally ill for he did not live beyond the third day; and indeed it turned out well and honourably for him that he did not last out with his comrades to the bitter end. This Roger, once a poor and needy knight, by his diligence and valour became the king's special friend, for which reason the king gave him his niece in marriage, and her third share of the earldom of Gloucester; but because he sided with the barons against the king, many marked him down as ungrateful.[436]

Thus the earl of Lancaster and the earl of Hereford, with all their supporters, were put to flight and came to Pontefract. After a short delay there it was finally decided to press on towards Scotland. They

---

between Feb. 1319 and Feb. 1322. Perhaps it was the loss of this position which finally showed him the great danger of opposing the monarch and prompted his desertion of Lancaster. He was murdered by Thomas Wyther, a Lancastrian knight, in 1328 (*Ann. Paul.*, p. 342; J. R. Maddicott, 'Thomas of Lancaster and Sir Robert Holand: a study in noble patronage', *EHR*, lxxxvi (1971), 449–72).

[435] The king was at Tutbury on 11 Mar. 1322; the household moved on to Derby between 12 and 14 Mar. (*Itin.*, p. 222).

[436] Amory died of wounds or illness on 13 or 14 Mar. 1322. The sentence of execution against him for treason was formally respited on 13 Mar., because of the king's former affection for Amory and because he was married to Edward's niece (*CP*, iv. 43 note f). For Amory's marriage to Elizabeth de Clare, see above, n. 294.

1322 iter arripuerunt. In Scociam sperabant habere confugium, quia Robertus de Brutz, ut dictum erat, contra regem promiserat auxilium.[437]

Cumque apud Borbrigge uenissent[438] ut ibidem saltem una nocte
requiescerent, ecce Andreas de Herkelee miles strenuus,[a] cui iam de
fuga comitis innotuerat, qui eciam progressum[b] eius et propositum
plenius explorauerat, quasi cum quatuor milibus uirorum uenerat
quos ad locum illum repente conduxerat. Audientes autem comites,
qui erant infra uillam quasi iam hospitati, quod uenerat Andreas et sui
sequaces ad expungnandum eos totaliter, exierunt uillam bipertito[c]
cum aduersariis congressuri. Comes Herfordie cum suis armatis per
pontem transiuit, set nullus eorum equum ascendit, erat enim pons
strictus, nec uiam equitibus ad bellum procedentibus prebere potuit.
Comes Lancastrie cum suis militibus ad uadum fluminis uiam
arripuit. Set Andreas de Herkeleye, tanquam miles prouidus, ad
utrumque exitum cuneum armatorum sapienter statuit.[439] Comes
Herfordie partem aduersam primitus aggreditur; decertando male
uulneratus tandem occiditur. Tres uel quatuor milites in ipso
certamine cum comite perierunt. Rogerus de Clifford[440] et alii
quamplurimi male uulnerati ad uillam redierunt. Alii uero, dum
uadum transire nituntur, ab ymbre sagittarum usque[d] atteruntur; set
post mortem comitis Herfordie sua uirtus tepuit milicie, et statim
reuertuntur. Pepigit autem comes Lancastrie cum Andrea de
Herkelee de treuga et pace seruanda usque in crastinum; et hoc
facto rediit unusquisque ad hospicium suum. Ipsa uero nocte
uicecomes Eboraci[441] cum magna cohorte uenerat inimicos regis
inuadere; cuius auxilio fretus[e] Andreas de Herkelee uillam intrauit
summo mane,[442] et cepit comitem Lancastrie et omnes pene reliquos
milites et scutarios sine uulnere, et perducens Eboracum reclusit in

[a] strenuis MS; strenuus St, Den-Y; the copyist uses this form above (p. 92) ed.
[b] progressu MS; progressum He, St, Den-Y   [c] bipertitam R; bipertito St, Den-Y
[d] usum MS; poss. usque or usquequaque or omit usum altogether He; misere St, Den-Y
[e] fertus MS; fretus He, St, Den-Y

[437] Rumours of Lancaster's contacts with the Scots led many to believe that the flight
north was to Scotland. The pro-Lancastrian author of the Brut tried to save Lancaster's
reputation by reporting that he was forced by Clifford to go beyond Pontefract (Brid., p. 76;
Lanercost, p. 242; Brut, p. 217).

[438] Boroughbridge, sixteen miles north-west of York, was on the main route to the
north, whether to Lancaster's castle at Dunstanburgh or to Scotland. The battle took place
on 16 Mar. 1322.

[439] The use of cuneus by the author of the Vita suggests that Harclay was copying the
close formation wedge or 'schiltrom' he had seen used by the Scots during his military
service on the northern border. This is confirmed by the detailed description of the battle
in the Lanercost chronicle which describes Harclay's scheltrum secundum modum Scottorum

were hoping to find a refuge in Scotland, because Robert Bruce, as it 1322
was said, had promised help against the king.[437]

And when they had reached Boroughbridge,[438] intending to rest
there for at least one night, who should be there but Andrew Harclay,
that active knight, to whom the earl's flight had already become
known, who had also more fully spied out the earl's advance and
plans, and who had arrived with nearly 4,000 men, whom he had led
there with all speed. The earls, who had already almost settled into
their lodgings in the town, hearing, however, that Andrew and his
followers had come to destroy them utterly, marched out of the town
in two columns to meet their opponents. The earl of Hereford crossed
by the bridge with his men-at-arms, but none of them was mounted,
for the bridge was narrow, and could provide no passage for horsemen in battle array. The earl of Lancaster with his knights made his
way to the ford of the river. But Andrew Harclay, as a knight with
foresight, wisely stationed a wedge of men-at-arms opposite each
crossing.[439] The earl of Hereford attacked the enemy first; badly
wounded in the fighting, at length he died. Three or four knights
were killed with the earl in the struggle itself. Roger Clifford[440] and
very many others returned to the town badly wounded. Others, trying
to cross the ford, were continually weakened by a shower of arrows;
but after the death of the earl of Hereford their eagerness to fight
cooled down, and they immediately retreated. But the earl of Lancaster made a truce with Andrew Harclay to keep the peace until the
next day; and when this was done each returned to his lodging. On
that same night the sheriff of York[441] had come with a large force to
attack the king's enemies; relying on his help Andrew Harclay entered
the town very early,[442] and took the earl of Lancaster and almost all
the other knights and squires unscathed, and leading them off to

(*Lanercost*, p. 243). For his service at Boroughbridge Harclay was made earl of Carlisle, but
he enjoyed the position for less than one year. He was executed for treason in Mar. 1323
for attempting to negotiate a treaty with the Scots without the king's permission (*HBC*,
p. 454). The Lanercost chronicler was fully aware that the action was treason, but was also
sympathetic to Harclay's attempt to obtain peace; this may reflect widespread northern
opinion (*Lanercost*, pp. 248–51). The terms Harclay arranged showed understanding of the
northern situation and had much in common with the treaty finally agreed in 1328. It is
unfortunate that the missing leaves later in this manuscript deprive us of this author's
views on Harclay.

[440] Clifford, aged just 22, was the son and heir of Robert Clifford who died at
Bannockburn (above, n. 167).

[441] Simon Ward was sheriff of Yorkshire from Oct. 1315 to Jan. 1317 and again May
1318 to June 1323, with a brief hiatus of three weeks in Nov.–Dec. 1318 during the purge
of sheriffs agreed at the York parliament (*List of Sheriffs*, p. 161).

1322 carcerem. Euitare*a* equos reliquerunt, et exuentes*b* arma sua ueteres attritas uestes quesierunt sibi, et more mendicancium uiam incesserunt. Set cautela non profuit, nam nec unus quidem famosus ex omnibus euasit.

O monstrum! uidere uiros purpura et bisso nuper indutos[443] nunc attritis uestibus incedere, et uinctos in compedibus recludi sub carcere! Res miranda et certe nutu Dei et auxilia promota, quod tam rara manu subito superatur tanta milicia. Pars*c* enim comitis numero armatorum partem persequencium excessit in septuplum. Capti sunt enim cum comite Lancastrie et ceteris baronibus milites ualentes centum et amplius. Set et scutariorum non minus*d* ualencium multo maiorem credo fuisse numerum. Quare igitur non restitissent et pro salute sua uiriliter dimicassent? Reuera cor delinquencium semper est pauidum et ideo minus ualens ad negocium. Videbant totam patriam a fronte excitatam, et per hoc uiam eorum impeditam. Sciebant a tergo iminere*e* regis exercitum, et propter hoc cursum retrogradum non esse securum. Vnde quasi homines non habentes consilium nec eciam tempus ad deliberandum, inciderunt in manus inimicorum, etc.

Quarto quintoue die post capcionem comitis Lancastrie ueniens rex apud Pontfreit iussit adduci comitem sine dilacione,[444] et statim iussu regis adducitur, et in quadam noua turri per noctem illam*f* recluditur.[445] Fertur comes turrim illam nouiter construxisse, et regem captum in ipsa recludendum perpetuum decreuisse, set et leonem more Lumbardorum principem constituisse.[446] Hec erat fama uulgaris, set non audiui testem ueritatis.

In crastinum producitur comes in aulam coram iusticiariis assignatis, et singillatim species transgressionis, ac pro quolibet articulo adicitur pena specialis, uidelicet, ut primo protraheretur, deinde suspenderetur, ac postremo capite truncaretur. Set ob reuerenciam regii sanguinis pena protraccionis est remissa, suspencio suspensa, set pena pro omnibus decreta. At comes, uolens se in aliquibus excusare,

---

a sic *MS*; *poss.* ut euitarent *He*; quidam *St, Den-Y*   *b* exuentes *R*; exuentes *St,*
Den-Y   *c* per *MS*; pro *He*; pars *St, Den-Y*   *d* unus *MS*; minus *He, St, Den-Y*
e sic *MS*; imminere *He, St, Den-Y*   *f* illa *MS*; illam *He, St, Den-Y*

---

[442] On 17 Mar. 1322.   [443] Luke 16: 19.
[444] The king was there 19–25 Mar. (*Itin.*, p. 222). Pontefract was reputed to be Lancaster's favourite castle and he spent long periods there in 1318–21 (*Anon.* p. 106; Maddicott, *Lancaster*, pp. 331, 346–7).
[445] The night of 21–2 Mar.

York, he imprisoned them. To escape, they left their horses and, 1322 taking off their armour, looked round for old worn-out clothes, and took to the road as beggars. But their precaution was no use, for not a single well-known man from among them all escaped.

Oh, calamity! To see men lately clothed in purple and fine linen[443] appear now in rags and, bound in shackles, shut up in prison! A marvellous thing and certainly one brought about by God's will and help, that so small a force should in an instant overcome so many knights. For in the number of men-at-arms the earl's side was more than seven times that of its pursuers. More than a hundred valiant knights were captured with the earl of Lancaster and the other barons. I believe the number of squires, no less strong, was much greater. Why therefore should they not have stood firm and fought manfully for their safety? In fact the criminal's heart is always fearful and therefore less effective in action. They saw that the whole countryside was up in arms in front of them, and thus their route was blocked. They knew that the king's army threatened them from the rear, and therefore their retreat was not secure. Thus as men having no plan or even time to deliberate, they fell into the hands of their enemies, etc.

On the fourth or fifth day after the capture of the earl of Lancaster, the king, coming to Pontefract, ordered the earl to be brought there without delay,[444] and he was at once brought there by the king's command, and for that night he was shut up in a certain new tower.[445] It is said that the earl had recently built that tower, and had determined that when the king was captured he should be imprisoned in it for life, and so he would make the prince a lion after the manner of the Lombards.[446] This was the common story, but I have not heard a witness to its truth.

On the following day the earl was led into the hall before the justices assigned for the purpose, and charged one by one with his crimes, and for each charge a particular penalty was awarded, namely, that first he should be drawn, then hanged, and finally beheaded. But out of reverence for his royal blood the penalty of drawing was remitted, the hanging was suspended, and one punishment was

---

[446] This is perhaps a general reference to the restraints put on the claims of the emperors in northern Italy by the independence of the Lombards, rather than to any specific imprisonment of a king. The affairs of the emperors in northern Italy were of topical interest throughout Edward's reign. Most major chronicles recorded Henry VII's acceptance by the pope, Henry's death, the election of Louis IV 'of Bavaria', and Louis's subsequent war with the pope.

1322 nitebatur quedam statim allegare; set iusticiarii noluerunt ipsum
audire quia uerba dampnatorum sicut nec nocent nec possunt*
proficere. Tunc ait comes: 'Fortis est hec curia, et maior imperio,
ubi non auditur responsio nec aliqua admittitur excusacio'.

O spectaculum! uidere comitem Lancastrie, qui nuper erat terror
tocius patrie, in castro proprio et domo iudicium recipere. Deinde
educitur comes extra castrum, et ascendens quoddam uile iumentum
conductus est ad capitolium.[447] Tunc comes quasi orando caput
extendit, et spiculator bis uel ter percuciens caput amputauit. Et
hec acta sunt mense Marcii anno regni quintodecimo.[448]

O comes Lancastrie! ubi est dominacio tua, ubi sunt diuicie tue,
quibus sperabas omnes subicere et nullum contra te posse resistere?
Si in primeua fide perdurasses, ad desolatum[b] nequaquam perue-
nisses. Si Sampson in cautela et Salomon in deuocione perstitissent,
nec hic uiribus nec ille sapiencia priuatus fuisset.[449] Forte latens
causa, non presens set preterita, comitem puniuit. Comes Lancastrie
caput Petri de Gauestone olim abstulit, et nunc iussu regis comes
Lancastrie caput perdidit. Sic uicem pro uice, forsan non iniuste,
comes reportauit, sicut scriptum est in sacris litteris: eadem mensura
qua mensi fueritis remetietur uobis.[450] Sic Abner occidit Asael
percuciens in inguine,[c] set Abner non euasit; nam postea interiit
consimili uulnere.[451] Sic in principio Iudicum cepit Iudas regem
Bezel et uinxit captiuum, ac summitates manuum eius prescidit et
pedum. Tunc ait rex ille captus, 'Merito fecit hoc michi Dominus,
ego enim septuaginta reges in bello ceperam et omnes hac[452]

[*Desunt sex folia*: Hearne][453]

. . . tempore comes Wyntoniensis, licenciatus a rege, ad partes
australes se transtulit ut maneria sua uisitaret, quia post destruccio-

---

a possent *MS*; possunt *He, St*   *b* *sic MS*; *poss.* desolacionem *He*   *c* igne *MS*;
inguine *He, St, Den-Y*

---

[447] *Capitolium* is an unexpected word to find here. The Capitoline Hill with its temples
was the religious centre of Rome. The author may be indulging in play on the word *caput*
as he had done earlier (see above, n. 84) to imply that Lancaster would lose his head on a
headland (Lancaster was executed on a small hill outside Pontefract). There may also be a
further allusion. The Tarpeian rock from which, in legendary times in Rome, traitors had
been thrown to their deaths is on the south-west side of the Capitoline Hill in Rome. This
would make an apt allusion to the death of Lancaster for treason, but it is not clear that the
author would know of the location of the rock. I am indebted to Mr Ian Moxon and Dr
W. Flynn for discussions on this use of *capitolium*.

[448] On 22 Mar. 1322.   [449] Cf. Judg. 16: 16–21; 3 Kgs. (1 Kgs.) 11: 1–13.

decreed for all three. Now the earl, wishing to speak in mitigation of 1322
his crimes, immediately tried to make some points; but the judges
refused to hear him, because the words of the condemned neither
harm nor can be of any advantage. Then the earl said: 'This is a
powerful court, and very great in authority, where no answer is heard
nor any mitigation admitted.'

Oh, what a sight! To see the earl of Lancaster, who was recently
the terror of the whole country, receiving judgment in his own castle
and home. Then the earl was led out from the castle, and, mounting
some worthless beast of burden, was led to the Capitol.[447] Then the
earl stretched forth his head as if in prayer, and the executioner cut
off his head with two or three blows. And these things happened in
March in the fifteenth year of the reign.[448]

Oh! Earl of Lancaster! Where is your power, where are your riches,
with which you hoped to subdue all, and that no one could resist you?
If you had been steadfast in your early faith, you would never have
come to be forsaken. If Samson had remained cautious and Solomon
devout, the one would not have been deprived of his strength nor the
other of his wisdom.[449] Perhaps a hidden cause, not immediate but in
the past, brought punishment upon the earl. The earl of Lancaster
once cut off Piers Gaveston's head, and now by the king's command
the earl of Lancaster has lost his head. Thus, perhaps not unjustly,
the earl received like for like, as it is written in Holy Scripture: 'for
with the same measure that you shall mete withal it shall be measured
to you again'.[450] Thus Abner killed Asahel, striking him in the belly,
but Abner did not escape, for he afterwards died by a similar
wound.[451] Thus at the beginning of the Book of Judges, Judah took
the king of Bezel and made him captive, and cut off his fingers and his
toes. Then said the captive king: 'What I have done, so hath God
requited me, for I had taken seventy kings in battle and all . . .'[452]

[*Six leaves are lacking: Hearne*][453]

time the earl of Winchester, with the king's leave, went south to
inspect his manors, as he had not seen them since their destruction a

---

[450] Luke 6: 38.   [451] Cf. 2 Kgs. (2 Sam.) 2: 23, 3: 27   [452] Judg. 1: 6–7.
[453] These six folios are equivalent to about twelve pages in the Stubbs and Denholm-
Young editions. This is a substantial loss, including all comment on the executions after
the death of Lancaster and on the York parliament at which the elder Despenser was
created earl of Winchester on 10 May (*HBC*, p. 488). The narrative is taken up again in
the late summer of 1322.

1322 nem iam dudum non uidit. Cum audis loqui de comite Wyntoniensi, intellige de Hugone Despenser seniore.

Accessit itaque Robertus Lewer ad maneria comitis Wyntoniensis, et cepit ibidem uictualia et alia necessaria pro sua uoluntate.[454] Visitauit eciam maneria Henrici Thyeys[455] et Warinii[a] de Insula,[456] comiti Wyntoniensi post dampnacionem eorum a rege collata. Et ibidem dominus Robertus [b]elemosinarum nomine[b] pro animabus dictorum baronum fecit magnam distribucionem pauperibus. Ex hoc tamen parum promeruit, quia[c] non quid fiat set quo animo Deus attendit. Non potest dici elemosina que sit[d] ex furto uel rapina. Nam, sicut dicitur alibi, species furti ex bonis alterius inuito domino quicquam largiri.

Audiens autem comes Wyntoniensis quod uenisset Robertus eum comprehendere, intrauit castrum de Wyndelsore, et fecit fieri excubias die et nocte, donec congregasset uirtutem sufficientem ad excipiendum Robertum et comitiuam suam. Venit eciam in auxilium eius comes Cancie missus a latere regis. Sic ergo Robertus caruit proposito suo, et sui cotidie diuertebant ab eo. Cumque uideret iam aliud subsidium nullum superesse, ueniens clam apud Hamptone super mare, cogitauit ibidem cum uxore sua transfretare. Set omnibus incolis facie notissimus, utpote apud illos diu conuersatus, latere non potuit. Quodam[e] die comprehensum in urbe minister regis in carcerem detrusit. Productus uero coram iusticiariis, interrogatus et accusatus in multis, nichil respondit. Quem discrecio iudicum ad peragendam sentenciam suam in carcerem retorsit.[f] Pena siquidem, scienter obmutescentibus debita, talis per regnum usitata. Sedebit incarceratus in area frigida et nuda captiuus, unica sola et tenuissima ueste uelatus, tanto pondere ferri quantum miserum corpus ferre ualerit oppressus. Cibus erit illi panis deterrimus[g] et modicus, et potus aque liquor turbidus et fetidus. Die qua commedit non potabit, nec die qua potauerit panem gustabit. Communis humane nature

[a] Wariny R; Warini St; Warinii Den-Y   [b-b] elemosinarius nam MS; nam om. He; elemosinarum nomine St, Den-Y   [c] que MS; quia He, St, Den-Y   [d] sic R; fit St, Den-Y   [e] quedam MS; quodam He, St, Den-Y   [f] sic MS; for retrusit He   [g] deterius MS; deterior He; deterior or deterrimus St; deterrimus Den-Y

[454] These attacks took place in Aug. and Sept. 1322. Ewer was finally arrested in Dec. and was dead by 8 Jan. 1323 (CPR 1321–4, p. 232). For his rebellion, see Fryde, Tyranny, pp. 153–5. For his earlier career see above, n. 412.

[455] For his part in the rebellion, Tyes was hanged in London on 3 Apr., in rebel livery (Ann. Paul., p. 303; for the livery, see above, nn. 395, 422). He had held lands in several southern counties, had been summoned to parliament from 1300, and held office from time

long time ago. When you hear speak of the earl of Winchester, you are 1322
to understand Hugh Despenser the elder.

So Robert Ewer came to the earl of Winchester's manors, and
carried off victuals and other necessaries of life as he liked.[454] He also
visited the manors of Henry Tyes[455] and Warin de Lisle,[456] granted
by the king to the earl of Winchester after their condemnation. And
there Sir Robert distributed a great deal to the poor in the name of
alms for the souls of the said barons. However, he had little benefit
from this, because God has regard not to the deed but to the
intention. That cannot be called alms which comes from theft or
robbery. For, as it is said elsewhere, it is a kind of theft to distribute
largesse from the goods of another without the consent of the lord.

When the earl of Winchester heard that Robert had come to attack
him, he took refuge in Windsor Castle, and set a watch night and day,
until he had gathered a force sufficient to capture Robert and his
retinue. The earl of Kent, sent from the king's court, also came to
help him. Thus Robert failed in his plan, and his men deserted him
day by day. When he saw that no other help was left, coming secretly
to Southampton on the coast, he thought that he might cross the sea
from there with his wife. But as he was very well known by sight to all
the inhabitants from long residence there, he could not hide himself.
He was arrested one day in the town and a royal official threw him
into prison. When he was brought before the justices, questioned, and
accused of many crimes, he did not answer. He was therefore
returned to prison at the discretion of the judges to undergo his
sentence. The customary punishment, indeed, for those deliberately
remaining silent is carried out thus throughout the kingdom. The
prisoner shall sit on the cold, bare floor, dressed only in the thinnest
of shirts, and pressed with as great a weight of iron as his wretched
body can bear. His food shall be a little of the worst sort of bread, and
his drink cloudy and stinking water. The day on which he eats he
shall not drink, and the day on which he has drunk he shall not taste

to time (e.g. keeper of Oxford, and of the Isle of Wight). He was the brother-in-law of
Warin de Lisle, and it is not clear what brought both of them so firmly to the rebel side.
Tyes had no obvious connections with Lancaster, and may have been closer to Amory and
Hereford. His father had supported Hereford's father in 1297 (*CP*, xii. 2. 102–4).

[456] Lisle was one of the six lords (two of them certainly Lancastrian retainers) who were
hanged at Pontefract on 22 Mar., the day of Lancaster's execution. Lisle had had lands in
Berks. and other southern counties, and like Tyes had held keeperships (e.g. Windsor
1318–19) from time to time. Also like Tyes, he had no obvious connection with Lancaster
nor, in his case, with the Marchers (*CP*, viii. 48–9).

1322 uirtutem superaret qui quintum uel sextum diem sub hac pena
transigeret.[457]

1323   Huiusmodi pene per aliquot dies Robertus astrictus tandem
occubuit, et ita *pro delictis*[a] dignam ulcionem et anime salutiferam,
si[b] tamen pacienter ipsam tum sustinuit, in fine reportauit. Ipse
Robertus, in curia regis olim educatus, in rebus bellicis cautus erat et
strenuus. Verumptamen de fauore curie confisus, et uariis moribus a
iuuentute consuetus, ad predas et homicidia semper erat precipuus.
Ceterum quia tum quendam bonum occidit, et uxorem eius super-
duxit, quam eciam in adulterio prius posuerat, omne aliud[c] delictum
longius excedit. Sic igitur Robertus cecidit ut meruit, et comes
Wyntoniensis indempnis euasit.

Aliud quoque non minus timendum accidit Wyntoniensi comiti
periculum.[458] Mauricius de Berkele, iam fere per annus detentus, tum
moram traxit in castro Walynfordie, ad quem solebat quidam armiger
qui diu steterat in obsequio ipsius frequenter intrare, et ob priorem
familiaritatem domino suo beneficium consolacionis impendere.
Accidit autem quadam die ut armiger ille cum tribus uel quatuor
sociis intraret castrum, de licencia custodis, propter solitum accessum
in nullo suspectus. Eadem nocte rogauit Mauricius constabularium ut
cenaret cum eo, insuper et[d] ianitores et uigiles quotquot[e] erant in
castro. Cenantibus autem illis subito surrexit armiger cum sociis suis,
et petiit claues castri sibi reddi, necnon et minas mortis intendebat
cuilibet repugnanti.

Videns ergo constabularius quod non posset resistere, tradidit
claues sine dilacione. Tunc armiger ille ad quamdam[f] priuatam
portam accessit, et circiter uiginti socios statim introduxit. Et hec
quidem facta sunt sub tanto silencio ut nec clamor nec murmur
resonaret in castro. Tandem puer quidam residens ad exteriorem
portam, postquam sentiit quod interior custodia insolito modo
tractabatur, latenter exiuit, *adiensque ⟨maiorem⟩ uille,*[h] castrum
perditum et multos extraneos intrasse protinus nunciauit. Primum
quidam[i] nuncius a predicto armigero cum litteris emissus testis

[a-a] per electis *MS*; pro *He*; pro delictis *St, Den-Y*   [b] sibi *R*; si *St, Den-Y*
[c] alium *MS*; aliud *He, St, Den-Y*   [d] e *MS*; et *He, St, Den-Y*   [e] in quotquot *MS*; in
om. He, St, Den-Y   [f] sic *R*; quandam *St, Den-Y*   [h-h] audiensque uelle *R*; adiensque
⟨maiorem⟩ uille *Den-Y*   [i] quid' *MS*; quidem *He, St, Den-Y*; quidam *MW*

[457] The procedure of returning a defendant to prison until he agreed to plead was
introduced from France in the 1250s; the conditions of eating and drinking on alternate
days, of skimpy clothing and heavy fetters began to be recorded between the 1270s and
1290s. By not pleading the defendant ensured that his goods and lands could not be

bread. He who survives this punishment beyond the fifth or sixth day would have strength beyond that of normal human nature.[457]   1322

Afflicted with this treatment for a few days Robert at length died, and thus received in the end a punishment fitting for his crimes and healthy for his soul, provided that he then bore it with resignation. This Robert, who had been brought up at court, was shrewd and active in military matters. Nevertheless, relying on his influence at court, and accustomed to lax morals from youth, he was always ready for plunder and killing. But because he then killed a certain good man, and made off with his wife, with whom he had previously committed adultery, he exceeded by far every other crime. Therefore he died as he deserved, and the earl of Winchester escaped unharmed.   1323

Another danger no less fearful befell the earl of Winchester.[458] Maurice Berkeley, in custody now for almost a year, was at that time detained in Wallingford Castle, where a certain squire who had long been in his service often used to visit him and to give his lord comfort, on account of his former close friendship. But it happened one day that this squire entered the castle with three or four companions, with the guard's permission, in no way mistrusted because his visit was usual. The same night Maurice invited the constable to dine with him, and all the doorkeepers and watchmen in the castle as well. As they were dining the squire and his companions suddenly rose and demanded the keys of the castle, threatening with death anyone who resisted.

Seeing therefore that he could not resist, the constable handed over the keys immediately. Then the squire went to a certain postern gate, and at once let in about twenty companions. This was done in such silence that not a sound or murmur was heard in the castle. At length a boy living at the outer gate, realizing that affairs in the inner ward were not as they should be, secretly slipped out, and going to [the mayor] of the town, at once reported that the castle was lost, and that many strangers had entered. A certain messenger sent out by the squire with letters came forward as a witness. For the squire had

forfeited and so lost to his heirs (H. R. T. Summerson, 'The early development of the *peine fort et dure*', in E. W. Ives and A. H. Manchester (eds.), *Law, Litigants and the Legal Profession* (London, 1983) pp. 116–25).

[458] This event took place in Jan. 1323. Berkeley had been in captivity since his surrender in Jan. 1322, and the king knew of this rising by 20 Jan. 1323 (*CPR 1321–4*, p. 257). Berkeley died in prison in May 1326, but his son, Thomas, who was also imprisoned in 1322 after Boroughbridge, survived and was released from Pevensey by Isabella in Oct. 1326 (*CP*, ii. 128–9; see above, n. 421).

1323 accessit. Disposuerat enim armiger ille quosdam socios premunisse, et in *ª*gallicinio dominum*ª* suum Mauricium et ceteros uinculatos*ᵇ* pariter eduxisse. Set nuncius machinacionis proditorie timens periculum subire accessit ad maiorem uille. Populus conuocatur, pulsantur campane, tonant cornua, et uox horrida*ᶜ* plebis extollitur.

Tunc qui erant infra castrum audientes *ᵈ*populi tumultum*ᵈ* suspicabantur consilium suum iam esse detectum, et per consequens propositum eorum impeditum, unde *ᵉ*statuerunt custodes ad singulas ⟨portas, et⟩ excubias per totum murum ordinauerunt.*ᵉ* Mane facto diuulgata est res per totam patriam, accessitque uicecomes ad uillam, et hortabatur interiores ad castri dedicionem. Illi uero asserebant*ᶠ* se regis auctoritate castrum intrasse, nec cuiquam homini sine regis mandato reddere uelle. Et hoc quidem responso*ᵍ* usi sunt ad cautelam, ut sic prodicionem suam palliarent et nacta oportunitate temporis a castro recederent.

Non credidit uicecomes responsum, quia non fecerunt ei fidem de regis mandato. Immo statim accesserunt robustiores tocius patrie, et fecit fieri uigilias circa castrum die ac nocte donec certificaretur super allegata regis auctoritate. Aduenerunt in auxilium uicecomitis comes Wyntonie et comes Cancie, quoniam tunc erant in partibus illis, et statim disposuerunt*ʰ* castrum inuadere et proditores ui et armis ad dedicionem compellere. Videntes autem interiores tot et tantos uiros ad obsidicionem,*ⁱ* et capcionem tandem euitari non posse, quantoque diucius rebellarent, tanto grauiori pene subiacerent,*ʲ* portas aperiunt et liberum introitum cunctis promittentes in quadam capella omnes conueniunt.

Tunc ingressi comites repererunt Mauricium in solita custodia, reliquos autem in capella. Non profuit eis immunitas ecclesie; nam protinus extracti truduntur in castrum. Ille uero interrogatus cur proditores in castrum regis aduocare presumpsit, nichil in preiudicium domini regis machinatum constanter affirmauit, et cognitorem*ᵏ* omnium cordium⁴⁵⁹ et omnes homines exceptis aduersariis suis testes adiecit. Tunc significauerunt domino regi omnia acta cum responso Mauricii. Rescripsit rex comiti Cancie . . . . consensu Mauricii

ᵃ⁻ᵃ galli cinodnu' *MS*; gallicinio dominum *He, St, Den-Y*   *ᵇ* uinculatores *MS*; uinculatos *He, St, Den-Y*   *ᶜ* homda *MS*; horrida *He, St, Den-Y*   *ᵈ⁻ᵈ* populum tumultu *MS*; populi tumultum *or* populum tumultuantem *He*; populi tumultum *St, Den-Y*   *ᵉ⁻ᵉ* statuerunt custodes ad singulas excubias per totum murum ordinauerunt *MS*; statuerunt ⟨et⟩ custodes *etc. He*; statuerunt custodes ⟨et⟩ ad singulas excubias; per totum murum ordinauerunt *St*; statuerunt custodes ad singulas ⟨portas, et⟩ excubias *etc. Den-Y*   *ᶠ* asserebantur *MS*; asserebant *He, St, Den-Y*   *ᵍ* responsio *MS*; responso

planned to warn certain friends and at cockcrow to get his lord Maurice away together with the other prisoners. But the messenger of this treacherous plot, fearing to take the risk, went to the mayor of the town. The townsmen were aroused, bells rung, horns sounded, and the harsh cries of the populace were heard.

Then, hearing the people in uproar, the men in the castle guessed that their plan was discovered and consequently their intention blocked, so they posted guards at all [the gates and] arranged watches all along the wall. By morning the news had spread throughout the countryside, and the sheriff came to the town and urged those inside to surrender the castle. They replied that they had entered the castle by the king's authority, and that they would not yield it to any man without the king's command. They gave this answer as a precaution, to disguise their treachery, so that if they found an opportunity they might leave the castle.

The sheriff did not believe this reply, because they gave him no proof of the king's command. The hardier country folk came up immediately, and he set a watch around the castle day and night until he was informed about the alleged royal authority. The earl of Winchester and the earl of Kent, since they were then in that area, came to the sheriff's aid, and they at once arranged to attack the castle and compel the traitors to surrender by force of arms. Seeing the strength of the besieging force, and that they could not in the end escape capture, and that the longer they rebelled the more severe would be their punishment, the men inside opened the gates and, promising unimpeded entry to everyone, they gathered all together in a certain chapel.

Then, having entered, the earls found Maurice in custody as usual, and the rest in the chapel. The immunity of the church was of no benefit to them; for they were dragged out immediately and hustled into the castle. When [Maurice] was asked why he had presumed to call traitors into the king's castle, he stoutly maintained that he had plotted nothing to the prejudice of the lord king, and called as witnesses Him who knows all hearts,[459] and all men except his enemies. They then notified the lord king of all that had been done and of Maurice's reply. The king wrote back to the earl of Kent . . . to

He, St, Den-Y   ʰ deposuerunt MS; disposuerunt He, St, Den-Y   ⁱ sic MS;
obsidionem He, St, Den-Y   ʲ sic MS; poss. subiacere He   ᵏ cogitorem MS;
cognitorem He, St, Den-Y

---

[459] This echoes the first collect of the mass: *Deus cui omne cor patet* (Legg, *Sarum Missal*, p. 216).

1323 diligenter inquireret, et dictum armigerum ceterorum sig . . . .
      suis

[*Deest folium unum: Hearne*][460]

1324 '. . . sepius promouit; et, si per lapsum temporis populum suum in
      unitate reduxerit, id quod prius profuit in uanum redibit. Preterea
      diutina pax homines nostros effeminatos reddet, et usus armorum
      suspensus inbellem gentem nostram efficiet. Set et hii qui nunc
      apti sunt ad prelium inutiles fient, uergentes in senium; et hec
      omnia nobis incommoda conferet[a] tempus uacacionis producte.
      Super hiis igitur consulimus quod regi Anglorum perpetua con-
      cordia offeratur,[b] et pax fiat, alioquin de treugis initis non multum
      confidat.[461] Et quia rex Anglorum, sicut creditur, certamen est
      habiturus cum Francis, eo cicius speramus optinere quod peti-
      mus.'[462]
         Tunc misit Robertus le Brutz ad regem Anglie, dicens: 'Domine,
      placet Scotis in pacem perpetuam treugas conuertere, et quid tibi
      placuerit, si bonum tibi uidetur, uelitis rescribere. Multi enim nostris
      treugis[c] initis egre consenserant. Vnde timeo ne forsan pace repulsa
      pacta seruabo, set multorum grassancium rabiem solus cohibere non
      potero. Nam et rex Getheus, qui satis in Dauid sibi complacuit, eum
      tamen contra uota satraparum sustinere non potuit.'[463]
         Animaduertens rex Anglie quod artaret eum negocium Vasconie,
      quod et Scoti ex nimia causa proni essent ad recidiuum[d] concordie,
      rescripsit se uelle in pacem perpetuam libenter consentire, placuit-
      que de communi consensu super tractanda apud Eboracum partes
      conuenire.[464] Quo cum uenissent, uidelicet rex Anglie ex parte una
      et quidam magnates Scotorum ex altera, pecierunt Scoti Scociam
      ab omni exaccione regni Anglie imperpetuum esse[e] immunem et

---

        [a] conferret *MS*; conferet *He, St, Den-Y*   [b] offerratur *MS*; offeratur *He, St, Den-Y*
        [c] tregis *MS*; treugis *He, St, Den-Y*   [d] reciduum *MS*; recidiuum *He, St, Den-Y*
        [a] et *R*; esse *Den-Y*

        [460] The lost leaf, equivalent to about two pages in Stubbs's and Denholm-Young's
editions, covers most of 1323 and 1324. The reference below to appointing negotiators,
which was done on 3 Nov., places the reopened narrative in the autumn of 1324.
        [461] A short Anglo-Scottish truce had been arranged in Mar. 1323 to negotiate a final
peace. When this proved impossible a thirteen-year truce was made 30 May 1323 (*Foed.*, ii.
1. 510–13, 518, 521–2; *CPR 1321–4*, p. 292; *CCR 1318–23*, p. 717; *Plac. Abb.*, p. 342).
Peace with the Scots was not popular with all the English; Henry Beaumont feared the loss
of his Scottish lands (Fryde, *Tyranny*, p. 159 and n. 42).
        [462] The situation in Gascony was grave. Open hostilities had already begun in Aug.

enquire diligently with Maurice's consent, and . . . the said squire . . . 1323
of the rest . . .

[*One leaf is lacking: Hearne*][460]

'. . . advanced more frequently; and if in the course of time he 1324
[Edward II] reunites his people, what formerly was profitable will be
worthless. Further, a long period of peace will make our men
unmanly, and lack of practice in the use of arms will make our
people unwarlike. Those who are now fit for battle will become
useless, bordering upon old age; a long-drawn-out time of rest will
bring all these disadvantages upon us. In this, therefore, we advise
that a permanent agreement be offered to the king of the English, and
let it be peace, otherwise he should not rely on any truces which were
set up.[461] And because the king of the English, as it is thought, is on
the point of fighting the French, we hope to obtain what we seek from
him more quickly.'[462]

Then Robert Bruce sent to the king of England saying: 'My Lord,
the Scots wish to turn the truces into a permanent peace, and, if it
seems good to you, may it please you to send a reply on what you wish
to do in the matter. For many men have agreed to our present truces
reluctantly. For this reason I fear that if peace is refused I will be
unable to keep the agreements, for I will not be able alone to restrain
the fury of a violent throng. For the king of Gath, though himself
much pleased by David, yet could not support him against the wishes
of his satraps.'[463]

The king of England, realizing that the Gascon affair limited his
scope of action and that the Scots had every reason to welcome the
restoration of peace, wrote back that he would willingly consent to a
permanent peace, and it was agreed by common consent that the
parties should meet at York to negotiate.[464] When they had come
there, that is the king of England on the one hand and certain Scottish
magnates on the other, the Scots demanded that Scotland should be
for ever exempt and free from every exaction of the English kingdom,

1324, and Agen and La Réole had surrendered by September. For the causes of the Anglo-
French war, see below, pp. 228–9.

    [463] Cf. 1 Kgs. (1 Sam.) 29: 1–11.

    [464] Scottish envoys had safe conducts from 3 Nov. 1324 to 13 Jan. 1325, and English
negotiators were appointed on 8 Nov. (*Foed.*, ii. 1. 577–8). In a letter to Ralph Basset,
seneschal of Gascony, Hugh Despenser wrote that a meeting with the Scots had been
arranged for 18 Nov. (Chaplais, *Saint-Sardos*, p. 76). The *Vita*'s description is the fullest
we have of the negotiations.

1324 liberam, pecierunt iure adquisicionis et dominii totam terram quam perambulauerant usque ad portas Eboraci.[465] Erat et quedam baronia in partibus Essexie quam Robertus de Brutz propter rebellionem dudum demeruit; hanc peciit Robertus sibi restitui, eciam cum fructibus quos medio tempore rex inde percepit.[466] Pecierunt eciam Scoti petram illam regalem sibi restitui quam Edwardus rex senior quondam de Scocia tulerat et apud Westmonasterium collocauerat iuxta tumbam sancti Edwardi.[467] Erat autem lapis ille apud Scotos celebris memorie, eo quod super hanc reges Scocie solebant gubernacula regni cum ceptro[a] recipere. Scota filia Pharaonis hanc petram secum a finibus Egipti eduxit, cum in partes[b] Scocie applicuit et terram subiugauit. Prophetauerat enim Moises quod qui petram illam secum afferret amplas terras suo dominio subiugaret. Vnde a Scota est dicta Scocia que prius ab Albanacto uocabatur Albania.[468] Ad hec in augmentum federis [c]ac cumulum[c] pacis optulit Robertus de Brutz filiam suam matrimonialiter copulari filio regis. Postremo uoluerunt Scoti quod, presentibus quorum interest coram domino papa, a rege Francie confirmarentur uota procerum, ut fedus pacis [d]iam initum[d] et tanta auctoritate uallatum nullum solueretur in euum.

Auditis peticionibus Scotorum ait rex: 'Scoti uenerunt non ut nos ⟨ad⟩ pacem[e] allicerent set ut occasiones dissencionis magis quererent et sponte treugas infringerent. Reuera preiudicialia nimis nobis

---

[a] sic MS; sceptro St, Den-Y   [b] parte MS; partes He, Den-Y   [c-c] ad tumltu MS; ac cumulum He, St, Den-Y   [d-d] tam in ta[u]m MS; tali He, St; iam initum Den-Y; the text remains uncertain ed.   [e] sic MS; pace He, St, Den-Y; ad pacem ed.

---

[465] The reference to lordship may be an allusion to the Scottish possession of Cumbria and Northumbria in 1137–57 (G. W. S. Barrow, 'Frontier and settlement', in R. Bartlett and A. MacKay (eds.), *Medieval Frontier Societies* (Oxford, 1989), pp. 3–21, at p. 4; R. R. Davies, *The First English Empire* (Oxford, 2000), pp. 64–5). I am indebted to Miss Barbara Harvey for this suggestion. However, the reference to conquest and York seems to refer also to recent events. Edward utterly refuted the claim.

[466] Bruce inherited Writtle and Hatfield Broadoak in Essex from his father (*CIPM Edward I*, iv. no. 220). These came into the family through his great-grandmother, Isabel, as part of her inheritance of one-third of the honour of Huntingdon (Barrow, *Bruce*, p. 331 n. 8).

[467] The Stone of Destiny, the Scottish royal enthronement stone, had been taken south from Scone by Edward I after he defeated John Balliol in 1296 as a symbol of his conquest of Scotland (Barrow, *Bruce*, p. 73; N. Aitchison, *Scotland's Stone of Destiny* (Stroud, 2000), pp. 113–18).

[468] This was one of several myths which linked medieval peoples to antique origins (see above, p. xxix). Scota, wife of a Scythian prince, daughter of Pharaoh, was part of an early Irish origin myth. It was claimed that she and her husband fled from Egypt in the time of

they demanded by right of conquest and lordship the whole land that 1324
they had traversed as far as the gates of York.[465] There was also a
certain barony in Essex which Robert Bruce had long ago forfeited on
account of his rebellion; Robert demanded that this should be
restored to him, with the profits, moreover, that the king had received
from it in the meantime.[466] The Scots also demanded that the royal
stone should be restored to them, which the elder King Edward had
long ago taken from Scotland and placed at Westminster by the tomb
of St Edward.[467] This stone was of famous memory amongst the
Scots, because upon it the kings of Scotland used to receive the
government of the kingdom with the sceptre. Scota, daughter of
Pharaoh, brought this stone with her from the country of Egypt when
she landed in Scotland and subdued the land. For Moses had
prophesied that whoever bore that stone with him should bring
broad lands under the yoke of his lordship. For this reason the
land which was formerly called Albany from Albanactus is called
Scotland from Scota.[468] To improve the treaty and strengthen the
peace, Robert Bruce proposed that his daughter should be joined in
marriage with the king's son. Finally the Scots wished that, with all
those concerned being present before the lord pope, the nobles'
wishes should be confirmed by the king of France, so that the treaty
of peace then agreed and strengthened by such authority, should
never be broken.

When the king had heard the Scottish proposals he said: 'The
Scots have come not to draw us towards a peace but to seek
opportunities for further discord and for unprovoked breaches of

Moses and settled for a time in Spain. Their descendants moved to Ireland and, later, to
Scotland. The legend was adapted in the 1290s by the Scots to bring Scota herself directly
to Scotland. This provided Scotland with a long independent history and a direct classical
link as part of the battle against Edward I's claim to overlordship. In particular it could be
used to combat the English use of their own legendary origin, in which Brutus (great-
grandson of Aeneas of Troy) conquered all Britain, and bequeathed Scotland to his son
Albanactus. The revised legend of Scota was used in the Scots' pleading at the papal curia
in 1301 and is clearly visible in the Declaration of Arbroath, although Scota is not
mentioned there by name. The author of the *Vita* is thus repeating a recently devised piece
of political propaganda. For Albanactus's inheritance see *Geoff of Mon.*, ii. 1; for the
development of Scota's legend, see E. J. Cowan, 'Myth and identity in early medieval
Scotland', *SHR*, lxiii (1984), 111–35, at pp. 119–23; Dauvit Broun, 'The birth of Scottish
history', *SHR*, lxxvi (1997), 4–22 at pp. 10–15; R. A. Mason 'Scotching the Brut: politics,
history and national myth in sixteenth-century Britain', in R. A. Mason (ed.), *Scotland and
England 1286–1815* (Edinburgh, 1987), pp. 60–84, at p. 64; A. A. M. Duncan, *The Nation
of Scots and the Declaration of Arbroath*, Hist. Assoc. gen ser., lxxv (1970), pp. 31–2, 34. For
variations on the myths associated with the origins of the stone, see Aitchison, *Stone of
Destiny*, pp. 19–36.

1324 exposcunt, unde et sine effectu ad propria remeabunt. Quomodo enim sine preiudicio corone nostre ius quod habemus in Scocia possumus remittere, que ab aduentu Britonum usque aduentum Saxonum et deinceps usque ad tempus nostrum antecessoribus nostris semper dinoscitur fuisse subiecta, que quamuis rebellando nostrum sepius declinaret imperium, ad iugum tamen debitum, licet inuita, non ambigitur fuisse reducta? Ius in Marchia uendicare non poterunt, cuius possessionem nunquam habuerunt. Pedis enim posicio priuato possessionem tribuit, non extraneo.[469] Quod si ob perambulacionem Marchiam petant, consequens est ut et ipsi magnam partem Scocie eadem racione nobis concedant. Hereditatem quam Robertus de Brutz petit, pater meus ei ob manifestum delictum quondam abstulit, et non decet filium irritare quod pater decreuit. Scimus eciam quod pater meus deuicta Scocia petram illam regalem secum tulit in signum uictorie; quod si restitueremus, uideremur forsan ius sic acquisitum tanquam degeneres repudiare. Verumptamen super petra reddenda dissencio breuis, si cetera non discreparent a limite racionis. Nupcias eciam quas offert Robertus ad presens non admittimus, quoniam prout offeruntur[a] nobis indecentes esse perpendimus. Denique pacem quam Scoti coram domino papa et rege Francie petunt confirmari, si contingeret eam debito fine concludi, coram quolibet principe mundi uellemus explicari. Set, quia preiudicialia nimis nobis exposcunt, infecto negocio ad propria remeabunt.'

Igitur responsum est Scotis formam oblatam regi non placere, nec regem in tantum artatum esse ut tam degenerem pacem cogatur inire.[470] Conuencionem tamen super treugis prius initam nichilominus censuit obseruandam, alioquin Scotis nunquam deinceps fidem adhibendam. Nuncii uero Scotorum, accepto responso, redeuntes retulerunt regi suo et hiis qui erant de consilio responsa regis Anglie et conclusionem in fine. Inter quos tandem deliberatum est et communiter consensum quod predicte treuge cum Anglis inite in suo robore starent, et religionem quam omnis nacio et etas conseruat

---

a offerruntur *MS*; offeruntur *He, St, Den-Y*

[469] Cf. *Dig.* xli. 2. 3 (1), xli. 2. 40 (1), *Corpus Iuris Civilis*, i. 652, 655. Bracton echoed the Roman law position, that livery did not need more than a token entrance to the property, but he emphasized that the donor must be willing, *De Legibus*, ii. 125–6. The *Vita* is the only source for these claims of the Scots to some rights in the March, which caused Edward such outrage.

the truce. In fact, they are demanding terms highly damaging to us 1324
and they will return to their own country without result. For how,
without prejudice to our Crown, can we surrender the right we have
in Scotland, which is known always to have been subject to our
ancestors, from the coming of the Britons to the coming of the Saxons
and from then down to our own time; which, although in rebellion it
often spurned our authority, was, nevertheless, as no one doubts,
restored to its proper state of servitude, though unwillingly? They
cannot claim any right in the March, of which they never had
possession. For the placing of the foot gives possession to the citizen
but not to the foreigner.[469] But if they claim the March by
perambulation, it follows by the same reasoning that they should
give up a large part of Scotland to us. Robert Bruce claims the
inheritance which my father once took from him for manifest crime,
and it is not fitting that a son should nullify what his father has
decreed. For we know that my father, when Scotland had been
conquered, took with him that royal stone as a sign of victory; and if
we were to restore it we should perhaps seem basely to give up the
right thus acquired. Nevertheless, we should make little difficulty
about returning the stone, if their other demands were not beyond all
reason. Even the marriage which Robert offers we do not agree to at
present, since we consider that, as offered, it is unsuitable for us.
Finally, we would be willing to have the peace, which the Scots seek
to have confirmed in the presence of the pope and the king of France,
recited before every prince in the world, if it were brought to a
suitable conclusion. But, as their demands are too damaging to us,
they shall return home unsatisfied.'

Reply was therefore made to the Scots that the draft offered to the
king did not please him, nor was the king under such pressure that he
could be forced to make such an ignoble peace.[470] But he thought
nevertheless that the agreement previously made concerning the
truces should be observed, otherwise no credence could ever be
given to the Scots. The Scottish ambassadors, having received the
reply, returned and reported to their king and his counsellors the king
of England's answers and final conclusion. At last it was determined
among them by common consent that the said truces made with the
English should stand firm, and that they would in no way dishonour
the scrupulous observation of an oath which every nation and age

[470] The king wrote to the pope that the Scottish demands were to the disinheritance of
his crown (*Foed.* ii. 1. 595).

1324 in nullo macularent. *"Nam et Israel Gabaonitis*[a] seruauit iusiurandum quamuis dolo in circumuencione fuisset extortum.[471]

Dum durarent inducie inter reges Anglorum et Francorum discurrebant nuncii et mediatores, hinc inde proponentes plures formas concordie; set nulla placuit regi Francie nisi satisfaccio sibi pro terra Vasconie.[472] Videns igitur rex Anglie quod per huiusmodi nuncios nichil proficeret, disposuit mittere reginam si forsan ipsa negocium ad effectum perduceret. Nam sicut inter duos reges erat sanguine media, ita efficacior uidebatur in pace procuranda.[473]

1325 Abiit regina ualde gauisa, dupplici gaudio letificata; gaudens quippe natale solum et parentes uisitare, gaudens quorundam quos non diligebat comitiuam[b] relinquere. Nimirum si Hugonem non diligat per quem auunculus eius periit, per quem famulis orbata et omnibus redditibus suis priuata remansit; iccirco a multis reuersura non creditur, donec Hugo Despenser a latere regis penitus seperaretur.[c][474]

Veniens autem regina ad fratrem suum regem transmarinum, nichil plus aliis nunciis optinuit, nisi quod rex frater eius amore ipsius usque ad gulam Augusti treugas prorogauit.[475] Cernens itaque rex Anglie ex actis iam nichil aliud restare, nisi aut transfretare et regi Francie satisfacere, aut terram[d] Wasconie indefensam perdere, transacto iam Paschate collegit exercitum copiosum, pedites uidelicet linea armatura[e] incinctos,[f] habentes arcus, secures aut gladios, singuli[g] arma singula in quibus se nouerant magis experts.[476] Est enim aliquis

---

[a-a] nan et Irael Gabaonis *MS*; nam et Israel Gabaonitis *He, St, Den-Y*
[b] commitiuam *MS*; comitiuam *St, Den-Y*   [c] sic *MS*; separaretur *He, St, Den-Y*
[d] terras *MS*; terram *He, St, Den-Y*   [e] armata *MS*; armatura *He, St, Den-Y*
[f] imminctos *MS*; aminctos *He*; incinctos *St, Den-Y*   [g] sic *MS*; poss. singulos *He*

---

[471] Cf. Josh. 9: 3–27.

[472] War had broken out between England and France in 1324 for two main causes: conflict over the building of a French bastide at St Sardos in the English territory of Agenais in the autumn of 1323, and Edward's constant delay in performing homage to the new French king, Charles IV. Charles finally confiscated Edward's French lands on 24 June 1324 (Chaplais, *Saint-Sardos*, p. 188 n. 1). The French army entered the Agenais on 15 Aug. 1324 and quickly reached La Réole, where they besieged the king's brother, Edmund, earl of Kent, who had been sent to defend the king's lands. After a five-week siege, he surrendered and arranged a six-month truce for 22 Sept. 1324 to 14 Apr. 1325 (Chaplais, *Saint-Sardos*, pp. ix–xiii, 61–3).

[473] Sometime before 13 Jan. French negotiators had suggested that both Isabella, who was Charles IV's sister, and Prince Edward should go to France, and in early Feb. the king's advisers agreed unanimously that the queen should go. The suggestion that Prince Edward should go (originally made by England in Nov. 1324) was dropped. Edward later said that the suggestion that Isabella should go had come from the pope (Chaplais, *Saint-Sardos*, pp. 193–6; *Foed.*, ii. 1. 599; M. Buck, *Politics, Finance and the Church in the Reign of*

upholds. For Israel kept its oath to the Gibeonites although it was ₁₃₂₄ extorted by treachery and deceit.[471]

While the truces lasted between the kings of the English and the French, ambassadors and mediators ran to and fro proposing many forms of agreement; but nothing pleased the king of France unless it gave him satisfaction for Gascony.[472] The king of England saw that nothing was to be achieved through these ambassadors, and arranged to send the queen, who might perhaps bring the matter to the desired conclusion. For, since she was related by blood to each king, so she seemed likely to be more effective in bringing peace.[473]

The queen departed very joyfully, happy with a twofold joy; ₁₃₂₅ pleased in fact to visit her native land and her relatives, pleased to leave the company of some whom she did not like. Certainly she does not like Hugh, through whom her uncle perished, by whom she was deprived of her servants and dispossessed of all her rents; consequently many think she will not return until Hugh Despenser is wholly removed from the king's side.[474]

When the queen came to her brother, the king, across the channel, she obtained nothing more than the other ambassadors, except that her brother, out of affection for her, prolonged the truce until the first of August.[475] So the king of England, seeing that there was now nothing left to do except either to cross the channel and satisfy the king of France, or to lose the defenceless land of Gascony, after Easter collected a large army, namely of foot soldiers equipped with linen armour, having bows, axes, or swords, each bearing the arms in which he knew he was more skilled.[476] For one is fitted for this, but not for

Edward II: Walter Stapeldon, Treasurer of England (Cambridge, 1983), p. 153 n. 178). Isabella landed at Wissant on 9 Mar. 1325 and by 20 Mar. reached Pontoise, where she met the queen of France (Chaplais, *Saint-Sardos*, p. 267).

[474] Isabella's uncle was the late Thomas of Lancaster; for the relationship see above, n. 94. Her lands were confiscated on 18 Sept. 1324 and she was given a cash allowance; her French servants were removed on 28 Sept. (*Foed.* ii. 1. 569; *CFR 1319–27*, p. 300). Confiscation was not unprecedented in times of war and Isabella's income was not ungenerous, but at 3,920 marks (£2,613. 6s. 8d.) a year it was just over one-third of her earlier income (Buck, *Stapeldon*, p. 152 n.).

[475] By 31 Mar. 1325 Isabella had negotiated an initial extension of the truce from 14 Apr. to 9 June. After further negotiations it was agreed on 31 May and confirmed by Edward on 13 June that he would come to France to do homage on 15 Aug. On 1 June the homage ceremony was postponed until 29 Aug. (Chaplais, *Saint-Sardos*, pp. 199–201; *Foed.*, ii. 1. 601–3; Chaplais, 'Duché-Pairie', pp. 156–7).

[476] Preparations for Edward's passage to France continued throughout the spring and summer. Easter was 7 Apr. 1325. The main muster at Portsmouth was first called for 17 Mar., postponed to 17 May, and then to 2 Aug. (*PW*, ii. 1. 683–90, 696–9, 702–4, 714–19).

1325 aptus ad hec, non ad illa; Saul ad gladium, Ionathas ad arcum, et
Dauid in[a] fundam.[477] Iussitque eos rex ad mare procedere cum
ductoribus suis, ibidemque residere donec aliud haberent in mandatis. Conuocauitque magnates regni sui Wyntoniam, disponere uolens
communi consilio negocium expedicionis sue.[478]

Interim pedites petierunt uadia sua, set non dabantur eis; quamobrem discurrebant per totam patriam spoliantes incolas uictualibus
suis. Mirabantur omnes quia non satisfaceret rex peditibus, cum rite
uiuere non possent sine uadiis, et satis habundaret thesaurus regis.
Multi enim progenitores sui congregauerunt denarios, ipse solus
supergressus est uniuersos.[479] Verumtamen imputatur Hugoni regis
duricia sicut et alia mala que fiunt in curia. Vnde et multi in necem
eius coniurauerunt, set machinacione detecta quidam eorum capti
sunt, reliqui fugerunt.[b][480]

Tunc iussit rex omnes pedites naues ascendere et in fluctibus maris
stacionem facere, donec adueniret tempus transfretandi in terram
Vasconie; preposuitque eis comitem de Warenna, Iohannem de
Sancto Iohanne, et alios magnates terre, qui similiter ingressi sunt
naues non audentes resistere.[481] Misit eciam rex litteras per singulos
comitatus mandans et precipiens omnes qui ab exercitu ad partes suas
sine licencia rediissent capi, et statim sine interrogacione suspendi.
Tantus siquidem rigor hodie creuit in rege, ut nullus quantumcunque
magnus et consultus uoluntati regis audeat obuiare. Iccirco parliamenta, tractatus et consilia hiis diebus de nullo decernunt.[c] Nam
proceres regni, minis et penis aliorum interriti,[d] uoluntatem regis
liberis habenis ambulare permittunt. Sic uoluntas hodie uincit
racionem. Nam quicquid regi placuerit, quamuis racione careat,
legis habet uigorem.[482]

---

[a] sic MS; poss. ad He   [b] fugierunt MS; fugerunt He, Den-Y   [c] desernmt MS;
decernunt He, St, Den-Y   [d] interiti MS; interriti He, St, Den-Y

---

[477] Cf. 1 Kgs. (1 Sam.) 15: 33, 17: 48–50, 20: 35–41.
[478] A council was summoned to Winchester for 3 Mar. 1325, but the king remained in
London for most of that month. The council was postponed to 14 Apr. at Westminster,
then on 8 Apr. postponed sine die (PW, ii. 1. 325–6, 328). On 6 May the king summoned a
parliament to meet at Westminster on 25 June (HBC, p. 555).
[479] Edward's wealth is well established. By the end of his reign he had paid off most of
his father's debt and amassed at least £69,000 in cash. The author of the Vita is not the
only chronicler to remark on his wealth, and the author of the Brut called him the richest
king since the Conqueror (Brut, p. 225). For details of his income see Buck, Stapeldon,
pp. 163–96.

that: Saul for the sword, Jonathan for the bow, and David for the 1325
sling.[477] And the king ordered them to advance to the sea with their
leaders, and to remain there until they received further orders. He
also summoned the great men of his kingdom to Winchester, wishing
to arrange the matter of his expedition by common counsel.[478]

Meanwhile the foot soldiers claimed their wages, but they were not
given them, because of which they overran the whole countryside,
plundering the inhabitants for their food. Everyone was amazed that
the king did not pay the infantry, since they could not live properly
without wages, and the king's treasure was abundant enough. For
many of his forebears amassed money, he alone outstripped them
all.[479] However, the king's hardness is blamed on Hugh, like the other
evils that take place at court. Hence many conspired to kill him, but
the plot was discovered, some were captured and the rest fled.[480]

Then the king ordered all the infantry to board the ships and stand
out to sea, until the time should come for crossing to Gascony; and he
put in command of them Earl Warenne, John de St John, and other
great men of the land, who likewise went on board the ships not
daring to resist.[481] The king also sent letters to every county
commanding and ordering that all who had returned from the army
to their homes without leave should be arrested, and hanged forthwith without trial. The king's harshness has indeed increased so
much today that no one, however great and wise, dares to cross the
king's will. Thus parliaments, consultations, and councils decide
nothing these days. For the nobles of the realm, terrified by threats
and the penalties inflicted on others, let the king's will have free rein.
Thus today will conquers reason. For whatever pleases the king,
though lacking in reason, has the force of law.[482]

---

[480] Earlier fears of conspiracy against Despenser are apparent in 1323 when the escaped
Mortimer was accused of encouraging the assassination of the king's counsellors, and when
accusations were made against a group of twenty-seven men for using sorcery to get rid of
the Despensers and the prior of Coventry (*CPR 1321–4*, p. 349; *Select Cases in the Court of
King's Bench*, iv. Selden Society, lxxiv (1955) pp. 154–7).

[481] Warenne contracted to serve in Gascony for six months in Mar. 1325 and was
appointed leader of the expedition on 1 Apr.; he was in Gascony from May to Oct. (*Foed.*,
ii. 1. 591–2, 594, 596; *CP*, xii. 1. 510). John de St John of Basing, king's banneret, was a
loyal supporter of Edward II throughout the reign and went with Warenne to Gascony
(*Foed.*, ii. 1. 592; *CCR 1323–7*, p. 279). After the Gascon campaign, he was entrusted with
organizing the defence of Hampshire against possible invasion in 1326. He left Edward
only after Edward's capture in Nov. 1326 (Phillips, *Pembroke*, p. 314; Maddicott,
Lancaster, p. 299; *CP*, xi. 325–6).

[482] *Inst.* i. 2. 6, *Corpus Iuris Civilis*, i. 1. For the author's views on kingship, see above,
pp. lii–lvii.

1325   Sub ista tempestate, dum rex moraretur Wyntonie,[483] accusatus est
Henricus de Lancastria comes de Leycestria,[484] quod foueret inimicum[a] regis episcopum[b] Herfordie.[485] Wyntoniensem et Lyncolniensem[c] clemencia regis in graciam admisit;[486] Herfordensis uero, quia
ceteris asperior, graciam inuenire non potuit. Scripserat autem
episcopus Herfordie Henrico de Lancastria comiti Leicestrie suppli-
cans quatinus apud regem pro eo uerba faceret, ut eo cicius graciam
regis ipsum promereri contingeret. Et quidem Henricus, prout erat
benignus et compaciens afflictis, huiusmodi uerba fertur rescripsisse:

Salutem in omnium Saluatore et tam infliccionum[d] pacienciam quam in
agone fortiter dimicare. Pater, utinam que pateris sustineas pacienter; omnis
enim cordis aut corporis afflictio premio caret sine paciencie adiuncto.
Paciencia reliquas uirtutes roborat et exornat, nam uidua est uirtus quam[e]
paciencia non firmat. Paciencia uincit maliciam, et si qua uirtus adiungitur
ipsam facit esse perfectam. Porro si legitime contendere[f] speras legitime
certa,[g] oportune inoportune insta,[487] et fiducialiter[h] perseuera. Nam et sacra
scriptura testatur quod licet omnes uirtutes currant ad brauium,[488] sola
perseuerancia coronatur. Spera in Deo et uiriliter age, quoniam, si pro Deo
ascendisti[i] ex aduerso, scito[j] quod non deseret in tempore malo. Deus et
Dominus dominancium, in cuius manu corda sunt regum, et qui procellam
conuertit in auram,[489] prosperum statum tibi restituat et regis mitiget iram.

Huiuscemodi uerbis consolatoriis usus est comes in litteris suis.
Delate sunt littere ad aures regis, quamobrem nitebatur rex arguere
comitem prodicionis. Adiecte sunt et alie cause, quod uidelicet
Henricus, ex gracia regis iam comes Leycestrie, relictis armis
propriis, deferret[k] arma fratris sui comitis Lancastrie; quod uisum

---

[a] inmicum *MS*; inimicum *He, St, Den-Y*   [b] spiritum *R*; episcopum *St, Den-Y*
[c] Wynton' *and* Lyncoln' *R*; Wyntoniensem, Lyncolniensem *He, St, Den-Y*   [d] *sic MS*;
in affliccionibus *or* afflictione *He*   [e] quod *MS*; quam *He, St, Den-Y*   [f] *sic MS*; *poss.*
coronari *He*   [g] circa *MS*; certa *He, St, Den-Y*   [h] fudicialiter *MS*; fiducialiter *He,
St, Den-Y*   [i] *sic MS*; *poss.* contendisti *He*   [j] scuto *MS*; scito *He, St, Den-Y*
[k] defferret *MS*; deferret *He, St, Den-Y*

[483] The king was in or near Winchester on 28 Apr.–9 May. He was also in the area on
4–27 Apr. at Beaulieu (Hants), and on 9–17 May at Porchester (*Itin.*, pp. 270–1).
[484] Henry, Thomas of Lancaster's younger brother and heir, had not taken part in
Thomas's rebellion in 1322. He was restored to the earldom of Leicester, but not to that of
Lancaster, on 29 Mar. 1324 (*HBC*, pp. 468, 469). He was approached by Orleton, who
wished for reconciliation with the king, at the end of April 1325 (Haines, *Orleton*, pp. 108,
152, 226).
[485] The bishop of Hereford, Adam of Orleton, had been strongly suspected by Edward
of connivance with the Mortimers in 1321–2 and was suspected of further complicity in
Mortimer of Wigmore's escape from the Tower on 1 Aug. 1323. He claimed benefit of

About this time, while the king was staying at Winchester,[483] 1325
Henry of Lancaster, earl of Leicester,[484] was accused of supporting
the king's enemy the bishop of Hereford.[485] The king's mercy
admitted the bishops of Winchester and Lincoln to his grace,[486] but
Hereford, more troublesome than the others, could find no favour.
However, the bishop of Hereford had written to Henry of Lancaster,
earl of Leicester, asking him to speak with the king for him, so that he
might more rapidly gain the king's favour. Henry, who was kind and
sympathetic to those in trouble, is said to have written back in these
words:

Greeting in the Saviour of all men, and patience in affliction as well as
strength to strive in suffering. Father, may you bear with patience what you
suffer; for all affliction of heart or body lacks its reward if patience is not
present. Patience strengthens and embellishes the other virtues, for virtue
which is not supported by patience is empty. Patience conquers malice, and
joined to any virtue makes it perfect. Further, if you hope to exert yourself
lawfully, do so, 'be instant in season, out of season',[487] and press on
confidently. For Holy Scripture bears witness that though all virtues run
for the prize,[488] perseverance alone is crowned. Hope in God and act
courageously, since, if you have risen in opposition for God's sake, know
that He will not desert you in the time of evil. May God, the Lord of princes,
in whose hand are the hearts of kings, who turns the storm into a breeze,[489]
restore prosperity to you and mitigate the king's wrath.

The earl used some such words of consolation in his letters. The
letters were reported to the king, who therefore tried to accuse the
earl of treason. Other charges were made, too, namely that Henry,
already by the king's grace earl of Leicester, had ceased to bear his
own arms and adopted the arms of his brother the earl of Lancaster;
which seemed to the king's party an insult to the king, as if the arms

clergy against prosecutions in 1324. His attempts at reconciliation were unsuccessful and
he continued to be suspect to Edward II (Haines, *Orleton*, pp. 108, 143–53).

[486] John Stratford was provided to the bishopric of Winchester in June 1323, when he
was at the Curia with Edward's instructions to seek the bishopric for Robert Baldock.
Edward was furious and kept Stratford from his temporalities, but he was reconciled in
June 1324 when Stratford offered a large fine (N. Fryde, 'John Stratford, bishop of
Winchester, and the Crown, 1323–30', *BIHR*, xlix (1971), pp. 153–61). Edward had fully
supported the provision of Henry Burghersh to the bishopric of Lincoln in May 1320 (see
above, pp. 178–81), but as Badlesmere's nephew Burghersh was tainted by his uncle's
rebellion. Edward tried to have him removed from his bishopric in 1322 and 1323, but the
pope refused without evidence of guilt. Most of his temporalities were restored in 1324,
but some were withheld in a further dispute over appointments in his diocese in 1325
(*Foed.*, ii. 2. 51–2, 60–1, 85; Smith, *Appointments*, pp. 86–94; *CPL 1305–42*, p. 469).

[487] 2 Tim. 4: 2.   [488] Cf. 1 Cor. 9: 24.   [489] Ps. 106 (107): 29.

1325 est regalibus regis iniuria, quasi dampnarentur pariter et arma. Et quia ⟨crucem⟩[a] erexerat extra uillam Leicestrie pro anima fratris sui comitis Lancastrie, quod uisum est regalibus in scandalum regis redundare, quasi dampnato corpore dampnaretur et titulus memorie.

Respondit comes ad litteras, non debere ascribi ad prodicionem uerba consolatoria in quibus nichil machinatum esset in principem. Ad arma respondit dicens se non arma fratris set patris pocius acceptasse, que eciam iure successionis dixit ad se pertinere, maxime cum primogenitus frater eius obiisset sine prole. Allegabat et comes non in scandalum regis crucem erectam, set ob deuocionem plebis pro anima fratris sui spiritualiter excitandam, et quidem pro fideli debet oracio bene fore licita, cum pro Iudeis et hereticis sancta frequenter oret ecclesia.[490]

Hiis tandem pretermissis interrogauit rex prelatos et proceres qui tunc conuenerant, quidnam ipsi de transfretacione sua consulerent. Nolens autem Hugo Despenser filius, propter imminens periculum, quod aliquis transfretandi daret consilium, fertur coram aliquibus arroganter[b] dixisse: 'Iam apparebit quis consulet domino regi ad inimicos suos transfretare; quoniam manifestus proditor est quicunque sit ille.'[491] Auditis eius minis responderunt prelati cum proceribus ad consultacionem domini regis dicentes: 'Domine, constat plures regni magnates absentes esse, unde non expedit nobis in tam arduo negocio sine paribus nostris respondere.'[492]

Tunc decretum est prelatos et regni magnates uniuersos in crastino beati Iohannis baptiste ad parliamentum Londoniis fore conuocandos.[493] Set et comes Leicestrie accepit mandata[c] ad eundem diem uenire finaliter responsurus[d] obiectis.

In crastino natiuitatis beati Iohannis baptiste conuenerunt Londoniis omnes prelati cum proceribus qui tunc erant infra regnum Anglie, consultique super regis transfretacione responderunt, saltem hii quibus

---

    [a] om. MS; supplied He, St, Den-Y   [b] arrogater MS; arroganter He, St, Den-Y
[c] mandatis MS; poss. mandata He; mandata Den-Y   [d] responsis MS; respondere or responsurus He; responsurus St, Den-Y

---

[490] Although Henry's loyalty was sufficient for him to be suggested as guardian for the prince should Edward go abroad in Aug. 1325 (see below, p. 238–9) he continued to be distrusted by Edward and did not receive his brother's full titles and lands until Isabella took over the government. He joined Isabella immediately she invaded in Sept. 1326, was styled earl of Lancaster from Oct. 1326, and was formally restored to the title in Feb. 1327. Nonetheless, in 1328 he rebelled against the new regime and was heavily fined (CP, vii. 396–401; G. A. Holmes, 'The rebellion of the earl of Lancaster, 1328–9', BIHR, xxviii (1955), pp. 84–8).

were condemned equally [with the earl]. And because he had set up [a   1325
cross] outside the town of Leicester for the soul of his brother the earl
of Lancaster, this was regarded by the king's party as an offence to the
king, as if, when his body was condemned, a man's memory should
also be condemned.

As far as the letters went, the earl replied that words of consolation
in which there was no design against the prince should not be
construed as treason. Concerning the arms he replied saying that
he had not taken the arms of his brother but rather of his father,
which he also said belonged to him by right of succession, especially
as his elder brother had died without issue. The earl also maintained
that the cross had not been erected to the dishonour of the king, but
to stir up the spiritual devotion of the populace for his brother's soul,
and indeed prayer ought certainly to be allowed for the faithful, since
Holy Church frequently prays for Jews and heretics.[490]

At length these matters were postponed, and the king asked the
bishops and nobles who had assembled what they advised about his
crossing to France. But Hugh Despenser the son, not wanting anyone
to advise the king to cross, on account of the imminent danger, is said
to have remarked arrogantly to some: 'Now it will become clear who
advises the king to cross over to his enemies; since he is a manifest
traitor whoever he may be.'[491] On hearing these threats the bishops
and nobles answered the lord king's enquiry saying: 'Lord, it is
known that many great men of the realm are absent, and it is not
fitting for us to give answer in so difficult a matter without our
peers.'[492]

Then it was decided that all the bishops and great men of the realm
should be summoned to parliament at London for the day after the
blessed John the Baptist.[493] And the earl of Leicester received orders
to come the same day to give a final answer to the charges against him.

On the day after the nativity of the blessed John the Baptist all the
prelates with the great men who were then in the kingdom of England
met in London, and having been consulted about the king's crossing

---

[491] Despenser may have had in mind not only his own safety, but also the safety of the
realm: there were rumours of a French invasion and the lack of a firm peace with Scotland
(Buck, *Stapeldon*, pp. 150 n. 155, 154 n. 182).

[492] Despite this evasive answer, the lords temporal and spiritual had already advised the
king before 13 June that the arrangements for homage were in principle acceptable
(Chaplais, *Saint-Sardos*, pp. 277–8).

[493] That is 25 June 1325. Parliament (without commons) had been summoned on 6 May
to meet at Westminster on that date (*HBC*, p. 555).

1325 ceteri non ualebant contradicere, oportere dominum regem omni modo
transfretare, nec posse eos sine lesione consciencie et fidei in aliud
consentire. *"Quid nunc* si rex non ierit? Rex Francie totam Vasconiam
statim occupabit, et rex noster alias, uel forsan filius eius cum ipsum
regnare contigerit, prodicionis et merito nos omnes accusabit.

Huiusmodi responso[^b] communiter prolato rex ad alios se conuertit,
et, amoto Exoniensi episcopo ab officio thesaurarii, archiepiscopum
Eboracensem eidem substituit. Erat enim Exoniensis ultra modum
cupidus, et durante officio suo uehementer diues effectus, unde
uidebatur tam regi quam populo terre concussione[^c] magis quam
fideli commercio tanta copia uiro prouenisse.[494] Iccirco amouit eum
rex a potestate, ut, si contigisset eum aliquos lesisse, necesse haberet
querelantibus respondere; et quidem bonum commune foret et
consonum iuri, ut tanta potestate predicti[^d] annales fierent, ut qui
tempore officii conueniri non possunt, saltem post annum iudicio
starent, et non diutina uexacione subiectos opprimerent.[495] Eboracensis iste, Willelmus nomine, olim curialis in omni commisso fidelis
extitit, et, quamuis inter curiales diu conuersatus, mores tamen a
conuictu non traxit, set, obuiata Anglorum cupiditate, per Dei
graciam impolutus[^e] semper permansit.[496] Sane est uberioris gracie,
inter malos bene uiuere: sic Iosep in Egipto,[497] Clusi cum Absolon,[498]
et Daniel innocenter uixit Babilone.[499]

Audiens archipresul Cantuariensis quod rex Eboracensem gazis
suis uellet preponere, respondit nequaquam sic fieri posse sine
preiudicio Cantuariensis ecclesie; crucem suam deferri[^f] faceret
quocunque rex diuerteret per totam Angliam [^g]'quod quidem[^g] ego',
inquid, 'sana consciencia sustinere non possem. Mota est enim illa
inueterata discencio[^h] super dilacionem[^i] crucis inter utramque

---

[^a-a] *sic MS*; quod nunc *He, St*; quid enim *Den-Y*   [^b] responsio *MS*; responso *He, St,*
Den-Y   [^c] cancassiome *MS*; concussione *He, St, Den-Y*   [^d] prediti *R*; predicti *St,*
Den-Y   [^e] *sic MS*; impollutus *St, Den-Y*   [^f] differri *MS*; deferri *He, St, Den-Y*
[^g] quia quod *R*; quod quidem *St, Den-Y*   [^h] *sic MS*; dissencio *He*; dissensio *St, Den-Y*
[^i] *sic MS*; delacionem *He, St, Den-Y*

[494] Walter Stapledon, bishop of Exeter 1308–26, was dismissed and William Melton,
archbishop of York 1316–40, took over on 3 July 1325. Stapledon had been treasurer from
1320–1 and again from 1322 until this dismissal (*HBC*, pp. 105, 246). He was strongly
associated with Edward's successful Exchequer reforms and money raising, and was very
unpopular for alleged heavy exactions, but his guilt in this is not manifest (Buck,
Stapeldon, pp. 155, 197). Following Isabella's invasion, he was murdered 15 Oct. 1326
in London, where he was particularly unpopular (*Ann. Paul.*, pp. 315–16, 345–6, 350;
Buck, *Stapeldon*, pp. 210–15, 220–1).
[495] The author's liking for annual appointments shows a more radical viewpoint than

they replied, or at least those whom the others did not have the power 1325
to contradict, that by all means the lord king should go, and that they
could not agree to anything else without injury to their conscience
and loyalty. For what if the king should not go? The king of France
will at once seize the whole of Gascony, and at another time our king,
or perhaps his son when he comes to the throne, will accuse us all and
rightly of treason.

When this answer had been given by all together, the king turned
to other matters, and having removed the bishop of Exeter from the
office of treasurer, he appointed the archbishop of York in his place.
For Exeter was greedy beyond measure, and during his term of office
had become extremely rich, whence it seemed to the king and the
people of the land alike that he had made such wealth by extortion
rather than by honest dealing.[494] Therefore the king removed him
from power, so that if he had harmed anyone he should have to
answer to the plaintiffs; and indeed it would be to the common
advantage and consonant with right, if offices of such great authority
were made annual, so that those who could not be summoned during
their period of office should at least stand to judgment after a year,
and not oppress those beneath them with long-drawn-out hardship.[495] The archbishop of York, William by name, was formerly a
courtier faithful in everything committed to him, and, although he
has dwelt a long time among courtiers, he has nevertheless not
absorbed their habits by living with them, but, resisting the greed
of the English, by the grace of God has always remained unconta-
minated.[496] It is truly a mark of more abundant grace to live well
among the wicked: thus Joseph lived innocently in Egypt,[497] Chusai
with Absalom,[498] and Daniel in Babylon.[499]

When the archbishop of Canterbury heard that the king proposed
to set the archbishop of York over his treasure, he replied that this
could in no way be done without prejudice to the church of Canterbury; he [York] would have his cross borne before him wherever the
king went throughout England, 'and this', he said, 'I could not
tolerate with a clear conscience. For that age-old dispute about the

that of most reformers, who simply wanted a check on suitable appointments (see
Ordinances caps. 14–17). For the author's support for the radical purges in 1318, see
above, pp. 156–9.
[496] William Melton remained treasurer until 14 Nov. 1326 when John Stratford, bishop
of Winchester 1323–33, took over for Isabella (HBC, p. 105).
[497] Cf. Gen. 39: 1–50: 26.
[498] Cf. 2 Kgs. (2 Sam.) 15: 32–37, 16: 16–18, 17: 6–16.
[499] Cf. Dan. 1: 6–16, 6: 3–4, 23.

1325 ecclesiam, pro qua sanctus Thomas certauit usque ad mortem; a cuius
diebus nullus archipresul Eboracensis per Cantuariensem prouinciam
hactenus crucem detulit, nisi forsan in stipite^a elacionis, aliquorum
magnatum auxilio suffultus, hoc presumpserit, uel nunc saltem in
parliamentis, quod, ne per dissencionem priuatorum impederetur^b
utilitas communis, hoc permittendum racio persuasit.' Paruipendebat
rex allegata ab archipresule, protestans se ob delacionem crucis uel ob
aliud cuiuscumque^c priuilegium necessarium ministrum nolle dimittere.^{500}

Comes Leicestrie in parliamento presens affuit, set de sibi prius
obiectis nichil audiuit, et forsan eo quod ceteris illustrior, filio domini
regis, patre^d transfretante, regno preposito uidebatur necessarius.^{e}
Nam licet Hugo Despenser, comes Wyntoniensis, cunctis prudencior
et magis expertus tanto negocio foret preponendus, omnibus tamen
incolis et ipsi filio regis habebatur exosus. Rex igitur iuxta consilium
magnatum transfretare disposuit, et iussit necessaria preparari.^{501}
Displicuit rex Hugoni Despenser, tam patri quam filio; sciebant
enim quod abeunte rege nescirent locum quo possent iuiere tuti.

Circa idem tempus bone memorie Norwycensis episcopus, pro
negociis regis ad transmarinas partes destinatus, in redeundo diem
clausit extremum;^{502} statimque misit rex ad Norwicense capitulum
uolens eos eligere Robertum de Baldok cancellarium suum. Monachi
uero non audentes regi displicere direxerunt uota sua in uirum
uoluntatis regie.^{503} Erat autem tunc temporis quidam clericus Willelmus Ermynne dictus, uir prudens et circumspectus et, precipue in
hiis que tangunt cancellariam domini regis, efficax et expertus. ^{f}Ipse
unus ex hiis transfretauerat cum regina.^{f} Optinuit ut et rex Francie
pariter et regina supplicarent domino pape pro promocione sua.

---

^{a} sic R; poss. for spiritu. This phrase is noted, with this possible meaning, in Revised
Medieval Latin Word-list, ed. R. A. Latham (London, 1965), p. 453. ^{b} sic MS;
impediretur He, St, Den-Y ^{c} sic R; cuiuscunque St, Den-Y ^{d} fratre R; patre
Den-Y ^{e} necessariis MS; necessarius He, St, Den-Y $^{f-f}$ sic R; perhaps . . . ex hiis
⟨qui⟩ transfretauera⟨n⟩t cum regina MW

^{500} The clash of jurisdictions between Canterbury and York stretched back to the reign
of William the Conqueror. York had won its independence, but both archbishops remained
sensitive to the privileges of their sees (see R. M. T. Hill and C. N. L. Brooke, 'From 627
until the early thirteenth century', in Aylmer and Cant, York Minster, pp. 31–4, 38–40).
^{501} For Edward's preparations from June to Aug, see Foed. ii. 1. 601–6.
^{502} John Salmon, bishop of Norwich 1299–1325, died on 6 July. He was on his way
home from France, where he had been negotiating alongside the queen, the earl of
Richmond, and William Ayrmin (HBC, p. 261; Foed., ii. 1. 579, 595, 597; CPR 1324–7,
p. 162).

bearing of the cross has been a cause of disturbance between the two ₁₃₂₅ churches; for this St Thomas strove until his death; and from his lifetime until now no archbishop of York has borne his cross in the province of Canterbury, unless perhaps he has presumed to do this in a spirit of arrogance, upheld by the support of some great men, or except now in parliaments, as is only reasonable lest the common good should be hindered by private quarrels.' The king took little notice of the archbishop's arguments, protesting that he would not dismiss any necessary official on account of bearing the cross or any other privilege whatsoever.[500]

The earl of Leicester was present in parliament, but he heard nothing of the former charges against him, and perhaps because he was of better blood than the others, his presence was considered essential to the lord king's son who would be in charge of the kingdom while his father was abroad. For though Hugh Despenser, earl of Winchester, shrewder than all and more experienced, had to be put in charge of such a business, yet he was hated by everyone and even by the king's son. The king therefore, according to the advice of the great men, made arrangements to cross the channel and gave orders for the necessary preparations.[501] This displeased Hugh Despenser, both the father and son; for they realized that with the king away they would not know where to live safely.

About the same time the bishop of Norwich of happy memory, who had been sent abroad on the king's business, died on the way home;[502] and the king at once sent to the chapter of Norwich, wanting them to elect Robert Baldock his chancellor. The monks not daring in truth to displease the king gave their votes for the royal candidate.[503] There was, however, then at the time a certain clerk, called William Ayrmin, a knowledgeable and informed man, and efficient and experienced especially in matters relating to the lord king's chancery. He was one of those who had gone abroad with the queen. He contrived that the king of France and the queen likewise should

[503] Robert Baldock, archdeacon of Middlesex, canon of St Paul's, was elected on 23 July 1325, given his temporalities on 12 Aug., but had to resign on 3 Sept. as the pope had already provided Ayrmin on 19 July. Baldock was a royal clerk, whom the king had already tried to have promoted to Winchester in 1323. He was keeper of the privy seal and controller of the wardrobe 1320–3, and chancellor 1323–6. He was closely associated with the Despensers and Stapledon, was captured with the king in 1326, and taken to Hereford. He was claimed as a cleric by the bishop of Hereford, but was later seized from Hereford's London house by the mob and put into Newgate, where he died 28 May 1327 (*HBC*, pp. 86, 93, 261–2; Tout, *Ed. II*, p. 316; Smith, *Episcopal Appointments*, pp. 39–41, 41–5; *Ann. Paul.*, pp. 320–1; Emden, *BRUO*, i. 96–8).

1325 Dominus uero papa nouit eum ex nomine, eo quod iam pridem
electus in episcopum Karlionensis^a ecclesie cessit iuri suo ad
mandatum domini pape. Vnde tum propter bonum obediencie,
tum^b propter preces regis Francie et sororis sue, consecrauit eum
dominus papa in episcopum Norwicensis ecclesie,[504] et sic supplan-
tatus est Robertus de Baldok en altera uice.

Veniens itaque rex ad mare, et quasi paratus nauem ascendere,
nuncios regis Francie in ipso portu maris obuios habuit; quelibet noua
optata protinus accepit. Nam rex Francie, multis precibus et arduis
negociis regem Anglie tangentibus allegatis inductus, hoc indulsit, ut,
si rex Anglie filium suum primogenitum transmitteret,^{c} idem filius ad
ducatum Vasconie eisdem condicionibus admitteretur, quibus et rex
pater eius si ueniret. Placuit regi et regis consilio conferre filio
Vasconiam,[505] et statim puer ad iussum patris nauigauit in Franciam.[506] Admisit eum benigne auunculus eius rex Francie. Admisit et
homagium ipsius pro terra Vasconie, set non permisit ei possessionem
nisi pro parte. Decreuit enim rex Francie partem quam ui occupauerat non debere restitui, nisi ^{d}satisfaccio ⟨fieret⟩^{d} sibi pro sumptibus quos fecerat occasione homagii retardati.[507]

Exoniensis unus erat ex illis qui uenerant cum filio. Curiales uero
Francorum ipsum quasi alicuius sceleris notatum respiciebant pre
ceteris. Ipse uero nichil sibi conscius uel ad uultus^e eorum caute
premunitus, familiares suos ibidem relinquens qui presenciam suam
fingerent, clam fugam iniit, clam de nocte mutata ueste usus
duplomate ad mare deuenit, et quasi mercator uel peregrinus
nauem conscendens in Angliam rediit; et ita si quid in eum
machinatum exstitit, prudenter euasit. Igitur si periculosa fuit ei
legacio sua, uideat ne uideatur iterum in Francia.[508] Quatuor sunt
quippe persone de maioribus Anglie, Exoniensis episcopus nuper

---

^{a} Karlionencis *MS*; Karliolensis *He*; Karlionensis *St, Den-Y* ^{b} tamen *MS*; tum *He, St,
Den-Y* ^{c} transmittet *MS*; transmitteret *He, St, Den-Y* $^{d-d}$ satisfaccio *MS*; *poss.* fieret *to
be understood He*; satisfacto *St, Den-Y* ^{e} adultus *MS*; ad uultus *He, St, Den-Y*

---

[504] William Ayrmin was provided to the bishopric of Norwich on 19 July 1325. The
pope appears to have thought he was acting in Edward's interests by appointing Ayrmin,
whom Edward had formerly supported for the bishopric of Carlisle in Jan. 1325, but
Edward now refused Ayrmin his temporalities, which he received only in Feb. 1327 (J. L.
Grassi, 'William Airmyn and the bishopric of Norwich', *EHR*, lxx (1955), 550–61).

[505] Edward postponed his passage again on 24 Aug., claiming illness. The possibility of
Prince Edward going to France had been raised in Nov. 1324 but not followed up. Prince
Edward was granted Ponthieu on 2 Sept. and Aquitaine on 10 Sept. 1325, on which day
Edward II wrote to inform Charles IV (*Foed.*, ii. 1. 606–8; Chaplais, *Saint-Sardos*, pp. 193–
4, 241).

petition the lord pope for his promotion. The lord pope indeed knew ⟨1325⟩ him by name, because already as bishop-elect of the church of Carlisle he had waived his right at the lord pope's command. Hence as much on account of the value of his obedience as on account of the prayers of the king of France and his sister, the lord pope consecrated him bishop of the church of Norwich,[504] and so Robert Baldock was displaced yet again.

When the king reached the coast and was nearly ready to take ship, he met messengers of the king of France at the sea port itself; he immediately accepted certain new agreeable proposals. For the king of France, persuaded by many entreaties and the weighty matters in which the king of England was said to be involved, allowed him this, that if the king of England would send over his eldest son, that same son should be admitted to the duchy of Gascony on the same conditions as the king his father if he had come. The king and the king's council agreed to grant Gascony to his son,[505] and by his father's orders the boy at once sailed for France.[506] His uncle, the king of France, received him kindly. He also accepted his homage for the land of Gascony, but allowed him only partial possession of it. For the king of France decided that the part which he had seized by force ought not to be restored, until he had been given satisfaction for the expenses that he had incurred by reason of the delayed homage.[507]

The bishop of Exeter was one of those who had come with the son. The French court officials regarded him more than the others as if he were guilty of some crime. He, either in truth with a clear conscience or providently forewarned by their grim looks, leaving behind his household to pretend that he was there, secretly fled and, having changed his clothes and travelling post-haste, came secretly to the coast by night, and embarking on board a ship as a merchant or pilgrim, returned to England; and so if anything had been plotted against him, with foresight he escaped. Therefore if his embassy was dangerous to him, he should see that he is not seen again in France.[508] There are indeed four greater persons among the men of England, the

---

[506] Prince Edward left on 12 Sept. 1325 (*Foed.*, ii. 1. 609).

[507] Prince Edward arrived in Paris on 22 Sept. and did homage on 24 Sept. 1325 (Chaplais, *Saint-Sardos*, pp. 241–5, 269). Charles's delay in returning the occupied lands led to renewed war with Edward II in 1326 and the matter was not settled until Edward III's treaty of 31 Mar. 1327 (Chaplais, 'Duché-Pairie', p. 157).

[508] Stapledon was present at Vincennes for the ceremony of homage on 24 Sept. and back in England by 29 Sept. (Buck, *Stapeldon*, p. 157). This passage was without doubt written before Stapledon's murder on 15 Oct. 1326.

1325 thesaurarius, Robertus de Baldoke nunc cancellarius, Hugo Despenser pater et filius, qui si reperirentur infra regnum Francie, non carerent utique mala mansione.[509] Asseritur enim quod de consilio Exoniensis predia regine capta erant in manu domini regis, et ipsa destituta Francis*a* familiaribus suis. Robertus de Baldoke fautor erat in nece procerum. Nimirum si exosus habeatur*b* parentibus eorum, quorum licet multi sunt in Anglia, quidam tamen eorum dominantur in Francia, et quidam ualentes exulant; omnes autem et singuli tempus ulcionis exspectant. Set quicquid in aliis arguitur, Hugoni Despenser tam patri quam filio pre ceteris imputatur.

Inter alia, cum mitteret rex filium suum in Franciam, mandauit uxori sue quod sine dilacione rediret in Angliam.[510] Quo quidem mandato tam regi Francie quam ipsi regine per nuncios exposito, respondit regina, 'Ego,' inquid, 'senciens, quod matrimonium sit*c* uiri*d* et mulieris coniunccio, indiuiduam uite consuetudinem*e* retinens, mediumque esse qui inter maritum meum et me huiusmodi uinculum nititur diuidere; protestor me nolle redire donec auferatur medius ille, set, exuta ueste nupciali,*f* uiduitatis et luctus uestes assumam donec de huiusmodi Phariseo uiderim ulcionem.' Set et rex Francie ne uideretur eam detinere respondit: 'Regina,' inquid, 'libere uenit, libere redeat si uoluerit. Sin autem maluerit in hiis partibus remanere, soror mea est, nolo eam expellere.' Reuersi sunt nuncii et narrauerunt hec omnia regi.

Tunc rex, conuocatis apud Westmonasterium prelatis et proceribus terre,[511] sic cepit prius acta breui sermone referre. 'Nostis,' inquid, 'omnes dissencionem et causas, inter regem Francie et nos pro terra Wasconie dudum exortas, et quomodo satis prouide, ut tunc uisum erat, pro formanda concordia regina transfretauit, habuitque in mandatis facta legacione sua statim rediisse. Quod et ipsa repromisit bona uoluntate. Nulli quoque in recessu suo uidebatur offensa. Licenciata enim omnes salutauit, et abiit iocosa. Nunc autem nescio quis animum eius immutauit; nescio quis in aduencionibus*g* ipsam

---

a Fancis *MS*; Francis *He, St, Den-Y*   *b* sic *MS*; *poss.* habebantur *He*   *c* sicut *R*; sit *St, Den-Y*   *d* uir *MS*; uiri *He, St, Den-Y*   *e* consuetudine *MS*; consuetudinem *He, St, Den-Y*   *f* *from this point we are reliant on Hearne's printed text only,* ed.   *g* sic *R*; adinuencionibus *Den-Y*

---

[509] *Mala mansio* was a punishment in which the captive was stretched out and tied fast to a board, *Dig.* xvi. 3. 7, xlvii. 10. 15, *Corpus Iuris Civilis*, i. 211, 783.

[510] When he had accompanied Prince Edward on 12 Sept. 1325, Stapledon had been authorized to pay the queen's expenses for her journey home. Clearly Edward II expected

bishop of Exeter lately treasurer, Robert Baldock now chancellor, the 1325 Despensers, father and son, who if they are found within the kingdom of France will certainly not lack bad quarters.[509] For it is declared that the queen's lands were taken into the lord king's hands and she herself deprived of her French servants by the bishop of Exeter's advice. Robert Baldock furthered the destruction of great men. It is not surprising that he is hated by their kinsmen, of whom, though there are many in England, some nevertheless are in power in France, and some thrive in exile; however, one and all await the day of vengeance. But whatever may be alleged about the others, the Despensers, father and son, are held guilty beyond the rest.

Amongst other things, when the king sent his son to France, he ordered his wife to return to England without delay.[510] When this command had been explained to the king of France and to the queen herself by the messengers, the queen replied, 'I feel', she said, 'that marriage is a union of a man and a woman, holding fast to the practice of a life together, and that someone has come between my husband and myself and is trying to break this bond; I declare that I will not return until this intruder is removed, but, discarding my marriage garment, shall put on the robes of widowhood and mourning until I am avenged of this Pharisee.' And the king of France, not wishing to seem to detain her, replied, 'The queen', he said, 'has come of her own free will, she may freely return if she wishes. But if she prefers to remain in these parts, she is my sister, I will not expel her.' The messengers returned and reported all this to the king.

Then the king having summoned the prelates and great men of the land to Westminster,[511] began thus to relate what had happened in a short speech. 'You know', he said, 'all the long-standing disputes and processes between the king of France and us over the land of Gascony, and how, wisely enough as it seemed at the time, the queen crossed to France to make peace, and she had instructions to return at once when her mission was accomplished. And she promised this with a good will. And on her departure she did not seem to anyone to be offended. For as she took her leave she bade farewell to everyone and went away joyfully. But now someone has changed her mind; someone has filled her with extraordinary stories.

her to return then and he may have sent specific instructions. The king demanded their return in letters to Isabella and Edward dated 1 and 2 Dec. 1325.

[511] Parliament (with commons) was summoned for 18 Nov. 1325 at Westminster; it lasted until 5 Dec. 1325 (*HBC*, p. 555).

1325 instruxit. Noui enim quod ex proprio capite nullam confinxit offensam, tametsi*a* dicit Hugonem Despenser aduersarium et inimicum esse.' Subiungit et hoc: 'Mirum unde contra Hugonem rancorem conceperit, que cum recederet nulli alii me excepto tam se iocundam exhibuit. Quamobrem Hugo tristis effectus est ualde; uerumtamen innocenciam suam paratus est quomodolibet ostendere. Vnde constanter credo reginam in huiusmodi errorem ad suggestionem alicuius inductam esse, et reuera malignus et inimicus est homo quicunque sit ille.[512] Nunc igitur sapienter consulite,*b* ut quam doctrina malorum in uersuciam instruit et instigat, uestra prudens et blanda corepcio*c* ad debitam unitatem inuitet*d* et reducat.' Tunc de consilio regis ordinatum est quod omnes episcopi regine scriberent, et singulas litteras sub eodem tenore uerborum eidem destinarent, quibus eam tanquam filiam carissimam ad uirum suum redire monerent,*e* rancorem sine causa conceptum dimittere, et Hugonem Despenser pariter excusarent. Singularum uero litterarum communis et unus tenor talis erat:[513]

Carissima et prepotens domina mea, de nouis et responsis tuis ad dominum nostrum regem a te nuper transmissis, turbatur tota patria; et ex eo quod in odium Hugonis Despenser differs reditum tuum, multa mala presagiunt omnes in futurum. Porro Hugo Despenser coram omnibus innocenciam suam solempniter ostendit, et se regine nunquam nocuisse, set omne commodum eius pro posse procurasse, et hoc semper inposterum se facturum fore corporali sacramento firmauit. Addidit quoque se non posse credere huiusmodi minas ex solo capite tuo*f* unquam prodiisse, set aliunde forsan procuratas esse, maxime cum ante recessum tuum*g* et in ipso recessu hillarem sibi faciem ostenderis, et litteras amicabiles postea ei transmiseris, quas in pleno parliamento in argumentum fidei protulit coram multis. Quamobrem, carissima, rogo te tanquam dominam, moneo te tanquam filiam, quatinus ad dominum nostrum regem, uirum tuum, redeas, rancorem dimittas, et que pro bono pacis abieras*h* pro bona pace redire non differas.*i* Timent enim habitatores terre nostre, eo quod redire negasti, multa mala contingere. Timent alienigenarum aduentum et

a tamen se *MS*; tametsi *or* tamen sibi *He*; tametsi *Den-Y*   *b* consulitur *R*; consulite *St, Den-Y*   *c* sic *MS*; correpcio *He, St, Den-Y*   *d* mitem *R*; inuitet *St, Den-Y*   *e* mouerent *R*; monerent *MW*   *f* suo *MS*; tuo *He, St, Den-Y*   *g* suum *MS*; tuum *He, St, Den-Y*   *h* adhibeas *R*; abieras *St, Den-Y*   *i* disperas *MS*; desperes *He*; differas *St, Den-Y*

[512] Edward explicitly named Mortimer as Isabella's counsellor only on 8 Feb. 1326, and on 18 Mar. urged his son to leave Isabella and Mortimer and return home. In June 1326 he wrote to the French peers and others asking them to urge the king of France to send Isabella and Edward home (*CCR 1323–27*, pp. 543, 576–9, 581–2). Isabella's most recent

For I know that she has not invented any affront out of her own head, 1325 although she says that Hugh Despenser is her adversary and enemy.' And he added this: 'It is surprising that she has conceived this grudge against Hugh, for when she left, towards no one was she more agreeable, myself excepted. For this reason Hugh has been made very unhappy; but he is nevertheless prepared to prove his innocence in any way whatsoever. Hence I firmly believe that the queen has been led into this error at the suggestion of someone else and, in truth, whoever he may be he is a man who is wicked and an enemy.[512] Now therefore deliberate wisely so that she, whom the teaching of evil men directs and incites to deceit, may be urged and brought back to rightful harmony by your sensible and kindly reproof.' Then it was ordained by the king's council that all the bishops should write to the queen, and that they should each send letters to her in the same words, by which they might persuade her as their dearest daughter to return to her husband, to put aside her baseless ill-feeling, and at the same time they might excuse Hugh Despenser. The one text common to all the letters was as follows:[513]

My most dear and powerful lady, the whole country is disturbed by your news and the answers which you have lately sent to our lord king; and because you delay your return out of hatred for Hugh Despenser everyone predicts much evil for the future. But Hugh Despenser has formally demonstrated his innocence before all, and that he has never harmed the queen, but done everything in his power to help her; and he has confirmed by his corporal oath that he will always in future do this. He added moreover that he could not believe that these threats ever came from your head alone, but that they were provided from some other source, especially as, before your departure and during it, you showed him a gracious countenance, and afterwards sent him friendly letters, which he produced in full parliament before many people as evidence of his loyalty. Wherefore, dearest lady, I beseech you as my lady, I warn you as a daughter, to return to our lord king, your husband, to put aside resentment, and, since you went away for the sake of peace, do not, for the sake of peace, put off your return. For the people living in our land fear that many evils will occur, because you refuse to return. They fear the arrival of foreigners and the plunder of their goods;

biographer shows that there is little evidence that she had any close relationship with Mortimer before she arrived in France in 1325, although she knew Mortimer and his family throughout the reign and her sympathy for his position may have increased after 1322–3 (Doherty, *Isabella*, pp. 81, 84–5, 86–8).

[513] The tone of these letters is very similar to those which the king sent to Isabella and Edward on 1–2 Dec., and it is likely that they were written at about the same time (*CCR 1323–27*, p. 580).

1325 depredacionem bonorum suorum; nec reputant ex debita affeccione proue-
nire, odio unius hominis, populum tam tibi deuotum uelle destruere. Quod
autem scripsistis, ea que frater tuus rex Francie et alii amici tui eiusdem
patrie pro uoto suo facere intendunt, non in preiudicium domini regis nec
alicuius alterius, set in exterminium solius Hugonis redundabunt, Carissima
et potentissima domina, noli tali negocio inicium prebere, cuius progressus
dampnum irrecuperabile uerisimiliter posset afferre. Presagit enim populus
Anglicanus ex huiusmodi minis aduentum alienorum, et dicit, si Franci
ueniant terram utique spoliabunt. Impossibile quin*a* tam insontes quam
sontes communiter dampna sustineant, et que non rapuerunt innoxii tunc
exsoluent. Heu quam sperabamus habuisse et patronam, si sic eueniant,
continget nos, proh dolor! sentire nouercam. Heu! querula uoce clerus et
populus frequenter ingeminat, timentes ne odio unius hominis se et sua
penitus exterminari contingat. Quocirca, domina regina, utere sano consilio,
et ad maritum tuum redire non differas. Nam desideratus aduentus tuus
malicias hominum refrenabit et occaciones mali sedabit uniuersas.

Set mater et filius huiusmodi litteris non obstantibus ad Angliam
redire noluerunt.

---

a qui *MS*; quin *He, St, Den-Y*

they do not believe that it stems from the goodwill that is due to them, that 1325
you wish to destroy a people so devoted to you for the hatred of one man. But
as for what you have written, that what your brother the king of France and
your other friends of that country intend to do on your behalf will turn out
not to the prejudice of the lord king or anyone else, but to the destruction of
Hugh alone, dearest and most powerful lady, refuse to give an opening to
such an undertaking, as its furthering can in all probability bring irreparable
loss. The English people has a foreboding from these threats that foreigners
will come, and says that, if the French come, they will plunder the land. It is
impossible that the innocent should not suffer equally with the guilty, and
the innocent who have stolen nothing will then pay the debt. Alas! if things
turn out like this, it may happen, oh! what grief! that we shall perceive as a
stepmother her whom we hoped to have as a protector. Alas! clergy and
people with a voice of complaint often repeat their fear, that they and theirs
will be utterly destroyed through the hatred felt for one man. Wherefore, my
lady queen, accept wise counsel, and do not delay your return to your
husband. For your longed-for arrival will restrain men's ill-will and check all
opportunities for evil.

But notwithstanding these letters mother and son refused to return
to England.

CONCORDANCE

In this concordance the page in the present edition and the page in the edition by W. Stubbs are those on which will be found the first word of each page of Latin text in the edition by N. Denholm-Young.

Den-Y	St.	This edition	Den-Y	St.	This edition
1	155	4	34	186	58
2	156	4	35	187	60
3	157	6	36	188	62
4	157	8	37	188	62
5	158	10	38	189	64
6	159	12	39	190	66
7	160	14	40	191	68
8	161	16	41	192	70
9	162	18	42	193	72
10	163	18	43	194	74
11	164	20	44	195	74
12	165	22	45	196	76
13	166	24	46	197	78
14	167	26	47	198	80
15	168	28	48	199	82
16	169	28	49	200	84
17	170	30	50	201	86
18	171	32	51	202	88
19	171	34	52	203	90
20	173	36	53	204	90
21	174	36	54	205	92
22	175	38	55	205	94
23	175	40	56	206	96
24	176	42	57	207	98
25	177	44	58	208	100
26	178	44	59	209	102
27	179	46	60	210	104
28	180	48	61	211	104
29	181	50	62	211	106
30	182	52	63	212	108
31	183	54	64	213	110
32	184	56	65	214	112
33	185	56	66	215	114

Den-Y	St.	This edition	Den-Y	St.	This edition
67	216	116	107	253	182
68	217	116	108	254	182
69	218	118	109	255	184
70	219	120	110	256	186
71	220	122	111	257	188
72	221	124	112	258	190
73	221	124	113	259	192
74	222	126	114	260	194
75	223	128	115	260	194
76	224	130	116	261	196
77	225	132	117	262	198
78	226	134	118	263	200
79	227	134	119	264	202
80	228	136	120	265	202
81	229	138	121	266	204
82	230	140	122	267	206
83	231	142	123	267	208
84	232	144	124	268	210
85	233	146	125	269	212
86	234	146	126	270	212
87	235	148	127	271	214
88	236	150	128	272	216
89	237	152	129	273	218
90	237	154	130	274	220
91	238	156	131	275	220
92	239	158	132	276	222
93	240	158	133	277	224
94	241	160	134	278	226
95	242	162	135	279	228
96	243	164	136	279	230
97	244	166	137	280	232
98	245	168	138	281	234
99	246	168	139	282	236
100	247	170	140	283	236
101	247	172	141	284	238
102	248	174	142	285	240
103	249	174	143	286	242
104	250	176	144	287	244
105	251	178	145	288	246
106	252	180			

INDEX OF QUOTATIONS AND ALLUSIONS

A. THE BIBLE

	Den-Y	This edn.
Old Testament		
Genesis		
19: 31	1	1–2
39: 1–50: 26	139	236–7
47: 20–22	41	70–1
47: 26	41, 77	70–1, 132–3
49: 7	43	74–5
Exodus		
1: 22	111	190–1
4: 10, 13	107	182–3
14: 28	111	190–1
21: 17	26, 86	46–7, 148–9
22: 28	86	148–9
Numbers		
1: 47–53	77	132–3
3: 5–10, 32	77	132–3
16: 46, 48	78	134–5
18: 2–3	77	132–3
Deuteronomy		
20: 10–12	34, 93	58–9, 160–1
32: 37	27	46–7
Joshua		
6: 20	78	134–5
9: 3–27	134	228–9
Judges		
1: 6–7	127	214–5
16: 16–21	126	214–5
20: 21–25	56	90–1
1 Kings (1 Samuel)		
2: 25	84	144–5
5: 2	107	182–3
15: 3, 9–11, 15–23	115	196–7
15: 33	135	230–1
17: 48–50	135	230–1
18: 1–4	15	28–9
19: 1–7	15	28–9
19: 1–2, 11–12	97	166–7
20: 1–42	15	28–9
20: 31	66	116–7
20: 35–41	135	230–1
21: 10	76	130–1

GENERAL INDEX

John XXII, pope (1316–34) 136–7,
    238–41
John of Brittany, *see* Brittany, John of
John of Salisbury xxviii, lii, 49 n. 93, 56
    n. 103
John of Wales xxviii
Jonathan, son of King Saul 28–9, 52–3,
    230–1
Joseph, son of Jacob 236–7
Judah 214–15
Julius Caesar xxx, 138–9
Jupiter 122–3
justice, criticism of xlii, 110–11, 156–9,
    170–1, *see also* Despenser, Hugh
    the elder, as forester; law

Kenilworth (Warwickshire), castle of
    208–9
Kent, earl of, *see* Woodstock, Edmund of
kingship xliii, lii–iii,
    king's power 38–9
    king's power to revoke 60–1, 64–5
    king's prerogative 58–61
    king's prerogative in Wales 184–5
    king's will as law 230–1
    threats to royal power 18–21, 58–9,
        60–1, 186–7, 192–3
    treatise on, presented to king's confessor
        128–31
    see also coronation oath; fealty;
        resistance; restraint; treason;
        tyranny
Kingston-on-Thames (Surrey) 198 n. 405
King's Langley (Hertfordshire) xlii,
    16–17, 100–3
Knaresborough (Yorkshire) 42–3, 154
    n. 301

Lacy, Alice, d. of Henry Lacy, wife of
    Thomas of Lancaster 5 n. 4, 50–1
    abduction of 138–9, 146–7, 150–1
Lacy, Henry, earl of Lincoln (1272–1311)
    xl, 4–5, 10–11, 14–15, 20–1, 50–1,
    108–9
Lancaster, Edmund of, earl of Lancaster
    (1267–96) 50–1, 140 n. 273
Lancaster, Henry of, earl of Leicester
    (1324–45), earl of Lancaster
    (1326–45) xxiii, xlviii, 118–19,
    232–5, 238–9
Lancaster, Thomas of, earl of Lancaster
    (1298–22)
    xv, xvii, xx, xxii, xxiv, xxvi, xxxii,

xxxiv–v, xxxix–xlvi, lvii, lx, 40–3,
    48–51, 56–61, 72–3, 98–9, 150–1,
    208–15, 234–5
author's laments on xlv, xlviii, l–li,
    168–71, 214–15
and Badlesmere l, 198–9
and Banaster 112–15
at Berwick (1319) xxix, 162–3, 174–5,
    177–9
at Boroughbridge (1322) 210–13
and the cardinals (1317) 142 n. 276
collusion with the Scots xxxii, xxxv,
    xliv–v, l, 130–1, 138–9, 166–71,
    174–5, 208–11, *see also* Bruce,
    Robert
as chief counsellor 120–1, 130–1
and Despenser the elder 150–1, 160–1,
    190–1
and Despenser the younger 150–1
failure to attend parliaments and
    councils xliii, 136–9, 150–1, 176–7
failure to go to Scotland 86–9
and Gaveston l, 16–17, 20–3
and Holand 208–9
and the Marcher lords xlv, l–li, 186–7,
    202–3, 206–7
negotiations with king (1312–13) 60–1,
    (1317–18) xliii–iv, 144–7, 148
    n. 289, 150–3
at Newcastle (1312) 42–3, 58–61
and the Ordinances, l, 38 n. 70, 146–7,
    150–1, 168–9
pardoned (1313) 74–5
and Pembroke l, 198–9
at Pontefract 140–3, 212–13
position and wealth 50–1
as steward xliv, 140–1
trial and death of 212–15
and Warenne 146–7, 150–1, 158–61
wife's abduction, *see* Lacy, Alice

Langley, *see* King's Langley
Langton, Walter, bishop of Coventry and
    Lichfield (1296–1321) 64 n. 115,
    102–3
La Réole (Gironde, Fr.) 222 n. 462, 228
    n. 472
law, author's interest in, see *Vita Edwardi
    Secundi,* author's interests
canon xxvii, 70–1, 144–5
    de multa 78–9
    see also papal bulls

Newcastle (Northumberland) lx, 42–3,
    58–61, 106–7
  musters at 140 n. 272, 160–3
Newport (Powys, formerly
    Monmouthshire, Wales), castle of
    184–5, 188–9
Norfolk, earl of, *see* Bigod, Roger;
    Brotherton, Thomas of
Norham (Northumberland), castle of
    150–1
Normans 138–9
Northampton (Northamptonshire), king
    at 148–51
Northumberland xlv
Northumbria 104–5, 120–1, 142–3, 146–7
  tributes taken by Bruce and Scots, 54–5,
    82–3, 176–7
Norwich (Norfolk)
  bishop of, *see* Ayrmin, William; Salmon,
    John
Norwich, Walter, treasurer (1314–17) 100
    n. 192
Nottingham (Nottinghamshire), castle of
    164–5
  see also councils
Nouvel, Arnold, abbot of Fontfroide,
    cardinal priest of St Prisca 56–7,
    81 n. 155

oaths, importance of 228–9
  see also barons; coronation oath; fealty
Ockham, John 100 n. 192
Odiham (Hampshire), castle of 200 n. 412
Ordainers xxii, xl, 20–1, 30–3, 36–7
  proposals to appoint (1310) 18–19
Ordinances xxii–iii, xxxiv–v, xxxix,
    xl–xliii, xlvi–vii, lv–vii, 20–1,
    30–41, 54–5, 60–1, 64–5, 75
    n. 142, 86–7, 98–101, 134–7,
    150–3, 177 n. 357
  inspired by Warwick 108–9
  supplementary ordinances 38–9
Orleton, Adam, bishop of Hereford
    (1317–27) xxxi, 202–3, 232–3
Oxford (Oxfordshire) 48–9, 100–1, 148–9
  earl of, *see* Vere, Robert de
  King's Hall at 148–9
  university xli, 46–7

Pagula, William de 128 n. 249
papal bulls 76–7
  clericis laicos xliii, 70 n. 131, 132–3

de penis xxiii, xliv, 142–5
  see also *de multa*
papal legates 80–1, 136–7, 144–5, *see also*
    Aux, Arnald d'; Nouvel, Arnald
papal provisions 80–1
papal truce with Scots (1318) 154–5
see also Boniface VIII; Clement V; curia;
    John XXII; taxation
parliaments xxxix, xli, xliv, xlvi, lv–vi,
    86–7, 136–9, 146–7, 152–3, 230–1
  1308 Westminster 10–13
  1309 Stamford xl, 16 n. 29, 81 n. 156
  1310 Westminster 16–19
  1311 London 30–3
  1312 Westminster 56–61
  1313 Westminster I 66–7
  1313 Westminster II 72–3
  1313 Westminster III 72–3, 74–7
  1314 York (called a council by the
      author) 98–9
  1315 Westminster 102–3
  1316 Lincoln xlii, 120–1
  1318 Lincoln postponed, finally at York
      140–1, 144–9
  1319 York (called a council by the
      author) 160–1
  1320 York 176–7
  1321 Westminster 190–5
  1325 Westminster I 230 n. 478, 234–9
  1325 Westminster II 242–3
patrocinium 162–3, see also *seruitium
    debitum*
Patroclus, companion of Achilles xxix,
    28–9
peine forte et dure 216–19
Pembroke, earl of, *see* Valence, Aymer de
Percy, Henry (d. 1314) 75 n. 142
Perigueux (Dordogne, Fr.), process of 22
    n. 41
perjury, *see* vices
Peter of Blois 56 n. 103
Pevensey (Sussex), castle of 219 n. 458
Pharoah 132–3, 190–1
Philip IV, king of France (1285–1314)
    8–9, 22–3, 42–3, 66–7, 72–3
Philip V, king of France (1316–1322)
    174–5, 178–9
Philotas, military commander under
    Alexander the Great xxix, 168–9
Poitou, county of (Fr.), Hugh Despenser
    the elder's exile in 196 n. 402
Pole, Griffin de la 16 n. 31

268 GENERAL INDEX

Scotland (cont.)
king of, see Alexander III; Balliol, John;
Bruce, Robert
March of 130–1, 176–7, 226–7
tributes paid to, see Northumbria
truces with 83 n. 161, 154–5, 174–7,
222–7
see also Berwick; Edinburgh; Roxburgh;
Stirling
Scots 68–9, 102–3, 138–9, 150–1, 204–5
boldness of 106–9
military forces of, see armies
raids by 54–5, 82–3, 104–5, 120–1, 154
n. 301, 176–7
see Bruce, Edward; Bruce, Robert;
Douglas, James; Fraser, Simon;
Randolph, Thomas; Strathbogie,
John; Wallace, William
see also Lancaster, Thomas of, collusion
with Scots
Seba, son of Bochri 114–15
Segrave, family 96 n. 184
Segrave, John 16 n. 31, 96–7
Segrave, Nicholas 16 n. 31, 96 n. 184
self-defence liv, 18–19, 52–3, 58–9,
130–1, 178–9, see also resistance
Semei, son of Gera 204–5
Senghennydd (S.Wales) 115 n. 221, 116
n. 224
seruitium debitum 20–1, 86–7, 88–9, see
also patrocinium
Severn, river 200–3
Sherburn (Yorkshire), meeting at (not
named by author) xlv, 190–1
sheriffs, of Berkshire 220–1
of Herefordshire, see Elmerugge, Roger
of Yorkshire, see Ward, Simon
Shrewsbury (Shropshire), king at 200–3
Sicily, see Messina
Skipton (Yorkshire) 154 n. 301
Solomon, son of King David, 180–1,
214–15
Song of Lewes lii
sorcery 231 n. 480, see also Gaveston,
called a sorcerer
Southampton (Hampshire) 216–17
Speculum Regis Edwardi III xix, 128
n. 249
Spain 110 n. 211, 200–1
king of 68–9, see Alfonso VIII; Alfonso
XI
see also Castile; Santiago de Compostela
Stapledon, Walter, bishop of Exeter

(1308–26) xix, xxvi, xlvii, 236–7,
240–3
stewardship, see Lancaster, Thomas of
Stirling (Stirlingshire, Scotland), castle of
xli, 84–5, 86 n. 166, 88–9
constable of, see Mowbray, Philip
Stratford, John (bishop of Winchester,
1323–33) 232–3
Strathbogie, John, earl of Atholl
(1284–1306) 24–5, 168–9
Stratton, Adam, chamberlain of the
exchequer (dism. 1290) 158–9
Stubbs, Bishop William xv–vi, xix–xx,
xxiv, xxxiv, lviii
supplementary ordinances, see ordinances
Surrey, earl of, see Warenne

taxation
of the laity (1313) xli, 76–7, (1319)
160–1
see also church, taxation of
Temple, Order of the xxxviii, 80–1
Thomas of Brotherton, see Brotherton,
Thomas of
Thomas of Lancaster, see Lancaster,
Thomas of
Thorpe Waterville (Northamptonshire)
xxxv, xlviii, 200 n. 409
Tibetot, Payn 92–3
Tickhill (Yorkshire), castle of 206–7
Tilh, Arnaud de 16 n. 31
Tintagel (Cornwall), castle of 38–9
tirades xli, xliv, l, 78–83, 170–5, 178–83
tournaments 40–1
at Wallingford 6–7
see also round table
treason xxix, liii–v, 168–71
lesa maiestas lv, 48–9, 54–5, 130–1, 168
n. 336
see also kingship; rebellion; resistance;
restraint; self-defence; tyranny
treasury, royal (fiscus, erarium) 20–1,
134–5, 184–5, 196–7; see also
Edward II, wealth of
Trent, river 206–9
Trevet, Nicholas, xxviii, xxx, 168 n. 337
tributes, see Northumbria
Troy xxix, 25 n. 48, 146–7, 168–9, 176–7
see also Achilles; Aeneas; Helen;
Patroclus; Priam
Turberville, Payn xlii, 114–17
Turberville, Thomas (d. 1295) 168–9

Tutbury (Staffordshire), castle of xlv,
208–9
Tyes, Henry 216–17
tyranny xliii, liii, lvii, 128–31, 230–1
see also kingship; rebellion; resistance;
restraint; self-defence

Ulster 106–7
earl of, *see* Burgh, Richard de

Valence, Aymer de, earl of Pembroke
(1307–24) xxxiv–v, xli–iii, xlv,
20–3, 40–7, 52–3, 74–5, 86–7, 92
n. 176, 104–7, 124–5, 136 n. 264,
140–3, 162–3, 192–3, 198–9, 206
n. 428
author's judgement of xlviii
Vashti, queen of the Medes and Persians
30–1
verses (quoted) 26–7, 28–9, 56–7, 110–11
Vere, Robert de, earl of Oxford
(1296–1331) 5 n. 4
Vescy, Isabella de 54 n. 100
vices xxii
avarice xxv, 128–9, 156–9, 170–5, 236–7
deceit 14–15, 108–9, 170–1
flattery 14–15, 54–7
king's use of 32–3
perjury 108–9
presumption 180–1
pride xxv, xli–ii, 28–31, 98–9, 108–9
Vienne, council of 80–1
Vincent of Beauvais xxviii, xxix
Vita Edwardi Secundi lvii
accuracy of xxxviii–ix
authorship of xxiv–xxxii, xxxvii–viii; *see*
Walwayn, John
author's education xxvi–xxx
author's interests in
astrology xxvii, 122–3
classical learning xxviii–xxx
history xxx, xxxviii, xlv
law, xxvii, liii
political ideas xxxviii, lii–vii
political personalities xlvii–li
author's West Country links xxiv–v, xxxi
date of composition of xix–xxiii
editions of lviii, *see* Denholm-Young,
Noel; Hearne, Thomas; Stubbs,
Bishop William
sources for xxiii–iv, 93 n. 177, 166 n. 329
style of xxvi–vii
value of xxii–iii, xxxvii–ix

Wales 38–9, 106–7, 114–19, 138–9,
184–5, 188–9
infantry of 22–3
March of xxi, 184–5, 198–9, 202–3
law of, *see* law, Marcher
Marcher barons of xxxi, xlv, 185 n. 378,
190–1, 198–9, *see* Amory, Roger;
Audley, Hugh; Bohun, Humphrey;
Clifford, Robert; Mortimer, Roger;
Mowbray, John
men of xxvi, 48–9, 56–7, 188–9
prince of (Edward II as) 4–5, 68–9
see also Bren, Llywelyn; Glamorgan;
Gower; Welsh
Wallace, William 24–5
Wallingford (Berkshire), castle of xv, xlvi,
38–9, 218–21
see also tournaments
Walter of Châtillon xxix n. 37, 39 n. 72,
147 n. 287, 168 n. 336
Walwayn, John, DCL (d. 1326) xxiv–v,
xxvii, xliv, 76 n. 143
Ward, Simon, sheriff of Yorkshire 210–11
Warenne, John, earl of Surrey (1306–47)
xxxiv, xl, 6–7, 16–17, 22–3, 86–9,
146–7, 150–3, 158–9, 200–1, 230–1
Wark (Northumberland), castle of 154
n. 301
Warley, Ingelard 100 n. 192
Warrington (Lancashire) 112 n. 216
Warwick 44–9
earl of, *see* Beauchamp, Guy
Welsh, characteristics of 106–7, 118–21
West, James xv–vii, xxiv
Westminster, 224–5
burial of Edward I at 6–7
palace of 17 n. 32
see also councils; parliaments; Scone,
stone of
Weyland, Thomas, chief justice (dism.
1289) 158–9
Willington, John 96–7, 126–7
Winchelsey, Robert, archbishop of
Canterbury (1293–1313) xxi, xxv,
xli, 8–9, 40–1, 70–3, 76–7, 179
n. 362
Winchester (Hampshire)
bishop of, *see* Stratford, John;
Woodlock, Henry
earl of, *see* Despenser, Hugh the elder
king at 232–3
see also councils